A History of the Soviet Union fro

Third Ed..

MW00489707

This concise yet comprehensive textbook examines political, social, and cultural developments in the Soviet Union and the post-Soviet period. It begins by identifying the social tensions and political inconsistencies that spurred radical change in Russia's government, from the turn of the century to the revolution of 1917. Peter Kenez presents this revolution as a crisis of authority that the creation of the Soviet Union resolved. The text traces the progress of the Soviet Union through the 1920s, the years of the New Economic Policies, and into the Stalinist order. It illustrates how post-Stalin Soviet leaders struggled to find ways to rule the country without using Stalin's methods – but also without openly repudiating the past – and to negotiate a peaceful but antipathetic coexistence with the capitalist West. This updated third edition includes substantial new material, discussing the challenges Russia currently faces in the era of Putin.

Peter Kenez is Emeritus Professor of History at the University of California, Santa Cruz. He is the author of numerous articles and books, including *The Coming of the Holocaust: From Antisemitism to Genocide* (Cambridge University Press) and *Hungary from the Nazis to the Soviets: The Establishment of the Communist Regime in Hungary, 1944–1948* (Cambridge University Press).

A History of the Soviet Union from the Beginning to Its Legacy

Third Edition

PETER KENEZ

University of California, Santa Cruz

CAMBRIDGE
UNIVERSITY PRESS

CAMBRIDGE
UNIVERSITY PRESS

One Liberty Plaza, 20th Floor, New York NY 10006, USA

Cambridge University Press is part of the University of Cambridge.

It furthers the University's mission by disseminating knowledge in the pursuit of education, learning, and research at the highest international levels of excellence.

www.cambridge.org
Information on this title: www.cambridge.org/9781107141056

© Peter Kenez 2017

First published 2017
3rd printing 2019

Printed in the United Kingdom by TJ International Ltd. Padstow Cornwall

A catalogue record for this publication is available from the British Library.

Library of Congress Cataloging in Publication Data
NAMES: Kenez, Peter, author.
TITLE: A history of the Soviet Union from the beginning to its legacy / Peter Kenez
(University of California, Santa Cruz).
DESCRIPTION: Third edition. | New York, NY : Cambridge University Press, [2016] |
Includes bibliographical references and index.
IDENTIFIERS: LCCN 2016020876| ISBN 9781107141056 (Hardback : alkaline paper) |
ISBN 9781316506233 (Paperback : alkaline paper)
SUBJECTS: LCSH: Soviet Union–History.
CLASSIFICATION: LCC DK266 .K43 2016 | DDC 947.084–dc23 LC record available at
https://lccn.loc.gov/2016020876

ISBN 978-1-107-14105-6 Hardback
ISBN 978-1-316-50623-3 Paperback

To P.K., as always

Contents

Acknowledgments

I am grateful to my friends Professors Norman Pereira, Denise Youngblood, and Hugh Ragsdale, who read the entire manuscript and made helpful comments.

Introduction

Leibniz, the great German philosopher and scientist, at the beginning of the eighteenth century, once expressed his envy of Russia. He argued that, because Russia had neither civilization nor history, the reforming tsar, Peter, could start with a tabula rasa. His line of reasoning was based on the assumption that people and institutions are infinitely malleable. Of course Leibniz lived in an age more innocent than ours, and no one today would make such a naive statement. We know that history never starts completely anew and that the past not only matters, but sometimes weighs heavily on the present.

Obviously both change and continuity are real. Modern Russia is not what it was a hundred or two hundred years ago, and to believe that Russians are condemned to repeat the past forever is a crude error. But, at the same time, there are trends and mental attitudes which continue for a long, long time. Church historians, for example, have shown that some unique tenets of the Orthodox faith and ideas held by such major authors as Tolstoi and Dostoevskii reflect features of Russian paganism, even though the people had converted to Christianity more than one thousand years ago. Stalin consciously modeled himself on the sixteenth-century tsar Ivan the Terrible, and Soviet propagandists at the time of the Second World War reminded Russians how Teutonic (i.e., German) warriors had behaved in the thirteenth century. Such examples could easily be multiplied.

We often hear the opinion that democracy in today's Russia is doomed because the nation has no democratic traditions. The implication is that, since Russia has always been autocratic, it is bound to remain so forever; the people want strong rulers and willingly accept tyrants. By contrast, some nineteenth-century historians argued that the Russians are basically anarchistic people. They pointed out that Russians did not even form their own state, but needed the services of foreigners, the Vikings. Sometime in the ninth century these nomadic traders and warriors came from Scandinavia on their own or, according to the Russian chronicle – that beautiful but not always reliable source – were invited by the Slav tribes living in the territory of modern Ukraine. Before that time the Slavs in this territory had lived under the rule of nomadic empires and paid tribute to them. These empires disappeared one after another, and it is an irony of history that a fundamentally agricultural people, knowing only the loosest form of political organization, managed to prevail while others, much better organized, possessing far more powerful armies, disappeared, often hardly leaving a trace behind.

The Vikings who arrived in modern-day Ukraine using the extensive north–south river system for trade could not have been very numerous, and they were soon absorbed into the Slav population. The kind of state that they created hardly deserves the name "state," for it was a loose federation of cities, headed by the prince in Kiev, the most important of the towns. The city-states collaborated with one another in order to protect the valuable trade routes from Scandinavia to Byzantium, the richest and culturally most advanced country outside the Orient in the early Middle Ages. Although the city-states were headed by princes from the same family, they spent as much time fighting one another as they did fighting foreigners. Both Ukrainians and Russians proudly claim the heritage of that Kievan state, and they regard this period of their history as a golden age. Indeed, during that period Russia, which became Christianized in 988, came to be accepted into the European family of nations, and by no definition could it be described as "backward." This fact is demonstrated by the degree of intermarriage between the Kievan princely family and other European ruling families. Several centuries passed before the Russian ruling family would once again be accepted as equal by European royalty.

In the Kievan political system, the city assembly, the *veche*, in which all heads of families participated, greatly limited the power of the prince. This was a participatory democracy that could best be compared to the Greek city-states of antiquity. It is therefore not quite correct to say that Russians have no democratic heritage. (To what extent it matters that a thousand years ago a rudimentary form of democracy existed in Kievan Russia is another issue.)

Given the nature of the Kievan state, it is not surprising that it was short-lived. As a result of internal dissension, the changing of trade routes which made the maintenance of the state less important, and the constant attacks from nomadic tribes from the southeast, the Kievan state fell apart even before the coming of the Mongols in the middle of the thirteenth century. The Mongol conquest was an event of epochal significance in the history of Eurasia. What emerged after the 250-year-long Mongol occupation of Russia was something profoundly different from what had existed before. First of all, the country broke apart, never to be completely reunified. Instead of Kiev, three new centers emerged: the southwest, which came to be dominated by pagan Lithuanians and was ultimately absorbed by powerful

Poland; the northwest, in which the Novgorod city and commercial state was able to maintain longest the Kievan political heritage (until that city was subjugated by Moscow at the end of the fifteenth century); and, ultimately most important, Moscow in the northeast.

Moscow, which started out as an insignificant principality within the Kievan realm, grew quickly during the period of Mongol rule. It did not become a copy of the Kievan state, but its dialectical opposite. In the new political system the *veche* had no place. People came to settle on lands that were already the prince's property, and consequently he could set the terms; there was no power to challenge his authority. The Muscovite prince ruled over an ever-larger area as if it were his own property. It is not important to decide whether the Russian princes learned autocratic habits from the Mongols, or autocracy was the consequence of domestic developments. It is, however, clear that the political system of Muscovite Russia was profoundly different from that of the pre-Mongol era.

A country's political system is inseparable from its social structure. Autocracy came into being because there was no social force capable of restraining the arbitrary power of the prince. Our terms for describing social classes and groups come from West European experience, and we apply these concepts to Russian history because we have no better ones. At the same time historians are aware that these terms fit the Russian situation only imperfectly. Russia had no feudalism, narrowly understood – that is, relationships in which more or less independent local lords owed service to the central ruler in exchange for protection. The Russian nobility was not as strong as its European equivalent; it never even attempted to act in unison to defend its class interests. There is no equivalent in Russian history of the Magna Carta, or of the Golden Bull that the Hungarian nobility managed to impose on their king in 1222. Status in Russia meant no more than closeness to the tsar, and nobility was largely acquired in service.

The Russian rulers time and again succeeded in defeating the aristocracy. The princes – or tsars, as they came to be called in the sixteenth century – went to great lengths to prevent the development of an independent aristocracy by confiscating their holdings, and by moving them from one part of the country to another to prevent the development of strong local ties. The Russian privileged classes had no unity: some were rich in landed wealth, while others had very little; some came from ancient Kievan princely families, and others had Mongol backgrounds; some achieved power and influence by serving a tsar, others attempted to stay aloof from the court. In modern times the country was not ruled by the nobility, which gradually lost influence in the army and in the administration, but by a socially heterogeneous bureaucracy. Although the top levels of this bureaucracy were constituted by people from noble families, the bureaucrats nonetheless considered themselves separate from the nobility, and they by no means acted always in defense of class interests. The state was poor and therefore could not pay those who worked for it decently; the concept of public service was largely absent. Under the circumstances it was not surprising that corruption was widespread.

The single most important fact in Russia's social history was serfdom, an institution that existed until 1861. At the time of the revolution of 1917, there were still people alive who had been born serfs, and a large majority had parents who had not been full-fledged citizens of their country. The memory of serfdom made a considerable impact on Soviet history.

Serfdom developed late. Russia was moving in the opposite direction from the rest of the continent. This institution became part of the social structure in Russia only in the sixteenth and seventeenth centuries, at a time when in Western Europe the obligations imposed on serfs were becoming less and less onerous. Although the institution of slavery did exist in Kievan Russia, the vast majority of the population consisted of free peasants – free in the sense that, even when they cultivated land that belonged to others, they retained the right to make contracts and, most importantly, the right to move.

Peasants came to be tied to their landlords as a consequence of two interrelated factors: the development of the centralized state and the duration of hard economic times. Kievan Russia was situated in an area favorable for agriculture, but the new Russia dominated by Moscow was not so blessed: in the northeast the climate was severe and the growing season short, while the southeast did not get enough rain. Russia was an agricultural country in a region that was not well suited to agriculture. In the best of circumstances the peasant lived a marginal existence. The sixteenth century, the time of Ivan the Terrible, was an age of constant and devastating wars; and wars and famines often went hand in hand. Peasants were compelled to borrow from their landlords to survive, even knowing that they would not be able to repay their loans, and thereby would lose their freedom.

The economic downturn endangered the livelihood of the lesser noble landlords – let us call them "gentry." The land was plentiful, but the country was thinly populated and labor scarce. In bad times people escaped from the center of the country to the thinly inhabited south, which after the disintegration of the Mongol Empire was a kind of no man's land. The large landlords – let us call them "aristocrats" – could protect themselves because they could attract peasants from the land of the smaller landlords (the gentry) by offering them better terms. The gentry faced ruin. This was a threat to the state, for it was precisely this element that made up the bulk of the armies of the tsar. In this subsistence economy, the state could pay its soldiers only by giving them land. However, the land was worthless if there was no one to cultivate it while the lord was away fighting in the armies of the tsar. The economic ruin of the poor nobility threatened the military strength of the state. Gradual limitations by the state on the ability of the peasants to leave their masters were introduced for the mutual advantage of the gentry and the central power. This alliance between the gentry and the tsar against the aristocracy and the peasantry was an enduring one. Russian autocracy and serfdom, the two most significant institutions of the premodern Russian state, were its consequences: the nobility gave up interest in politics, and the state guaranteed them unlimited rights over the serfs.

Muscovite Russia differed from Europe not only in its social and political institutions, but also in its religion. Kievan Russia was a state of free peasantry, democratic institutions, and a flourishing culture. By accepting Christianity from Byzantium, Kiev came under the influence of the most civilized country in Europe. Greek missionaries had already translated religious material for their proselytizing efforts among the Slavs of the Balkans and in Moravia; they therefore possessed an alphabet suitable for a Slavic language, and religious works comprehensible to the Russians. Having immediate access to a significant body of written material allowed a quick flourishing of culture – as is shown, for example, by the Primary Chronicle – but there was a price to pay. In the West, where priests and monks had to learn Latin and Greek, some learned men became acquainted with the great culture of the ancient world. This knowledge was a precondition of the Renaissance. The Russians were excluded, and their intellectual world remained limited for a long time to the material that happened to be translated for them. Although the Russians accepted the Greek form of Orthodoxy and the superior authority of the patriarch in Constantinople, nevertheless, perhaps unconsciously, they transformed Christianity to suit their own spiritual needs. The Russian image of Christ was a more human and suffering figure than the original Greek, which was severe and remote. The Russians particularly admired humility, and the idea of suffering for Christ.

During the Mongol period the church in effect freed itself from Byzantine tutelage and, when Constantinople itself fell to the Turks in 1453, it became fully independent. In Byzantine history there was no competition between worldly and religious authorities; the emperor was the head of the church. The Russian church inherited this ideology of cesaropapism: that is, it was content to act as ideological supporter of Muscovite autocracy. It was this tradition which allowed Peter the Great at the beginning of the eighteenth century to reduce the Orthodox Church simply to one department of the government. Separation of church and state would not happen in Russia until 1917.

Up to the seventeenth century Russian culture was essentially religious. From that time on, however, there were ever-increasing contacts with the West; and in the eighteenth century, at the time of Peter and Catherine, these contacts made an ever more powerful impact. At first the court, and later a growing number of nobles, became acquainted with Western ideas, customs, and art and acquired a taste for foreign possessions and a European lifestyle. The consequences were profound. An increasing but still small group of people came to live in a different world from the vast majority of the Russian people, and the unity of culture was broken. In the nineteenth century, great intellectual sophistication in the realm of art and science came to coexist with a rich but static traditional Russian peasant culture and illiteracy.

A vague awareness on the part of at least some Russians that their country was not as rich and powerful as some others (i.e., that it was backward) resulted from the encounter with Western military strength and wealth. Since that time, there have always been two points of view: some argued that Russia must and would follow the Western path and had much to learn from the advanced countries, while others saw in Western influences primarily a danger that would undermine Russia's distinctiveness and spiritual values. The two groups at different times had different names, but the fundamental difference in Russian intellectual life remained. In the first half of the nineteenth century "Slavophiles" and Westerners confronted one another with distinct visions of Russia's past and future.

In a grand effort of social engineering, serfdom was abolished by the state in 1861. Since the military, judicial, and educational institutions were all based on that outdated institution, all had to be reconsidered and reformed. In the following two decades, within a remarkably short time, the statesmen serving Alexander II, the reforming tsar, created the rudiments of a modern military and judiciary. They also established institutions of local government, the *zemstva* (sing. *zemstvo*), and thereby brought government closer to the citizens. But of course, the most significant of the reforms was giving personal freedom to the peasants, freeing them from feudal obligations to their landlords. The great spurt in industrialization which took place at the end of the century could not have happened without these reforms. At the same time, it is clear that bringing about economic growth was not uppermost in the minds of the reformers. The peasants assumed a heavy financial obligation to the state for the land they received, which robbed them of resources.

The emancipation manifesto preserved that peculiar Russian institution, the peasant commune. Whether the peasant commune was an ancient institution, as Slavophile thinkers believed, or relatively modern in its nineteenth-century form, does not much matter. It is clear, however, that this institution played a crucial role in the life of the nineteenth-century Russian peasantry. In most instances these institutions of peasant self-government periodically redistributed land among their members to accommodate ever-changing family sizes and available land. The government supported the communes by assigning collective responsibility for taxes and redemption payments, and thereby, in fact, tied the peasants to the land. Even after the liberation of the serfs, the peasants could leave their villages only with the permission of the commune. The reformers were moved only partly by Slavophile sentiment – that is, by the belief that this institution best corresponded to the "naturally collectivist mentality of the Russian people." The government tied the peasants to the land because it believed that the communes would prevent formation of a landless proletariat and thereby would ensure stability. There was a price to pay, however. At a time of great agricultural overpopulation, the communes delayed economic growth.

Delayed, but not prevented. In the 1890s, under the able and pragmatic leadership of Finance Minister Sergei Witte, the Russian economy enjoyed extremely high growth rates. Witte, a conservative man, succeeded in persuading the reactionary Tsar Alexander III that without modern industry the country would be at the mercy of stronger powers. Industrialization was a precondition of military strength, and those who did not modernize would fall victim to those who did. In the industrialization that took place at this time, the state played a major role: it heavily taxed the peasantry, reduced imports and encouraged exports, and thereby achieved a favorable trade balance. This made possible the adoption of the gold standard in 1897, which made Russia attractive to foreign investors. The state subsidized the building of railroads and provided protective tariffs. Tsarist industrialization was similar to what would take place decades later under Stalinist auspices: heavy industry benefited most, and the production of consumer goods was neglected. The industrialization drive favored large factories and major projects, rather than small entrepreneurs.

The establishment of new factories, of course, created an urban proletariat. Most of the new workers retained their ties to the village: they remained members of the commune and often left their wives and children behind, sending them money periodically. Living and working conditions were abominable. This proletariat would play a major role in the revolutions of 1905 and 1917.

The tensions increasingly visible in Russian society at the turn of the century were the consequence not of stagnation, but of dynamic change. The tsarist government attempted to preserve autocracy undiminished at a time of profound economic and social transformation. The country needed educated people to run the new industry; it needed engineers, lawyers, and doctors; but the tsarist ministers so feared the subversive power of education that they refused to support general education. The contrast with the other important modernizing country, Japan, could not have been greater. The revolutionary movement was gaining strength. Assassinations of tsarist functionaries and members of the imperial court created an atmosphere of crisis.

As a major power, Russia was neither willing nor able to stay out of the significant international conflicts of the time. It had imperialist ambitions: it was deeply involved in the confused affairs of the Balkans, and the newly completed Trans-Siberian Railroad allowed it to project its strength to the Far East, where it quickly came into conflict with Japan. The Russian government stumbled into a war with Japan, which it undertook lightheartedly, grossly underestimating the enemy's strength, technological sophistication, and determination. The Russian military, especially the navy, performed poorly in this war, lowering the prestige of the empire.

The social developments in a fast-changing society, combined with the impending defeat in a misconceived and poorly led war, resulted in the revolution of 1905. It was a messy affair. No leadership was able to take control of the revolutionary movement. The waves of revolutionary activities among workers, soldiers, and peasants remained uncoordinated, and therefore could not reinforce one another. Although at times it seemed that the autocracy might be toppled, the government – by a combination of repression and timely concessions, as expressed in the Manifesto of October 1905 – managed to divide the opposition and thereby put off the demise of the tsarist system.

The revolution failed, in the sense that Nicholas II managed to retain his throne, but it was nevertheless an event with far-reaching consequences. On the one hand, it gave much-needed training to the revolutionaries. The workers at the height of the upheaval in October 1905 spontaneously created soviets (a word meaning council). These organizations were one of Russia's most important contributions to twentieth-century revolutionary politics. None of the theorists of the revolution, neither Marx nor the much more practical-minded Lenin, foresaw these workers' councils. Created by striking workers in order to coordinate activities, they turned out to be admirably suited to the requirements of a revolutionary situation. They were capable of quickly mobilizing proletarian forces and thereby channeling revolutionary energies. At least for a moment, in the fall of 1905, the St. Petersburg Soviet seemed almost as powerful as the government.

Although at the outset in 1905 the soviets, including the most important one in St. Petersburg, were genuine working-class organizations, gradually radical socialist intellectuals came to play an important role in them. Leon Trotsky proved his oratorical and organizational talents with the St. Petersburg Soviet. It was this experience that allowed the workers and soldiers in 1917 instantaneously to return to this form of organization.

The revolution changed the character of the Russian state. The tsar, in order to consolidate the situation, was compelled to grant concessions. Preliminary censorship was abolished, which meant that opposition papers could be printed. The Bolshevik paper *Pravda*, for example, although periodically repressed, could be legally published. The workers could organize trade unions, though these were on occasion harassed by the police.

The constitutional system introduced after the revolution would no longer be considered democratic in our time. However, one must avoid being anachronistic: to expect Russia to introduce universal suffrage and a government responsible to a parliament was hardly realistic (no European country at the time had full universal suffrage). The problem was not that the constitutional system was insufficiently democratic, but that the tsar and his government accepted it under duress, in bad faith, with no intention of observing it. The government was no more respectful of the rule of the law than was the revolutionary opposition.

As soon as the revolutionary wave subsided, the government reduced the concessions it had given just a few months before. In April 1906, it introduced a constitutional system, which with some changes remained in existence until the revolution of 1917. Russia acquired a two-chamber legislature. The lower house, the Duma, was elected on the basis of estate suffrage, meaning that a handful of landowners elected 31 percent of the delegates, while the vast majority of the citizens, the peasants, elected 42 percent. The system treated the working classes especially poorly because the government regarded them as most dangerous. The urban poor (i.e., the workers) elected only 2 percent of the delegates. The upper house came as a surprise to the electorate, for it had not been mentioned in the October Manifesto at all. Half of its delegates were named by the tsar, the other half elected by institutions such as the church, the Academy of Sciences, and the *zemstva*. The legislature could neither remove the government nor override the tsar's veto.

Even this Duma elected on the basis of restricted suffrage was far too radical for the government. Premier Peter Stolypin, in a virtual coup d'etat in June 1907, dissolved the Duma and for the new elections readjusted the percentages assigned to different estates. After 1907 landowners elected more than half of the members of the Duma, and the representation of the peasantry was reduced to 22 percent.

Despite the limited franchise and the limitations on the powers of the assembly, the Duma was not an insignificant institution: important matters were discussed openly in a public forum. The Duma, for example, took an intelligent interest in military and educational reforms. Perhaps most importantly, elections to the Duma implied the legalization of political parties. For the first time in Russian history, politicians were allowed to develop and to present to the electorate political platforms.

The political spectrum ran from the extreme right to the socialist left. The Union of Russian People, a reactionary organization, intended to disrupt the Duma from the inside. Its electoral base was small but significant, for it enjoyed the not-very-covert support of the tsarist court. Arguably, this organization was proto-fascist: it romanticized violence and used the crudest demagoguery to gain support from the urban lower classes. The Union of the Russian People was involved in anti-Jewish pogroms and competed with the revolutionaries in bloody terror, organizing assassinations of leftist politicians.

The liberals, with their political base of professional people, the bourgeoisie, and a segment of the nobility, were well represented in the Duma. In the First and Second Dumas the strongest party was the Kadets (Constitutional Democrats). This was a party of the Westernizing gentry: the party stood for land reform with compensation, concessions to the nationalities, civil liberties, and further constitutional reform. Its left wing was republican, while the right wing was satisfied with constitutional monarchy. The other major party of liberals was the Octobrist Party, which gained its name from the October Manifesto of 1905. These were people who preferred constitutional monarchy and, as their name implied, wanted to base the political life of the country on the concessions already given by the tsar. The Octobrists were much more willing than the Kadets to cooperate with the government, were dubious about the wisdom of breaking up large estates, and tended to look at matters from the point of view of Great Russian national interests.

The left was made up of two types of Russian socialists: the Socialist Revolutionaries (SRs) and the Social Democrats. The Socialist Revolutionaries were heirs to the rich tradition of Russian populism. They intended to base themselves on the peasantry and attempted to defend the interests of this class. In a genuinely free election they would undoubtedly have received the largest number of votes. The Socialist Revolutionaries, while respectful of Marx and Marxism, saw a different path for Russia than for the West. They made much of Russian institutions, primarily the peasant commune, which they regarded as a germ of Russian socialism and an example of the communitarian mentality of the Russian peasant. A large and heterogeneous party, the Socialist Revolutionaries also included people responsible for some of the worst acts of terror.

Socialist Revolutionaries and Social Democrats both believed in the necessity of revolution, but the Social Democrats, as Marxists, saw industrialization as something inevitable and already changing the face of Russia. They assumed that the workers would be the moving force in the coming revolution. From the very outset the Social Democrats were split between Mensheviks and Bolsheviks. The difference between the two trends in Russian social democracy was not yet clear to the Russian electorate.

The Bolshevik Party was the left wing of Russian social democracy. The party to an extraordinary extent was the creation of V. I. Lenin, who from the very outset tolerated only those who deferred to him. He not only created the party by causing a split with the Mensheviks at the 1903 "founding" party congress, but he also laid the theoretical basis that distinguished Bolshevism from other Marxist currents. Lenin's starting point was that the workers left to their own devices could see no further than their immediate economic interests. Therefore, in order to bring about the transformation of society, the proletariat needed a disciplined organization, the party, which could channel the energies of the workers to bring about the revolution. Revolutionaries educated in Marxist theory had the task of bringing class consciousness to the workers. The stress on organization and discipline helped the Bolsheviks when they were struggling underground, and would help them again during the years of upheaval, 1917–21. The Mensheviks, who considered themselves just as revolutionary as the Bolsheviks, differed little in theory from their Marxist colleagues, but they lacked a leader who dominated their organization the way Lenin dominated the Bolsheviks.

The First and Second Dumas were dominated by opponents of the government, the Kadets. The government responded by dissolving them and unconstitutionally changing the electoral system in order to produce a more docile assembly. Only the Third Duma lived out its five-year tenure, from 1907 to 1912. The Fourth Duma, elected in 1912, was dissolved at the time of the 1917 revolution.

Changes in the economic life of the nation during the last decade of the monarchy were just as profound as the political reforms. After the economic slump caused by war and revolution, the economy once again grew impressively. The state played a somewhat smaller role in directing industrialization than before; its place was taken by banks. The country still seemed an eminently safe place for foreign investors, promising large returns on investment.

Witte concentrated on industrial development and temporarily neglected the problems of agriculture. His able successor, Stolypin – who acquired his reputation by firm repression of peasant uprisings in his province and acted as premier from 1906 to 1911, when he was assassinated – paid primary attention to agriculture. It turned out that the government had been wrong to regard the peasant commune as a bulwark of stability in the villages. During the revolution the communes provided the peasantry with the organizational base necessary for the occupation of land and other attacks on the outposts of authority in the countryside.

Stolypin regarded the commune as a hindrance in the modernization of agriculture: the peasants had no incentive to improve land they might lose at the next repartition, and the land came to be divided into inefficiently small strips. He understood that the dissolution of the communes would lead to increased stratification in the village, since some peasants might lose their land while others, presumably more efficient, could acquire more. From his point of view the development of a stratum of rich peasants – the kulaks, as they were called – was an advantage, since the government was likely to find support among those who had a vested economic interest in the existing regime and in the maintenance of order. Stolypin simply abolished those communes that had not redistributed land, and made it possible for peasants to claim their share of land from the repartitional type. Thereby he made land individual rather than communal property.

Whether within a reasonably short time Stolypin's reforms would have done away with the communes and thereby substantially improved Russian agriculture is impossible to know, because the process was interrupted by the outbreak of the First World War. That war ended an epoch. The period of almost universal optimism about the future, about the improvability of human nature, was over. After the mindless slaughter of millions it was difficult to believe in reason, in rationally organized societies. When the weapons fell silent, it seemed impossible to return to the old order.

Ever since, historians have disagreed over which nation was most at fault. It is fair to say that Russian responsibility was neither less nor more than that of the other major European countries. The war into which the statesmen of Europe had foolishly entered was not the kind of war that they had anticipated. They did not know and could not have known the consequences. They assumed that this war would be like other wars in the previous century: fought for limited goals and calling for limited sacrifices. It cannot be said that the Russian military was eager for a fight. In fact the high command, more aware than civilians of the weaknesses of the army, advised restraint. It was only after the outbreak of the war that the military men could not bear the idea of ending the fight without victory. The war was a disaster for all its European participants, but especially for Russia.

Almost immediately the army suffered a shortage of equipment and munitions and, because of the thoughtless sacrifice of thousands of young officers in the early campaigns, of competent leadership as well. Yet one should not exaggerate the weaknesses of the Russian military. Soldiers fought valiantly and usually successfully against the Turkish and Austrian enemies. The German army, on the other hand, was unquestionably superior in matters of organization, discipline, and leadership. It was the government and administration that failed abysmally. Governmental institutions have never worked well in Russia on any level. The state was authoritarian, but it lacked organization – the intervening institutions between the individual and the central authorities. The bureaucracy was too small for satisfying the needs of a modern state, and it was incompetent. Under the stress of a modern war requiring mass mobilization, the system broke down: the government was incapable of providing for the needs of the army and of the population. Ad hoc organizations were compelled to take on governmental tasks. Although the overall output of Russian agriculture did not significantly decline, the collapse of the transportation system made it difficult to feed the cities. Liberals in the Duma, who had always criticized the administration, saw the danger for the country of such lack of leadership in wartime, and even more bitterly denounced the government. They had good reason to do so, for the moral and intellectual level of the last Russian tsarist government was much below that of other countries. The tsar appointed shady and incompetent men to responsible posts.

The problem was not just incompetence, but an entire worldview. In January 1917, the British ambassador, Sir George Buchanan, had his last audience with the tsar. He said:

> "Your majesty, if I may be permitted to say so, has but one safe course open to you – namely, to break down the barrier that separates you from your people and to regain their confidence." Drawing himself up and looking hard at me, the Emperor asked: "Do you mean that I am to regain the confidence of my people, or that they are to regain my confidence?"[1]

This brief exchange shows the obtuseness of the tsar. It also shows that the tsarist regime was based on hopelessly anachronistic principles. The defenders of the monarchy did not consider it their task to convince people; they naively believed that it was the responsibility of the people to obey and follow. The monarchists did not possess an ideology with which to mobilize; nor were they aware of the need to have one.

Historians have often posed these interrelated questions: was Russia successfully modernizing its economic and political systems before 1914? Had the war not intervened, would the country have joined the more advanced nations of Europe? Or, on the contrary, were revolutionary tensions so high, and the tsarist regime so inflexible, that a revolutionary outbreak was bound to occur sooner or later? Indeed, some historians have argued that the war actually postponed the great explosion.

These questions, of course, cannot be answered with certainty, since the war did occur and we know that the tsarist regime failed to cope with the ensuing crisis. The political consequences of these questions are considerable. If we believe that the revolution was only a historical accident, then we are likely to regard the child of that revolution, the Soviet regime, as an unfortunate and tragic detour. But if we conclude that the tsarist regime was incapable of reforming itself, then we are more likely to regard the revolution as inevitable and attribute somewhat greater legitimacy to the Soviet regime.

Soviet historians, as long as that regime lasted, took it for granted that the revolution was inevitable and, indeed, historically foreordained. Among Western scholars answers to these questions have evolved over time. In the 1960s some historians challenged the then-prevailing opinion that the collapse of the old regime was primarily the consequence of defeat in the war. Most historians today would agree that the old regime failed not because of the unforeseeable emergency created by the war, but as a result of deep-seated cleavages in Russian society and the inability of the tsarist regime to adjust to changing circumstances.

2

The Revolution, 1917–1921

No event since the French Revolution has occasioned such an outpouring of historical scholarship and such passionate debate as the Russian Revolution. The interest and the engagement are understandable, for the issues are complex and the stakes are high. The revolution was not simply a most significant event in Russian history, transforming an antiquated society and changing the way of life of millions: it was also a catalyst in the development of our world. For better or worse, the interpretation of the revolution was not confined to historians; people from all segments of the political spectrum have always been aware of the political significance of historiography.

All aspects of the revolution have been well covered by historians, but none has received as much attention as the history of the revolutionary movement. This is understandable: revolutionaries fighting against the repressive tsarist regime were often willing to sacrifice their lives for a cause they deeply believed in. Many of them were extraordinary men and women, and their stories are fascinating. However, it may be an error to look for an explanation of the revolution in the work of underground subversives, for neither the tsarist government nor the Provisional Government were brought down by revolutionaries, or even primarily by discontented workers and peasants.

It may be more fruitful to think of the events of 1917 as the collapse of two different systems of government, first the autocratic and then the liberal. The decisive questions were not why the workers were dissatisfied and what exactly they wanted, but how and why different forms of government disintegrated. According to this view the revolutionary events were the manifestation of a crisis in authority. The fundamental question was a political one: how could Russia be governed? It follows from this under-standing of the revolution that the Bolshevik success in October was not the culmination or end of the revolution, but the nadir of the crisis. The question of what form of government was necessary for Russia under exceptionally difficult circumstances was truly resolved only by the civil war.

THE FEBRUARY REVOLUTION

The events that came to be called the February Revolution can be briefly summarized. On February 23, 1917 – International Women's Day – workers of the textile factories, mostly women, went on strike and demonstrated for bread. They knew that the city had a flour supply lasting for only ten days. The first demonstrators were soon joined by workers from the metal factories, most important among them the vast Putilov works, the largest armament factory in Petrograd.[1] There was nothing particularly new or unusual about the strikes and demonstrations, which had been taking place with increasing frequency; and at first the authorities were not overly concerned. They believed the disturbances were caused only by worry about the food situation and that they could suppress any possible uprising. Not only did the demonstrations, however, continue, but the number of protesters also grew and their slogans acquired an increasingly political character.

On February 24, according to police records, there were between 150,000 and 200,000 demonstrators, making this the largest such action in the city since the war had begun. The next day there were even more people in the streets, and observers noted an increasing reluctance among the Cossacks, the traditional defenders of the autocracy, to disperse the crowds. Now the authorities became alarmed. The tsar, from the headquarters of his army in Mogilev, telegraphed the hapless military commander of the city, General Sergei Khabalov, ordering him "to stop the disorders as of tomorrow."

February 26, a Sunday, was the turning point: the soldiers, who had freely mingled with the crowds for days, now were ordered to shoot to kill. Although dozens of labor leaders were arrested, and at least for a brief moment the city was calmer, a fatal break occurred in the willingness of the soldiers to defend the tsarist order. In the course of the next few days Petrograd was engulfed by anarchy. An ever-larger number of soldiers joined the revolutionaries, and within a couple of days almost nothing remained of the city garrison. The absence of authority led to lootings and senseless killings.

On February 27 the last tsarist government under Prince Nikolai Golitsyn resigned. The following day the tsar dismissed General Khabalov, who had lost his nerve and failed to pacify the city, and named an aged general, Nikolai Ivanov, military dictator of the capital. It was obviously, however, too late: Ivanov had no loyal forces left at his disposal, and the fate of the tsarist order was sealed. Learning that he could expect no support from the army, Nicholas on March 2 abdicated in favor of his brother, Michael, who, fearing for his life, did not accept. On March 3 the 300-year rule of the Romanov dynasty ended.

Disaffection culminating in strikes and demonstrations was not unexpected. After all, Russia had already experienced a revolutionary wave in 1905–07, and other belligerent countries had also suffered the effects of civil strife, as the cost of the war became more and more evident. Nevertheless, the timing and the ease with which the imperial system collapsed were surprising. Trotsky, a brilliant chronicler of the revolution, posed the question, "Who led the revolution?" He concluded that a handful of Bolsheviks had given it the necessary guiding spirit. In his version of the story, the nameless workers who had taken to the streets were acting in the name of the Bolsheviks. Even a cursory examination shows this view to be untenable, for it is absurd to assume that the workers needed the Bolsheviks to tell them that they were hungry and tired of the war. There is no evidence whatever to demonstrate that class-conscious revolutionaries played an important role during those chaotic days. But, even if we conceded this point to Trotsky, it would make little difference. The important event in February was not the workers' demonstration: it was the soldiers' refusal to obey. Once the chain of command and the bonds of authority were broken, the imperial order collapsed with amazing speed.

The soldiers defied their officers because of personal hatred, a sense of oppression, and disgust with the conduct of the war. In their eyes the officers, the army, and indeed the entire tsarist system had lost prestige as a consequence of the dreadful mismanagement of the war. The most demoralized regiments had been stationed in the capital, and these soldiers felt the greatest hostility toward their officers. These regiments, the weak link in the army, were understandably the first to defect.

It is easier to understand the behavior of the soldiers than that of the officers. It is striking how easily they, too, abandoned their monarch. General Mikhail Alekseev, the tsar's chief of staff and the de facto commander of the Russian armies, helped to persuade his sovereign to abdicate; and the most powerful generals, the commanders of the five "fronts," all expressed support for Alekseev's arguments. Of the tens of thousands of officers, only two corps commanders offered their services to the tsar, and only a couple of men resigned rather than swear loyalty to the Provisional Government. Such behavior needs an explanation. Surely the majority of the officers, if they held political views at all, were monarchists. In the spring of 1917, however, it seemed to them that to come to the aid of the tsar would lead to civil war, and that such a development would gravely compromise the national effort to resist the foreign foe. The war seemed crucially important to the officers. After all, in three years of fighting they had sacrificed millions of their countrymen – they had to believe in the importance of that war in order to preserve their sanity.

DUAL POWER

The Russians greeted the demise of tsarism with enthusiasm. Although the revolution did not resolve the controversial problems facing the nation, at least for a short time it created an appearance of unity. Different groups could interpret events in their own way, and for a moment contradictory goals and expectations could peacefully coexist: some expected that the revolution would bring the end of the war nearer; others hoped a "democratic" army would fight better.

The tsar's government had had two enemies: the workers and soldiers – peasants in uniform – revolting against oppression, and the liberals who had lost confidence in the ability of the government to defend the nation's interests. Those who wanted a social revolution and those whose goals were limited to political reform had briefly cooperated in an uneasy alliance. Now that tsarism was gone, these two social forces, socialists and liberals, established their separate institutions.

The Duma, the Russian parliament, had been last elected in 1912 on the basis of restrictive suffrage. In spite of the fact that members of the Duma represented privileged Russia almost exclusively, it nevertheless became the best forum for criticizing the policies of the tsar and his government. Prominent politicians time and again had demanded a government responsible to the legislature and a general (though limited) democratization of the political system. Before resigning, the last tsarist government had prorogued the Duma, and the deputies had not defied the authorities. An unofficial meeting of deputies took place on February 27 in which representatives of the right refused to participate. This meeting elected a provisional committee that was to be the parent body of the future Provisional Government. A paradoxical situation was thus created: the liberal bourgeoisie, whose point of view was represented in the new government, not only did not make the revolution, but in fact feared it. Most liberal politicians hoped that the monarchy could be saved one way or another. Respectable citizens as they were, they had no stomach for social revolution, which was now an ever more obvious threat.

Contrary to the desire of most liberals, the tsar abdicated on March 2, and the provisional committee formed itself into a government in order to prevent anarchy. The liberals regarded themselves as natural successors to the defunct government, and expected to stay in power until a constituent assembly could be called. Since the meeting that elected the provisional committee had been unofficial, and the ministers had more or less named themselves, the legitimacy of the Provisional Government was open to question. For liberal politicians, believing in the rule of law, this was a significant handicap.

Russia's new government was dominated by people who had made their reputations in the Duma during and before the war, demanding liberal reforms. Politicians from the two main liberal parties, the Kadets and the Octobrists, who stood somewhat to the right, got the most important portfolios. Prince Georgii Lvov, a somewhat colorless nonparty politician and ex-president of the Union of Zemstva, became premier; an Octobrist, Aleksandr Guchkov, the foremost spokesmen in the Duma on defense matters, became minister of defense; and Pavel Miliukov, a prominent historian and a leader of the Kadets, took the foreign portfolio.

The other center of power that would dominate the political landscape during the coming months was the Petrograd Soviet of Workers' Deputies. The soviet was established almost at the same moment as the provisional committee of the Duma. Although at the outset in 1905 the soviets, including the most important one in St. Petersburg, were genuine working-class organizations, radical socialist intellectuals had gradually come to play a dominant role in them. The same phenomenon occurred in 1917. At first, Socialist Revolutionary and Menshevik leaders were the most influential. The importance of the Petrograd Soviet was out of proportion to the number of soldiers and workers it represented, because it was in a position to put pressure on the government. It was a loose organization, which at one time had included more than 3,000 representatives. Procedures were haphazard. Given the large number of deputies and disorganized procedures, the executive committee acquired dominant influence. But soon even this committee grew to an unwieldy size of more than fifty people. It was through the executive committee that socialist politicians exercised their influence over the genuine worker and soldier delegates.

Aleksandr Kerensky, a moderate Socialist Revolutionary politician and Duma deputy, was elected as one of the two vice chairmen of the Petrograd Soviet. Without explicit permission from the soviet, he also accepted the portfolio of justice in the government, and thereby became the only person with a foot in both camps, a fact that propelled him to prominence and power during the following months. Kerensky, an able and charismatic speaker, quickly acquired a following in the revolutionary circumstances.

On March 1 the Petrograd Soviet issued its famous Order Number One, according to Trotsky the single worthwhile document of the February Revolution. Although the order was addressed only to the Petrograd garrison, its impact was soon felt by the entire army. It called on the soldiers to form soviets in every military unit down to the size of companies; it asked the soldiers to obey orders of the Military Commission of the State Duma (the Provisional Government had not yet been formed) only if they did not contradict orders from the Petrograd Soviet; it abolished old forms of address of officers; and it conferred on soldiers all rights of citizenship, including full participation in politics, when off duty.

Although undoubtedly this order was conceived in a spirit hostile to officers, its significance should not be exaggerated. It expressed the hostility that soldiers felt, rather than created it. In February 1917, the officers lost control over their soldiers, and they could never reestablish their authority. The majority of the officers believed that it was Order Number One that was most responsible for destroying the fighting capacity of the army. Instead of evaluating their situation realistically, they preferred to blame the socialists for their frustrations.

Thus out of the February Revolution a novel constitutional situation arose. The country now had a government that was quickly and enthusiastically recognized by all foreign Allied powers. This government took charge of the old administrative machinery of the tsarist state without difficulty and had, at least for the time being, the support of the high command of the army. The government, however, had less actual power than the Petrograd Soviet of Workers' and Soldiers' Deputies. Although the socialist politicians who led the soviet by no means directed the revolution, nonetheless the masses of workers and soldiers in Petrograd, and soon after in the entire country, recognized this institution as their own. The soviet in Petrograd, unlike the Provisional Government, could call on workers and soldiers to demonstrate and to carry out revolutionary actions. The ministers well understood that they held their offices at the tolerance of the socialists in the soviet.

The question arises: why did the moderate socialists not take all power into their own hands when their opponents were not in a good position to resist? Lenin was unquestionably right when a short time later he blamed them for timidity. The socialists, many of them freshly out of jail, had trouble thinking of themselves as ministers; to them it seemed natural that the liberals should be entrusted with power. They lacked that will to power that Lenin so obviously possessed. Further, the Mensheviks at least were influenced by their deeply held Marxist beliefs, according to which Russia was ready to get rid of the remnants of feudalism and embark on the road of capitalist development, but not yet ready for a socialist revolution.

Discord was bound to arise between those who had authority but no power, and those who could command the workers and soldiers but had no formal responsibility.

PROBLEMS FACING THE PROVISIONAL GOVERNMENT

The liberals found themselves in an ironic situation: the forces that brought them to power ultimately destroyed them. The tsarist government failed because Russia could not be governed during a modern war on the basis of principles in which the tsarist elite believed. It was, however, also impossible in 1917 to build governing institutions on the basis of liberal principles. The problems the country faced were too great, and there was no consensus on how to approach them; therefore the liberal experiment was bound to fail. Although the members of the Provisional Government can be blamed for making errors and needlessly alienating various important constituencies, it is impossible to see, even in hindsight, what policies, consistent with their deeply held beliefs, would have enabled them to retain power. The Provisional Government collapsed because it was unable to resolve the burning issues of the day: war, land reform, and autonomy for the national minorities.

Of these issues, the question of participation in the war was the most immediate and difficult. Russia's educated and privileged classes and the great masses of the people had different concepts of patriotism. The peasant soldiers were tired of fighting in a war that was dragging on for the third year, with no end in sight. The concept of national interest, dear to the hearts of the liberals, made little sense to them. They did not much care about making Constantinople Russian, or about the sanctity of international treaties. By contrast, members of the Provisional Government, who represented the privileged classes, firmly believed that Russia had to remain faithful to its allies. The officers in the army and the politicians failed to understand the depth of dissatisfaction among peasant soldiers, just as the tsarist government had earlier failed to recognize the mood of the people.

In the course of 1917 one political crisis followed another, and in each the underlying issue was the nation's war effort. The members of the first Provisional Government were just as intent as the tsarist government had been on vigorously pursuing the war to a victorious conclusion. Between the position of the war-weary soldiers and workers and that of the Provisional Government stood the Petrograd Soviet. The leading figures in the soviet appreciated that the war could not be stopped simply by Russian soldiers' leaving the battlefields. They took a "defensist" position: they favored the continuation of the war as long as Russian territory was occupied, but opposed a policy of annexing foreign territories and demanding indemnities from the defeated.

The Provisional Government and the soviet leaders have been blamed by historians for not stopping the war. It is true that all liberal and many socialist politicians believed in the importance of the war and did nothing toward disengagement. On the other hand, had they wanted to, it is most unlikely that they could have succeeded. As the experience of the Bolsheviks in 1918 demonstrated, the Russians could not have obtained peace terms from the Germans acceptable to the politically powerful. The Germans regarded themselves as victors, and they were in no mood to compromise.

The first political crisis came in April. Foreign Minister Miliukov wrote to the Allied governments informing them that Russia would observe all obligations to its allies and would fight until "decisive victory." The publication of this note in the newspapers caused a storm of indignation. The government's policy obviously contradicted the announced principles of the leaders of the soviet, who regarded the publication of the note as a challenge. Demonstrators in the streets, along with the Petrograd Soviet, forced Miliukov to resign, and Defense Minister Guchkov soon followed him. A new coalition government had to be formed, and it had a different makeup: it included six socialist members, among them Kerensky, who now took the crucial defense portfolio. The April events proved that the Provisional Government could not act without the explicit support of the Petrograd Soviet.

The next crisis came in June, when Kerensky initiated a major and ill-considered offensive. He had two motives: first, the Russian high command before the February Revolution had promised the Allies that it would undertake active military operations to facilitate a long-expected breakthrough on the western front. Second, he recalled the experience of the French Revolution, when the troops of democratic France fought successfully against the coalition of autocratic states; he believed that a successful offensive would help to rekindle the fighting spirit in the army. The offensive turned into a disaster. After some initial and local Russian successes, the Germans, who had been forewarned, pushed back the attackers with ease, inflicting heavy casualties. Clearly, the demoralized Russian troops were not in a position to carry out successful offensive operations. Kerensky, who had hoped to reap political benefit from military success, in fact had to pay a heavy price for failure.

At the beginning of July serious disturbances took place in Petrograd. For the first time the soldiers and workers of the city showed themselves to be more radical than the socialist leadership of the soviet. The troubles started when a regiment, fearing it would be sent to the front, mutinied. Soon the soldiers were joined by workers, and for a while the survival of the entire dual system of government was in doubt. The government, supported by the soviet leadership, succeeded in bringing fresh troops to Petrograd and reestablished order. In the aftermath of this affair, Prince Lvov resigned and Kerensky finally became premier.

A few weeks later it was the turn of the right to attempt to change Russia's existing political order by force. In July Kerensky appointed Lavr Kornilov as commander in chief of the Russian armies, largely because the general promised to restore order among the demoralized troops. The military men were increasingly unhappy with the course of events. They blamed the government for not taking energetic steps against the "troublemakers" and suspected treason among the leaders of the soviets. The newly appointed commander in chief decided to take matters into his own hands. He sent troops to Petrograd in order to disperse the soviet. When the prime minister ordered him to relinquish command, he refused. General Kornilov's fault was not simply that he mutinied – even worse, he mismanaged his mutiny. He overestimated his forces; he did not personally lead his troops; and he did not properly prepare by ensuring support from conservative groups. The failure of his undertaking was rapid and complete: soldiers did not carry out orders, and railroad workers stopped trains taking his troops to the capital. Kornilov and his fellow mutineers were arrested.

The combined effects of the July disturbances in Petrograd and the Kornilov affair were disastrous for the Provisional Government. The liberals and the moderate socialists alienated first the left and then the right. At a time when danger obviously threatened from both political extremes, the government's attempt to balance between increasingly hostile forces was doomed.

The right believed the existing government could not successfully pursue the war, and the left saw that it could not or would not stop the fighting.

While the politicians' inability to deal with the question of land reform did not lead to such spectacular crises as did the question of participation in the war, it just as surely undermined the government's ability to govern. It is a great deal more difficult to describe the peasant disturbances of 1917 than the movement of the revolutionary workers and soldiers, because the peasants possessed no national leadership that articulated goals and coordinated revolutionary acts. Nevertheless, the role of the peasants in preventing the consolidation of liberal rule was every bit as important as that of the workers.

The peasants had long been preoccupied with a desire for land. When the serfs were liberated in 1861, they had received approximately half of the land they had cultivated before; but this was an arrangement that most considered unfair – they wanted all of it. As the population grew in the decades preceding the First World War, demand for land increased. In 1917, when the central authority collapsed, the peasants wanted to make their own revolution, which to them meant above all a redistribution of land. Few understood that even taking all the lands of the nobility was not a long-term solution: given methods of cultivation in Russia, there was simply not enough land for everyone who wanted to cultivate it. Members of the government, of course, were well aware of the significance of the issue of land reform, and did not in principle oppose the idea. In practice, however, they did nothing. In the first place, carrying out land reform at a time of war, when millions of peasants were in the army, would have ended the effectiveness of the troops. Peasant soldiers would have left their regiments to go back to their villages to claim their allotments. Second, the government did not possess the machinery to carry out an inevitably complex process. Third, the liberal ministers took it for granted that landlords had to be compensated for their property. In 1917, the government obviously lacked the means necessary to compensate those who were about to be dispossessed. Given these difficulties, the government procrastinated by arguing that the resolution of the land question had to await the convocation of the Constituent Assembly.

Because of this inaction the peasants turned ever more decisively against the Provisional Government. The government's foothold in the villages had never been strong, even at the outset. In tsarist times the main agents of governmental power were the land captains, appointed officials who supervised judicial and police agencies. The land captains had been unpopular, and the Provisional Government had abolished the office. According to the reform plan, the functions of the land captains were to be taken over by elected district committees. These committees, and the age-old village commune, became the real rulers of the village. Now the peasants possessed a degree of self-government they had never had before. Unfortunately for the government, peasant self-rule did not become a bulwark of stability. On the contrary, peasant institutions became the instruments through which the peasants attacked private property.

This was something of an irony. The tsarist government for decades had supported the peasant communes in the expectation that they would encourage stability. At the time of the revolution, however, it was precisely the peasant communes that organized forcible land seizures. These communes were the equivalents of the soviets in the cities; without them the peasant revolution could not have succeeded. Before the revolution, socialist and liberal intellectuals believed that the commune was a disappearing remnant of the past. But now that the peasants had acquired some power over their own lives, these institutions received a new lease on life. Confiscation of landlord land was not done by individuals, but by the peasant communes, which then divided the land among their members. Unauthorized land seizures and attacks on landlord property began in May and grew ever more threatening during the summer. The government could neither satisfy the peasants nor suppress their revolutionary actions. It could gain neither the allegiance of the peasants nor their respect.

The third source of conflict during the days of the Provisional Government was the increasing desire of the national minorities for autonomy. Russia has been a multiethnic state from its inception. The minorities, which made up half of the population of the empire, differed greatly from one another in economic and cultural development and in degree of national consciousness. As long as the empire was strong, minority nationalism could not threaten the stability of the state. With the exception of the Poles and perhaps the Finns, nationalist aspirations were limited to small circles of people primarily interested in cultural autonomy. In 1917 the nationality issue still did not have the same burning significance as the questions of peace and land; however, it foreshadowed a major source of instability during the civil war. The Provisional Government could not satisfy the ever-growing nationalist aspirations of a large number of people, nor could it suppress them. Imperial Russia was a multinational empire; Russians made up only approximately half the population. As long as the state was powerful, the minorities' desire for autonomy was rarely heard. Only the Poles, who had had a long history of national independence, remained thorns in the side of the russifying government of the imperial regime. As the state was disintegrating following the February Revolution, the growth of national self-awareness came quickly. Most of Poland was under German occupation in the summer of 1917, so the Poles did not present the government with an immediate difficulty. In 1917, the most troublesome challenge came from the Ukrainians.

Ukrainians set up their own parliament, the Rada. The socialist members of the Provisional Government were willing to concede de facto autonomy to Ukraine, but the Kadets within the coalition resisted, believing that conceding to the Ukrainians would be the first step toward unraveling the empire. It was this difference that led to the demise of Lvov's government just before the July days, and to Kerensky's assumption of the premiership. The issue of the position of Ukraine within the future democratic Russian state was far from resolved when the Provisional Government ceased to exist.

THE BOLSHEVIKS AND THE WORKERS

In February 1917 there were fewer than 25,000 Bolsheviks in the entire country; only about 3,000 operated in the capital. The well-known leaders were in exile. The Bolsheviks, following Lenin, had opposed Russia's participation in the First World War and denounced it as imperialist. They called for transforming the international conflict into a civil war, urging the exploited everywhere to turn their weapons on the exploiters. Under the circumstances it is understandable that the tsarist government persecuted them more resolutely than other socialists.

At the time of the February Revolution, Lenin was in exile in Switzerland. Joseph Stalin and Lev Kamenev were the first senior leaders to return to Petrograd from their Siberian exile and take charge of party policy. Theirs was a moderate course. Recognizing the weakness of their position, they saw no alternative to working with Mensheviks and Socialist Revolutionaries in the Petrograd Soviet and thereby tacitly accepting cooperation with the Provisional Government.

Such a policy was anathema to Lenin. Not for a moment was he seduced by the idea of socialist unity. He accepted a German offer to aid his return to his country through German territory, although he well understood that such apparent cooperation with the enemy during wartime entailed political risks. The Germans allowed him to return home, believing that his presence in Russia would contribute to the disintegration of the government. Lenin's party later received financial aid from Germany. Anti-Bolsheviks at the time and ever since have attributed great significance to this fact, even describing the revolution as the product of foreign subversion. Such charges are unwarranted. The fact that the interests of the Bolsheviks and the Germans temporarily coincided did not make one into the puppet of the other. First of all, the amount of money the Leninists received could not have made a great deal of difference. As far as financial resources were concerned, the Bolsheviks were much worse off than their enemies. In any case, the revolutionaries believed that the German empire would soon collapse as a result of the victory of the world revolution. The Leninists did not worry about the morality of taking money from the enemies of their country. They believed that the interests of social revolution outweighed nationalist concerns, and that under the circumstances it did not matter which imperialist camp derived short-term benefits from Bolshevik actions. Ironically, many of the people who most vociferously denounced Lenin as a traitor did not hesitate to accept aid from the Germans after the Bolshevik Revolution, and thereby proved the point: the interests of class struggle under some circumstances supersede the interests of national struggle.

In Lenin's extraordinary career one of the most extraordinary moments was his return to Petrograd after years of exile. He did not allow himself to be moved by the general enthusiasm generated by the victory over tsarism. He was unwilling to pause, but eager to move on to face the next task. Immediately at the railroad station he announced his famous April theses. Their essence was that Bolsheviks should not support the existing political order, but must immediately start to work for the overthrow of the government, which Lenin regarded as a mouthpiece for the bourgeoisie. His concrete demands – all power to the soviets, nationalization of land, workers' control in industry, an immediate end to the war – were all based on the assumption that, contrary to Marxist analysis, the country did not require a lengthy period of capitalist development but was ready to proceed immediately to socialist revolution.

In April 1917 such a program was breathtaking in its radicalism. The soviets, to which Lenin wanted to give power, belonged to his political enemies: the Bolsheviks made up only small minorities in the important soviets of the country. As far as the war was concerned, while the idea of continued fighting was increasingly unpopular, it is unlikely that a majority would have been willing to accept peace at any price. Hostility toward the Germans was still profound. Nevertheless, within a few weeks Lenin succeeded in winning over his party. The Central Committee at the end of April passed resolutions in the spirit of his new radicalism. Then Lenin won the support of important socialist leaders not hitherto identified with the Bolsheviks. Among these, the most important was Leon Trotsky, who had also just returned from exile. By the end of May the Leninist policy also had important working-class support.

Did the Bolsheviks express the views and feelings of the revolutionary workers and peasants and act in their interest or, to the contrary, manipulate them for their own political advantage? Of all aspects of the history of the revolution, the role of the Bolsheviks – the character of their party and their relationship to the workers – is the most controversial. During the early days of the cold war most Western scholars depicted the Bolsheviks as a tightly knit, well-organized group that succeeded during the turmoil of the revolution in imposing its will on the workers. According to this interpretation, Lenin's party was essentially a manipulative one that carried out a coup d'etat in October, supported neither by the majority of the Russian people nor by the workers. Post-Soviet Russian historians are also inclined to this view.[2]

More recent scholars, many of them inspired by Marxist theory, have taken a different approach. They stress the indigenous radicalism of the working classes. According to their view, in the course of the revolutionary struggle the workers acquired class consciousness and came to support the Bolshevik Party because that party represented their well-understood interests. The October events, therefore, should be regarded as a genuine proletarian revolution.[3]

It is evident that in the course of 1917 the working classes came to be radicalized. This radicalization occurred largely as a result of the deteriorating economy. The workers understood ever more clearly that the Provisional Government could not help them and could not solve the country's problems. Believing that the existing government would not protect their interests, they started to look to their own organizations and to the Bolsheviks for leadership. The Bolsheviks had consistently represented the most radical point of view. The most important working-class organizations were the factory committees established shortly after the February Revolution. The committees were more popular and powerful than the trade unions because they represented a kind of direct democracy that suited the chaotic circumstances. They could quickly change policies as circumstances demanded. When Lenin talked about the need for workers' control in industry, he had in mind the factory committee as the instrument of such control. Indeed, the committees had begun interfering with every aspect of management well before the October Revolution. Already in the era of the Provisional Government the Bolsheviks had taken over the leadership of these committees.

Soviet historians saw the key to Lenin's success in his "consistent class analysis." But it may be that Lenin was simply lucky. He had opposed the war for reasons of principle. He craved revolution and insisted on radical politics largely as a matter of temperament. Now the Russian people, primarily the workers and the soldiers in the rear echelons, came to ideological positions that Lenin had already advocated. It makes little sense to believe that the workers were won over to Bolshevik policies by clever Bolshevik propaganda. In fact, the nonsocialist parties had far greater resources than did the socialists, and the Bolsheviks were disadvantaged even within the socialist camp. To be sure, the Bolsheviks did not shrink from demagoguery, but neither did their opponents. The anti-Bolsheviks also used all available means. For example, they rather successfully kept Bolshevik newspapers out of military units. Obviously, the Bolshevik appeal succeeded because there was an eager audience for radical positions. There is no reason to think that in matters of technique the Bolsheviks were superior propagandists.

Support for Bolshevik positions grew steadily during 1917, except during a short period following the July days when the radicals suffered a setback. While many rank-and-file Bolsheviks certainly were involved in organizing demonstrations and creating disorder, the top leadership of the party, including Lenin, clearly did not believe that a Bolshevik takeover could be successful at this point. On the other hand, once the disorders started and numerous people were killed, the Bolsheviks could not abandon the demonstrators without suffering great political damage. When the government succeeded in reestablishing order, it arrested some of the Bolshevik leaders. Lenin and his close comrade Grigorii Zinoviev were forced to go into hiding, and a band of soldiers wrecked the offices of the party newspaper *Pravda*. It seemed that Lenin had suffered a serious defeat.

The Bolsheviks were further embarrassed by the publication of documents designed to show that Lenin and his comrades were German agents. Although the documents were forgeries, the basic allegation that the Leninists had received aid from Germany was true. Soldiers and workers may have been fed up with the war, but such an accusation still carried considerable political force, and without doubt undermined Bolshevik support in the factories and regiments. The setback, however, was only temporary. Anarchy – which after all was the main source of Bolshevik strength – continued to spread. The single event that helped the Bolsheviks most was the ill-fated Kornilov mutiny. The mutiny seemingly demonstrated that it was the political right that threatened the revolution, as the Bolsheviks had always maintained, and that Leninists were the only ones uncompromised by cooperation with the bourgeoisie. They had called upon workers and soldiers to take power, and during the Kornilov mutiny, the workers and soldiers showed that they did possess considerable force. Support for the Bolsheviks jumped. For the first time they achieved majorities in both the Petrograd and Moscow Soviets. These victories had decisive significance for the future of the Provisional Government. The Bolsheviks and the radical workers had taunted the Petrograd Soviet for not daring to take power. Now that the Bolsheviks controlled the soviets, the decision when to attack was in their hands.

THE OCTOBER REVOLUTION

Historians have asked whether the Bolshevik seizure of power in October 1917 was a coup d'etat, carried out by the impetuous Bolsheviks, or a true revolution, the work of the radical workers and soldiers of Petrograd. But perhaps the most striking aspect of the events was neither the Bolsheviks' daring, nor the behavior of the workers, but the complete disintegration of governmental authority.

Lenin determinedly urged his followers to act, arguing that waiting might prove fatal. He finally succeeded in winning over the Central Committee of his party, with the exception of two important dissenters, Zinoviev and Kamenev. Lenin's old comrades were so opposed to what seemed to them a rash decision that they decided to publish the date of the planned uprising in a noncommunist journal. They chose *Novyi Mir*, a journal edited by Maxim Gorky, the famous radical writer. By this time the

Provisional Government had lost all power and authority: every politically aware person in Petrograd knew that the Bolsheviks were about to act, but the government could not defend itself. Under the circumstances one could hardly speak of a coup d'etat, much less a conspiracy. The Bolsheviks seized power because the country was in the throes of anarchy.

The Bolshevik Revolution is such a significant moment in world history that the observer looking back is often surprised and even disappointed to learn that the actual events of October 24–25, 1917, were not particularly dramatic. Restaurants and theaters were open that night. From the point of view of weary contemporaries, the country simply experienced another crisis. The Bolsheviks, now in control of the Petrograd Soviet, used its military revolutionary committee to organize and carry out a revolutionary move. They took over key public buildings and the offices of the major newspapers and railroad stations. The last holdout was the Winter Palace, in which the Provisional Government was meeting – without Kerensky, who had succeeded earlier in escaping from the city. The storming of the Winter Palace, so well known to posterity from Eisenstein's film *October*, did not take place as depicted by the great director. The besiegers were disorganized and few, but that did not matter, since the government in the last minutes of its existence could count on practically no armed support. The Bolsheviks timed their action to coincide with the Second Congress of Soviets. By maintaining that they were acting in the name of the soviets, they hoped to achieve a measure of legitimacy. In fact they presented the congress with a fait accompli. Although moderate socialist leaders left the meeting in protest, the Bolshevik majority passed a resolution approving the revolutionary moves.

It was the issues of land and peace which had brought down the Provisional Government, and Lenin was resolved to deal with these issues as decisively and expeditiously as possible. On the day after his victory he presented his decree on peace and land to the Congress of Soviets. The first of these decrees was an appeal to all belligerent countries to commence negotiations for a just and democratic peace without indemnities or annexations. The second declared the land to be national property, but allowed peasants to cultivate it as their own. In practice this meant that the Bolsheviks officially recognized the peasants' land confiscations. Creating a class of landed peasants tended to conflict with the Bolsheviks' Marxist image of the future. As Marxists, they believed that the possession of property by the large majority of the Russian people would make the establishment of a socialist society more difficult. Lenin, however, realized that it was essential to allow the peasants to carry out their revolution in order to win them over, or at least to render them neutral. After October the main task of Bolshevik agitators in the villages was to spread the land decree: it was the chief argument of the agitators in their attempt to persuade the peasants that the Bolsheviks were on their side.

V. I. Lenin

The new government, called the Council of Commissars and headed by Lenin, was an exclusively Bolshevik body. The list of commissars was a disappointment to the majority of the radical soldiers and workers who had helped the Bolsheviks to power, because they had expected a coalition government of socialists. A sizable portion of the top leadership of the party would also have preferred a coalition. Some leaders felt so strongly about this that they resigned rather than participate in a one-party government, but Lenin and Trotsky were adamant. Their conception of the new regime did not allow concessions to those who had opposed taking power. A month later the Bolsheviks did admit a few left Socialist Revolutionaries into their government. The new commissars took their portfolios on Bolshevik terms, however, and since they had no organized power base they could not effectively oppose Bolshevik policies. In any case, the left Socialist Revolutionaries remained in the coalition for only a short time. They left the government in protest over Lenin's decision to conclude peace with the Germans in March 1918.

In view of the bitterness of the civil war that was to begin within a few months, the question arises: what were those future passionate anti-Bolsheviks doing in the crucial hours? Why did they allow their adversaries to take power so easily? As we have already seen, the Bolsheviks did not surprise them: every politically aware person in Russia knew about the well-advertised intentions of the revolutionaries.

The paralysis had several causes. The military men, followers of Kornilov who would soon make up the leadership of the anti-Bolshevik White movement, had recently been defeated and were disappointed in the Russian people. On the one hand, they hated Kerensky's liberal regime with such passion that they would not come to its defense under any circumstances. On the other hand, they underestimated the Bolsheviks. They did not imagine that a band of radicals with outlandish ideas could succeed where tsarist ministers and educated and experienced statesmen had failed: to wit, in governing the country. Moreover, they were so preoccupied with the need to fight the foreign foe that they refused to abandon their positions at the front. They came into open opposition only when it became impossible for them to continue to fight the Germans.

The Mensheviks and the Socialist Revolutionaries failed to act because they underestimated the differences between themselves and the new government. In their eyes the Bolsheviks were fellow socialists. The country was preparing for elections to the Constituent Assembly, and the moderate socialists were afraid of compromising their position in the eyes of the voters. The fact that the Bolsheviks managed to retain a semblance of legitimacy by obtaining majority support at the Second Congress of Soviets also helped them significantly. In some sense the anti-Bolsheviks were right: the conquest of power was a relatively minor matter. The truly difficult task, providing the country with a functioning government and overcoming anarchy, still lay ahead.

The Bolsheviks took power with an extraordinarily ambitious program aimed not only at reorganizing society and politics, but also at remaking humanity. Their program was based on abstract principles derived from their reading of Marx. Perhaps not surprisingly, the precepts of theory and the concrete needs of the moment almost immediately clashed, and the Bolsheviks were forced to improvise. In that process of improvisation they became the great innovators of twentieth-century politics. They developed institutions, methods of mobilization, and even a vocabulary that would be not so much imitated as rediscovered again and again. The interplay between the demands posed by unexpected and harsh reality and an ideology to which the revolutionaries were deeply committed is a complex and fascinating topic.

It would be a mistake to imagine that all the unattractive aspects of Bolshevik policies were the consequence of the cruel and unexpected demands of the time. The Bolsheviks were not democrats and liberals converted to a different mode of politics by their desire to survive. They obviously brought with them the mental attitudes that enabled them to transform themselves quickly from revolutionaries to administrators, from freedom-fighters to oppressors.

They came to power in circumstances completely unforeseen by their ideology. Instead of taking over a fully mature industrial society, their inheritance was illiteracy, anarchy, industrial ruin, and hunger. Instead of participating in a world revolution, after which they could have benefited from the help of more advanced nations, they had to face further attacks from the mighty German army. That army seemed unstoppable because the Russian army had lost its capacity to resist – at least partially as a result of previous Bolshevik antiwar propaganda.

Internationalism was deeply ingrained in the mental framework of the Bolsheviks: they regarded themselves as an advance regiment in the international proletarian army. It was disturbing to them that, contrary to Marxist theory, the revolution had not first occurred in the economically most advanced countries. They explained this anomaly to their own satisfaction by arguing that the Russian proletariat was in a position to break the chain of world capitalism at its weakest link. According to this reasoning, the primary purpose of the Russian Revolution was to break that chain and thereby initiate a world revolution. As they saw it, their revolution could be successful in the long run only if it was aided by sympathetic, more advanced, and above all socialist nations. The expectation of a socialist revolution following the mad devastation of the First World War was by no means nonsensical. Today we know that the revolution did not occur, that the old order reasserted itself. At the time, however, everyone, friend and foe alike, hoped for or feared just such a cataclysmic transformation.

This expectation of world revolution was not a theoretical issue to the Leninists, but a matter that affected their everyday behavior. The victorious Bolsheviks faced a phalanx of hostile governments. Such hostility was expected and even necessary for the Bolsheviks. Those who believed in the internationalism of the working classes also had to believe in the internationalism of capital. The Bolsheviks half-expected that the capitalist powers, understanding that their deadliest enemies were not one another but the socialists, would forget about the war and unite against the revolutionaries. Such a development, in the Bolshevik view, was most likely to lead to a revolt of all exploited peoples, and was thus perhaps desirable.

The immediate problem, however, was not a hostile coalition but the German army. The Bolsheviks entered peace negotiations with the enemy and ultimately accepted severe German terms. On March 3 they signed the Treaty of Brest-Litovsk. The dispute over the terms of that treaty came to be the first bitter debate in Soviet history, a debate that almost tore the party apart.

Negotiating with an imperialist foe could be regarded as the starting point of Soviet foreign policy. When the Bolsheviks took power they believed that their regime had no need for a foreign policy. The governments of the world would be implacably hostile, and the world proletariat supportive; foreign relations could be reduced to revolutionary appeals. The Bolsheviks saw the solution to their difficulties in immediate world revolution. That this revolution never came was their greatest disappointment.

A large and influential segment of the leadership of the party continued to believe that it was a mistake to conclude any treaty or even to maintain diplomatic discourse with the capitalist powers. These people, led by Nikolai Bukharin and dubbed the left communists, wanted to continue the war not so much to defend Russia's national interests, but because they believed that the German soldiers would refuse to fight against their Russian comrades and that this refusal would spark a long-awaited German revolution. If in the process the new soviet regime were eliminated, that, in the view of the left communists, was a worthwhile price for advancing the international cause. Such an argument was compelling to those who were certain that the new revolutionary regime could not long survive in any case without the help of the world proletariat.

Lenin, the great realist, did not allow himself to be seduced by revolutionary dreams. With remarkable energy, determination, and clear vision, he forced his views on his recalcitrant colleagues. By signing the Brest-Litovsk treaty he ensured the immediate survival of his regime; after all, the Germans could easily have overthrown the Bolsheviks, who possessed no serious military force. The Germans stopped their advance because they realized that any regime imposed on the defeated Russians would require a considerable investment of German troops; they preferred to use their soldiers on the western front.

The second great disappointment for the Bolsheviks was the behavior of the Russian people. According to their understanding the party directed the revolution of the working classes. That revolution was carried out in order to benefit the great majority of the Russian people, the workers and the peasants. In the course of 1917 there was a great deal of talk about the convocation of the Constituent Assembly that was to resolve the major national questions. Elections to the assembly had been scheduled for November, before the October Revolution took place, and the Bolsheviks decided to go through with the elections. It is not entirely clear what the Bolsheviks expected, for the results were not surprising. The Socialist Revolutionaries, who had support in the countryside, succeeded in electing the majority of the deputies, while the Bolsheviks could count on about a quarter of the delegates.

The assembly duly met in January 1918, expressed anti-Bolshevik sentiments, and then was dispersed by the Bolsheviks. It was a dramatic move, because by disregarding the clearly expressed will of the electorate the Bolsheviks repudiated once and for all any pretense of acting on the basis of the principles of "bourgeois" democracy. Their legitimacy was not to be based on popular sovereignty, but on the conviction that they understood the movement of history. They stood for a better, socialist future for all mankind. It is hard to see, however, how the Bolsheviks could have acted otherwise, for to accept the authority of the Constituent Assembly would have meant to undo the October Revolution. Unlike the Brest-Litovsk negotiations, which had caused a major crisis within the party, this time there were no differences of opinion among the leaders. Everything in their experience and theoretical outlook prepared the Leninists to take precisely these steps.

While repudiating electoral democracy did not cause them much soul-searching, suspension of freedom of expression did lead to a passionate debate among the Bolsheviks. On November 4 in the central executive committee of the soviets, a number of prominent Bolshevik leaders argued eloquently for freedom of the press. They confidently – albeit no doubt wrongly – believed that, if presented with a number of conflicting views, the Russian people would be able to see the correctness of the Bolshevik position. Lenin passionately opposed this position and spoke contemptuously of the principle of the freedom of the press. Once again, he prevailed. The new rulers could not immediately eliminate all non-Bolshevik publications. However, within the first eight months of their rule they succeeded in doing so. As the civil war began and the revolutionaries found it necessary to use harsher and harsher methods, all non-Bolshevik newspapers disappeared from territories under their control.

Suspension of freedom of the press went hand in hand with suspension of freedom of association: in areas under their control the Bolsheviks suppressed first the nonsocialist parties and later all parties. In order to carry out such policies, the new rulers needed a coercive force. Those who had suffered at the hands of the tsarist political police, the Okhrana, soon after their victory established their own political police, the All-Russian Extraordinary Commission for Struggle Against Counterrevolution, Sabotage, and Speculation, known simply as the Cheka (the Russian abbreviation for extraordinary commission).

THE COURSE OF THE CIVIL WAR

The old order had ceased to function and the country faced extraordinary difficulties. Both the socialist and the nonsocialist camps were deeply divided over how to deal with the problems. Within a short time, however, out of the dozens of competing points of view, only two – the Bolsheviks and the military counterrevolutionaries – remained serious contenders. The Socialist Revolutionaries, who undoubtedly possessed the support of the majority of the Russian people, never had a chance. The moderate socialist politicians had no way of turning electoral support into regiments. They did not possess an ideology, or a mentality, that would enable them to take the necessarily harsh steps to resolve the national crisis.

The civil war, therefore, was soon reduced to a contest between the Whites and the Reds. On one side were revolutionary intellectuals and semi-intellectuals, who had suffered repression during the tsarist regime and were committed to change on the basis of their deeply held Marxist beliefs. They were politicians of a new type, who clearly understood the need for mass mobilization and propaganda. On the other side, the leadership was made up exclusively of army officers, men who had been at home in tsarist Russia, who were contemptuous of politics, and who envisaged military solutions to most problems. They had no vision of a future Russia but felt it necessary to combat the Bolsheviks, for they believed that communist rule would bring only evil to the fatherland. However different the two groups were, they faced the same problems: how to provide the country with a functioning administration, furnish food for the starving, make the railroads run; in short, how to overcome anarchy.

The anti-Bolsheviks were slow to organize. The ex-leaders of the Kornilov mutiny, who had subsequently been imprisoned, used the confusion created by the Bolshevik rising to escape from their confinement and flee to the Cossack district of the Don. They were soon joined by the tsar's ex-chief of staff, General Alekseev. This small group of officers included many, but by no means all, of the most prominent leaders of the Russian forces during the war. They came to the Cossack district of the Don because there was no other region in Russia where they could find security. The Cossacks, descendants of freebooters, by the early twentieth century had become rich peasants; they were receiving taxation and landholding privileges from the tsarist government in return for heavier military obligation. Unlike other Russian peasants, they enjoyed a tradition of self-government. Now they felt their privileges threatened by the less fortunate fellow inhabitants of their districts, the Russian peasants. These Russian peasants were much poorer, owned much less land, and often had to rent from Cossacks. They resented their Cossack exploiters, and were willing listeners to Bolshevik appeals. The Don and the Kuban districts were embarking upon their own civil war, a contest for power that partially overlapped the larger national struggle. The Cossacks came to play a decisively important role in the White movement, largely because the White generals did not have another force to count on; they never succeeded in winning over the majority of the Russian people, the peasants.

During the first few months of 1918 the generals attracted only a pitifully small following. After several months of organizing, the incipient White movement's military force, the volunteer army, had only about 3,000 fighters, mostly officers. It reflects the weakness of the new Bolshevik government that it did not have the strength to disperse even such a minuscule army; a civil war is always a struggle between the weak and the weaker. Later during the spring it was the Germans, ironically, who enabled the Whites to survive. German policy was to encourage anti-Bolsheviks in the peripheries of the country, while tolerating Bolsheviks at the center. A country torn by civil war best served German interests. One consequence of this policy was their support for a conservative Cossack government on the Don. Thus the White generals, who had not so long ago denounced the

Bolsheviks as German agents and sworn loyalty to the Allies, now became the main beneficiaries of the policies of the enemies of their fatherland.

A turning point in the history of the civil war was the rebellion of the Czech troops, surely one of its most curious episodes. The Habsburg monarchy, Russia's enemy in the First World War, was – like imperial Russia – a multinational empire. The large Slav minority within it felt oppressed, and at the time of the war showed little loyalty to the Habsburgs. A large number of Czech soldiers, for example, allowed themselves to be easily captured by the Russians. The tsarist government hesitated to play the nationality card. They refused to form an army from these prisoners of war and allow them to fight on the Russian side. That situation changed in 1917: Kerensky had no scruples on this score and encouraged the Czechs to form an independent corps and fight the Germans. The Czechs were enthusiastic soldiers, for they rightly believed that only the defeat of the Central Powers, Germany and the Austro-Hungarian monarchy, would allow them to form an independent state. When the Russian army fell apart, this tiny force alone wanted to continue fighting, but the Brest-Litovsk treaty made it impossible for them to continue their struggle. After long negotiations with the Soviet government, it was decided to allow them to travel to the western front through Siberia, the Pacific, and the United States. The Czechs, however, never reached their destination, because while traveling through Siberia they started to fight the Bolsheviks. In May 1918 Bolshevik rule in Siberia was still so weak that 50,000 Czechs could overthrow it. This totally unexpected development allowed the anti-Bolsheviks to establish themselves and organize. After a great deal of quibbling the Whites established a liberal regime in which the Socialist Revolutionaries played a major role. However, this government lasted only for a short time. In November 1918 the military overthrew the socialist government and named Admiral Aleksandr Kolchak, the ex-chief of the Black Sea fleet, as supreme ruler.

The end of the war in Europe had far-reaching consequences for the course of the civil war in Russia. As long as the Allies and the Central Powers were fighting one another, they looked at their involvement in Russia as far less important. Although the Allied governments regarded the Bolsheviks and everything they stood for with fear and loathing, had the Bolsheviks continued the war against the Germans, they could have received Allied support. The Allies first assisted the Whites with the illusory hope that the anti-German front might be reconstructed. The British and the Americans, who in early 1918 sent small detachments to the Far North in Murmansk and Archangel and to the Far East in Vladivostok, justified their intervention in Russian affairs in terms of their need to fight the Germans.

Once the First World War ended, any rationale for the intervention fell away while the opportunities for practical aid to the anti-Bolsheviks vastly improved. Immediately after the defeat of the Germans, French troops landed in Odessa, and shortly after in Crimea. The British sent small detachments to the Caucasus and to Central Asia, and soon began the delivery of valuable military hardware to Kolchak and to Anton Denikin, the commander of the volunteer army.

The Bolsheviks, of course, then and ever since, had a great incentive to believe, or at least to pretend to believe, that they were fighting not against domestic enemies but against the combined forces of world imperialism. It became an article of faith in Soviet historiography that the young Soviet state struggled against the combined forces of world imperialism. In fact the contribution of foreigners to the outcome of the civil war was slight. Foreign governments had only the vaguest understanding of Russian affairs; they based their policies and dispensed their advice on the basis of false premises. But however much the Allies would have liked to overthrow the Bolsheviks, given the politics of postwar Europe they were not in a position to do so. French troops were the only ones who actually did a bit of fighting, and their performance was dismal. They did more harm than good to the White cause. British military aid, and to a lesser extent American, was undoubtedly helpful to Denikin and Kolchak; but such aid could only prolong the war.

German withdrawal increased the scope of the fighting. Bolsheviks and anti-Bolsheviks rushed into the vacuum, hoping to take advantage of the opportunity. The greatest threat to Bolshevik rule in the first months of 1919 came from the east. As Kolchak marched west, it seemed that he might be able to link up with Denikin in the south. The Red Army managed to turn the tide on the eastern front in June 1919, but the Bolsheviks could not yet relax. That summer Denikin occupied Ukraine, and in October he reached Orel, about 250 miles from Moscow. At the same time Lenin's regime faced a new danger. General Nikolai Iudenich had organized yet another anti-Bolshevik army in Estonia that now threatened Petrograd. October 1919 was a decisive moment in the civil war. The Reds at this crucial time managed to mobilize new forces and to stop both Iudenich and Denikin. Denikin's lines had become overextended and were mercilessly harassed by Ukrainian anarchist partisans, most significantly Nestor Makhno.

By 1920 it was fairly certain that the Reds would ultimately win. In the spring of 1920, Denikin once again was restricted to the Kuban. He succeeded in getting his troops to Crimea, but then went into exile. Petr Wrangel, the last commander, an able and charismatic figure, could pin his hopes only on outside circumstances. Poland, which became an independent country at the end of the war, had great territorial ambitions at Russia's expense. The Polish leader, Jozef Pilsudski, believing he could get a better deal from the Bolsheviks than from the victorious Whites, waited until the defeat of the main White forces and then started his campaign. The Russo-Polish war, which inspired nationalist passions on both sides, saw changing military fortunes; at one point the victorious Red Army threatened the Polish capital. The war ultimately ended in the compromise peace of Riga in March 1921. Following the decisive phase of the Polish campaign, the Red Army defeated Wrangel and forced him and the remnants of his army into exile. By the end of 1920 the Bolsheviks had defeated all their enemies with the exception of a few scattered peasant bands.

THE CAUSES OF BOLSHEVIK VICTORY

Although the Bolsheviks ultimately won the civil war, their victory at the outset was by no means assured, nor did it seem so to weary contemporaries. Several times the survival of the revolutionary government hung in the balance. In the spring of 1918, for example, the regime was almost overcome by sheer anarchy; the next spring, Kolchak seemed unstoppable; and in the fall of 1919 the combined forces of Denikin and Iudenich presented such a military threat that many expected Lenin's regime to soon collapse.

The Whites enjoyed many significant advantages. They had the support of the church. Their armies were almost always better led, and they did not have to fear treason among their officers. In the prevailing conditions, where the front line moved quickly, the Cossack cavalry was an extremely valuable force. The Whites occupied better agricultural lands, and had to feed the populations of fewer large cities. These factors, combined with Allied aid, made living conditions better in White-held territories. When the Whites occupied a city, the price of bread almost always fell. Naturally, at a time of starvation, lower food prices held a great appeal and far-reaching political significance.

Still, the Bolsheviks won at least in part because of the weakness of their enemies. The Whites did not have an attractive ideology or the right frame of mind to accomplish their most important task: imposing order on an unwilling population. Since they saw their task as primarily a military one, they made no serious attempt to win over the population with an attractive vision of the future. Indeed, they themselves lacked such a vision. The generals had been comfortable in imperial Russia and, although the more enlightened among them realized that some reforms might be necessary, they all fervently wished that the revolutions of 1917 had never happened.

When they were forced to articulate their goals, the Whites had to fall back on a newly developed and exaggerated sense of nationalism. They proclaimed that they were fighting for "Russia." The trouble with such an ideology was that it had little appeal to those who were politically the most important, the peasants. Perhaps even more significantly, it fatally alienated the national minorities, who might have become useful allies in an anti-Bolshevik crusade. Since the Whites of necessity were fighting in areas largely inhabited by non-Russians, hostility from the minorities had fateful consequences.

The disintegration of the once-powerful empire, and the obvious weakness of the central authorities, resulted in an extraordinarily rapid growth of national self-consciousness among the minorities. Politicians who had professed to be internationalists and socialists now came into power in newly independent states and came to embrace the nationalist cause with passion. The Bolsheviks and the anti-Bolsheviks adopted different policies toward the newly established states on the peripheries. The Bolshevik attitude was a great deal more expedient: as long as they had no power to prevent the establishment of these states, they did not openly oppose them. They seemed to have accepted the principle of national self-determination, although adding that it applied as long as it served the interest of the proletariat. The Whites would make no comparable concession.

The Russian peasants were not moved by a nationalist ideology; they were interested in getting the lands of the landlords. White politicians labored for many months to come up with a land reform plan. They were slow to produce one, for they did not fully appreciate the political significance of winning over the land-hungry peasants. By the time they published a land reform project, in the summer of 1920, it was far too late. Even this plan offered very little. After all, the Whites drew their social support from the right and could not alienate their supporters. The peasants saw that, in the wake of the White armies, the landlords and ex-tsarist officials reappeared to reclaim their wealth and power. No matter what White politicians said in their manifestos, the peasants correctly understood that the Whites stood for restoration.

But the Bolsheviks won the civil war not only because of the weaknesses and errors of their opponents. Their understanding of the needs of the moment and the principles of revolutionary politics helped them as well. The political program with which they came to power could not be realized, and therefore the revolutionaries constantly had to improvise. But, fortunately for them, their background and their ideology allowed them to improvise successfully.

The Bolsheviks, as Marxist-Leninists, instinctively understood the significance of organization and mass mobilization. They worked tirelessly and ceaselessly both to bring their program to the workers and peasants and to create organizational forms that could restore order. A major share of the credit for winning the civil war belonged to the party. Originally an organization of revolutionaries, it was quickly transformed into an instrument of rule. In the circumstances it would be wrong to think of it as a tightly knit, disciplined, and hierarchical organization. Top leaders frequently quarreled, and the center often had only nominal control over the distant cities. Nevertheless, as an organizational base it conferred on the Bolsheviks an inestimable advantage. The party was involved in every aspect of national life: it was responsible for developing a strategy for winning the struggle; it was a recruitment agency that brought forward able and ambitious cadres; it was the chief indoctrination agency; in enemy-controlled territories, it organized an underground; and, perhaps most importantly, it attempted to supervise the work of other governmental and social institutions.

Bolshevik organizational skills and principles were best shown in the creation and building of the Red Army, which was Trotsky's great achievement. Both Trotsky and Lenin quickly realized that, contrary to utopian notions they themselves had entertained, the services of experts were essential for running a modern state. In the case of the military, this meant that the young Soviet state needed the expertise of the officers of the ex-imperial army. These men had to be forced or cajoled into the service of an ideology that they in almost all instances found distasteful. Furthermore, the policy entailed risks: it created indignation among some old communists, and the officers were by no means fully reliable. Treason was a constant danger. Yet Trotsky was correct: only a disciplined force, led by professional men, could defeat the enemy.

By the end of the civil war the Bolsheviks, using extensive propaganda in addition to conscription, had built an army of 5 million – incomparably larger than the combined forces of their enemies. Only a small percentage of this army ever served in battles; the rest provided support and administrative services. At a time of anarchy, the new state needed all the support it could get.

The Cheka also made a contribution to the Bolshevik victory. Terror was equally bloody on both sides; Reds and Whites alike committed acts of extraordinary brutality. However, political repression by the two sides had a different character. The Whites, whose views were more appropriate to the nineteenth century than to the twentieth, had little appreciation of the role of ideas in politics and tolerated a far greater diversity of political opinions. The Cheka, by contrast, allowed only one political organization, and one political point of view, that of the Leninists.

The Bolsheviks successfully tailored their social and economic policies to the needs of winning the war. Lenin presented his famous decree on land on the day following his victory. As a concession to the peasants, the decree legalized previous land seizures and allowed the peasants to cultivate land previously held by the landlords as their own private property. Lenin, the great realist, clearly saw the political benefits. Yet, despite the fact that the Reds gave them land and the Whites gave them nothing, the Bolsheviks could win only a few active supporters among the peasants. The great weakness of the Bolshevik position was that they needed to feed their cities but had nothing to give the peasants in exchange for grain. In such circumstances the principles of a free market obviously could not operate, and the Bolsheviks requisitioned grain by force. This policy was bound to alienate the peasants, but it is hard to see what else the revolutionaries could have done.

The economic policies introduced by the Bolsheviks in the middle of 1918, chief among them the suspension of a market mechanism for grain, were called war communism. This system mobilized the economy for the purpose of winning the war by means of coercion. The Bolsheviks nationalized trade and industry. Although such developments were clearly the result of improvisation, at the time theorists professed to see in the disappearance of private enterprise and even money a step toward the coming of communist society. The system caused great misery and hardship for the population and in the long run led to the devastation of the national economy. Nevertheless, in the short run it was effective: factories did produce enough arms to fight the enemy, and people in the cities were fed, however poorly.

The Bolshevik Revolution, like all great revolutions, was fought for social equality. The revolutionaries did a great deal to recruit a new political elite. Young and ambitious peasants and workers, through a mixture of conviction and careerism, threw in their lot with the Bolsheviks. They were able to approach their fellow workers and peasants far more successfully than any White propagandist. By mobilizing this hitherto-untapped source of talent, the Bolsheviks gained a great deal. Conscious Bolshevik policies, as well as the misery imposed by war and war communism, did in fact greatly reduce inequality.

New Economic Policies, 1921–1929

As long as the Soviet Union existed, Soviet historians depicted the history of their country as an unbroken unit. Paradoxically, the most determined opponents of that failed regime agreed on that point. Although of course they had different attitudes toward the revolution and the Soviet regime, both groups saw the outlines of Soviet history as already inherent in Lenin's revolution. Liberal Western historians, and some Marxist dissidents in the Soviet Union, disagreed: they saw profound discontinuities and maintained that the direction of history was not predetermined at its critical turning points. By stressing the contingent nature of Soviet history, they were able to identify themselves with the emancipatory goals of the socialist revolution without accepting Stalinism or the undeniably unattractive aspects of the era of Brezhnev as a natural outcome of the revolution.

In this important though often only implicit debate, the interpretation of the 1920s had a crucial place. This period stands out in Soviet history. Many saw it as a golden age: the victorious revolutionaries had destroyed the old order and eliminated, or at least narrowed, the appalling cleavage between the poor and the rich that had characterized imperial Russia. The new regime gave opportunities to the talented and ambitious to rise in the social hierarchy and filled millions with hope. At the same time, the Bolshevik government still allowed a considerable degree of cultural pluralism. Artists, imagining themselves the equivalents of the Bolsheviks in their respective spheres, embarked on experimental ventures without suffering harassment. It was a period during which intelligent and articulate Bolsheviks, profoundly conscious of being pathbreakers in the history of mankind, discussed alternative strategies for economic and social development. No one could then even imagine the dreadful bloodletting that was to follow.

In 1921 the Bolsheviks gave concessions to the peasants, allowing free trade in grain and opening the way for free enterprise within a rather narrow framework. Historians with more or less favorable attitudes toward the

Soviet experiment have argued that the New Economic Policies (NEP) were the natural strategy of the victorious revolutionaries, and that war communism was an aberration imposed on the Leninists by cruel circumstances.[1] Other historians, in contrast, have maintained that the Leninists' preferred policy was the social and economic radicalism of war communism. They abandoned such policies only because they had to, only temporarily as a tactical retreat. These historians point to the great reluctance of the majority of party members to accept the NEP and to the numerous statements of Lenin and his closest comrades according to which the NEP was merely a temporary phase.

It is possible to establish an intermediate position between the two extremes. It is indisputable that the Bolsheviks regarded the NEP as a temporary phase; after all, those who had worked for a communist society could not be satisfied with the halfway solutions of the NEP. However, different leaders had different understandings, and indeed the same leaders at different times had different views on how long a "temporary" period the NEP ought to occupy. The Leninists, flexible politicians that they were, adopted both the policies of war communism and the NEP under duress. As the leaders came to believe in the policies that they were carrying out, they tended to forget the circumstances of their introduction and came to see positive good in them. Nikolai Bukharin, a most articulate ideologue of the party, waxed eloquent in 1919 on the disappearance of money as a sign of the coming communist society; yet he came to be a passionate defender of the social system of the NEP. Bukharin was perhaps an extreme case; nevertheless, other communists also managed to believe both in the policies of war communism and in the NEP. As we shall see, the NEP was genuinely and significantly different from the era of Stalin; but at the same time it contained the seeds of the coming totalitarianism.

THE CONSEQUENCES OF THE REVOLUTION

In November 1920, the Reds defeated the army of General Wrangel, the last major counterrevolutionary force. Although the war against Poland dragged on for several months, it was clear that the revolutionary system of government had survived the test of the civil war. If, at that historical moment, the Bolshevik leaders had been inclined to look around them and ask how much they had accomplished, how much had Russia changed, the answers to these questions could not have been fully pleasing. Their chief goal, to spark a world revolution, still eluded them. The bourgeois world order had consolidated itself, and Soviet Russia remained a backward and isolated country within a hostile world system.

The changes that had occurred were far-reaching. The world had never seen a comparably profound change in the relationship of classes in such a brief period. As important as conscious policies were, the unforeseen and unforeseeable consequences of the enormous destruction, the years of anarchy and extraordinary misery that the people of the new revolutionary state had to suffer, were even more profound. Numbers cannot express the human misery that the destruction of war, revolution, and civil war caused, but they are suggestive. In 1921 Soviet agriculture produced less than two-thirds of what the Russian empire had produced in 1913.[2] The decline of large-scale industry was truly catastrophic: industrial output was only one-fifth of what it had been during the last year of peace. As long as the Bolsheviks insisted on the policies of war communism and did not allow free trade, the peasants had no incentive to produce, and certainly no incentive to part with the fruits of their labor. As traditional authority broke down, a multiplicity of armies fought one another. In areas devastated by civil war, people did not know who might come tomorrow to take food from them, to draft them into their armies, to subject them to blind and senseless terror. Bands of orphans roamed the streets of cities and the countryside trying to survive at the expense of others. The social fabric had disintegrated. It is not surprising that in these circumstances the relationship between classes, and indeed all social institutions, greatly shifted.

Perhaps the most obvious change was the destruction of the traditional ruling class. A few individuals from the upper classes managed to adjust to the altered circumstances and make careers in the new world. However, 2 million people emigrated, and those who stayed behind lost their wealth, the basis of their power. Two worlds had uneasily coexisted in imperial Russia: the culture of the unprivileged, the workers and peasants, and the culture of the intelligentsia and the privileged. The customs, ways of life, and even the languages of the two groups had been far apart. The revolution abolished this cleavage – perhaps its greatest achievement.

Ironically, it was not the proletariat but the peasantry who gained most tangibly from the revolution. As the landlords' property was distributed, 3 million previously landless peasants received some land. By 1919, for practical purposes all agricultural land was in their hands. The revolutionary events, most significantly land seizures, reversed the process of economic differentiation that had begun before the First World War. For ideological and strategic reasons the Bolsheviks wanted to encourage class struggle in the villages: to win the support of the poor, to gain the benevolent neutrality of those neither poor nor well-to-do (middle peasant, in Bolshevik terminology), and to struggle against the rich, the kulak. Such a strategy, however, could achieve only limited success at a time when the peasant class was becoming more than ever economically undifferentiated.

The peasants benefited from the extreme weakening of state authority. Their heavy debts were canceled, and the state was not in a position to interfere in their lives. Peasant self-government in the form of the commune, an institution that had been diminishing in importance before the war,

Famine victims, 1920

acquired a new lease on life. The peasantry turned inward, showing hostility toward all outsiders. They bitterly resented Bolshevik policies, in particular the prohibition of grain sales in the free market and requisitioning. Needless to say, the peasants also suffered. They too were victims of the general economic collapse and of marauding armies, conscription, and forced requisitioning. However, in the prevailing conditions of subsistence economy and poor communications, those farthest from the scenes of conflict could protect themselves best.

It was the workers, in whose name the revolution had been carried out, and who provided the backbone of support to the revolutionaries, who suffered the most during the years of the civil war. The proletariat, never very large in backward Russia – perhaps 3 million strong before the war – was almost disappearing. Workers were the first to volunteer for the Red Army and later were drafted in disproportionate numbers. They suffered extremely heavy losses. The new rulers needed an administrative machinery and naturally, given their ideology, removed workers from the factory bench and gave them responsible posts. But the most significant cause of the reduction of the size of the working class was the economic collapse.

Factories closed down, and workers could not earn a living. As the normal market economy broke down, the cities were inadequately supplied with food, and the collapse of the transportation system made matters worse. Under such circumstances it was understandable that the workers, and to a lesser extent all other city dwellers, left the cities in droves. Since the Russian working class was new, and since most of the workers had retained ties with the villages from which they had come, it was all the easier for them to return. Moscow lost half of its population, and Petrograd two-thirds. In smaller cities the exodus was not as extraordinary, but nonetheless all cities suffered.

THE INTRODUCTION OF THE NEW ECONOMIC POLICIES

The need for survival at a time of a bitter civil war necessitated the policies of war communism. At the end of the war, the Bolsheviks probably would have introduced changes into their economic and political system in any case. However, their hand was forced by a wave of disturbances around the country. During the civil war the majority of the peasants opposed the Whites with greater fervor than they opposed the Bolsheviks, though it cannot be said that the peasants actually supported the government in Moscow. Peasant interests and peasant mentality were best represented by various anarchist (or so-called Green) bands, who fought against both the Whites and the Reds. Among these, the most important and best led was the army of the anarchist, Nestor Makhno, who fought in Ukraine. Makhno first dealt severe blows to Denikin's armies, making thereby a significant contribution to Red victory; but after the civil war he took on the Reds and was finally defeated by them. Even more threatening to Lenin's government than Makhno was the uprising of the Tambov peasants, led by Aleksandr Antonov. Although Makhno, Antonov, and the other lesser leaders were formidable enemies, they could not possibly defeat the Bolsheviks in the sense of overthrowing the government in Moscow. These uprisings, which stemmed from the peasants' great misery and bitterness against the policies of their new rulers, raised the specter of anarchy.

The workers were just as desperate as the peasants. Aside from the dreadful hardships they had to endure, it seemed to them that the new government was not carrying out the promises of the revolution. The workers actually ran neither the economy nor the state, because the government could not dispense with the services of experts. Many workers were dismayed that the hated class enemy was not altogether dislodged, but continued to have influence and power. The Bolshevik Party, losing even the support of the working class, came to operate in a vacuum. At the beginning of 1921 there was a series of threatening strikes in Petrograd, and the Bolsheviks feared that the defeated Socialist Revolutionaries and Mensheviks might make political capital out of their difficulties.

Since legal political organizations could not operate in Bolshevik-held territories during the civil war, disputes took place within the party itself. Members of the "democratic opposition" deplored the increased bureaucratization and the disappearance of democracy within the party. In 1920 the leaders passionately debated the role of trade unions in the new society. The most significant faction within the leadership, however, was the "workers' opposition," led by Aleksandr Shliapnikov and Aleksandra Kollontai. The group advocated eliminating bureaucracy and giving greater power to the workers in running the factories. This group, unlike most other intra-party factions, could count on support from the workers themselves, and this fact made it extraordinarily dangerous.

But the greatest blow to the Leninist leadership at this time was the uprising of sailors at the naval base of Kronstadt. Militarily, the uprising was no more dangerous than the chronic peasant disturbances around the country. However, the Bolsheviks could rather easily rationalize peasant hostility. The peasants, they believed, were infected by bourgeois private property consciousness, and therefore their hostility could be anticipated. The sailors, by contrast, were the "pride of the revolution" who had time and again performed the most valuable services for the Bolsheviks. In March 1921 these sailors, expressing the disaffection of their peasant and worker brothers, called for what amounted to a new revolution.

The program of the Kronstadt sailors demanded new and secret elections, soviets without Bolsheviks, and the extension of democratic freedoms to the workers and peasants – but only to them. The sailors were never democrats or liberals. Bolshevik politicians at the time, and Soviet historians as long as the Soviet regime lasted, maintained that the sailors had been in touch with and were led by foreign and domestic "counterrevolutionaries." In fact, there were no such contacts; the uprising of the sailors was a great blow to Bolshevik politicians precisely because the sailors represented the bulk of the Russian workers and peasants. These people did not need to be told that their revolution had not turned out as they had expected.

There is no evidence that any of the leading Bolsheviks hesitated even for a moment about what to do: the uprising had to be suppressed and suppressed quickly before it could spread to nearby Petrograd. Between March 16 and 18 the approximately 10,000 sailors were defeated by loyal troops, and the captured rebels mercilessly punished. The symbolic and emotional significance of Kronstadt was far-reaching. By defeating the sailors, the party in effect repudiated some of the utopian, but nonetheless emotionally powerful, goals of the revolution.

The uprising took place while the Tenth Party Congress was in session, a congress that was perhaps the single most important in the history of the party, its decisions affecting every aspect of the life of the country. Under the

Red Army troops fighting against the Kronstadt rebels

impact of the Kronstadt rising, the delegates to the congress accepted a resolution that outlawed factions within the party. That decision, originally aimed at the workers' opposition, had far-reaching consequences for the life of the party in the following decade.

Politics and economics were closely intertwined. The crisis in self-confidence produced by the rising at Kronstadt no doubt contributed to the relatively easy acceptance by the congress of significant economic concessions. The heart of the change was the abolition of requisitioning and the substitution of a tax in kind. This tax remained in effect until 1924, when as a result of the stabilization of currency it was superseded by a tax in money. The measure seems simple enough, but its consequences were important. It meant that the peasants were free to dispose of their surplus products, and implied the legalization of trade and traders, a social group for which the Bolsheviks felt great hostility. Lenin, in particular, feared the corrosive influence of the small trader even more than that of the capitalist. No wonder, then, that the Bolsheviks accepted the reforms with great misgivings and fear. The severity of the crisis, however, was such that they had no choice.

The substitution of a tax for requisitioning was followed by other reforms that dismantled the economic system of war communism and introduced a new order. In May 1921, the government revoked the law that had nationalized all branches of industry. The economic system that succeeded war communism can be described as a mixed economy. Private individuals were allowed to form small enterprises or to lease them from the state. The government, however, continued to control what was called at the time the "commanding heights," meaning large-scale enterprises, mining, banking, and foreign trade.

In the long run, NEP made reconstruction possible. However, the relaxation could not immediately end the crisis. In 1920 and 1921 some of the most fertile areas of the country were hit by drought. Natural disaster and manmade confusion led to widespread famine, especially in the Volga region. Millions starved to death and millions more were threatened. Weakened by starvation, people fell victim to epidemics. More people died in these terrible years than perished in the First World War, the revolution, and the civil war. Without large-scale famine relief organized by the Americans, many more millions would have died.

The Bolsheviks struggled against chronic shortages of food and fuel. Returning to more or less orthodox principles of economics was difficult, and the recovery was painfully slow. In order to save money the government was compelled to abandon a number of projects it had favored for ideological reasons. Under war communism the factories had operated regardless of cost, but now government enterprises had to make a profit. In an effort to stabilize the currency, cost accounting was introduced, which among other things meant firing workers.

THE POLITICAL SYSTEM

In the heady days of October 1917, the Bolsheviks believed that they were at the threshold of a new era, that their revolution was a first step toward ending the world capitalist order. They came to power against great odds. It seemed to them that the rules of politics were suspended – now everything seemed possible. But the revolutionaries were soon disappointed, for the capitalist world turned out to be far more sturdy than they had imagined, and holding onto power in a backward, beleaguered country was very difficult. But in one sense the Bolsheviks were correct in stressing the uniqueness of their revolution: their accomplishment was not a simple transfer of power from one group of politicians to another. They instituted a new political order, and their regime was like nothing that had ever existed before.

The Bolsheviks created a new political system not by following some sort of blueprint, but by responding to unforeseen and unforeseeable problems. Because the Leninists faced problems they had not anticipated, one is tempted to say that ideology was irrelevant, that Bolshevism was simply the outgrowth of the exigencies of the civil war. Such an underestimation of the role of ideology would be a great error. The revolutionaries' background and ideology predisposed them to make certain decisions and to avoid others. All important Bolshevik leaders of the 1920s had acquired their reputations as revolutionaries. Their school for statesmanship was underground work against the antiquated and inefficiently repressive tsarist state.

The Bolsheviks' ideology was a form of Marxism, presupposing the perfectibility of man and the possibility of building a just and rational society. As Marxists, believing in progress and that societies advance through predictable stages, they saw their own country as backward compared to Europe. The Bolsheviks were the most extreme Westernizing wing of the Russian intelligentsia. It is one of the paradoxes of history that politicians who wanted above all to make Russians more like Europeans ultimately cut off their country from the West.

The extraordinary character of Bolshevik policy followed above all from the breathtaking ambitions of the new rulers. They had no interest in administering society; they wanted to transform it. It was clear from their program, background, and ideology that democratic means would not suit the victorious revolutionaries. After all, the Bolsheviks did not believe that all views were in some sense equally valuable. They had no romantic respect for folk tradition and wisdom. Nor did their experiences in the revolutionary movement encourage a tolerance for opposing points of view.

In the 1920s, however, Soviet Russia was not a totalitarian society. First of all, the Bolsheviks still defined the boundaries of politics somewhat more narrowly than they would in the following decade. For example, they allowed a certain degree of autonomy to the sphere of culture. Also, the regime did not yet possess sufficient organizational strength. This was most evident in the countryside, where Bolshevik rule over the great majority of the Russian people, the peasants, remained tenuous. One might say that the Bolshevik Revolution was carried out in stages. In 1917 a new regime came into being, but it succeeded only by a tacit compromise with the peasantry. This compromise enabled the revolutionaries to set up their government and rule in the cities, and allowed the peasants in their villages to live more or less as they saw fit.

The Bolsheviks attempted to carry out extremely ambitious plans, but they possessed very little power; the gap between intentions and reality was extraordinarily wide. In a peculiar way the very weakness of the party at a time of anarchy encouraged utopian thinking. It made little sense to be "realistic" when no realistic solutions seemed available. The period of the civil war was a utopian one, when the Bolsheviks attempted fanciful schemes, undertaken with high hopes, but usually with little result.

Both because of their background as revolutionaries, and because of their ideology, the Bolsheviks possessed a keen appreciation of the significance of propaganda and mass mobilization. They constantly attempted – sometimes in prosaic ways, sometimes using imaginative methods – to bring their message to the people. Such an approach was extremely useful in winning the civil war – after which they did not abandon such efforts, but on the contrary expanded them. One cannot but be impressed by the sheer imagination and determination with which they tried to establish their influence among the peasants. They used the literacy drive for agitation. They artificially created a Lenin cult to supplant religious feelings. They set up a network of village reading rooms to act as propaganda centers. They established a number of meaningless holidays and campaigns to use as occasions for agitation. They periodically sent out communist workers from the cities into the villages in order to organize the peasants. They reached out to the village youth through a special youth wing, the Komsomol.

Yet it is striking that, despite all these efforts, the communists achieved little. They could not overcome the peasants' suspicion and hostility toward a city-based, revolutionary ideology. Their vision of the future and the desires of the peasants obviously clashed. The Bolsheviks could not attract enough reliable cadres among the villagers to act as an organizational nucleus. In the mid 1920s Soviet Russia had approximately a quarter-million communists living in the villages. When one remembers that the country had about a half-million rural settlements, it is evident that even if all the communists were able and diligent, they could not have made much impact on village life. In remote villages people lived their lives very much as if there was no Soviet government in Moscow.

The regime's authority in the villages was exceptionally weak, but so was the entire governmental apparatus. In this respect also, the tsarist government had left a deplorable heritage. The imperial governmental structure had been too small, too ill organized, and too lacking in honest, intelligent, public-spirited administrators to act effectively as a link between the government and the individual citizen. When the Bolsheviks took power they had to give jobs, aside from the very top positions, to the bureaucrats of the old regime. Some gave their services grudgingly, others wholeheartedly collaborated. As could be expected, many old Bolsheviks looked askance at the continued domination of the bureaucracy by people they had never fully trusted.

The chief distinguishing feature of Soviet polity was the party, for Soviet Russia was the world's first one-party state. From its inception the Bolshevik Party, aside from its name, had very little to do with political parties as these existed in pluralist societies. It was created as an association of revolutionaries for the concrete purpose of bringing about a bourgeois and later a socialist revolution. After the revolutionaries assumed power, their tasks completely changed, and it was necessary to reshape and reorganize the party.

From the time of the October Revolution, the party coexisted with the government. It was not clear how responsibilities should best be divided between the two structures. As far as the central administration was concerned, it seemed at first that the major center of power would be the government or, as it was called at the time, the Council of People's Commissars. Lenin definitely considered his most important office the chairmanship of this body. Gradually, however, after Lenin's death, the party organization came to surpass the government in power and importance. This development first took place in the provinces. There the old governmental structure had been the weakest and had finally disintegrated completely. Since the local soviets could not assume the responsibilities of the old bureaucracy, the party committees from the outset played governmental roles.

The party adjusted to the new role by changing its membership policy. During the civil war the regime had tried to attract support and had relatively easily accepted people from various backgrounds into the party. At the beginning of the NEP period, the party had almost 750,000 members. To reimpose discipline, the membership by 1924 had been reduced to 350,000. Then following Lenin's death, the party started to grow again; at the end of the decade it had 1 million members. The party made great efforts to enroll workers and thereby, from its own point of view, to "improve" its membership. As a consequence of this reduction and expansion the overwhelming majority of communists had no prerevolutionary or even civil war experience as party members. They came to be indoctrinated not with the ethos of the revolution, but with the more mundane spirit of the 1920s.

During the civil war and immediately afterward, two simultaneous but connected processes took place. One was the decline and disappearance of internal party democracy. The death of democracy within the party was related to circumstances in national politics. The idea of "democratic centralism," supposed to govern the working of the Bolshevik Party, became increasingly meaningless. Democratic centralism was a principle according to which lower bodies elected all higher organs and participated in making decisions, but all communists were obliged to carry out decisions of the higher bodies whether they agreed with them or not.

The indigenous institutions of participatory democracy that were important in 1917, such as factory committees and soviets, were emasculated. While struggling for power, the Bolsheviks benefited from anarchy, and the relatively loose party organization suited the spirit of the times. After October, however, the Bolsheviks turned against the factory committees that had served them so well during the era of the Provisional Government. Since they had lost working-class support, they could not afford the luxury of working-class democracy. The goals of the workers and those of the party increasingly diverged.

The establishment of a Bolshevik government ended the significance of the Petrograd Soviet. The new government in theory was responsible to the Congress of Soviets, but in reality it obviously did not depend on it. The local soviets for some time continued to play significant political roles, but their character changed completely, and they lost their autonomy. The Bolsheviks succeeded in gradually removing the Socialist Revolutionaries and Mensheviks and used these institutions to extend their power.

One might have anticipated that winning the civil war would lead to a general relaxation, a return to a greater degree of participatory democracy and toleration of dissenting views. In fact, nothing of the sort happened. To the Bolsheviks, just because the fighting had stopped did not mean that there were no more dangers. The introduction of the NEP clearly demoralized many party functionaries. Moreover, it was necessary to give concessions to the "class enemy," as the Bolsheviks saw it, which made that enemy stronger.

As one faction after another within the party leadership was defeated, the leaders took an increasingly intolerant attitude toward dissent. It made little sense to suppress political enemies and then allow the very same opinions to be expressed within the party. Dissident views were repressed within and outside of the party; repression had its own logic. It was at this time in 1922 that the Menshevik Party, already an insignificant shadow of its former self, was finally destroyed. The Mensheviks had advocated policies similar to those of the NEP for a long time, making it all the more necessary to get rid of them. The destruction of the Menshevik Party was followed by a trial of leading Socialist Revolutionaries, a preview of events of the following decade.

During the difficult years of the civil war the central organizations of the Bolshevik Party assumed an ever-larger role. The local organizations did not have the cadres and therefore were willing to abdicate responsibility. They often welcomed an influential person sent out from Moscow to take charge. As the party ceased to be a democratic organization, and as the central offices' workload increased, the importance of the apparatus steadily grew. At the time of the revolution the machinery was still rudimentary. Yakov Sverdlov, a brilliant organizer, created the party secretariat that directed organizational matters. He died in 1919, and his place was taken by three secretaries. It was Stalin who united the office once again when he became general secretary of the party in 1922. By this time much of the bureaucracy Stalin was to use so effectively was already in place. In fact, the new general secretary was not a particularly able organizer; details could not hold his attention. He was, however, a master politician, and he knew how to take advantage of the bureaucratic machinery by placing ideological allies and people indebted to him in positions of leadership. Politics never bored him.

Aside from the party, mass organizations were the most significant distinguishing feature of Soviet polity. These were called in contemporary parlance "transmission belts." It was a mechanistic image: the party drove the machinery of society ever forward, and the mass organizations took the energy generated by the party to the "masses." Since the party was elitist in the sense that only the "best," the "most class-conscious," could join, the mass organizations gave an outlet for participation to ordinary citizens. These organizations extended the reach of the party, enabled the party to fashion propaganda messages most suitable for particular audiences, and gave scope for the talent of numerous activists. Through these organizations many Soviet citizens became accustomed to Soviet political language. The party jealously controlled these organizations and conceded them not the slightest amount of genuine autonomy. They took the message of the party to a particular target audience, but they were never allowed to become representatives of a segment of society. The rule of the party was based on the incorrect assumption that there was no divergence of interests among groups in Soviet society.

The organization for women was the Zhenotdel. The youth organization, the Komsomol, was particularly important. It had twice as many members in the villages as the party, and played a crucial role in agitating for government policies. Its campaigns not only brought these policies to the attention of the villagers, but also taught the youth Soviet-style politics. Thus the Komsomol became a training ground for the party. The trade unions functioned in a similar way. In addition there were dozens of other "voluntary" organizations, such as the society Down with Illiteracy, the Society of the Friends of the Red Fleet, a society for aiding needy revolutionaries abroad, and a society for fighting alcoholism.

The era of the NEP was a period of preparation. As the economy was catching up with prewar standards, and as society was recovering from the dreadful blows of the period of the revolution and civil war, the party was transforming itself. It gradually trained those cadres who would carry out the assault on the rest of society. The regime taught the future activists and to a lesser extent the rest of the population to speak a new political language. It instilled new political habits.

THE BIRTH OF THE SOVIET UNION

Imperial Russia was a multinational empire: approximately half of its citizens were not ethnic Russians. The minorities were extremely different from one another in terms of economic and cultural development and degree of national self-consciousness. The defeat of the empire and the revolutions of 1917, in the course of which central authority disintegrated, changed that situation with extraordinary rapidity; suddenly minority nationalisms became a potent force. The skill with which the Bolsheviks handled this explosive issue contributed greatly to their ability to emerge victoriously from the civil war.

The famous Marxist slogan, "Workers of the world, unite!" implied that the workers had no fatherland. Indeed, the Bolsheviks as Marxists took their internationalism seriously, and consequently regarded themselves merely as the Russian detachment of the international army of the world proletariat.[3] In their view nationalism was the ideology of the bourgeoisie for the purpose of protecting local markets and deflecting the proletariat from a revolutionary path. In other words, nationalism was a nuisance – a problem that, together with so many other ills, would be remedied after the worldwide victory of the proletariat. As a practical thinker and revolutionary, however, Lenin understood that nationalist aspirations could be used as a weapon

Anti-illiteracy poster from the 1920s

against the tsarist state and denounced his fatherland as a prison of nations. Lenin's attitude toward nationalism was similar to his attitude toward the peasant question: he sympathized neither with the desire for private owner-ship of land nor with nationalist aspirations; nevertheless he saw concessions in these matters as essential preconditions for victory.

At the very heart of Lenin's thinking was the need for a tightly organized revolutionary party. He firmly believed in the necessity for discipline and organization, and therefore his principles inevitably led to centralization. Already at the moment of the creation of their party, the Bolsheviks rejected the notion of federalism within the socialist movement and excluded the Jewish Bund, which claimed for itself organizational autonomy within the larger party. Bolshevik policies were marked by a certain ambivalence: on the one hand they had little sympathy for nationalists of any kind and were instinctive centralizers, but on the other as internationalists they did not look at problems from the point of view of Russian nationalists, who could not envisage Russia deprived of the borderlands. Since they believed that they knew where history was going – toward a socialist world state – temporary concessions could easily be granted. They were pragmatists, able to concede where necessary.

When the Bolsheviks established their government, they included in it a commissariat of nationalities, and Joseph Stalin became commissar. He was an obvious choice for heading that institution. Stalin was a Georgian who, with Lenin's support and encouragement, had written an essay on the topic of nationalism from a Marxist perspective. In the first and crucial years of the Soviet regime, when the union had to be more or less reassembled from parts of the defunct empire, Stalin and his commissariat had a crucial role to play. His commissariat was instrumental in issuing a Declaration of Rights of the Toiling and Exploited Peoples in January 1918. This document promised self-determination to the minorities, and described Soviet Russia as a federation of Soviet republics.

Bolshevik policies were based on principles that arose from their intellectual background. They took it for granted that they were engaged in an international struggle and believed in the solidarity both of the workers of the world and of the capitalists. Helping the working classes in foreign countries to bring about their revolution was not considered subversive or shameful, but an obligation. When the Red Army was fighting on Polish soil, or later when it invaded the de facto independent states of Georgia, Armenia, and Azerbaijan, from the Leninist point of view these were not acts of aggression, but simply the meeting of their international obligations.

As the Bolsheviks understood the concept, "self-determination" applied only to the proletariat of each nation. "Proletariat" did not mean the actual working class – the sum total of workers in factories and shops – but was an abstract entity of "class-conscious" workers. "Class-conscious" workers by definition would not want to be excluded from the proletarian state. The Bolsheviks to their bitter disappointment soon discovered in the course of their war against Poland that the vast majority of workers were Poles first, and "class-conscious" workers not at all.

Playing with concepts allowed the Bolsheviks to give the most far-reaching concessions – even to the extent of secession, when there was nothing they could do to prevent it – and to repress nationalist risings when they were in the position to do so. In this way Lenin's government ultimately recognized the independence of Poland, Finland, and the Baltic states, Estonia, Lithuania, and Latvia, although in each of these newly independent countries the Bolsheviks at one time or another hoped to reverse the process by more or less openly supporting communist forces. Flexible policies induced the three states in the Caucasus – Georgia, Armenia, and Azerbaijan – to favor the Reds in the civil war rather than the Whites, who were seen as hopeless Great Russian nationalists. Bolshevik nationality policies successfully divided the camp of their enemies.

From the point of view of the future Soviet Union, developments in Ukraine were by far the most important. This land, inhabited by brother Slavs, contained a fifth of the population of the Russian empire, some of the most valuable industrial districts, and the best agricultural lands. Ukraine was also that part of the old empire where the civil war was most bitter and confused, where regimes changed most often. In the course of three years, governments changed twelve times in Kiev. Whites and Reds, Ukranian nationalists and anarchists, fought against one another, and foreign powers became involved. In 1918 the Germans supported a puppet government in Kiev; after the armistice, the French sent troops; in 1920 the Poles invaded. The ethnic and social situation was complex: the working class in the newly established industrial areas was Russian; the landowning classes Polish in the west and Russian in the east; the petite bourgeoisie largely Jewish; and only the peasantry was predominantly Ukrainian-speaking. As elsewhere, social and national issues came to be intertwined. The Russian working class, of course not drawn to Ukrainian nationalism, was most likely to support the Bolsheviks.

The nationalist movement was largely the creation of the intelligentsia and semi-intelligentsia, such as village school teachers. The nationalists placed their hopes in the peasantry and developed an ideology that was closest to that of the Socialist Revolutionaries. They were, however, not particularly successful in getting peasant support. In 1917 the demand of the Ukrainian assembly (the Rada) for autonomy, the limits of which remained unspecified, became one of the most contentious and difficult issues that the Provisional Government faced. From that bitter and long struggle, ultimately the Ukrainian Bolsheviks – with the decisively important help of the Red Army – emerged victorious.

It is disputable how strong the power of nationalism was in Ukraine, but it is evident that in neighboring Belarus national consciousness among the overwhelmingly peasant people had reached only the most rudimentary stage at the time of the civil war. An "independent" Belarus was created under German protection, and it lasted as long as the Germans were there. Nevertheless, this most ephemeral of states could serve seventy years later as the foundation of a more robust nationalism. The Treaty of Riga, which ended the war between Soviet Russia and Poland in 1921, divided Belarus between the two parties.

In Central Asia one could hardly talk about national consciousness at this time. The basis of self-definition here was religion, Islam. The Muslims were of course not uniform: on the one extreme, the Tatars had a native intelligentsia, self-governing institutions, and a degree of national consciousness; on the other, the Kazakhs were largely nomadic. The Bolshevik faced a dilemma: as Marxists they of course opposed Islam, as they opposed all religions. On the other hand they – Lenin in particular – understood that colonial peoples could be valuable allies all over the world against the imperialist West. The Bolsheviks organized under the auspices of the Communist International in 1920 in Baku a "Congress of Eastern Peoples," which had the task of mobilizing the exploited colonial peoples, many of them Muslim, against the common enemy – the West. After the regime consolidated itself, it pursued a more aggressive policy in the east. The Bolsheviks labeled those who resisted sovietization as "bandits," and the Red Army gradually overcame opposition. Ultimately Stalin's commissariat turned against those Muslim socialists who had the temerity to consider the Russians as one of their Western oppressors.

The Declaration of the Rights of the Toiling and Exploited Peoples spoke of a federation, but in January 1918 this was of course only a theoretical matter – the government in Petrograd hardly controlled Russian territories, much less the regions where the national minorities lived. The nature of the federation was, perhaps understandably, left undecided at this point. The declaration was more an announcement of intentions than a policy document. The first Soviet constitution, issued in July 1918, reiterated the declaration, without spelling out further the character of federalism of the Soviet state.

When circumstances changed, when the civil war was over, the Bolsheviks succeeded in reconquering at least some of the territories that they had lost, without having to make great changes. The Caucasian republics fell before a combination of Bolshevik internal subversion and the invasion of the Red Army. In the spring of 1921 independent Georgia was destroyed, and after the removal of the last interventionist forces from Siberia in 1922, the territory that was to constitute the Soviet Union until 1939 was under the control of Moscow. The Russian empire, destroyed by war and revolution, was now more or less restored.

At this time the task of working out the terms of federation had to be faced by the Soviet leadership. At first the relationship between the republics (Ukraine, Belorussia, Georgia, Azerbaijan, and Armenia) and the Russian Republic, itself a federation, was governed by treaties – that is, these political entities preserved at least the appearance of sovereignty. In the course of 1923 a commission prepared a constitution that was officially accepted by the Congress of Soviets in January 1924, and the Union of Soviet Socialist Republics (USSR) was born. The constitution, though it preserved some of the niceties of a federation, in fact created a highly centralized state. The logic of a communist state demanded centralization. While the government existed in a federal form, there was no talk of creating a similar organization for the Bolshevik Party.

This is not to say that the aim of those who created the Soviet Union was to advance Russian nationalist interests. Arguably Lenin was more concerned about Russian nationalism as a danger than about the nationalisms of the minorities. According to Soviet policy, the task was to raise the cultural level of the "backward" peoples to the level of the Russians, because only then would it be possible to create a genuine sense of Soviet nationalism. The policy was called "indigenization," which meant that the state made considerable efforts to find local people to fill the administration and gave them preference over Russians who lived in the minority areas. It also meant the promotion of national languages and cultures. Written languages were developed for those minorities that had not had one before, and the alphabet used was Latin rather than Cyrillic. The ironic consequence of this policy was the growth of national consciousness among the non-Russian population of the union.

ECONOMICS AND SOCIETY

In their effort to rebuild the economy the Bolsheviks returned to the principles of capitalism.[4] After they made their first crucial and ideologically difficult concession, accepting private ownership, they showed considerable flexibility and were willing to use heterodox methods to bring about national recovery. Lenin, who had high hopes of attracting foreign capital by offering concessions, went further in promising foreigners the possibility of unhindered exploitation of the country's natural resources than some of the White leaders, such as for example General Denikin. The young Soviet state, however, had little success in attracting foreign capital. Given the prevailing economic conditions and the understandable suspicions of capitalists, it is not surprising that only an insignificant amount of foreign capital entered the economy. Even at the end of the decade, when the Soviet economy was stable and the regime had shown its ability to survive, only 0.6 percent of the total output of the economy was produced by foreign concessions.[5] It is therefore fair to say that foreign help had played little or no part in the revival of the economy.

Recovery was blocked by bottlenecks: industry could not operate without a functioning transportation system, and the trains, in turn, could not run without fuel. Under the circumstances, the government had to concentrate scarce resources in the critical areas. The first priority was the production of coal – the miners in the Donets basin and elsewhere received extra food to enable them to perform their heavy work. Soviet Russia used its small supply of convertible currency to buy railway engines and rolling stock abroad. There was a high price to pay, however, for these necessary steps: providing one group with better nourishment could come only at the expense of others. Economizing with scarce resources and capital led to the closing of numerous inefficient factories. During war communism the workers had frequently received their wages in food; losing jobs often meant starvation. The immediate consequence of the introduction of the New Economic Policies meant increased hardship for many, and the standard of living of the working class fell even further. For some time the market did not function normally: the relationship between agricultural and industrial prices wildly fluctuated. (At a time of high inflation, all prices rose; the issue was the relationship of prices.) In the middle of 1922, as compared to the prewar situation, the exchange was excessively favorable to agriculture. This imbalance was partially the result of the desperate need for food: at a time of famine, those who had surplus food could demand very high prices.

The relative decline in industrial prices, paradoxically, was also partially the consequence of the extreme disorganization of industry. The factories, suddenly denied resources from the government, desperately needed capital. Since the factories did not have a functioning network for selling their products, in some instances they were forced to trade in the streets of the cities in order to raise money. On occasion factories were even compelled to sell some of their machinery. At a time when Soviet industry produced only a fraction of what Russian industry had produced before the war, goods were unsalable.

In the following year, prices changed in such a way as to become grossly unfavorable to the village. This was because it was more difficult to reconstruct industry than agriculture: famine had been alleviated, but industry remained extremely inefficient, with low productivity and a high cost of production. In addition, the distribution system continued to perform poorly. The consequence of high industrial prices in a market economy was predictable. The peasants once again had little incentive to part with their products. This was the so-called scissors crisis – a name given by Trotsky, who had a knack for the vivid phrase. The two widening blades respectively stood for agricultural and industrial prices. Since in the Soviet economy all major economic issues had political overtones, the government, fearing another crisis in its ability to feed the cities, took energetic measures to force down industrial prices in October 1923.

A major step toward normalization was the stabilization of the currency. The Soviet government was not entirely responsible for the hyperinflation, which was as deep as the better-known German one. The depreciation of the currency began when the imperial government decided to cover war expenditures by printing more money; the revolution and the civil war greatly exacerbated the problem. At its nadir, the country was reverting to barter economy; paper money had become worthless. In order to save the situation, the government had to draw up balanced budgets and revive the banking system. Between 1922 and 1924 the government managed in several steps to create a stable currency based on gold.

After the first two or three years of the new economic system, the government had reason to be pleased with the results. Life was gradually returning to normal. Private enterprise dominated the economy, producing more than 50 percent of the national income. Agriculture was almost entirely in private hands: even at the end of the period, state farms and collective farms occupied less than 2 percent of the land under cultivation. Small-scale industry was private, while large-scale heavy industry was state-owned. The government retained control over the mines, the banking system, and foreign trade, and thus had a decisive influence in running the economy.

The rate of recovery was uneven in different sectors of the economy. Agriculture was first to catch up with prewar production standards. Light industry (factories that produced consumer goods) was next to improve, and heavy industry was slowest to recover. Foreign trade revived, though it remained far below what it had been before the war. The mixed economy and the one-party state created a society profoundly different both from what had existed before the revolution and from what was to come as a result of Stalinist industrialization.

The revolution and its immediate aftermath brought about a great social leveling. In the new economic system, however, differentiation once again emerged. The NEP spawned a new social phenomenon, the NEPman. This new social stratum came into being in order to take advantage of the economic opportunities offered by the regime. Enterprising people traveled to the villages, selling clothes, shoes, razor blades, and so forth. The prices were high and the quality invariably low; nonetheless, at a time when the normal distribution network did not function, the NEPman provided a useful service. Peasants could not be expected to take their products to the consumer. The NEPman took this task on himself, frequently making exorbitant profits in the process. But food once again became available and plentiful in the cities, at least for those who could afford to pay the high prices.

The new class was a heterogeneous one. Its members came from different social backgrounds: enterprising peasants, descendants of the prewar petite bourgeoisie, and even some former members of the aristocracy now tried to make a living in unaccustomed circumstances. Some of the NEPmen were well off. People who traded in the cities or operated factories could make a great deal of money, but others remained petty traders barely eking out a living. This social class was emblematic of the world of the 1920s. The newly rich were visible: conspicuous consumption in the midst of poverty was especially disturbing following a great revolution fought in the name of equality. For most Bolsheviks the NEPman represented everything they disliked: petit bourgeois desire for property and profit, lack of ideological interests, and a middle-class lifestyle. In the second half of the decade, many of the NEPmen found that they could not continue their business activities. From the beginning such people had operated on the margins of legality, and as regulations became stricter and more numerous, as the government trade network was able to perform some of the tasks itself, the activities of the NEPmen seemed more and more like black-market operations.

From the point of view of the working class, the results of the great revolution were ambiguous. In theory, Soviet Russia was a state of workers and peasants, and the Bolshevik Party, in particular, claimed to represent the workers. It is impossible to say to what extent the workers accepted this claim at face value, but Bolshevik appeals were obviously not without effect. It may be that many workers derived psychological benefits from living in a political system that was described as the "dictatorship of the proletariat."

The workers did also make some tangible gains. The state was building a bureaucracy. There was a constant need for functionaries, and the party, on the basis of its ideology, trusted the workers more than others and whenever possible attempted to promote them. Paradoxically, the greatest gain the workers enjoyed was the opportunity to cease being workers. The possibility of making a career in the new system was open to all intelligent and ambitious workers. One would guess that even those workers who had no ambition to leave the factory bench came to identify with the new state because they saw their friends promoted.

The labor legislation of the NEP modified the policy of war communism: forcible labor conscription was abolished. Workers could freely sell their labor in either the private or the state sector of the economy. The regime abandoned its early egalitarian policies. Skilled workers now received much better wages than the unskilled. The trade unions, at least in the private sector, regained a limited ability to protect the economic interests of the workers. Although strikes were legal, the party leadership above all was interested in reconstruction and therefore prevented the spread of strikes through its control over the trade unions. Labor legislation in other aspects was in advance of that existing at the time in capitalist countries: it limited the length of the working day, forbade child labor, and provided paid vacations and health insurance.

As far as concrete economic gains were concerned, the situation was not so favorable. The standard of living could not rise until the economy recovered, and that was a slow and painful process. In the first half of the 1920s the cities recovered their populations, with the exception of Petrograd. The new urban influx meant the housing situation deteriorated. Since labor productivity remained below prewar standards, rising labor costs came at the expense of accumulating capital for industrialization. The government therefore resisted wage increases.

The most severe problem was unemployment. Even after the economy recovered, in the second half of the 1920s, unemployment did not diminish but worsened. Since the countryside was tremendously overpopulated, once conditions in the cities became bearable the peasants flocked into industry, just as before the war. Both private industry and state enterprises were cost-conscious and conservative in hiring workers. Unemployment hit various sectors of the working classes unevenly. Older, skilled, and experienced workers were less likely to suffer than young workers and women. The Komsomol, however, was not allowed to champion the interests of the younger workers, for the regime feared setting one section of the working classes against another. Unemployment benefits depended on how long a worker had been employed. Consequently, seasonal workers and the young who had never held jobs remained ineligible. The chronic problems of industry, such as unemployment and inability to accumulate capital for industrialization, created an atmosphere of crisis. This atmosphere colored the debate concerning the economic future of the country.

In 1917, it was only because they had no choice that the Bolsheviks had allowed the peasants to take the land and cultivate it as if it were their own. Like the Provisional Government before them, the Bolsheviks lacked the strength to prevent forcible land seizures. In the course of the 1920s, however, they looked apprehensively at the countryside, where private property consciousness was taking ever firmer roots. In theory the Bolshevik solution was to persuade the peasants to give up their lands and join collective farms. In the utopian era of the civil war, agitators had made serious attempts to convince the peasants that collective agriculture was superior to individual. The agitation, however, had backfired. The peasants hated even the idea of collectives, and anti-Bolshevik propagandists took advantage of this hatred. They told their audiences that in case of Red victory everything would be collectivized. The Bolsheviks had to abandon even agitation for the time being.

During the great economic debates of the 1920s Bolshevik theorists returned to the topic of collective agriculture. They argued that, once the state became rich enough to support collective farms with machinery and fertilizers, and the peasants could see the advantages of cooperation, they would voluntarily join. Since in fact the state was not in a position to support collective farms, the discussion remained theoretical. In reality there was no evidence whatever that the peasants would easily give up their land.

As the rural self-government system of the tsarist regime, the *zemstva*, was dismantled, and as the village soviets could not take their place, the traditional peasant village commune came to play a greater role than ever before. It was this institution rather than the village soviet that made the important decisions in the village, and the village communes continued to elude the influence of Soviet power. Although the Bolshevik government distrusted them, it took no immediate steps against them. As prewar economists and politicians recognized, the commune was a hindrance to economic growth. A strange blend of communalism and individualism, the peasant commune periodically redistributed land; therefore the peasants had little incentive to improve their holdings. The very foundation of the commune was the egalitarian sensibility of the peasantry, which required that the better and worse agricultural lands be fairly distributed. The consequence of such distributions was that families often received small strips of land in different parts of the village, making efficient cultivation, especially mechanized cultivation, difficult if not impossible. It is likely, however, that the main reason for Bolshevik hostility to the communes was not their economic inefficiency, but the inability of the regime to control them.

Under the conditions of the NEP, class differentiation in the villages – which had greatly diminished as a result of the revolution – started to increase again. Differentiation, however, remained very slight, the gap between the poor and the rich very narrow. The Bolsheviks, for reasons of their own, in their writings and discussions always exaggerated the extent of stratification. They feared and mistrusted the peasant class, but it was impossible for them to say this aloud, or perhaps even to admit it to themselves. Instead, they aimed their animosity at the richest layer of the peasant class, the kulaks, who made up approximately 5 percent of the peasantry. The kulak category remained ill defined. Possessing some sort of agricultural machinery or occasionally lending grain to poorer neighbors was sufficient to be considered a kulak. Since only 1 percent of the peasantry hired labor, it was impossible to define kulaks as peasants who exploited others.

The leaders of the regime faced exactly the same dilemma in connection with the kulaks as they did with the NEPmen. It was a dilemma at the heart of the contradictions of the NEP, one that led to the ultimate demise of the system. On the one hand, the Bolsheviks needed the services of the kulaks. Only the better-off peasants could produce for the market, and without them the regime could not properly feed the cities and would have no grain for export. On the other hand, as communists, they feared that the increased economic power of the kulaks would inevitably lead to political power. They explicitly considered the richest peasants hostile; implicitly they feared the entire peasantry, still 80 percent of the population. As a result governmental policies vacillated: at times the government issued regulations favorable to enterprising peasants, at other times unnecessary restrictions hindered the improvement of agriculture. Measures taken against the kulaks hurt the entire economy: the bulk of the peasantry understood that it was not worthwhile to strive to improve their lot, because there was a high price to be paid for economic success.

After a disappointing harvest in 1924, caused again by a drought, a series of good harvests followed. By the second half of the 1920s agriculture recovered, and overall production figures approached the prewar level. These few years were the best years for the Russian peasantry. The weakness of Soviet power in the villages, and the political system of the NEP based on the theory of worker–peasant alliance, did not allow the government to tax the peasants as heavily as they had been taxed in imperial Russia. The consequence of agricultural improvement, reduced taxation, and lessened differentiation was that the bulk of the peasants were better off than before the war. But because they used their products primarily to feed themselves better, rather than selling them on the open market, the amount of grain that entered the market remained well below prewar levels.

The peasants benefited from the revolution because they came into possession of all agricultural lands. Furthermore, the government, which they had always regarded as alien and hostile, was now too weak to interfere in their lives. Never in modern Russian history was the peasantry as autonomous as in the 1920s. However, the revolution did not help to overcome the traditional problems of Russian agriculture: a backward peasantry, primitive methods of cultivation, and great agricultural overpopulation. In fact, the changes made by the revolution were a step backward. It was the most modern sector of agriculture that suffered the most. The destruction of industry meant that factories could not siphon away the great village over-population. The peasantry, satisfied with being left alone, showed little interest in innovation or improvement.

BOLSHEVIK CULTURAL POLICIES

We tend to assume that a profound transformation in the political, social, and economic life of a nation must be accompanied by cultural change as well.[6] In fact, the real turning point in the cultural history of the Soviet Union occurred not in 1917, or during the civil war, but only at the end of the NEP period, at the time of the so-called cultural revolution.

Whether the Bolsheviks liked it or not, they were descendants of the nineteenth-century Russian intelligentsia, sharing a larger number of attitudes and assumptions than perhaps they themselves realized. Members of that intelligentsia took it for granted that ideas mattered greatly. Only this assumption allowed them to think of themselves as making a contribution to society and gave purpose to their lives. Because of their deep conviction that ideas mattered they upheld their ideologies with passion, and from passion often followed intolerance toward the views of others.

The Bolsheviks' faith in the power of ideas was reinforced by their reading of Marx. As the Marxists saw it, in order to change social relations, one first had to understand them. Once they had a chance, the Bolsheviks did everything within their power to propagate their own ideas. At the same time, since they knew the subversive power of their own message, they attributed similarly subversive power to the ideas of their numerous enemies. The only way to deal with those was to repress them. Russian Marxists, more than Marxists elsewhere, regarded their ideology as a science, which alone allowed a correct interpretation of historical phenomena. This conviction that they alone were in possession of the truth allowed them later to repress others – for, as they saw it, that repression was never an attack on truth, but only on falsehood.

According to the Bolsheviks, Russia was not different from other societies, with a particular genius, special achievements, and a unique future. It was simply backward. As they saw it, Russians lacked not merely Western Europe's capitalist development, but also European culture. This consciousness of backwardness was a main motivating force for Bolshevik policies after the victory. The victorious revolutionaries saw no contradiction between their determination to suppress heterodox thought on the one hand, and their desire to advance "culture" on the other.

The issue of cultural backwardness had political meaning for Lenin and his comrades. The Mensheviks had attacked them by arguing that the country was not yet ripe for socialist revolution. This was a powerful charge, for the Bolsheviks themselves had doubts on this score; they were painfully aware of the backwardness of their fellow Russians. However, they could not concede the crucial point that Russia was not ready for historical transformation, as that would have compromised the legitimacy of their revolution. The conclusion was inescapable. In order to build a socialist society, the immediate task was to bring the cultural level of the Russian people at least to that of Western Europe. Lenin believed that in Russia, unlike Western Europe, the socialist revolution had preceded the attainment of a certain necessary level of culture. The fact that the proletariat was in power made it possible to achieve a great deal within a short time. Russians would catch up quickly and soon overtake the West.

There was no time to waste. The work had to begin, even at a time when the regime was engaged in a life-and-death struggle. In the Leninist understanding, culture primarily meant material civilization: electrification, a well-functioning postal service, good roads, hygiene. Without these cultural preconditions it was impossible even to talk about socialism. But culture also meant the internalization of discipline, which the Leninists rightly considered a necessary component of industrial civilization. Spontaneity, so much distrusted by Lenin, was a feature of backwardness.

Culture also meant high culture, the great human achievements in the arts and sciences. At this point the Bolsheviks were convinced that the values inherent in science and the arts were congenial to the principles of socialism. Culture was to be a helpmate in the building of socialism. The Bolsheviks assumed that, unless there was a particular reason to distrust some artist or scientist, these people were working for the same goal they were: to bring about enlightenment, and through it a better future for mankind. They did not yet understand that some values inherent in the arts might be contrary to their own.

There was not much the Bolsheviks could do right away to advance material civilization. As long as the civil war continued, as long as the new rulers could not protect their people from cold and famine, plans for the electrification of the countryside was just empty talk. But the question immediately arose as to what steps the Bolsheviks could take to raise the cultural level of the people, and how they should treat the "workers of culture," the members of the scientific and cultural intelligentsia.

By and large the intelligentsia, especially the scientists and professors, were hostile. Given this hostility, the Leninists exhibited from the very beginning remarkable tolerance. Since science impressed them, they treated scientists better than artists. They saw science as a component of modernity, and they were passionate partisans of the modern age. They regarded the scientists almost as comrades: scientists were establishing the laws of nature, in the same way that Marxists were uncovering the laws governing social change. In a more practical vein, the Bolsheviks took it for granted that scientists would be needed for rebuilding the economy. Scientists were experts, and the new rulers admired expertise in all fields.

"Organize reading huts": poster from the 1930s

In their treatment of scholars, the Bolsheviks observed hierarchy. The more famous the person was, the more the Bolsheviks respected him and the better he was treated by them. The organization of school teachers, dominated by the Socialist Revolutionaries, was perceived by the Bolsheviks as an enemy and was treated as such. The universities and especially the Academy of Sciences, by contrast, were able to retain a degree of autonomy. S. F. Oldenburg, who had served as minister of education in Kerensky's government, headed the academy throughout the NEP period.[7] A descendant of an old aristocratic family, he was the only member of the defunct Provisional Government who continued to play a significant role in the vastly changed political environment. Individual scientists, such as Oldenburg himself, were won over by the interest and commitment of the new authorities to intellectual endeavor. However, the bulk of the professors and scientists remained unsatisfied.

In spite of the obvious good will of Lenin's government, there were bound to be conflicts between the new authorities and the scientists. At times of extreme privation and scarcity, the Bolsheviks could hardly afford to give much material support to scientists. The revolutionaries aimed to make the universities accessible to the lower classes, and this effort went contrary to the notions of good scholarship held by the professors. In the provinces, less-enlightened Bolsheviks often regarded intellectuals simply as members of the hated bourgeoisie and treated them as such. However, the revolutionaries had not yet attempted to interfere in the scientific enterprise; it had not yet occurred to them to rule some topics out of bounds for ideological reasons.

The party's relationship with artists was even more complicated. The ideological commitments of artists varied a great deal. Most of them were hostile to the revolution. Many of the most famous left the country even before the outcome of the civil war was certain. The film industry, for example, was devastated. Prominent film directors and actors first went to the south, which was controlled by the Whites, and then moved to European capitals, primarily Paris and Berlin. Only a minority of well-known artists greeted the revolution enthusiastically, and even they were not in fact Bolsheviks. They were attracted to the apocalyptic vision of the revolutionaries and to their announced desire to destroy the old order. But their enthusiasm for the revolution was based on a misunderstanding. They loathed the previous social order because it seemed to them "petit bourgeois"; they deplored the tastes of the common people and wanted to demolish old cultural norms. Rather naively, they believed that Bolshevik goals were similar to their own; they saw themselves as the equivalents of the Bolsheviks in their own fields. Many of them claimed to speak for the "proletariat," even though their artistic methods and concerns held no interest whatever for actual workers. Like the Bolsheviks, they created in their own minds an ideal "proletariat," one which had never existed and could not possibly exist.

The Bolsheviks understood that in spreading their ideological message the services of writers, musicians, and painters could be useful. However they never extended the same degree of respect and admiration to artists as they did to scientists. While it was sufficient to leave the scientists alone, giving them as much support as was possible under the circumstances, the Bolsheviks were determined to take an active role in the realm of the arts.

Lenin's government supported the publishing industry. During the months following the revolution, the government for all practical purposes exercised no censorship; the presses, like the rest of industry, remained in private hands, and the publishers continued to print what they believed would make money. Most of the books published were romances and adventure stories; but books on religious subjects, on idealist philosophy, and others equally undesirable from the Bolshevik point of view could also be printed. The problem for the publishers was not government censorship, but the collapse of the economy. Private publishing houses closed down because of the lack of raw materials and the disintegration of the distribution system rather than governmental intervention.

In May 1919 the government set up a state publishing house, Gosizdat, in order to centralize publishing. Although some feared that this move would result in increased government control, the main impetus was economic difficulties. The country suffered from an extreme shortage of paper, and to deal with the problem the government established a paper monopoly. All supplies not issued by the government became subject to confiscation. This regulation, however, like so many others at the time, remained unenforced. Private publishing houses evaded the regulation by hiding their supplies and managed to remain in existence until the very end of war communism. Gosizdat had a dual relationship with these firms: on the one hand they were competing against one another; on the other, Gosizdat had censorship powers over them. The announced policy of Gosizdat was to encourage the publication of works considered useful, remain neutral to those with no political significance, and oppose the publication of those which were anti-Marxist. The censors were liberal, and in practice they rarely interfered. Even then it was always possible to take advantage of the prevailing confusion and publish anti-Marxist works in the provinces.

The Bolsheviks were willing to make sacrifices to provide readers with books: the state invested precious foreign currency in buying paper abroad. The introduction of the New Economic Policies transformed the life of the country and made reconstruction possible. It also had far-reaching ideological implications; the revolutionaries now accepted that socialism would be built gradually. The great transformation in the life of the nation, however, brought few changes in the realm of intellectual freedom. Economic liberalization was not accompanied by political reforms or greater openness in discussing social and political problems. The principles that governed Bolshevik policies at the time of the civil war remained in force.

The Bolsheviks gave economic concessions because they believed that they had to: in order to feed the population, restrictions on peasants marketing their produce had to be loosened. There was no comparable pressure for political reforms or for extending intellectual freedom. On this occasion, unlike the time of collectivization, a reorganization of the economy, as far as the Bolsheviks were concerned, did not call for a new vision of politics. The end of the civil war did not allay the fears of the new rulers. The time was not propitious for broadening the public sphere. On the contrary, the Bolsheviks thought they were living in an especially dangerous moment. On the one hand, they had to watch their enemies grow stronger, and on the other they had to deal with the disappointment of the activists. Many devoted communists, especially among the young, who had taken previous slogans seriously, now felt abandoned and betrayed.

To make matters worse, in order to revive the economy the Bolsheviks had to return to the principles of financial orthodoxy. Expenditures had to be cut, and consequently subsidies for cultural work, and for propaganda and indoctrination, had to be seriously curtailed. In the new economic environment there could be no free distribution of books and newspapers. The government, which had once contributed a great deal to the literacy drive, now attempted to make society assume the burden. Hundreds of literacy schools had to be closed down.

There was no question of allowing non-Bolsheviks to publish newspapers. In fact, measures against the remnants of Socialist Revolutionary and Menshevik organizations became more severe than ever. There was to be no competition with the Bolsheviks in the interpretation of the news. Newspapers were now expected to be self-financing, but their character did not change. They reflected only indirectly the bitter struggle taking place among the leaders; the major issues, played out in a tiny political arena, were not discussed openly.

The principles of NEP were introduced in publishing, but only with some delay. The leaders understood that this industry was not exactly like others, that it required careful oversight; they were determined to protect themselves from ideological and political damage. Once again private publishing houses could be licensed. At the same time, however, the Politburo ordered agencies of state control to follow carefully what was printed and distributed. The Bolsheviks wanted to prevent the spread of religious literature, pornography, and "counterrevolutionary works." Because in the political climate of 1921 they considered the writings of Socialist Revolutionaries most dangerous, their fellow socialists were most likely to suffer the effects of censorship.

In the 1920s private publishing houses printed only a small and ever-declining share of the total output. Yet they made a considerable contribution to the variety of books available for the Soviet reader. These publishers brought out a considerable proportion of books on philosophy and psychology, translations, and belles lettres. Gosizdat continued to exercise supervisory authority – that is, censorship –over the publishers. Under Commissar Anatolii Lunacharskii's ultimate authority (Gosizdat was a part of his commissariat), few manuscripts were rejected.

The small number of rejections might give a mistaken idea concerning the laxity of censorship, for there is no way to count the number of authors who decided not to submit their works because they considered submission hopeless. During the beginning stages of NEP, authors such as

D. S. Merezhkovskii, N. A. Berdiaev, S. L. Frank, and V. Loskii were published in Soviet Russia. In retrospect it is clear, however, that such liberalism was born of weakness and an inability to control rather than any respect for freedom of speech. As time went on and Bolshevik rule became more secure, censorship became more strict.

The Bolsheviks were primarily interested in preventing the spread of "harmful literature" among the simple people. They did not particularly mind that some esoteric scholarly books might contain veiled anti-Marxist references. In this respect they followed the example set by their tsarist predecessors. The commissariat of enlightenment periodically issued circulars about purging village libraries and book collections kept by the cultural departments of trade unions. Their lists were extraordinarily comprehensive. They included Plato and Kant, but also (ridiculously) some writings of Lenin that had appeared under a pseudonym, "outdated" agitational pamphlets (i.e., writings that did not reflect the current political line), adventure stories, and lives of saints. The authorities followed exactly the same policies regarding the cinema. City dwellers, who were considered more politically "mature," were allowed a far broader choice of films than the peasants. The most interesting and commercially successful films of the decade, such as *The Bear's Wedding*, *Aelita*, and *Three Meshchanskaia Street*, were considered far too risky for peasant audiences. On occasion filmmakers prepared bowdlerized versions to be shown in the villages.

In an era of moderate repression, cultural life could still flourish. The intellectual trends of the prewar era continued; artists living in the Soviet Union kept up with their Western colleagues. In almost every area of cultural life, the most able Soviet artists remained in the avant-garde and made great contributions in literature, architecture, the fine arts, and music. There is general agreement that films produced in the studios of Moscow, Leningrad, Kiev, and Tbilisi between 1925 and 1930 were among the finest made anywhere in the world.

SOCIAL INSTITUTIONS: THE FAMILY, THE CHURCH, AND THE SCHOOLS

The revolution was fought not only for social equality but also for the equality of the sexes. In the social order of imperial Russia women were second-class citizens, dependent on men. Perhaps for that reason, women played an extraordinarily significant role in the revolutionary movement. Like all socialists, the Bolsheviks in theory were committed to bringing about equality of the sexes. After coming to power, the new government introduced an enlightened set of laws that greatly eased divorce, allowed abortion, and made marriage a civil affair. While some feminists wanted the government to play a more active role, the leading Bolsheviks were content to leave the establishment of genuine equality to the arrival of a classless society.

Although proportionately fewer women than men died, the years of war, revolution, and civil war were hard for the former. A demographic imbalance began that lasted for most of the rest of the century: Russia had many more women than men. The First World War forced a large number of women to take jobs in factories; between 1913 and 1920 the percentage of women in the urban labor force doubled. Then, as a result of chronic unemployment, many women were fired, and at the end of the NEP period the percentage of women in industrial labor was practically the same as before the First World War. During the war, when men were away in the army, women had to do their work and were left alone to take care of the children. When the peasants distributed the land of the landlords in 1917, women also benefited; however, as soldiers returned from the front and the communes redistributed the land, women often lost what they had acquired.

Bolshevik emancipatory attempts found little sympathy among women, especially in the countryside. What most women wanted was not easier divorce, but protection of the family in difficult times. Paradoxically, while utopian Bolshevik leaders talked about the disappearance of the family, in fact the opposite happened: men and women craved personal security and married in record numbers. The large number of marriages can only partially be explained by the fact that young people during the war had postponed weddings. After all, in the rest of Europe presumably the same phenomenon obtained, yet in 1919 Russia had the highest marriage rate in the world.

The great industrial transformation that was taking place in Russia before the revolution started breaking down the traditional patriarchal family. The revolutionary events accelerated the process. The Russians gradually moved toward the pattern of living in nuclear families. It is difficult to say to what extent governmental policies furthered this development. The Bolsheviks regarded the family as a bulwark of conservatism in which women were inevitably exploited, and so were hostile to it. Moreover, they wanted women to participate in the life of society, and it seemed to them that the family was a competitor, something that took the energies of women away from socially useful work.

In the villages the patriarchal family, in which several generations lived together, was disappearing. At first young people found it advantageous to establish their own households and claim land from the commune; later, when the government showed great hostility to the kulaks, it often became beneficial for the extended family to divide its wealth. For the women, in most instances getting away from their parents-in-law was a benefit, but there is no reason to think that the traditional relationship between males and females in the countryside changed a great deal. In urban families, where the nuclear family pattern was already the rule, the changes were even less significant. Time-budget studies show that, even in instances where women worked, all the household chores fell on them also. Men had more free time.

Contemporaries saw the changes around them more clearly than the continuities. For the first time divorces were legal, and some 20 percent of marriages ended in divorce. After the deaths of millions of men, there were a large number of single females. The country also had a distressing number of orphans, many of them simply left to their own devices. This experience, coupled with some radical theories of free love, gave the impression to many that the family structure, and the stability associated with it, was breaking down. In fact a much more profound change in the position of women in society and in the structure of the family was to come, with the introduction of Stalinist industrialization.

The Bolsheviks considered the church, just as they considered the family, a bulwark of conservatism. Obviously, there could be no amicable relations between the Russian Orthodox Church and the Bolshevik Party – the two worldviews were bound to clash. The church had a history of unthinking and uncritical support for the tsarist regime; at the time of the civil war the church did not even pretend to be neutral but acted as a propaganda arm of the White movement. Lenin, a master politician, immediately understood that a frontal attack on the church would backfire. The Bolsheviks in Moscow were circumspect in their relationship with the priests. In the rest of the country, however, instructions from the center were not always carried out, and as a result many priests suffered martyrdom at the hands of local Bolsheviks. As Lenin foresaw, in almost every instance the persecution of priests created hostility toward the new regime.

After the civil war antireligious agitation intensified. The Bolsheviks found the ideological competition with the church intolerable. Theorists debated the best means of confronting this particular enemy. Some activists argued that religion was a class phenomenon and that therefore active struggle against it was necessary. This tendency was best reflected in the Komsomol, which carried out antireligious campaigns and organized anti-Christmases and "Komsomol Easters." These events occasioned the crudest form of atheistic propaganda. All available evidence shows that such methods generated hostility and convinced few. Other communist leaders argued that religion would wither away because its class basis was disappearing. According to this point of view no special effort against Christian belief was necessary. After the obvious failures of radical Komsomol efforts, the party came to support a compromise position that called for "scientific atheist education" but repudiated crude forms of propaganda that offended believers. The regime created a "voluntary" society with the task of combating the religious worldview. In the late 1920s the society had approximately half a million members.

It is difficult to say how successful the regime was in undermining the faith of the people. Whatever success was achieved was probably among the young and in the cities. The great majority of the peasants continued to have the same relationship to church and God as they had before. We have a great deal of evidence showing that priests in the 1920s continued to enjoy the respect of the villagers, and therefore continued to possess considerable power. On one occasion, for example, the communist authorities tried to persuade the peasants to attend schools for literacy without success. Then they turned to the village priest for help, and on the following day hundreds appeared.

The Bolsheviks saw the power of the church as a characteristic feature of a backward society. Lenin in particular was keenly aware of the backwardness of his country and repeatedly described it as "Asiatic." In his last years he was preoccupied with the problem of how to overcome backwardness and make Russians into civilized Europeans. Indeed, imperial Russia had left an unenviable legacy. Tsarist bureaucrats before 1900 had taken a cautious if not hostile stance toward mass education, fearing its political consequences. The developing industrial society needed trained and educated people, but the government did little to provide for the industrial transformation. Only in the last decades of the empire did this attitude change, but by then it was too late. At the time of the revolution, approximately 60 percent of the people were illiterate. Overall figures, however, might be misleading, for illiteracy was unevenly distributed. Urban dwellers, the young, and males were far more likely to be able to read and write, so revolutionary agitators could always reach their target audiences with the written word.

The gap between the extraordinary ambitions of the new revolutionary regime and the miserable realities was enormous. The Bolsheviks believed that the success of their revolution depended on education, and therefore set themselves difficult tasks. They wanted to bring enlightenment to the entire people, to bring them up to the cultural level of West Europeans. They wanted to train new cadres to replace the old intelligentsia they had always distrusted. The regime needed party functionaries who understood at least the rudiments of Marxism, and therefore the government heavily invested in political education. The Bolsheviks were determined to use education for the purpose of spreading their ideology. The notion that education should stand above politics they considered dangerous nonsense.

At the outset, the Bolsheviks did away with those characteristics of the old educational system they found most distasteful. The church, which had played an important role in elementary education, was immediately excluded. Tsarist Russia had had three tracks of schools: an elementary school system, largely maintained by the church, for peasant children; vocational schools in the cities for the middle and lower-middle classes; and gymnasia, which trained students to enter the universities. It was difficult to move from one track to another, as each track was almost autonomous. This was a self-consciously elitist system, based on the assumption that people should get the education appropriate to their class standing.

The problems facing the Bolshevik educational program were formidable. The most significant was material poverty. School buildings had been destroyed, and even simple things such as pencils and paper were scarce. The introduction of the NEP necessitated economizing; per-student expenditure remained well below prewar standards until the end of the decade. Another major problem was the availability and political reliability of teachers. Village teachers had been traditionally attracted to the political ideology of the Socialist Revolutionaries. From the Bolshevik point of view this political orientation represented a great danger. In the early years many teachers simply refused to cooperate with the new authorities. Since the government was unable to make major investments in education, it shifted the burden to local budgets, and teachers were grossly underpaid. At a time when workers and peasants had more or less caught up with their prewar earnings, teachers were receiving no more than 45 percent of their prewar real income. Not surprisingly, in these circumstances, many village teachers wanted to leave the profession.

Given the poverty of the country and the shortage of competent teachers, it is understandable that the educational plans of the government largely remained on paper. The new government did establish a single type of school, to be attended theoretically for nine years. In reality, however, there were not enough schools in the villages for even one or two years of instruction. Talk about a single type of school remained meaningless at a time when the villages were so much worse off than the cities. At the end of the NEP period, in the 1928–29 school year, only about three-quarters of the peasant school-age children received any education at all. Each year approximately 1 million illiterate adolescents entered the population. While about half of the graduates from city elementary schools went on to middle schools, only one in thirty from the villages did so.

The utopian leaders in the Commissariat of Enlightenment wanted to introduce decentralized education. They were impressed by the principles of progressive, child-centered education and wanted to combine education with work experience. In the face of the teachers' resistance, however, their schemes remained largely unrealized.

The regime's accomplishments in education remained limited at least partially because the government chose to use its scarce resources outside the regular school system. The party organized an extraordinarily ambitious literacy and adult education drive. A "voluntary" society, Down with Illiteracy, was created to help illiterates learn and to agitate for attending literacy schools. The drive was thoroughly politicized. Approximately 8 million adults attended literacy schools in the course of the decade. Some contemporary observers recommended that the government maintain a small system of adult education for those eager to learn, but use most of its money to expand the regular school system. The government rejected this recommendation – which would have overcome illiteracy most quickly – because it was determined to use education for the indoctrination of the politically crucial adult population.

The government also financed an entire political educational system that on a small scale mirrored the regular system. These schools trained agitators and middle-level party and state functionaries. It opened workers' schools, enabling workers to improve their qualifications. The drop-out rate was extremely high: few workers had the determination to attend classes after exhausting hours of work. Nevertheless, these schools did contribute to the training of a new intelligentsia and encouraged further social mobility.

THE STRUGGLE FOR POWER

The Bolshevik Party to a very large extent was Lenin's creation. It was built on his principles, and its prominent figures were his personal disciples. He was a strong leader who insisted on having his way. However, he possessed such prestige that his fellow leaders willingly deferred to him – he rarely had to use dictatorial methods. People who disagreed with him, even on the most important issues, could always be forgiven, once the question was resolved. No successor to Lenin could rule the party as he did, since no one possessed comparably great and unquestioned authority.

In the spring of 1922 Lenin suffered a stroke which removed him from day-to-day participation in decisionmaking. In his isolation, the maker of the revolution reflected on his achievements, and was less than fully satisfied. The new socialist human being with a communitarian worldview had not yet been born. Instead, Lenin saw the growth of bureaucracy, the decline of the old revolutionary spirit within his party, and the revival of Russian nationalism among communists. Like many strong leaders before and since, he had no confidence that any of his disciples could take his place and carry on his work. Indeed, his illness started a struggle for power that lasted for the rest of the decade.

In the 1920s Soviet society and the political system were in the process of evolution. The leaders time and again faced problems for which there had been no precedent. The struggle for power and the resolution of the many difficult issues came to be inextricably intertwined. Every issue – the proper organization of the party, foreign policy, economic policy, ideology – became a battleground among the protagonists. The points of view of the protagonists actually did not differ much, because all Bolshevik leaders, perhaps without realizing it, shared basic assumptions. They all believed in building a modern industrial society, and all took the system of the NEP for granted. However, because of their rhetoric, the issues became divisive and entangled in personal politics. That the politicians indulged in rhetorical flourishes does not mean that they did not take the issues seriously and cared only about political advantage. None of them were purely careerists, and it is likely that all of them, including Stalin, believed that their positions were necessary for the victory of the Bolshevik cause.

On some occasions the positions of the protagonists were determined by their own political situations. It stands to reason that those who had lost control over the decisionmaking bodies became the most fervent advocates of party democracy. These leaders conveniently forgot that a short time before, when they had possessed political power, they had been just as intolerant and arbitrary as the present victors. Stalin won, and in the 1930s the Soviet Union embarked on a radically new path. We must not conclude, however, that if the outcome of the political struggle had been different – say, if Trotsky or Bukharin had emerged victorious – the relative freedom that characterized the 1920s could have continued and the Soviet Union could have become a more or less democratic state. The problems to which Stalinist totalitarianism was an answer were real, even if the Stalinist solution was not the only one.

The course of the struggle for leadership can be quickly summarized. Shortly before he died, Lenin dictated a political testament in which he characterized all the members of the Politburo – that is, the most important leaders of the party. His characterizations were rather acid; he had something damning to say about each major figure. He remembered that Zinoviev and Kamenev had erred in October 1917 by opposing the plans for revolution. He regarded Bukharin as too scholastic and too young. Although Lenin admired Trotsky's abilities, the commissar for war received heavy criticism: Lenin regarded him as arrogant and incapable of getting along with people. Although few of his contemporaries recognized this, Lenin rather perspicaciously noted that, aside from Trotsky, the most powerful figure in the leadership was Stalin. Stalin received the most unflattering characterization: in a postscript Lenin wrote that Stalin was crude, had accumulated too much power, and should be removed.

The two major antagonists at the outset were Trotsky and Stalin. Trotsky had considerable support in the army, which he had created and had led to victory, and among the young, who admired his revolutionary fervor and his oratory. In retrospect, however, it is clear that Trotsky had little chance of assuming Lenin's mantle. He showed a great ineptitude for political infighting, arrogantly underestimated the strength of his opponents, and lacked the talent for political timing. His fellow leaders neither liked nor trusted him. The political struggle for succession in the Soviet Union in the 1920s was not decided by popularity in the country at large, but by a rather small group of political actors; and within this all important circle Trotsky's strength proved insufficient.

Stalin, by contrast, was a master of infighting. He would bide his time and come forward only when he possessed the political strength to defeat his opponents. He succeeded in getting political allies to serve his purposes. He skillfully removed the supporters of his opponents from key positions, replacing them with his own people. He knew how to define the terms of disagreement in such a way as to gain benefits in politically relevant parts of the population. He managed to present his own positions so that the middle-level cadres found them attractive and worthy of support.

The first stage of the struggle was the most dangerous period for Stalin. Using Lenin's testament, Trotsky could probably have removed him from competition. Stalin, however, gained the support of Zinoviev and Kamenev, who feared Trotsky's ascendancy, and Trotsky stupidly acquiesced in the collective decision not to publish Lenin's testament. He never had another chance to deal a decisive blow to Stalin. By early 1925 he had lost most of his important jobs. Zinoviev and Kamenev soon realized that it was Stalin who had gained most from Trotsky's defeat, and watched with dismay as Stalin consolidated his position by placing his followers in critical posts. Zinoviev and Kamenev came over to Trotsky's side when it was too late. Stalin then allied himself with Bukharin, and by 1927 succeeded in politically destroying what came to be known as the left opposition. There remained only one powerful opponent, and that was Bukharin. The decisive struggle between these two leaders came to be associated with the end of the NEP and the beginning of forced collectivization.

The most contested issue between the left opposition and the Stalin–Bukharin leadership of the party concerned the strategy for economic development. Their passionate and often articulate exchange of opinions on economic strategy deserves attention, even though the outcome of the debate did not determine Soviet policy – indeed, what ultimately happened was not foreseen by any of the protagonists. The debate shows the mentality of the Bolshevik leadership at the time: their visions of the future, their fears, their goals. As in so many other matters, the Bolshevik theorists were path-breakers. In dealing with immediate problems, they were also dealing with the major issues of developmental economics: how could the state bring about rapid economic growth and modernize a backward society? All Bolsheviks agreed that growth of the industrial sector of the economy was necessary and that the state had a leading role to play in bringing that about. They also all assumed that a mixed economy should survive for an indefinite period.

The most able theorist of the left was Yevgenii Preobrazhenskii. He and his political allies disagreed with the economic policies pursued by the regime because they considered the pace of industrialization too slow. The question was where to get capital with which to finance industrial growth. In Pre-obrazhenskii's view, it had to come from the private sector – that is, largely from the peasantry. The peasantry had to be taxed more heavily. Further, the socialist industrial sector of the economy had to siphon away resources by "exploiting" the peasantry, that is, by raising the prices of industrial goods that the peasants needed. On the basis of Marxist analogy with the process of industrialization in Britain, Preobrazhenskii called this policy "primitive socialist accumulation." Preobrazhenskii and his comrades also criticized governmental policies as too favorable to the rich peasants. They feared that the Bukharin–Stalin economic policy line would encourage the growing political strength of the kulaks.

The debate, as usual with political debates, was not resolved by intellectual arguments. Both sides had valid points to make. Preobrazhenskii's point that under the circumstances it was impossible to accumulate enough capital for sustained growth and industrialization was obviously well taken. But Bukharin was also right to be concerned about the political consequences of violating the spirit of the NEP by shifting the economic burden onto the peasantry. The NEP system had inherent flaws, and the two articulate and intelligent debaters inadvertently pointed them out.

At first Bukharin and his allies on the right prevailed. The neopopulist, pro-peasant policies received a try, and in some ways the second half of the 1920s was a golden period for the Russian peasantry. But this victory was short-lived, and it led to the economic and ultimately political crisis of 1928. Neither the right nor the left in the great controversy of the mid 1920s envisaged the course on which the country was to embark a few years later.

The economic debate became entangled with an ideological dispute. That dispute could be reduced to a slogan used by Stalin and his political allies at the time: "Socialism in one country." Stalin presumably did not mean to challenge the Marxist notion that socialism could be realized only when capitalism had been destroyed worldwide. He meant that the country could work to bring about socialism by creating an industrial base and by raising the cultural level of the people without waiting for international revolution. The Trotskyists did not disagree with these propositions and did not have a competing strategy. After all, they were more consistent supporters of industrialization than the Stalinist–Bukharinist leadership. Nor was there any reason to accuse the Trotskyists of wanting a more adventurous foreign policy. To the extent that there were disagreements over foreign policy, they could not be reduced to a distinction between cautious and adventurous policies.

Nonetheless, for Trotsky and his political friends, Stalin's slogan seemed a repudiation of the Marxist-Leninist internationalist heritage. To their own satisfaction they demonstrated that Stalin was betraying the most sacred ideas of the revolution. However correct they may have been from an ideological point of view, what mattered was political appeal, and in this area they were drawn into a battle they were bound to lose. Although the two sides agreed on matters of concrete policy, and even on questions of ideology, the middle-level party leaders perceived that Stalin stood for national independence and pride and Trotsky for revolutionary adventures, when the country needed peace above all. In view of the fact that Stalin was about to embark on an exceedingly adventurous policy, his image as a man of caution and peace was ironic.

4

The First Five-Year Plan

THE DISINTEGRATION OF THE NEP SYSTEM AND THE
SEARCH FOR NEW SOLUTIONS

The NEP was an inherently unstable social and political system: it contained the seeds of its own destruction. The Bolsheviks carried out policies in which they did not fully believe and whose implications worried them. For the sake of economic reconstruction they had allowed the reemergence of private enterprise and, as time went on, many of them came to be convinced supporters of this mixed economic order. Others, however, based on their reading of Marxist texts, found such policies distasteful. They feared that the New Economic Policies would strengthen those social forces that were, in the long run, bound to be hostile to socialism.

The Bolsheviks were particularly concerned about developments in the countryside. While in the cities the new order was firmly established, in the villages the Soviet government lacked the organizational strength to enforce its will; and therefore, as the revolutionaries saw it, the power of the kulaks was especially threatening. The peasants were encouraged to produce because the government desperately needed their products, but at the same time the successful peasants faced the threat of being defined as kulaks, and therefore enemies. Ambivalence led to confused policies. The leaders of the regime abandoned the policies of the NEP not so much because they were eager to resume the advance toward a socialist society as because the existing system was unraveling. The country was suffering an extraordinarily severe economic and political crisis, a crisis that ended only with the dismantlement of the existing social and political order and the introduction of an unparalleled social experiment.

The period 1928–29 marked a transition, perhaps the most decisive turning point in the history of the country. While the NEP system was not formally repudiated, official policies increasingly came to contradict its fundamental assumptions. (Indeed, the NEP was never renounced. Soviet historians always considered the period of the first two five-year plans as part of the NEP. According to their interpretation, the turning point was 1937, the moment of "victory of the socialist methods of production.") The leaders of the regime were looking for ways to transcend the crisis. They grappled with genuine problems, and in searching for solutions created a new Stalinist order.

The crisis resulted from the coincidence of several problems of varying magnitudes. One of them was an expectation of war. Today we know that war was, in fact, not on the horizon, and that, contrary to contemporary talk, the capitalist powers were not about to recommence intervention. By the mid 1920s all major European powers had reestablished diplomatic and commercial relations with Soviet Russia, and the country was gradually regaining its place in the international arena. The Bolsheviks, implicitly and temporarily, gave up their hope for world revolution – peace was necessary for the return of normality, and trade was essential for reconstruction. But then the Soviet Union suffered some setbacks. The Chinese communists, on the advice of Moscow, pursued an unwise policy and as a consequence were slaughtered by the troops of Chiang Kai-shek; this debacle was followed by recriminations in the Comintern leadership and within the Politburo. In 1927 the United Kingdom canceled its trade treaty with the Soviet Union and broke off diplomatic relations. The Soviet ambassador to Warsaw was murdered. However, these unrelated events did not add up to a likelihood of renewed hostilities. Indeed, it is likely that Stalin manufactured the war scare. But, whether or not he was responsible for creating it, he clearly benefited from it, for the extraordinary means he recommended for industrialization seemed more plausible at a time of crisis.

The chief source of crisis was not foreign but domestic policy. Once reconstruction was completed, the economy needed larger investments just to maintain the previous level of growth. But, as Bukharin in his controversy with Preobrazhenskii had pointed out, an excessively high rate of growth, requiring large investments, was inconsistent with the balance of political forces in the country and with the concept of the worker–peasant alliance. Stalin's change of heart in the vital matter of industrialization led to a break between him and Bukharin, who along with his allies were now dubbed the right-wing opposition. Stalin could risk this political confrontation because he had already succeeded in getting rid of his enemies on the left. To Bukharin and to many other contemporaries it seemed that Stalin had stolen the program of the defeated left. Stalin found it more difficult to defeat Bukharin than Trotsky, because the right enjoyed support not only among segments of the population but also among the middle-level party functionaries. Stalin won because he ultimately succeeded in persuading the communist activists, who at this point were decisively important within the political system, that his policies were realistic as well as within the Leninist tradition.

The general secretary now threw his weight behind the most extreme industrializers. In an unprecedented effort to plan the industrialization of a backward society, the State Planning Agency had been drawing up increasingly ambitious projects. Although the first variant of the five-year plan, drawn up in 1927, was already extraordinarily optimistic, the planners, pressured by politicians, presented ever-higher target figures. The final document called for impossible goals and was internally inconsistent: investment and consumption were to rise, and both industrial and agricultural production were to grow fantastically. Even before the plan was formally accepted by the Sixteenth Party Conference in April 1929, large-scale projects, such as building a great dam on the Dnieper, were under way.

The great economic reconstruction was accompanied by an attack on a segment of the population whose services were sorely needed in backward and uneducated Russia: the old intelligentsia. Even before the introduction of collectivization, the Stalinists had embarked on a campaign against planners and engineers. The centerpiece of the campaign was a series of trials, in which the accused were compelled to confess to imaginary crimes. The point of these trials was to frighten the old intelligentsia, to establish scapegoats for failures, and to show young militants that the regime was taking a "revolutionary" line and did not fear an old elite. The future order of the Stalinist Soviet Union was already taking shape.

It is possible but unlikely that the Stalinists had another, cynical reason for their attack on this new "class enemy." Planned or unplanned, the attack greatly contributed to the atmosphere of crisis. It conveyed the idea that the normal and old-fashioned ways of doing business would no longer suffice. The government would no longer bow before the necessities created by mundane reality. In the new era, it was enthusiasm that counted, not the sober measurement of resources. The attack on the old intelligentsia found support among enthusiasts, who had always disliked this remnant of the old order. They also knew that the removal of the educated specialists would open up places for the new cadres and bring about social mobility.

The most important element in the atmosphere of crisis was the deteriorating food situation in the cities. Although overall agricultural production approximated prewar standards, the share that reached markets remained very much lower. The situation was especially bad in grain, the mainstay of the Russian diet. While grain production was 90 percent of what it had been in 1913, the peasants brought to market less than half of what had been sold in prerevolutionary times. Part of the problem was structural: the segment of agriculture that had produced primarily for the market, the large estates, had been destroyed. The very success of egalitarian policies contributed to the crisis. Given the abysmally low standard of living, the peasants preferred to eat their surplus product rather than sell it, at a time when industry could not produce goods at affordable prices. The shortsighted policies of the government greatly contributed to the difficulties. Since the government desperately needed capital for investment in industry, it tried to economize by keeping grain prices low. The consequences in a market economy were predictable: the peasants switched from cultivating underpriced products to others that promised a better return. The unwillingness of the peasants to sell to the government at artificially low prices directly threatened the ambitious industrialization project. The government also had great trouble in maintaining an export program, which was essential if they were to buy foreign machinery that domestic industry could not yet produce.

The situation in the winter of 1927–28 was becoming critical. The peasants did not have much grain, and what they did have they preferred to sell to private traders, who offered much higher prices than the government. Those who could afford to wait in anticipation of higher prices were, of course, the better-off peasants, those the government classified as kulaks. For political reasons the Stalinist leadership blamed these people for the entire crisis and initiated an attack on them. In some areas, especially in the Ural mountains and in Siberia, forcible requisitioning was reintroduced. The reintroduction of a brutal form of "class war" came to be called the "Ural–Siberian" method.

Governmental policies created confusion. After all, "kulak" was never a precisely defined term; the authorities could use it against anyone who resisted. Nor was the concept of "surplus" defined. Any peasant who had foodstuffs in addition to his immediate needs was in danger. When the authorities defined someone as a "kulak" and established that he had "surplus," they took everything. Obviously, the peasants tried to hide what they had, but concealment was a crime. The line between speculation, which was a criminal offense, and trade, an essential part of the NEP system, was vague.

The Communist Party structure had been weak in the villages; the government needed help to carry out the new and unpopular policies. It sent tens of thousands of workers into the countryside in search of food. Such policies, however, courted the danger of unifying the entire peasantry against the regime. The Stalinist leadership turned once again to its longstanding policy of fanning class war in the villages. It attempted to enlist the services of the poor by promising them a share of the loot for their help. Poor peasants now had a material interest in denouncing their rich neighbors for concealment. It is difficult to say how successful the policy of dividing the peasantry was. The worse the situation became and the harsher the attacks, the more likely it was that the entire peasantry would unite against Bolshevik policies.

The attack on the peasantry was carried out with great violence, which undermined the fundamental assumptions of the peasants about the communist regime. Forcible collections of grain made the return to a functioning market more difficult. The peasants lost confidence in their ability to market their products and lost their incentive to produce. Requisitioning grain one year increased the need to repeat it next year. It was in this situation of ever-present crisis that the government hit on the solution: forcible collectivization.

COLLECTIVIZATION

It is difficult to describe the period of the first five-year plan.[1] For purposes of analysis we must discuss individual topics separately, but such an approach obscures a complex historical process in which various aspects of the transformation coincided and reinforced one another. Violence against the peasants, the "cultural revolution," the politically inspired show trials, the new ways of conducting politics, and the fantastic industrialization plans went hand in hand; they could not have existed without one another. Of the various aspects of the extraordinary transformation, it was collectivization that was the most difficult to carry out and had the most profound consequences.

The Bolsheviks had distrusted the peasants even before the revolution, regarding private ownership of land as a major obstacle to the victory of socialism and always approaching the rural way of life with hostility. They would have liked to organize agriculture on the pattern of industry – that is, to make workers out of peasants. Only under the pressure of events did the Leninists accept as inevitable the de facto private ownership of land. But even at that difficult time Lenin in his famous manifesto of November 1917 was careful to describe land as the property of society – even if peasants could cultivate it as if it were their own. During the civil war it seemed wise not even to talk about the ultimate goal of collectivizing agriculture, for the peasants obviously hated the idea.

In the 1920s it became clear to the Bolsheviks that agriculture needed reorganization. Like previous knowledgeable observers, they understood that the traditional Russian pattern of land-holding, according to which the village commune periodically redistributed the land, was economically unsound. Such a land tenure system perpetuated the cultivation of small strips of land and thereby precluded the modernization of a backward agriculture. They also saw that a state-directed industrialization drive would not succeed as long as the authorities had no firm control over agricultural production and, most importantly, over marketing.

In their debates during the 1920s Bolshevik theoreticians continued to take for granted the superiority of collective agriculture. They assumed that when the modernized Soviet economy managed to supply collectives with fertilizers, machinery, and agricultural expertise, the peasants would see the superior standard of living of their fellows in the collectives and would want to join. Since during the period of the NEP the regime was unable to provide for the existing collectives, it naturally failed to increase its influence among the peasants, and their way of life was little changed. However much the theoreticians favored large-scale collectivized agriculture, it never occurred to any of them that it would be desirable or possible to coerce the entire Russian peasantry to give up its way of life.

Since the revolution there had been a few state-operated farms and a tiny collective movement. The collective farms succeeded in attracting only the very poorest; they were incompetently managed and uneconomically small, and suffered from rapid turnover of membership. Under the circumstances they could not possibly serve as advertisements. In 1928 hardly more than 1 percent of the arable land was cultivated by collectives. Concurrently with drawing up the plans for industrialization, party leaders and theoreticians discussed the role of collective farms in the new economic system. State and party organs started to take a more active interest and, by 1928, sometimes used coercion to collectivize entire villages. However, in the late 1920s even the most ambitious proposed only that 15 percent of the total output be produced by collectivized agriculture at the end of the first five-year plan.

Despite all the previous talk about collectivization, what occurred in the fall of 1929 and winter of 1930 was totally unexpected. The Stalinist leadership, having rid itself of all vestiges of opposition in the highest echelons of the party, carried out a frontal attack on the way of life of the peasantry. At first in selected regions, and soon in the entire country, the peasants were forced to join collectives. The speed with which the transformation was carried out was remarkable. At the end of September 1929 only 7.4 percent of peasant households were collectivized. This rose to 15 percent by the end of the year, and then the great rush began. In January and February 1930, 11 million households joined the collectives, and the share of collectivized peasant households rose to 60 percent. At this point Stalin, apparently fearing the consequences of his policy, called a temporary halt. With extraordinary hypocrisy, he dissociated himself from the "excesses" of collectivization. In early March he published an article in *Pravda*, under the heading "Dizzy with Success," in which he blamed the local authorities for violating the voluntary principle for joining. Within a few weeks, half of the recently collectivized peasantry left the kolkhozes (collective farms). Probably Stalin took this action because he feared that the confusion created by collectivization would interfere with spring sowing and create a disastrous famine. By reversing course he allowed time for consolidation. In the fall of 1930 the offensive was resumed in a more orderly fashion. In the following four years almost the entire peasantry was collectivized, and by 1937, at the end of the second five-year plan, private agriculture had been destroyed.[2]

The de facto declaration of war on the peasant way of life was obviously a risky undertaking. In view of the fact that the peasants bitterly resented the necessity of joining the collective farms, and the party at the outset of the campaign possessed only limited organizational strength in the villages, it is remarkable that the task could be accomplished at all. This war was carried out with the greatest brutality. The local party secretary or chairman of the soviet, often in the presence of cadres from the cities, would announce the formation of the kolkhoz. At the same time the Soviet authorities set impossible procurement and tax obligations on the recalcitrants, and those who spoke among their fellow villagers against the new institution were declared to be kulaks and mercilessly punished.

The destruction of the kulak stratum and the establishment of collective farms went hand in hand. At the beginning of the collectivization campaign Stalin called for the "elimination of the kulaks as a class" and insisted that they not be allowed to join the collective farms. At first glance, it is not evident why the attempt to create a modern agriculture had to be accompanied by the physical destruction of the most able peasant producers. Yet it is clear that the attack on the kulaks was an essential element in coercing the peasants to give up their farms. The dreadful danger of being classified as a kulak made many peasants accept the lesser evil of life in a kolkhoz. The fate of the kulaks was an irrefutable argument that there was no future in private agriculture. Many Bolsheviks could hardly wait to resume the "heroic age" of class struggle that had been suspended during the years of the NEP. For them, deporting kulaks and confiscating their property was not essentially different from fighting the Whites in the civil war. The violent attack on the better-off peasants started during the procurement crisis. Only the richer peasants could have a surplus, and it was only from them, therefore, that it could be taken away. By fighting the kulaks, the government attempted to create the impression that it was only the kulak stratum that opposed collectivization.

There was no precise definition of a "kulak," and this vagueness suited the Bolsheviks' purposes, allowing them to use the definition as a political weapon. Being relatively well off and opposing Soviet policies were identical from the Bolshevik perspective. Under the guise of the war against the kulaks, the regime got rid of potential and genuine opponents, for example priests (although priests could by no definition be considered rich). Also, by declaring war on the kulaks, the party and the government aimed at and to some extent succeeded in dividing the peasant class.

According to contemporary party estimates, there were 1 million kulak households in the entire country, consisting of approximately 5 million people.[3] Local authorities had a great deal of latitude in classifying people as kulaks. Although central plans were drawn up and local districts even received quotas of kulaks to identify, the destruction of the kulaks was inevitably a somewhat haphazard operation. Enthusiastic local officials often exceeded their quotas. In order to carry out the actual work of deportation, local officials called on the help of the OGPU (political police), mobilized workers, and the militia. The property of the kulaks was to revert to the newly formed collective farms. In reality, however, the disorder created by the state allowed a great deal of looting and settling of private scores.

The kulaks were divided into three subgroups. Those whom the local authorities found especially dangerous were deported by the political police to distant regions in the Far North and in Siberia. Approximately a million and a half human beings were subjected to this punishment. These people were abandoned with a minimum of resources in most inhospitable regions, where they had to fend for themselves. Many did not survive. Kulaks in the second category also had their property confiscated and were required to leave their native provinces; however, they were not deported to distant areas. The authorities wanted to remove them from their villages because they believed such people had influence among their fellow peasants and might use it against the collective farms. Kulaks in the third category were allowed to remain in their villages, but most of their property was confiscated. As compensation they received the worst land and were subjected to heavy taxation. They were demoted to a second-class citizenship. Rules and regulations made the lives of these ex-kulaks miserable.

The regime could not have carried out the attack exclusively with its forces in the countryside. At the outset of the collectivization drive it had only about a third of a million rural party members, many of them unreliable, corrupt, and uneducated. Therefore the party sent out teams of workers to help in the procurement and collectivization campaigns. In addition, at the time of the decision of full collectivization, in November 1929, the party decided to mobilize 25,000 reliable worker cadres for permanent work in the villages. These workers, most of them genuinely enthusiastic about the task of the great transformation, took on jobs in party and soviet administration, and in particular served as chairmen of collective farms. Some of them became disillusioned within a few years and drifted back to the cities, but others spent the rest of their days in the country. The peasants naturally resented this invasion of outsiders, who knew nothing about agriculture and village life but nevertheless came to rule over them. They frequently became objects of violence.[4]

No matter how much the peasants hated the new institutions, they were unable to protect themselves. Resistance was almost exclusively passive, taking forms such as the slaughter of domestic animals. (The peasants killed them to avoid giving them to the hated collectives.) Such behavior had lasting consequences for Soviet agriculture and made recovery very difficult. Active struggle amounted to nothing more than occasional haphazard, senseless, and desperate violence – assassinations of party and soviet leaders, the burning down of soviet buildings. Such acts convinced the Bolsheviks that they were in fact engaged in "class struggle" and seemingly justified their own violence. As so often in Russian history, the peasant class proved unable to overcome its organizational weakness in order to protect its interests.

The Bolsheviks feared that the commune might serve as an organizational base of peasant resistance. Therefore, along with the establishment of the collective farms, the Soviet regime, ironically enough, abolished that age-old expression of peasant collectivism, the village commune. The nature of the village commune was such that communists could not penetrate it and subvert it, but had to abolish it altogether. Given the brutality with which the struggle against the kulaks was carried out and given the danger of being classified as an enemy of the Soviet state, any discussion of the "voluntary" nature of the kolkhoz movement was purely illusory. Stalin and his fellow leaders gambled that they would be able to prevail against the peasantry, and they won the gamble.

The Bolshevik Revolution of 1917 was a thorough social revolution that destroyed the basic class structure of imperial Russia by abolishing the gulf between the privileged and unprivileged. From the point of view of the peasants, the most significant act of the revolution was the removal of the hated landlord from the village. The revolution of collectivization was a different kind of transformation, though it created a no less significant change. While it was a directed revolution, a "revolution from above," it caused just as much trauma and had just as many victims. Rather than changing the relationship of classes – though that also happened, as the relative position of the peasantry within the social structure greatly declined – it destroyed a way of life. In the course of the 1920s the Leninists had managed to make very few inroads in the villages and had left the structure and institutions of peasant life untouched. Collectivization changed that by destroying centers of peasant autonomy and gradually creating a political base for the Bolshevik rulers.

Many of the changes brought about by collectivization were bound to occur eventually in any case. The patriarchal peasant family was slowly breaking down. Industrial growth, and with it urbanization, was likely to accelerate. Collectivization, however, made the changes extraordinarily rapid and traumatic. Despite the overt industrial and urban orientation of the Soviet regime, its special genius was found not so much in its organization of industry or in its particular methods of industrializing, but in its organization of agriculture and treatment of the peasantry. Other countries have carried out thorough social revolutions, and other countries have had rapid industrialization drives. But the Soviet Union was the first country in the world that forced its peasants into collectives, and that particular feature of the regime has been imitated only by other communists.

Collectivization created havoc in agriculture. Fortunately for the regime, in 1930 the weather was unusually favorable, so the adverse effects did not show up immediately. However, the reckoning was not long in coming. The ills of Soviet agriculture, from which the country would not recover for decades, were the consequence of collectivization.

Forcing the peasants to give up their way of life was a turning point in Soviet history. Even before this, the regime had suppressed civil liberties. Persecuting out millions of human beings who had committed no wrong, had participated in no opposition movement, just because they belonged to a vaguely defined category, however, was a new departure, a new violation of a moral code. How were the Soviet leaders capable of such a crime? With their constant talk about class struggle in the previous decade, the Bolsheviks had unwittingly prepared themselves. They had convinced themselves that the kulaks were determined "class enemies" who were innately hostile to the Soviet order and who had successfully mobilized the bulk of the peasantry against them. The regime established a bloody precedent. The great blood-letting of the later 1930s, in which millions of human beings lost their lives, probably could not have occurred without this earlier atrocity. Mass murder for vaguely defined political goals became a possibility – this was the most important legacy of collectivization.

INDUSTRIALIZATION

The Bolsheviks, before their revolution, had always assumed that the prole-tariat would take power only after the country had been industrialized under a capitalist system of production. But reality refused to follow the demands of theory, and the Bolsheviks found themselves ruling over a backward and impoverished country. Under the circumstances, it fell to the Leninists to finish the task the capitalists had only begun. Once power was securely in their hands, and the country had survived its worst period of devastation, the new rulers set themselves as their primary task the industrialization of the country.

In the great industrialization debate of the 1920s, the only controversial issues were the methods and speed of industrialization; all Bolsheviks agreed that the industrialization of the country was essential. This conviction followed from the Marxist belief in progress, a progress predicated on economic development. In the Bolshevik worldview an industrial civilization was ipso facto superior to a nonindustrial one. The Soviet Union was to follow the West European experience, and that above all meant building a modern economy.

Stalin, after the victory over his rivals, brought a new element into Bol-shevik thinking. He justified the need for rapid industrialization by an injured sense of Russian nationalism. He best expressed this very non-Marxist and non-Leninist thought in an often-quoted speech in 1931. He insisted that the breakneck tempo of industrialization could not be slackened but, on the contrary, had to be further increased. Otherwise, he said, the USSR would fall behind, and those who fell behind would be beaten. He recalled the humiliation of imperial Russia at the hands of stronger adver-saries, by implication claiming the heritage of imperial Russia and promising to seek revenge for past humiliations. In the Stalinist view, such an extraor-dinary effort was needed in order to make the Soviet Union a powerful participant in the international arena.

When the reconstruction following the destruction of war, revolution, and civil war was completed, and the country was ready to turn to new economic tasks, planners prepared ambitious yet still reasonable and thoughtful plans for accelerated growth. In 1928 and 1929, as the political climate changed, the planning process acquired a dynamism of its own. One of the ironies of Soviet economic history is that, when the USSR entered the age of planning and five-year plans, planning became meaningless. Competent planners were removed from their jobs and tried for their "wrecking" activity. "Wrecking" meant the planners' desire to incorporate into their work a professional approach – that is, to insist on the maintenance of internal consistency. In the new world, "planning" was reduced to naming target figures which had little more than propaganda significance.

Party leaders in charge of the economy promised not only vast increases in the output of heavy industry, but also dramatic improvements in the standard of living of the Soviet people. How unrealistic the plans were can be seen by the fact that some of the target figures promised by the party leaders were achieved not in 1932, at the end of the first five-year plan, but in 1960, fifteen years after the end of the Second World War. The goal of the first five-year plan was reached by fiat: after four years the Soviet leaders simply announced that the plan had been fulfilled.

During the years of the first five-year plan, the citizens of the Soviet Union experienced a sensation that they were living in extraordinary times, when normal rules had ceased to apply. Indeed, the possibility of suspending the rules of economics became an article of communist faith. The slogan of the day expressed that faith: "there are no fortresses that the Bolsheviks cannot storm!" The party demanded not careful planning and balancing of resources and tasks, but enthusiasm; the leaders considered it treason when economists pointed out irrationalities in their plans or argued that impossible goals were bound to create crises, which in turn would lead to waste and inefficiency.

The Soviet method of industrialization turned out to be an immense improvisation, a revival of the war economy. The times shared a great deal with the period of war communism. The Stalinists resurrected the utopian mentality, suspended the market mechanism, and reintroduced rationing. But there were differences as well: the new revolution promised neither liberation nor equality, and terror provided a sinister backdrop for genuine enthusiasm.

To what extent euphoria was government-inspired and to what extent it was real and deeply felt is impossible to say. Indeed, perhaps the two could not be separated. The regime made every effort to manipulate and propagandize for the purpose of construction. On the other hand, the success of the propaganda drive shows that there was at least a politically significant minority eager to listen. The Stalinist promise to build an industrial economy in the shortest possible time fired the imagination of many. Many young activists, convinced of the superiority of the communist ideology and way of life, were willing to accept hardships for the sake of a brilliant future.

The Soviet economy was particularly geared to undertake gigantic tasks. In these years construction of a new industrial city, Magnitogorsk, was started; hydroelectric stations were built; and an important railroad line was constructed, connecting Central Asia to the trans-Siberian line. The very magnitude of projects was a source of appeal to the activists. Some of the projects were ill conceived, such as the White Sea Canal, built by convict labor with only the most primitive tools. Built at the cost of terrible suffering, the canal was almost useless when completed – it was so shallow that only small boats could use it.

Soviet industrialization was not planned to bring about balanced growth. The planners established Class A and Class B industries. Class A industries included producer goods, such as coal, iron, and machine-building, and Class B included consumer goods. All variants called for much higher rates of growth in Class A than in Class B industries. In reality, however, the disproportion of growth was far greater than even originally envisaged. In an economy of scarcity, where decisions constantly had to be made about the allocation of scarce resources, the economy functioned on the basis of the so-called priority method. This meant that when resources were not easily available – which was most of the time – preference was given to heavy industry. As a consequence, a remarkably dynamic heavy industry coexisted with a stagnating, and on occasion even declining, light industry.

Economists disagree about the extent of industrial growth during the first five-year plan, because Soviet statistics are not altogether trustworthy. The problem was not that the Statistical Bureau made up figures. It was that as each agency reported to a higher level the figures were padded, and the overall figures came to be distorted. The totals, after all, could be only as reliable as the raw data on which they were based. Furthermore, Soviet statisticians expressing national product according to preplan prices over-stated the extent of the growth, since the product mix to which those prices corresponded was altogether different. (For example, some relatively sophisticated machines that were produced in 1932 had not been produced at all in 1928. Assigning high monetary values to such products overstated growth.) There was an enormous amount of waste. To be sure, waste exists in every economy. However, during the first five-year plan the performance of factories was evaluated exclusively in quantitative terms, with no attention paid to quality. A considerable portion of the finished goods, though reported in the statistics, were in fact useless.

According to figures issued by the Soviet government, the annual rate of growth in industrial production during the first five-year plan was 19.2 percent. Although Western economists dispute these figures, no one doubts that the growth rate was impressive. The Soviet government, by keeping down consumption and investing an extraordinarily large share of the national product in the production of producer goods, managed to bring about an industrial transformation. The foundation of the great industrial power that was to be the Soviet Union had been laid. The character of the

Soviet economy in 1932 was very different from what it had been at the outset of the industrialization drive.

As in the case of every industrializing country, the capital for the building of industry was squeezed out of the peasantry. In the Soviet Union the situation was complicated by collectivization. Forcing the peasants to give up their private farms created such havoc and destruction that there was a net outflow of investment from industry to agriculture. For example, as noted, the peasants slaughtered their animals rather than give them to the hated collectives; the animals had to be replaced by tractors relatively quickly in order to avoid disaster. Still, the simple facts remain: peasants moved from villages to cities, where their productivity increased, and peasants who remained in the villages had less to eat than people in the cities. In this sense, the peasantry paid for industrialization.

The fundamental features of the Soviet economy were created during the great industrialization drive. At the outset, when the economy was still relatively primitive, it was an exceptionally dynamic system. The country needed a great deal of steel and iron and almost everything else. Later, the many dysfunctional elements of the system came to the surface, and the Soviet Union had to pay a significant price for its particular methods of modernization. The highly centralized and hierarchically organized economy necessitated a large bureaucracy, which attempted to control, supervise, and allocate resources. The bureaucracy struggled to control enterprises; enterprises, attempting to perform well and fulfill the plan, struggled to circumvent control. As long as the factory manager was successful, he was often allowed to get away with violating rules but, when he failed, he was punished. A system in which planning was expressed in terms of physical output placed little premium on quality and discouraged innovation. The risk of failure was too high. A large bureaucracy that attempted to control a huge economy could best coexist with a repressive political system.

The communists have always considered the industrialization of the country as their most important achievement. They believed that it was only the Soviet, and specifically Stalinist, method of industrialization that could have accomplished so much in such a short time. As long as their regime existed, Soviet publicists regarded an economy that was capable of catching up with the advanced capitalist West as the best proof of the superiority of their political, social, and economic system.

As the egalitarian and utopian goals of the October Revolution increasingly receded, an economic system producing rapid growth and national might came to be the main justification for the revolution. The communists' successful industrialization drive in their eyes became the decisive legitimizing factor. Had Soviet industry not been able to produce weapons in sufficient numbers and quality, they argued, the Nazi armies might have been unstoppable.

THE CREATION OF AN URBAN LABOR FORCE

Rapid industrialization created a vast social transformation. Collectivization destroyed the institutions and way of life of the peasantry. The transformation of the working class was perhaps not as obvious and violent, but nevertheless a mentality, a set of traditions, was also destroyed. In its place something new emerged: modern Soviet labor. Not even during the time of the revolution was Soviet society in such a state of flux.

The workers benefited from the new social mobility. The avenue for advancement for the ambitious and the intelligent was open. The hostility toward the technical intelligentsia and the great need for specialists allowed workers with little formal education to become engineers. On the one hand, tens of thousands of workers left the workbench and became engineers, took jobs in administration, or went to the countryside to assume responsible positions. On the other hand, millions of people who had had no experience in industrial labor swelled the working class.

All through the 1920s the Soviet Union had suffered serious unemployment. By 1930 this was not only eliminated, but the economy came to suffer from a shortage of labor. Between 1928 and 1932 the total number of employed increased from 11.5 million to 24 million, and the size of the industrial labor force from 3 to 6 million. The bulk of the new workers came from the countryside. The urban population grew from 26 million in 1926 to 38.7 million in 1932.[5] This influx was far greater than the planners had anticipated. Labor productivity did not grow as fast as expected and therefore the new factories needed more workers; collectivization created such misery in the villages that millions escaped to the cities in search of a better life.

In principle the Bolsheviks approved the transformation of peasants into workers. However, this vast, indeed unparalleled, demographic change over which the authorities had little control disturbed the Stalinist politicians. In order to establish control, the government in 1932 reintroduced domestic passports, which had existed in tsarist Russia but were abolished by the revolution. The new regulations established two classes of citizenship: the urban dwellers, who were in possession of their passports and therefore had freedom of movement, and the collective farm peasants, whose passports were kept in the offices of the chairman of the farm. This system gave the chairman power over his workers, because they needed his permission to leave the village even temporarily. The government – at times even individual factories – negotiated with collective farms over the delivery of workers.

The second important source of new labor was women. They made up less than a quarter of the industrial labor force during the years of the NEP, but by the end of the 1930s their proportion had increased to 40 percent. In the course of the second-five year plan, for example, 82 percent of the newly employed were women. Women participated in every branch of the economy, including construction and mining; but they were an especially important element in farm labor. They comprised 55 percent of the farm labor force in 1937. The greatly increased participation of women in the labor force was a boon to the Soviet economy. Only because women worked was it possible for the government to lower wages dramatically while ensuring that family incomes did not sink below subsistence levels. Furthermore, if the authorities had to bring in even more workers from the villages to supply the factories, it would have been necessary to construct more apartment buildings. Such investment in social overhead could have come only at the expense of heavy industry. As it was, the regime was able to use workers who already lived in the cities. Without the contribution of women, the Soviet method of industrialization could not have succeeded.

It is difficult to estimate the importance of forced labor for industrialization. We do not know and probably will never know the exact number of prisoners working during this period. It is indisputable, however, that in some distant and harsh regions such as Siberia and the Far North, and in some branches of the economy, such as lumbering and mining, convict labor was a significant factor. It was cheap. It was the ultimate form of exploitation. However, this method of using human beings was also wasteful. Skilled engineers worked in construction at a time when the economy desperately needed engineers, and of course the productivity of unfree labor was especially low. This kind of wastefulness was a chief characteristic of Soviet industrialization.

The productivity of free laborers was only slightly higher than that of the prisoners. The newly created labor force was of extremely low quality. The new workers not only lacked industrial skills, but also had trouble adjusting to a different way of life. One of the serious problems the regime faced with untrained labor was extremely rapid turnover. In some cases the turnover reached fantastic proportions. In the most extreme case, in the Donets basin in 1930, a quarter of the miners left their jobs every month. On the one hand, the peasants who entered industry were not prepared for what they encountered; on the other, the very rapid growth of industry created a constant shortage of labor, with factories bidding against one another for workers. Labor turnover of such proportions acted as a brake on the development of labor discipline and depressed productivity.

Turnover was not the only problem. The workers lacked labor discipline. They were not used to arriving on time, did not know how to take care of machinery, had very little interest in learning, and drank on the job. The result was a great deal of waste; breaking of expensive, often foreign-made machinery; and poor-quality work. The Soviet regime ultimately dealt with the problem in its own characteristic fashion. It introduced ever more severe laws to punish the offenders. By the time of the outbreak of the Second World War, workers were mobilized and treated like soldiers in wartime.

The great social transformation of the first five-year plan was traumatic, like any social transformation of this magnitude. Workers and peasants alike suffered great privations. The leaders who decided on rapid industrialization were not primarily interested in raising the standard of living of the Soviet people, and did not hesitate to impose suffering when they believed that their goals justified it. They did not, however, foresee the extent of the sacrifices that would be demanded. The original plans actually called for an improvement in the standard of living. It did not turn out that way. No one foresaw the extent and bitterness of the peasants' resistance to collectivization, and the consequences of that resistance. Nor did the planners foresee the amount of waste and mismanagement. They also could not have predicted the international economic crisis. This crisis brought great prestige to the Soviet cause everywhere in the world: people saw a remarkable contrast between the collapsing economies of the capitalist West and the fantastic tempo of growth in the world's first socialist state. In concrete terms, however, the international economic crisis was costly to the Soviet Union. The country needed Western machinery and Western technology. The imports had to be paid for by Soviet exports, and the only possible export was food. Agricultural prices were depressed on Western markets, and there was a famine in the Soviet Union. Without the economic crisis abroad, there would have been no need to export so much in order to gain so little.

The main reason that the plan turned out to be wildly optimistic in terms of improvement of living standards was that, wherever there was a shortage, the loss was made up at the expense of the production of consumer goods. Since almost everything was in short supply, the priority method, which gave primacy to heavy industry, implied a disastrous neglect of the welfare of the Soviet people. According to the calculations of economists, real wages of 1932 were only about half of what they had been in 1928. The decline in family incomes was smaller, since there were more wage earners per family.

The decline in incomes meant poor diet, clothing, and housing for the urban population. Although bread remained available in the cities, meat and milk consumption fell significantly. Since the production of textiles actually decreased during this period, it is obvious that the standards of clothing also deteriorated. The situation was worst in housing. Since the planners had not foreseen the extent of urbanization, they could not have planned for it. Living conditions for workers had been very bad in tsarist days and had further deteriorated during the war and revolution. The plans called for a slight improvement in the per capita living space available; what happened instead was a disastrous decline.

During the first five-year plan the population of Soviet cities almost doubled.[6] What this meant in terms of living conditions can be easily imagined. The Soviet state was determined to invest in heavy industry and was not about to be diverted by spending scarce resources on social overhead, meaning construction of apartment buildings and provision of various city amenities such as transportation and water. Living conditions became appalling: usually several families had to share a kitchen, and often a family could not have even a single room to itself. It would take a long time for the Soviet Union to make up for this dreadful neglect.

The answer to the question of who paid for Soviet industrialization is simple. Primarily the peasants paid. Hundreds of thousands of them lost their property through confiscation and were forced to work as convict laborers. Those who stayed in their villages had not only their way of life and institutions taken away, but also most of their food. Much of the peasantry was condemned to starvation. But the workers also paid: their standard of living declined, and they lived in misery.

COLLECTIVIZED AGRICULTURE

Collectivization was a vast improvisation. Its organizers did not foresee how it would be carried out and what its consequences would be, and had only vague ideas about what kind of collectives they wanted. If collectivization was a revolution from above, the revolutionary army was marching in uncharted territory. The major features of the new order emerged gradually as a result of a great learning exercise. The system was completed only in 1935 with the publication of a model collective farm charter.

The Soviet agricultural system was the outgrowth of a series of compromises between Bolshevik theoretical notions about socialist village life on the one hand, and harsh reality on the other. The communists would have liked to make agriculture into a branch of industry, so that the peasants would cease to be propertyowners and become wage earners. In any case, according to the decree on land of 1917, the land was the property of society – or, to put it more precisely, the property of the state, even if the peasants were allowed to cultivate it as if it were their own.

From this it followed that the authorities' preferred form of organization was the state farm (sovkhoz). At the time of the civil war the first state farms were established by carving lands out of large estates, but in the course of the NEP they fell, like the collective farms, into a deplorable state. They made only a minimal contribution to the national economy: in 1927–28 state farms produced only 1 percent of the total grain output of the USSR. When collectivization was put on the immediate agenda in 1928, the government also attempted to expand the land under cultivation in state farms, mostly by bringing virgin lands under cultivation. In some instances, however, privately cultivated lands were confiscated. Sovkhoz-cultivated land jumped from 3.6 million hectares in 1928 to 93.5 million in 1935. The government used its scarce investment resources lavishly on these farms.

Despite the investment and government encouragement, the economic failure of the state farms was even more evident than that of the collective farms. Reality did not bear out the theories concerning the economic rationality of enormous size, and this gigantomania of the planners was costly. The country possessed neither the equipment for large-scale cultivation nor the agricultural expertise. Giant farms produced giant failures. Motivation to work was even lower than in collective farms. Excessive specialization in state farms also turned out to be harmful. Some, for example, grew only sugar beets or cotton. After the first five-year plan, the state farms were, relatively speaking, deemphasized and the dominant form of organization remained the collective farm. After all, however poorly workers were paid on state farms, the state retained an obligation to pay wages. In the case of collective farms, the peasants directly paid for the failure.

The second crucial organizational decision was not to distribute agricultural machinery among the collective farms but to concentrate them in machine tractor stations (MTSs). By the fall of 1929 not a single one remained in private possession. At first the confiscated tractors were distributed among the collective farms. Soon the representatives of the government realized that it made no sense to distribute the tractors, because the majority of the kolkhozes were too small to use them efficiently. There were not enough tractors to satisfy the needs of the collective farms; and, after the slaughter of horses and oxen by the peasants, mechanical power was crucial for the success of agriculture. Even if some larger collective farms could have used tractors efficiently, they could not perform proper maintenance.

But, even aside from the economic considerations, the Soviet regime had other reasons for concentrating machinery. The concentration of implements allowed centralization and control. The kolkhozes drew up contracts with the MTSs according to which the kolkhoz handed over a percentage of the produce (usually 20 percent). By and large in collectives that were served by MTSs, the peasants received even less compensation than in farms without the benefit of mechanization. From the point of view of the peasants the MTS was just one more exploiter. Since the state managed the MTSs, it received two shares of the harvest: one as general procurement, which every collective had to pay, and another as payment for the labor rendered.

The MTSs were fortresses of the city in the hostile countryside. It was natural to make them supervisors of the political education system in the villages. Each MTS had a political department, which was independent of the local party organizations and reported directly to a national body. The department played a role in assuring that procurements would be carried out in the interest of the state and in setting up production plans. Ironically, because departments came to identify too much with local villagers and for a while became defenders of the peasantry, they were reorganized in 1934. The head of the political department, also deputy head of the MTS, remained responsible for political education work, but he was now put under the local party organization.

The third decision made about collectives was their optimal size. At first the Bolshevik leadership was attracted to giant farms. This attitude was part of an utopian attempt to transform peasants into workers. The Bolsheviks were keenly aware of the American example. They knew that in the United States large farms existed and enjoyed superior productivity. They wrongly assumed that the secret of American success depended on size, and hoped to surpass American productivity by surpassing the American scale of production. However, in the absence of scientific management and good communications, large kolkhozes and state farms made little economic sense. The peasants in particular were hostile. When the collectivization drive resumed in the fall of 1930, the communists did not insist any longer on the establishment of giant farms. In the system that finally emerged, the size of the average collective farm came to depend on the size of the village. Typically each village formed a collective farm.

The fourth issue was the degree of cooperation. In the course of the 1920s three types of collectives existed. The loosest form was the so-called TOZ, in which some of the agricultural work was carried out in common, but livestock and even most farm implements remained private property. This form was the least objectionable to the peasants. In the artel, the field work and implements were collectivized, as was most of the livestock. The commune was the most ambitious form of cooperation, in which everything, including buildings, was common property. Since the commune required extensive subsidies to function, and since the communists regarded the TOZ as insufficiently cooperative, after some hesitation the party chose the artel as the basis of the Soviet collective farm.

This decision implied that in addition to the arable land, the horses and plows became the property of the kolkhoz. The peasant was allowed to retain a small kitchen garden plot and to keep some animals such as chickens and pigs. The sale of such products became an important part of the total income of the peasant and an important part of the national economy. However distasteful this remnant of individual enterprise was for the communist leaders, the products of private plots were too important for the national economy to be abolished.

Fifth, the authorities had to decide the basis of compensation for the collective farm workers. The regime soon retreated from its attempt to make the peasants into workers by paying them wages. Such a system was undesirable because the regime wanted the produce as cheaply as possible, and payment of wages was too expensive. How should the workers be compensated? Different collective farms had different systems. Some, on the basis of old peasant custom, paid families according to the number of members in the household, others according to the hours of collective work performed. Eventually the "labor day" system came to be favored. This meant that the peasants' earnings were commensurate to the amount of labor delivered. A labor day, however, was not necessarily a chronological day. What was considered to be a labor day depended on the skills necessary for the performance of the task. Four hours of actual labor by a tractor driver, for example, was the equivalent of eight hours of work by a milkmaid. How much one labor day was worth depended on the performance of the kolkhoz. The farm first had to pay its obligation to the state, then to the MTS, then had to put aside seeds for next year's sowing. What remained was divided among the peasants according to the number of labor days accumulated.

The collective farm as it came into being in the 1930s was by no means egalitarian. The collective farm chairman, who often came from the city, and the brigade leaders had power and were materially better off than the peasants. The private plot became an essential feature of the system. These were and remained immensely more productive than the collective lands, since the peasants had every incentive to work on them. In order to have such a plot, a peasant had to earn a certain number of labor days. Stratification as it continued to exist in the village under collectivized agriculture depended on access to political power and the availability and productivity of private plots. Although functionaries in the villages had only rather modest economic advantages over their fellow villagers, in circumstances of extreme scarcity such advantages made a significant difference.

The trauma of collectivization, the lack of incentives, and the peasants' hatred of the new institutions led to a considerable decline in overall agricultural production. According to estimates, crop production declined 10 percent between 1928 and 1932, and the output of animal husbandry declined 50 percent. At the same time the state became far more efficient in removing produce from the countryside. Delivery quotas were high, usually 40 percent of the product of the farm. During the first five-year plan deliveries were two or three times higher than the quantities the peasants had previously marketed. The result was predictable: great misery and ultimately starvation in the countryside.

Overall production figures conceal a great deal of regional variation. While in better-functioning collectives the peasants could maintain a reasonable standard of living, elsewhere they were on the verge of starvation. After the good harvest of 1930, two bad years followed, and in 1932–33 disaster struck. The Soviet Union suffered the costliest famine in its history. Precisely in the best grain-growing regions in the country – Ukraine, the northern Caucasus, and the lower Volga region – mass starvation reached dreadful proportions. Survivors describe the most horrible scenes. People resorted to cannibalism, and entire villages came to be deserted. In some places so many people died that there were not enough survivors to bury them decently; the corpses had to be dumped into pits and covered with a little dirt.

This famine was different from previous ones. It was manmade in two different senses. The starvation was clearly the result of the giant social experiment of collectivization and, unlike on previous occasions, the regime took no steps to assist the people. Instead, the government insisted on carrying out the procurement plans, whatever the cost, and grain continued to be removed from the famine-struck villages. The cities were spared from starvation, and grain exports continued.

At the time, of course, the truth could not be kept from the majority of the Soviet people. Although no newspaper mentioned it, signs of the catastrophe were everywhere. Yet the government refused to acknowledge reality and consequently did not ask for foreign help, nor undertake any effort to save lives. Admitting the existence of famine would have undermined the claim for the success of the collectivization drive, and would have affected the country's international prestige. It would also, of course, have made further grain export difficult. The cost in human lives for protecting the prestige of the Soviet Union was very high. As long as the Soviet Union existed, the great postcollectivization famine could not be discussed openly by historians or by survivors.

Charges have been made, primarily but not exclusively by Ukrainian nationalists, that the Stalinist leadership was punishing Ukraine for its continued nationalism and for its particularly fierce resistance to collectivization.[7] Several contemporary observers noted that villages on the Ukrainian side of the border had no food at a time when bread continued to be available in the nearby Russian and Belorussian villages. Some survivors even reported that roadblocks were placed at the border to prevent the importation of food into Ukraine.

Since the Stalinist government never discussed its actions, we have no clear evidence concerning the motivation of the leadership; we can only guess. While there is nothing in the record of this government that allows us to dismiss the charge out of hand, it is possible that the government decided to restrict the famine to certain areas in order to help conceal it, and that therefore policies were not directed against the Ukrainians as such. We do not know the exact number of victims, but estimates by Western scholars vary between 5 and 7 million; so this famine was costlier in terms of human lives than collectivization itself. Collectivization might be regarded as an inhuman act, but also as a heroic undertaking aimed at changing Soviet life and society. The party activists who participated in the brutal acts believed that what they were doing was in the name of a better future. There can be no similar excuse for the Soviet government at the time of the famine. The government violated a basic implied social contract: it failed to save the lives of its citizens.

"A CULTURAL REVOLUTION"

The years of the first five-year plan were a remarkable interlude in the history of Soviet culture. Given the revolutionary transformation of Soviet society and politics, it was to be expected that the cultural life of the country would also be profoundly affected. The repudiation of the NEP system meant a declaration of war on "class enemies," as defined by the new Stalinist leadership. As NEPmen were dispossessed and the kulaks destroyed, the leadership also brutally attacked what it considered a remnant of the bourgeois social order, the old intelligentsia. The activists called for a new "cultural revolution," which would contribute to the transformation of the social-political order. The phrase was confusing, for Lenin had used it earlier to describe something very different. When Lenin had spoken of the need for a cultural revolution, he had meant the necessity of raising the cultural level of the people to that of advanced Europe. In his "cultural revolution," the enemies were ignorance, backwardness, and the lack of civilization.

Many activists, especially the young, had found the policies in the 1920s unacceptably liberal. Even at that time, heavy attacks were made on some artists and intellectuals for their perceived apoliticism. Indeed, many of the themes that dominated the age of the cultural revolution had appeared in the mid 1920s. The difference was that at that time the radical views had been only one of the variety of perspectives, while by the end of the decade they had become the only acceptable view – and disagreement cost not livelihoods, but lives.

The great transformation that was taking place in Soviet economics and politics unleashed an element within the party and the professions that felt the revolution had not gone far enough. The radicals objected to allowing the "bourgeois" intelligentsia to hold onto its powers and subvert the creation of a genuine "proletarian" culture. The cultural revolution would be carried out in the name of the "proletariat." Perhaps it is needless to add that the slogans and policies advanced in the name of the working classes had nothing to do with actual workers. Those who spoke in their name rarely knew much about working-class life and were as likely to have come from bourgeois families as those they denounced.

The cultural revolution was iconoclastic. Disrespectful of authority, it was directed against the entrenched by those who felt they were on the sidelines. The party leadership managed to tap a genuine radicalism existing within the professions, especially among the young. What took place in those years was partly a generational conflict. The attitude of the Stalinist leadership to the cultural revolution was complex. Clearly that leadership was responsible for the milieu in which the cultural revolution took place and benefited from it. It was the new leadership that commenced the attack on the old intelligentsia in 1928 by staging trials on trumped-up charges. The Stalinists turned the talk of intensified class struggle and vigilance to their political advantage by bringing cultural activities under closer political control. It must be acknowledged that many of the utopian, even eccentric ideas that came to the surface at this time clearly could not have been initiated from above. One activist suggested, for example, that workers bring their diaries to workshops; the task of writers would be only to assemble them. Another figure, a film critic, argued that there was no need for feature films and that the industry should produce only agitational shorts.[8] Nonetheless, when the party leadership felt that the cultural revolution had gone far enough, it had no trouble whatever in bringing it under control: the new rulers got rid of ideas they considered undesirable and retained only what seemed to them useful.

By extending their definition of politics to include all cultural activities, the Bolsheviks did immense harm to Russian intellectual life. The "cultural revolution" was profoundly anticultural and even anti-intellectual; it created a far more radical break in Russian intellectual history than had the revolution. It finally ended that glorious period of intellectual life that had begun in the early nineteenth century. The aspects of Soviet culture that suffered most at this period were those aimed at satisfying the cultural needs of an intellectual elite. This elite had survived surprisingly well. Ironically, when Stalin explicitly repudiated the notion of egalitarianism as a petit bourgeois idea, proponents of anti-elitism gained the upper hand. Writers and film directors who produced works that were not immediately accessible to a mass audience were denounced. These policies, of course, did not imply that artists were encouraged to produce what the majority of workers and peasants wanted. They were to produce what the people *should* want.

The first five-year plan established a framework for Soviet economics within which the country operated as long as it existed. By contrast, in the cultural life of the Soviet Union this period was not a seminal one, but an aberration. The party leadership knew what it did not want much better than what it did want, and this was a period of experimentation. After three or four years of turmoil the Stalinists called a halt, and only then did the new Soviet culture emerge. This culture lacked the verve, the utopian elements, and the madness of the age of the cultural revolution. It was tame, conformist, and profoundly petit bourgeois.

5

High Stalinism

TERROR

Those who have never believed the emancipatory promises of the revolution, and have seen only evil in that great social upheaval, point to the dark age of Stalin as the ultimate justification for their beliefs. By contrast, the partisans of the revolutionary ideology have had the painful task of coming to terms with the sad and inconvenient fact that it was Stalin who ultimately emerged victorious. It is hard for them to answer the question: has there always been a worm in the communist apple? Stalinism is at the heart of Soviet history. Rightly or wrongly, we are often tempted to regard the history of the 1920s as preparation for Stalin, and the post-1953 period as a long recuperation from the ravages of tyranny.

The preconditions for the rise of Stalin and the main outlines of the era of terror are not in doubt, but the reasons for the mass murder remain elusive. As long as the Soviet Union existed, historians had no access to party and secret police archives. In any case, the answers to the most significant questions cannot be found in documents. The important decisions were never put on paper; Stalin, it seems, ordered the destruction of his closest comrades by a nod of the head. It is unlikely we will ever know all that we would like to know.

The historian is compelled to describe and analyze mass murder on an extraordinary scale, a self-immolation of society. One cannot avoid psychological explanations, and the historian is always on thin ice in such matters, for it is difficult to find rational explanations for irrational phenomena. As a consequence, at the very heart of Soviet history there is a blank spot, a large area open to widely different interpretations, none of them fully satisfactory.[1] Our knowledge of the era cannot be complete without understanding the person who controlled events, but Stalin was an extremely secretive person. While we have a good idea of Hitler's mind and motives, we know

J. V. Stalin, 1933

almost nothing about Stalin's mind. He did not have Hitler's desire to appear on the stage, holding forth and giving his views on every conceivable topic. Hitler was an actor; Stalin was a puppeteer, who liked to move figures from behind the scenes. In trying to envisage that elusive figure, we must recognize that he changed greatly as time went on. The man who came to power in the late 1920s was not the same Stalin as the tyrant of the 1930s, the warlord of the Second World War, or the old Stalin, who increasingly lost touch with reality and lived in a world of his own.

Lightning never strikes from a clear blue sky. Stalin's terror could not have existed without certain preconditions. First of all, terror had been part of the Leninist system from its inception. The Bolsheviks called their regime the "dictatorship of the proletariat" and believed that as revolutionaries they had to be hard and pitiless. The first instrument of terror, the Cheka, was created already in 1917; it became the OGPU in 1922, which in turn in 1934 became a part of the People's Commissariat of Internal Affairs, NKVD; under that name it functioned during the darkest years. The machinery vastly expanded during the struggle against the Russian peasantry at the time of collectivization – as a result, Stalin had extermination machinery, camps, interrogation facilities already in place.

Second, a characteristic feature of the 1930s, the show trials, also had precedents. The Soviet regime had already held trials in which innocent people were made to confess to fantastic crimes at the time of the first five-year plan. Although compared to what was to follow there were relatively few victims, and the purpose of the trials was limited – namely to find scapegoats for genuine problems – in retrospect they appear as sinister forewarnings. Third, for the terror to reach its bloodiest extreme, Stalin had to become a dictator. As long as he did not rule the party absolutely it was impossible to order the extermination of venerable ex-leaders. But the most significant precondition was a general cheapening of the value of human life. Twentieth-century Russian history is a series of demographic catastrophes and purges. Mass deaths began with the First World War and continued in the civil war and during the famine, and millions more died at the time of collectivization and in the famine that followed.

The Seventeenth Party Congress in 1934 was a turning point: Stalin had already defeated his rivals; violence and terror had already become part of Soviet life; the country was set on the road to industrialization; the peasants had been forced to give up their land and the organization of the Soviet collective farm was taking shape; the worst of the famine was over; and, by the elevation of "socialist realism" as the only tolerated artistic style, the cultural heterogeneity of the NEP had come to an end. The Bolsheviks had fought many battles and had faced genuine problems, and now the issues had all been resolved to their satisfaction. It was for these reasons that the Seventeenth Congress designated itself "the Congress of Victors." At the congress Stalin himself said: "There is nothing more to prove and, it seems, no one to fight."

The peoples of the Soviet Union, and also many members of the political elite, desperately wanted a time of relaxation. While we have no firm evidence, there are hints that there was a faction in the party leadership that wanted to get rid of Stalin, or at least to limit his dictatorial powers as a precondition of returning to normality.[2] Stalin's response was an attack on the party, unleashing mass terror that ultimately demanded millions of lives. Terror for the first time was turned against the party itself. Among the victims were the "victors": by the time the next party congress met in 1939, more than half of the almost 2,000 delegates had been arrested – the higher one was in the hierarchy, the worse the chances for survival.

Sergei Kirov, the first secretary of the Leningrad party organization, a good orator, and unlike Stalin an ethnic Russian, was assassinated on December 1, 1934. The assassin, L. V. Nikolaev, had been associated in the past with the left opposition, but it is likely (though there is no firm evidence) that it was Stalin who plotted the murder. The historians who take for granted Stalin's involvement in this matter make assumptions concerning Stalin's character and the nature of the political system. These are good reasons, but by no means conclusive. Kirov's public record was neither better nor worse than that of other leaders, and if he harbored liberal sentiments he kept them to himself. What was Stalin's motive? Did Stalin fear Kirov as a rival, or was the tyrant already planning the elimination of his past opponents and needed a good excuse? We can only speculate.

Kirov's assassination was followed by thousands of arrests and hundreds of executions. In the following period of terror, mass murder was carried out on different levels. The most spectacular were the trials of ex-leaders of the Bolshevik Party, Lenin's comrades. With a few exceptions, the entire leadership of the revolution was exterminated. The first to be tried were Zinoviev and Kamenev for "moral responsibility" – and, of course, they were found guilty. In a closed trial they were sentenced to five years in prison. The next act was a second Zinoviev–Kamenev trial in August 1936; with them were tried major figures of the left opposition. This was the first of the great show trials that the Stalinists were to stage repeatedly in the following years. The sixteen accused were charged with carrying out Trotsky's orders to attempt to overthrow Stalin with the use of terrorist methods. Lenin's old comrades were accused of organizing Kirov's murder, and of failed attempts on other leaders, including Lenin and Stalin. They were also accused of being agents of foreign espionage services. These represented a curious assortment of countries, from Britain, France, Japan, and Germany to Poland. Only one major country was conspicuously missing: the United States. Presumably the United States was not considered important enough to be accused.

In January 1937 a second group of old Bolsheviks, including Yurii Piatakov, one of the architects of the industrialization drive, and Karl Radek, a brilliant publicist, were put on trial. The accusations were the same: these Bolsheviks wanted to overthrow the Soviet system by carrying out sabotage and were the agents of foreign powers and of Trotsky. A few months later, in June, the most self-destructive event occurred: the top leadership of the military were tried in a closed trial. The Stalinists eliminated the high command of the armed forces by carrying out a bloody purge. In March 1938 the event that is sometimes referred to as the "great purge trial" took place, indicting Bukharin, Aleksei Rykov, and nineteen others. Here the stakes for Stalin were the highest. Bukharin still possessed vestiges of authority within the party and a degree of popularity in the country. It was therefore especially necessary for the Stalinists not only to destroy him personally but also to discredit his past. He and his comrades were depicted by the prosecution as double agents from the beginning of their careers.

The destruction of the leadership was extraordinary because of the public nature of the trials, and because of the spectacle of previously powerful people standing in open court confessing to the most fanciful, and highly improbable, criminal activities. The confessions, carefully scripted, resembled contemporary novels and movies: the scripts were hallucinatory, and the authors paid very little attention to believability and psychological motivation. The accused were bad just because they were bad. None of them had motives for opposing the Stalinist system, for there could not be any good motives. In the Soviet mind there was no such thing as a good comrade who had lost his way. The wicked had been wicked from the beginning, just as Lenin and Stalin had exhibited their extraordinary talents practically from the cradle. Stalinist ideology allowed no development of character. It could not, for if there was change, then there had to be intermediate stages, something between black and white. Such a proposition was subversive of Stalinist ideology.

The audience was asked to believe that people who had suffered for their revolutionary activities, who had devoted their entire lives to the struggle for a socialist future, had never in fact had been genuine revolutionaries. Many contemporaries in the Soviet Union and elsewhere were willing to accept such confessions on face value. The inherent implausibilities, the factual errors that would have discredited the confessions in normal circumstances, did not seem to matter; there was no one to point out the contradictions or even voice doubts aloud. Although the prosecution never presented material evidence against anyone, everyone who appeared in court confessed. At the time some wondered why old communists, courageous revolutionaries, confessed to crimes that they had not – and could not possibly have – committed, which besmirched their careers and everything to which they had devoted their lives. Some contemporary foreign observers speculated that the accused confessed because they had morally collapsed: they knew no secure moral foundation outside the Communist Party, and they wanted to serve the party even in their dying moments. However, no complex psychological explanations are necessary. In the NKVD prisons the victims were treated with such extraordinary brutality that few human beings were able to resist. The representatives of the regime at times bargained with the accused: for a confession, the victims were promised either their own lives or the lives of members of their families. The Stalinists almost never kept their word, for no one remained to enforce a promise. There were some differences among the victims. Some were never put on open trial, presumably because the torturers could not trust their victims to "behave." Others, such as Bukharin, steadfastly denied some of the accusations to the end and sparred with the beastly prosecutor, Andrei Vyshinskii. Bukharin obviously attempted to make points that seemed important to him before his last audience. Whether people in the audience appreciated and understood Bukharin's strategy, however, must remain an open question. N. Krestinskii behaved heroically: at one point in open court he withdrew his confession, even though he must have known that the consequences of his act would be swift in coming. Indeed, the next day – presumably after a difficult night – he reaffirmed his original confession. But, if anyone cared to observe, he had already made his point. Most of the accused were sentenced to death, but the formal sentences did not matter much – almost everyone, whatever the sentence, was killed.[3]

Many of the leaders of the French Revolution paid with their lives. Hitler, in 1934, just before the great trials, exterminated in a brutal fashion a

Gulag

segment of the Nazi leadership. Stalin's terror was far more thorough than the French or the German, and he made it particularly gruesome by the show trials and torture; but the purge trials were only a small part of the terror. The arrests spread, ultimately involving millions of people. From a moral point of view, the elimination of the top leadership of the party – i.e., people who themselves in the past had not shied away from the use of terror – was less reprehensible than the incarceration and killing of millions of people who were guilty of nothing, neither according to the existing criminal code nor according to any moral reckoning.

The exact number of victims cannot be precisely established; the numbers are passionately debated among scholars. (Approximately 1 million people were executed, and maybe as many as 10 million were sent to camps.) Of course, it does matter whether the number of victims was 3 million or 30 million; and yet, for our understanding of the working of that particular political order, it cannot make much difference. Even if we accept the lowest reasonable number suggested by scholars who have studied the evidence, we cannot but form the picture of one of the most criminal regimes that ever existed on the face of the earth.

Marshal Mikhail Tukhachevskii

The top leadership of the nation – whether in politics, military, economics, or culture – was exterminated, but workers and peasants also became victims in their millions. The capital and the provincial cities suffered alike. It is possible to establish statistical probabilities for becoming a victim: although no group was altogether exempt, people in certain categories were in exceptional danger. Those who had contacts with foreigners rarely escaped. Foreign communists in the Soviet Union were treated with special venom: Stalin killed more German communists than Hitler. The Polish communists who had the misfortune of residing in the "motherland of socialism" were almost entirely eliminated. Members of past opposition groups did not survive. The higher the post of the party leader, the more he was in danger of being destroyed. But the newly created elite, those who had fought on Stalin's side, those who were to be members of the new elite, also suffered. An unintended (or perhaps intended?) consequence was a constant renewal of elites. The intelligentsia of national minorities suffered especially, perhaps as a result of the Stalinists' fear of the growth of non-Russian nationalisms. A peculiarity of the madness was that those who abused others were not likely to benefit. The NKVD was one of the organizations hardest hit: all of its leaders, Genrikh Yagoda, Nikolai Yezhov, and

Lavrentii Beria, were ultimately killed, though Beria survived Stalin by a few months. Those who had carried out interrogations a short time before often shared cells with their victims. Unlike Nazi Germany, where the torturers were safe, in the Stalinist USSR there was no clear division between "them" and "us."

What kind of politics could exist in an age of terror and repression? It would be ludicrous to suggest, of course, that Stalin was involved in all the arrests. He must have signed hundreds of lists with thousands of names of victims, but there was no need for him to be involved in all the arrests. No doubt, matters got out of hand. As one might imagine, the atmosphere was used by thousands to take revenge on their enemies, or in some cases to destroy their superiors in order to get ahead. No doubt, there were also genuine issues at stake. It is likely, as suggested by some Western historians, that leaders disagreed concerning the best methods of carrying out policies and used the purges to advance their own programs. Local bosses in the provinces took advantage of opportunities to enhance their powers, and the center struggled desperately to maintain discipline. At the same time, there is nothing in the newly uncovered documents to suggest that Stalin was not fully in control.

Control, however, did not mean that the apparatus functioned well. The Soviet Union was an underdeveloped country with poorly functioning governmental machinery and an ill-educated, venal bureaucracy lacking in public spirit. The country had no well-developed communication system, which increased local power and confusion. It is a mistake to think that totalitarianism implies efficiency, that in such a system all orders are carried out as intended. In fact, the world has never known an efficient totalitarian regime.[4] It would be a great jump in logic, however, to conclude that because Stalin did not control everything and not all orders were efficiently carried out in the provinces, he did not have overall control or that events developed contrary to his desires.

The terror profoundly changed the character and even the role of the party. One could no longer talk about the dictatorship of the party. The Soviet political system in the 1930s was the dictatorship of Stalin, who stood above and aside from the party, using it when he needed it as he did other instruments of power, most notably the secret police. From 1933 to 1938 the composition of the party changed. As an institution the party was among the main victims of the attacks. Those who were purged were replaced by new elements, representing the new Soviet elite.

Party organizations lost their assigned functions. After the "Congress of Victors" in 1934, the congress met only twice in Stalin's lifetime, in 1939 and 1952, and never discussed significant issues. The Communist Party, which contained within itself the nation's elite, was designed to play the role of reconciling competing interests, but at a time of oppression and terror the party could not carry out its assigned task. The suspension of normal politics, however, did not mean that there were no longer interest groups. Even if the major issues facing the nation were not openly discussed, those issues did not disappear. While Stalin's lieutenants agreed on a breakneck tempo of industrialization, for example, the question still remained exactly how much of the national income should be invested in the national economy.

Stalin and members of his ever-changing circle accumulated enormous power. They made their decisions not on the basis of law, not even on the basis of bureaucratic predictability, but according to whim. What mattered was not a party or government functionary's official position, but whether he was able to gain Stalin's attention and approval. In the absence of official forums, it was Stalin alone who was to reconcile competing interests and points of view. This was a haphazard political system, with an ill-functioning machinery, in which local leaders could sometimes sabotage directives from above.

Possibly a more important institution than the party was the political police, the NKVD. Although as one of the commissariats it came under the supervision of the Council of Commissars, in fact the heads of the agency reported directly to Stalin. In the 1930s the NKVD possessed an enormous network of paid and unpaid agents, who penetrated all levels of society and all institutions, including the party itself.

TERROR AND PROGRESS

At a time of bloody terror the Soviet Union experienced impressive industrial growth and a profound social transformation. These were not unconnected phenomena, for the kind of industrialization that took place could have occurred only against a background of terror.[5]

The industrial sector of the economy during the second five-year plan was less chaotic, at least compared to the extraordinary period at the beginning of the industrialization drive. According to Soviet figures – admittedly unreliable, they certainly overstate growth – national income and industrial output doubled in the course of the second five-year plan. The planners still set impossible goals, and the standard of living continued to be extremely low (although significantly improved), but there was a sense, especially during the middle of the decade, that normality was gradually returning. The abolition of rationing in 1935 was a sign of improvement. At the end of the decade, however, as a consequence of the purges and war preparations, the pace of economic growth slackened.

As the ex-peasants slowly adjusted to industrial discipline, labor productivity gradually improved. To bring about this improvement the regime used a number of different methods. One was moral appeal – we should not underestimate its significance. Such appeals, especially at the outset of the industrialization drive and among the young, must have been powerful. Many believed that they were in fact working for a better, richer, and more just society, and that it was necessary to make sacrifices for this cause. Some young communists did go voluntarily to distant parts of Siberia and endured extraordinary hardships for a cause they believed in.

Moral appeal, however, was never sufficient, and so the regime provided material incentives. The new factories required skilled workers and, in order to encourage people to learn skills, the gap between the earnings of the skilled and unskilled workers was increased. Stalin explicitly denounced the earlier egalitarian promise of the revolution and mocked it as "petit bourgeois." The compensation system was designed to give incentives for working hard. Soviet workers operated under the system of piecerates. Norms were established, and these norms were gradually raised, which meant that in order to receive the same salary a worker constantly had to increase his output.

The Stakhanov movement came into existence in this context. In 1935 Aleksei Stakhanov, a miner in the Donbass region, overfulfilled his norm by 1,400 percent. Obviously Stakhanov's great achievement was artificially created: several people stood behind him in order to carry out auxiliary tasks and assist in his superhuman achievement. He was built up as an example. He became the central figure of a vast propaganda drive, called socialist competition. Stakhanovists on the one hand received all sorts of benefits and privileges from the factory management, and on the other the norms for everyone else were raised, since the Stakhanovists showed that it was possible to produce more. Undoubtedly the movement – while it might have contributed to raising the productivity of some individual workers – made the confusion already rampant in Soviet industry worse. The more farsighted managers understood that Stakhanovite methods were incompatible with the rational organization of production and therefore resisted the officially inspired campaign. In addition, the campaign created a great deal of bitterness and division within the working class. This divisiveness, though perhaps not planned, also served the purposes of the regime. The creation of a new labor aristocracy was yet another factor that made workers' solidarity in the Stalinist state impossible. Stakhanovite methods – that is spectacular, spurt-like achievements, rather than a rationally organized and steady tempo – appealed at least to some among the Soviet leadership. After a couple of years, the leadership realized that the movement was more harmful than helpful, that the cost in confusion was greater than the benefit of some increased productivity. While the name was retained, the content of the movement was quietly abandoned.

The social transformation that occurred in the Soviet Union in the 1930s was largely the consequence of the vast industrialization drive. Nevertheless, it is significant that it took place against the background of terror. On the one hand, the great industrial expansion, and the struggle against the old intelligentsia, opened up avenues for social advancement. On the other, the draconian methods used for the creation of labor discipline – at a time when the working class was new, ill disciplined, and unused to conditions of modern labor – could have occurred only in an extraordinarily repressive state.

In the course of the 1930s the government used increasingly harsh methods to impose discipline. In the case of mishaps, workers were accused of sabotage, which in the atmosphere of the 1930s was a serious matter indeed.[6] For violations of discipline, such as absenteeism, workers were administratively punished, at times even losing their ration cards, which was likely to mean starvation. Workers had to carry with them a "labor book" in which violations of labor discipline were entered. The process culminated in the 1940 labor code, a fitting instrument of the Stalinist state. According to the labor code, leaving a place of employment without the permission of the employer became a criminal offense, liable to punishment by imprisonment and forced labor. Now ministries became legally empowered to move workers where they saw fit, even if that meant dividing families. This was a military-type mobilization of labor, unparalleled in peacetime. Life in "freedom" and in the concentration camps were not so very different after all.

In spite of the unenviable conditions of labor, life in the countryside was immensely harder than in the cities. By the end of the decade, almost all agricultural work was done in collectives or state farms. Even more than in the cities, labor was reduced to something resembling slavery. The state specified the number of days the peasant had to work on collective land, and it took a large share (usually a third) of the fruit of the peasants' labor for almost nothing in the form of compulsory deliveries. At the same time the state assumed no responsibility for the social welfare of the peasantry. There was no safety net. The collective farms, and within them the peasant households themselves, were compelled to take care of the sick and old. There was no minimum salary and, of course, no one had even heard of the idea of paid vacations. Under the circumstances peasants were not motivated to work efficiently, and it was not surprising that productivity remained abysmally low. Overall output in grain (again according to dubious Soviet statistics) increased by one-third between 1932 and 1937, but that increase occurred not because of any improvement in productivity but because of the inclusion of new areas under cultivation. Recovery from the immense trauma of collectivization was slow.

From the point of view of living standards, there was a large difference among collectives. Some were able to provide for their members decently; in many others the peasants remained close to starvation. Everywhere the private plot provided a large share of the peasants' yearly income. The regime faced a dilemma: not only were private plots were ideologically obnoxious, but the leaders also rightly feared that they took away the attention and energy of the peasants from their work on the kolkhoz. On the other hand, these plots not only provided a large share of the peasants' income, but also made a major contribution to feeding the population. At the time of collectivization, the most determined resistance was occasioned by the government's attempt to deprive the peasant household of its horse and especially its cow. By 1935, when the collective farm model charter was published – when the collective farm and the Soviet village assumed their final form – the regime had reconciled itself to the existence of the private plot, including the right to own one cow, a specified number of household animals, and unlimited poultry. The regime found it necessary to watch constantly whether the peasant was not enlarging his plot and animal holdings at the expense of the collective farm. Every time the regime attempted to "bring order," to clamp down, total output suffered – and that the Soviet Union could ill afford.

The peasant family received from the plot half of its money income, and almost all the animal products and vegetables it was able to enjoy. The collective farm itself supplied the peasant only with grain. In instances where the farm was near a city, the peasant was fortunate because money could be made by selling in the market. On the other hand, individual peasants taking their produce to the market were a primitive method of distribution, leading to a great deal of wasted time and energy. Most of the work on the plots was done by women, further increasing the disproportionate share of the burden on their shoulders. It is not too much to say that, without these plots, the system of collective farms could not have survived.

The system could exist only because there was force behind it. The MTSs were centers of Soviet power, and the collective farms themselves became focal points for communist education. The party organization network in the 1930s remained weak. Nevertheless, it was powerful enough, having the backing of the NKVD, to enforce the decisions of the party. The Soviet village remained backward; nevertheless the new power, in the form of representatives from the city and a new bureaucracy, transformed the lives of the Soviet peasantry.

TERROR AND SOCIETY

In 1946 a sociologist, Nicholas Timasheff, described the Stalinist age as "the great retreat."[7] The phrase appears paradoxical when one considers that this was a period of extraordinarily rapid and profound social and economic transformation. It is true, however, that this transformation was accomplished by a regime that was socially conservative, one that had repudiated the emancipatory ideas of the October Revolution. In this sense, Stalinism in fact was a retreat.

Although the Bolsheviks rather quickly abandoned their idealistic goals, we ought not forget how daring their original vision had been. They aimed

The Soviet high command: Yezhov, Kalinin, Stalin, Molotov, Kaganovich

to remake not only society, but also human beings and the oldest and strongest human institutions. They were hostile to the family, because they saw it as an institution that transmitted conservative, traditional values, and did everything within their power to weaken it. The Bolsheviks believed that women, like men, should take jobs outside the household. They recognized that it was necessary to help women by providing child-care facilities, but they lacked the necessary resources. These ideological commitments in the circumstances of the 1920s remained without consequence. The country suffered from unemployment, and the proportion of women in the labor force remained static, approximately 25 percent.

The Soviet family was transformed because at the time of the industrialization drive the political leadership understood the economic benefits of employing female labor. Collectivization and industrialization, from the point of view of the everyday lives of simple citizens, brought more significant changes than the revolution itself. Although the government did enlarge the service sector – providing more kindergartens, organizing after-school programs for children, building laundries – these could hardly keep up with the greatly increased need. The extremely ill-developed state of Soviet retail trade meant that everyone, but primarily women, spent an extraordinary amount of time just trying to buy the necessities – above all food. Under the circumstances it is hard to consider the vast changes that occurred at the time of industrialization as an aspect of the liberation of women. On the contrary, the lives of women became considerably more difficult. In the villages they worked in the collective farms and in addition did most of the work on the private plots; in the cities they worked in the factories, but also had to take care of the children and remained responsible for household chores. Women had less free time and their chances for political, social, or economic advancement came to be even more circumscribed.

The situation was ironic: women's entry into the labor force, the dreadful housing situation, the movement into the cities all combined to break down the traditional patriarchal family characteristic of peasant societies. The process that had started before the revolution now greatly accelerated. This development was in line with the oft-announced desire of the revolutionaries to encourage the "withering away of the family" that the Marxists had prophesized; but Stalin's government did not approve. The Stalinists instinctively understood that the sexual freedom of the earlier promise was incompatible with the kind of society they were intent on creating. Now the regime's legislation aimed to strengthen the family as an institution that reinforced values and hierarchies. The regime's policy toward the family and toward women in general illustrates well that, in bringing about change, it is not so much the intention of the government that matters, but the underlying social and economic realities.

The Stalinists, however, were correct in their understanding: different aspects of human behavior indeed were connected. The person who pursued an "undisciplined" sexual life was in fact likely to chafe under the restrictions imposed by the Stalinist state. A film like *Father and Son* by M. Barskaia, which depicted a factory director who because of his heavy responsibilities could not take good care of his son, could not be exhibited and was mercilessly criticized. A good factory director, a good communist, could not possibly be a bad father. (The director, incidentally, became a victim of the purges.) As far as the prevailing ideology was concerned, there could be no conflict between being a good husband and father on the one hand, and a responsible member of society on the other. The ideologues declared free love together with egalitarianism to be aspects of a "petit bourgeois" ideology. In order to strengthen the family, the Stalinist rulers harshly stigmatized illegitimacy and passed laws against prostitution and sodomy (i.e., homosexuality).

The country was in need of labor. The regime, eager to encourage women to give birth, passed a stringent anti-abortion law in 1936, allowing abortions only when the mother's life or health was in danger. The government promised allowances for large families, and carried out a propaganda campaign advertising the psychological and political advantages of having many children. On the positive side, although the government could not provide decent housing and child-care facilities, it did pass legislation designed to protect mothers. It guaranteed a paid maternity leave of three-and-a-half months, and allowed nursing mothers to work shorter hours. Although the number of child-care facilities did not keep up with demand, they did grow impressively during the years of industrialization, increasing approximately tenfold in the decade between 1928 and 1938.

The measures aimed at increasing the birth rate were very much needed because the material conditions prevailing in the Soviet Union had led to an extraordinary drop. Combined with the devastation produced by the collectivization drive, famine, and the purges, the country was experiencing a demographic catastrophe unparalleled in the twentieth century except in wartime. In 1937 the authorities carried out a census, and they themselves must have been surprised by the disastrous results: the population was 14–15 million fewer than expected. The NKVD arrested and shot the statisticians and suppressed the figures. A new census was carried out two years later, showing somewhat higher numbers. There is good reason to doubt the reliability of the second census.

Women's increased participation in the labor force did not lead to a corresponding rise in political power. On the lowest level, party membership, the percentage of women in the party, in the 1930s was a respectable 15 percent; but, as one went higher up the political ladder, the percentage of women decreased. By contrast with the time of the revolution and civil war, there were no women in the highest leadership of the party.

The changes in the educational policies of the regime were a part of a general conservative turn that included the repudiation of egalitarianism, rejection of experimentation in art, and the introduction of legislation protecting the traditional family. In the 1920s the leaders of the Commissariat for Enlightenment (Narkompros) had experimented with ideas and policies based on radical – indeed, utopian – notions of reforming education. Given the backwardness and material poverty of the country, however, very little could be accomplished. "Project"-based education, child-centered education, eliminating authority from the education process may all have been attractive and progressive ideas, but they were ludicrously irrelevant. Pupils and parents, and especially teachers, had a more realistic view: they wanted schools to teach the fundamentals – how to read, write, and do a bit of arithmetic.

In educational policies, as in other aspects of national life, the cultural revolution represented a radical interlude: the critics of Narkompros, who now had the upper hand, insisted on greater efforts to proletarianize the student body and further politicize the content of education. They mercilessly attacked the existing institutions – especially the universities, where they carried out a thorough purge of the faculties. At the end of the five-year plan, however, the radical impulse petered out. The Stalinist leadership understood that in the new age neither the mad utopianism of the revolutionaries nor the relative pluralism of the staid 1920s was suitable: a new set of policies, a new synthesis was needed.

In the early 1930s, one after another the main tenets of progressive education were abandoned. In a Stalinist society an education based on the principle of equality of students and teachers was obviously inappropriate. Gradually the teachers regained their authority in the classroom and their right to dispense punishments. A sign of the changed times was that the schools required both boys and girls to wear uniforms. The regime also abandoned the goal of proletarianizing the student body, which in practice had meant preferential treatment in admissions to "working-class" and peasant youth. "Working-class" background had become for all practical purposes an inheritable trait. Party officials and bureaucrats who had left the factory bench decades before managed to retain the coveted "working-class" appellation.

Despite the retreat from the principles of progressive education, vastly increased educational opportunities were one of the major achievements of the Soviet Union. The regime finally succeeded in enlarging the educational system, above all on the primary level, and by the end of the decade, for the first time in Russian history, the country was able to make good on its promise to provide at least some schooling for all children. Thousands of new schools opened in the countryside, and tens of thousands of teachers, willingly or unwillingly, left the cities to teach village children. The circumstances in which the teachers had to work were extremely primitive and difficult, and many had to be compelled to give up their relatively comfortable lives in the cities. Only a dictatorial regime could have forced people to undertake such jobs and accept such unattractive transfers. The great expansion of the educational system was a major step in transforming backward Russia into an industrial Soviet Union. To be sure, village schools remained much inferior to what was available in the cities; nevertheless, it was a remarkable achievement of Stalinist industrialization that every child was able to spend at least some years in school. It was the general availability of primary schools that enabled the regime finally to take decisive steps toward the elimination of illiteracy. By the end of the decade, four out of five Soviet citizens under the age of 50 could read and write.

The industrialization drive and the concomitant attack on the prerevolutionary intelligentsia necessitated paying immediate attention to the training of technical cadres. The industrialization drive was carried out at a time of great confidence in the power of technology, but that technology remained unavailable without trained personnel. The new curriculum stressed the teaching of mathematics and sciences. The views of some of the previous leaders of Narkompros, such as Commissar Lunacharskii – who regarded the goal of education as the training of broadly educated citizens – had little appeal in the age of Stalinist industrialization. The number of students in middle-level educational institutions in the course of the decade tripled.

TERROR AND IDEOLOGY

When the Bolsheviks came to power in 1917, they based their legitimacy on their conviction that they knew the workings of history and therefore could construct a society more just, democratic, and free than any other on the face of the earth. This conviction allowed them to violate the most elementary principles of democracy. They became particularly adept at finding ideological justifications for these violations, and always abridged freedom in the name of purer democracy and higher freedom. Freedom of the press was suspended because Lenin believed that ideas were like weapons, and that weapons, at least temporarily, had to be denied to the class enemy. National self-determination was qualified out of existence by adding the clause that the decision had to serve the interests of the working classes; obviously remaining part of the Soviet Union served the interests of the working classes.

Over time the regime's ideology went through significant changes. The revolutionaries carried out their revolution in the name of social justice. To be sure, they also believed that a socialist society would be more efficient; but efficiency was a byproduct, not the central aim. Indeed, it is difficult to imagine a revolution that had as its most significant promise a better functioning economy. Stalin shifted emphasis. The sacrifices borne by the people were worthwhile, the agitators maintained, because these would bring about the creation of an industrial society and wellbeing for all. The explicit purpose of industrialization was not merely to improve the standard of living of the people, but also to make the Soviet Union a great power. Such thinking involved a reincorporation of nationalism into the ideological arsenal of communism. Soviet patriotism came to play a greater and greater role in Stalinist propaganda, reaching extraordinary heights during the Second World War and going even further, into lunatic extremes, during the last years of Stalin.

In 1936, at a time when terror was reaching its peak and the purge trials were taking place, with great fanfare and public discussion, a new constitution was adopted. This constitution contained all democratic rights: universal and equal and secret suffrage, equality before the law, freedom of association and press, the inviolability and privacy of the home and the mails. All the democratic rights, however, were qualified out of existence by adding the phrase: "in the interests of the working classes and for the purpose of strengthening the socialist system." The new constitution for the first time spoke of the leading role of the party, which alone – or, more precisely, the Stalinist leadership alone – was entitled to decide just what exactly was "in the interests of the working classes." Ironically, the clause concerning the party was incorporated just when that institution had been reduced in power as a consequence of Stalinist persecutions.

Beria, Voroshilov, Molotov, Andreev, Kaganovich, Stalin, Zhdanov, Kalinin, Mikoian, Khrushchev, Shvernik

How is one to explain the charade of publishing a new constitution that claimed to be the most democratic in the world at a time when the Soviet Union in fact was a totalitarian state? The constitution was perfectly harmless from the point of view of the rulers. It was evident that it did not restrain them for a moment from carrying out their policies, however lawless, however murderous. The new constitution had many uses. It allowed sympathetic Westerners to contrast the Stalinist USSR with Hitler's Germany, a more or less explicitly terrorist state. "The most democratic constitution in the world" became a useful argument in the arsenal of communists everywhere against those who criticized the antidemocratic character of the Soviet state. But the constitution was not only for foreign consumption. Many citizens of the Soviet Union also believed that the formal acceptance of a new legal foundation by the Soviet state might herald genuine changes. The very process of working out the constitution and the ensuing public discussions were used as a mobilization device.

The publication of the democratic constitution, making citizens equal before the law, coincided with Stalin's greatest ideological innovation: he proclaimed that the successful building of socialism, the elimination of private property, did not in fact end class struggle. On the contrary: according to the Stalinist metaphor, the cornered enemy fought back all the more bitterly. Consequently, but paradoxically, as the Soviet Union progressed toward socialism, the class struggle sharpened. This theory was Stalin's most significant contribution to Marxism. The sharpening class struggle provided ideological justification for the purge trials and purported to explain the mass arrests.

The Soviet Union had long ago abandoned the internationalist promise of the October Revolution. That promise, based on utopian Marxist premises, could no longer act as a legitimation or mobilization device. From the beginning of the 1930s, in an ever-accelerating fashion, there was a revival of a particular form of Russian nationalism. Citizens of the Soviet Union were to be motivated by two types of nationalism: they were expected to be patriots of the empire (i.e., the Soviet Union) and also of their own nation. At the same time it became ever more explicit that the Russians were to be the leading nation in this family of nations. Most likely the revival of Russian nationalism – meaning the reclaiming of the national past, the national heroes and culture – would have occurred in any case. Nevertheless in this matter Stalin's personal predilections played a particularly important role. Stalin, a Georgian, had been a Russian nationalist from the earliest phase of his career. In the 1930s he more explicitly came to identify himself with the Russian tsars Peter the Great and Ivan the Terrible.

The turn to nationalism necessitated a reevaluation of the past, and therefore the historians needed new directions. Marxist historians, most prominently Mikhail Pokrovskii – an important Bolshevik revolutionary and one of the leaders of Narkompros in the 1920s – had a dismissive attitude toward the Russian past. These historians deplored the country's imperial past and wrote with appreciation about national leaders who had rebelled against tsarism. In other words, they were genuine internationalists. Stalin had never liked this approach. In 1931 Pokrovskii and his followers were repudiated, and historians were compelled to write about the imperial past in positive terms.

The film industry in the late 1930s produced one film after another aimed at making heroes of Russian tsars and the generals who had served tsars, even if they had fought against revolutionaries, as Suvorov did against Pugachev. Curiously, both Suvorov and Pugachev, although they had fought against one another, were regarded as heroes and a film was devoted to each. It would be wrong to imagine that the revival of nationalism was something imposed on the people from outside. Social conservatism and resurgent nationalism were genuinely popular. It is possible to look at the changed ideology as a kind of compromise, or a coincidence of tastes and ideologies between the governing elite and the people as a whole. Some aspects of the prevailing ideology, but by no means all, actually found widespread public support.

Putting Russian nationalism at the heart of the ideological appeal in a multinational empire was a risky undertaking. Already in the 1920s, at a time when the state encouraged the development of national languages and cultures, it also advanced the use of Russian as a lingua franca within the Soviet Union. In a period of increasing Russian nationalism, the teaching of Russian acquired a different meaning. In 1938 the Central Committee of the Communist Party passed a resolution making the study of Russian compulsory in all middle-level schools. Nationalities that had barely a decade ago acquired written languages using the Latin alphabet were now compelled to switch to Cyrillic, even if that made the acquisition of literacy more difficult. Historians had depicted tsarist policies of the nineteenth century as imperialist, but in this new age they were forced to depict those same policies as "progressive." This change, as one would expect, was perceived by the intelligentsia of the minorities as an insult to their heritage.

Another feature of Soviet ideology that must be noted was the ever-increasing "personality cult" of Stalin, leading to a virtual deification. Lenin's cult, created largely by Stalin immediately after the death of the founder of the Bolshevik Party, in retrospect appears as a pale precursor of the deification of the leader. Stalin's pictures appeared almost every day on the front pages of the newspapers; every speech began by paying tribute to his wisdom; there was hardly a scholarly book published in the Soviet Union that did not contain footnotes refering the reader to his speeches; poems were addressed to him; there was practically nothing that did not somehow come to be connected with his name. Most likely, the deification was not entirely the result of Stalin's vanity; in fact, there is reason to think that at least at the earliest stages he retained a rather ironic attitude to his own personality cult. The Bolsheviks believed that the cult of the leader would enable them to spread their message to the simple people. Stalin was to take the place of the tsar, and he increasingly came to think of himself in these terms.

The Soviet Union was a totalitarian dictatorship. A modern dictatorship is never based on coercion alone. Those in position of power do not disregard public opinion; on the contrary, they do everything within their power to influence it, and try to make every citizen into an accomplice. In the course of the 1930s the party greatly expanded the political education system. Now that the peasantry was concentrated in collective and state farms, it was possible for the agitators to reach them. Reading circles, traveling movie theaters, and especially loudspeakers spouting slogans became a ubiquitous part of rural life. In factories the workers once or twice a week were compelled to participate in "political education meetings." These consisted of meaningless speeches denouncing domestic and foreign enemies, and the reading of articles from newspapers. The listeners were exhorted time and again to be vigilant and to work better. No doubt, most of the workers found such speeches and meetings insufferably boring. At election time every year, teams of agitators went door to door to talk to and report on citizens.

One would like to know how much impression the political education network, the stilted newspaper articles, the speeches, and the agitators actually made on the citizens. According to some observers a new Soviet human being was in fact created, one who did not think for himself and spoke a strange language full of clichés. It is, however, impossible to tell whether these were only superficial changes. As long as no alternative way of looking at the world could be presented, the very issue of believing or not believing in the slogans remained meaningless. Once the vast propaganda machine was turned off, the fragile new belief system collapsed.

The "cultural revolution" destroyed the relatively heterogeneous culture of the NEP period. That culture, while containing the seeds of Stalinism, also retained much from the vibrant prerevolutionary intellectual life. At the conclusion of the "cultural revolution," however, it was not at all clear what kind of cultural life was appropriate in the age of Stalin. The artists themselves were compelled to work out the outlines. After some trial and error, the artists and party activists developed the "theory" of socialist realism, and from that time until the era of Mikhail Gorbachev this doctrine was recognized as the basis of all Soviet art. It is possible to find antecedents for socialist realist art both in nineteenth-century Russian literature – writers were expected to be instructors and play a social role – and among the avant-garde artists in the pre-Stalinist period, who disdained realism and wanted to depict the heroic, to paint pictures that were larger than life. Socialist realism was first defined in 1934 at the First All Union Congress of Writers. That definition spoke of "truthfulness," of showing "reality in its revolutionary development," of the task "of ideological transformation and education of workers in the spirit of socialism." All this, however, was meaningless doublespeak. Many then and since have attempted to give a better description of what socialist realism really was. Andrei Siniavskii in a witty essay described socialist realism as a variety of romanticism; Vera Dunham saw in socialist realism a triumph of petit bourgeois values. An American literary critic, Katerina Clark, argued that it is possible to find a "master narrative" in socialist realist novels and films. All such narratives are about the acquisition of superior, revolutionary, communist consciousness in the course of overcoming an obstacle, unmasking an enemy. We have, aside from the naive hero, who acquires superior class consciousness after the completion of the assigned task, a communist sponsor, a "real" revolutionary, who acts as an instructor and mentor. We also have a negative hero, one who hates – always without sufficient reason – the Soviet system. He hates the socialist system without reason, for there can be no conceivable reason why anyone would be in opposition to a just and democratic society. In Clark's opinion only those works that follow the "master narrative" can be regarded as socialist realist.[8]

Socialist realism can best be understood in terms of what it excluded. It excluded above all ambiguity: a text that could be interpreted on several levels, one that had multiple meanings, could not serve the interests of the political order. It implied that truth could be multilayered. This was a notion more subversive than an open expression of hostility to socialism. Furthermore, socialist realism could not include irony, for irony was always subversive. Socialist realist art created an alternative reality that seemed to have the features of the real world but in fact was a totally imaginary universe. The creation of this fictional world was the greatest service artists provided. In this world all behaved as they were supposed to according to Stalinist ideology: the workers were enthusiastic about their tasks; the enemy vicious, cowardly, and ever present; and the party always emerged victorious in every contest. Such art could exist only as long as there was no alternative to it. There was no point in creating a fictional world as long as that picture could be contradicted by others. The main characteristic of socialist realist art was, therefore, that it completely lacked opposition and contradiction. The primary necessity for the establishment of socialist realist art was not the presence of able and willing artists, but the existence of a brutal political police and prison camps. Socialist realist art could exist only as long as there was a police state to ensure not its success, but its absolute monopoly. Russian literature suffered the heaviest blows in this period. Some of the finest writers of the land, such as Osip Mandelshtam, Boris Pilniak, and Isaac Babel, were shot or died in concentration camps; and others who survived, for example Boris Pasternak, Mikhail Bulgakov, and Anna Akhmatova, were unable to publish their best work.

Socialist realism applied not only to literature, but to all arts. Among these, cinema was particularly important. The leaders of the regime attributed great power to cinema in influencing audiences and therefore paid particular attention to it. Party leaders assigned topics to directors, and censors examined films at every level of production. Even after all these precautions approximately a third of the films made were not exhibited, in effect discarded as ideological waste. Censorship was not only proscriptive, but also prescriptive: it was not so much that artists could not touch certain topics (though that was of course true), but that they had to deal with required issues. Films of the 1930s greatly contributed to the hysteria of looking for "enemies of the people" everywhere. The state became the coproducer, indeed the coauthor. As a consequence it became very difficult to make a film, and the number of films produced greatly declined from the 1920s to the 1930s. The highest censor was Stalin himself, who insisted on seeing and approving every film to be exhibited in the Soviet Union.

In the fine arts and music, socialist realism meant prohibition of experimentation and the imposition of a single style, one immediately comprehensible even to the least educated. The great painter Kazimir Malevich was compelled to give up his individual style, and the finest composer still working in the Soviet Union, Dmitrii Shostakovich, had the misfortune to have Stalin personally denounce his modernist opera *Lady Macbeth of Mtsensk District* as "formalist."

The imposition of socialist realism on all artists meant that no great work could be produced. After all, every first-rate artist has a distinct and individual style, and the Stalinists forbade precisely that type of individualism. On the other hand, writers still wrote novels that people were happy to read, and studios still produced films that audiences wanted to see. Indeed, the number of movie tickets sold in the 1930s was three times greater than a decade before. More people went to the movies, even if the available choices came to be greatly reduced. Some of the films, though by no means masterpieces of cinema art, were amusing enough. *Chapaev*, a skillfully made film about a naive hero of the civil war, was the most popular film of the decade. The musical comedies of G. Aleksandrov, such as *Circus, Volga, Volga*, and *Shining Path*, gave pleasure to millions.

Since in the prevailing atmosphere the spirit of free inquiry was suspect, science also suffered. Normal contacts with the Western world were for all practical purposes interrupted; thousands of scientists were arrested and sent to the camps. Some branches of science were harder hit than others; understandably, sciences with even a remote connection to ideology and politics suffered the most. Entire sciences, such as sociology and psychiatry, were abolished – according to the vulgar Marxism of half-educated party leaders, they were incompatible with Soviet ideology. Particularly shameful was the destruction of Soviet genetics, a field in which Russian scientists in the 1920s were among the most prominent in the world. The ignorant Trofim Lysenko set the tone; and, since he enjoyed the backing of the authorities, it was impossible to contradict him. Mathematics and physics, on the other hand, seemed to be beyond the purview of Marxism, and in these fields Soviet scientists were capable of great achievements even during the worst moments of oppression. But, even in physics, Einstein's theory of relativity – which the Nazis also considered unacceptable – was denounced as "bourgeois" pseudo-science.

The totalitarian state claimed authority over all aspects of human life – political, economic, social, and cultural – and in the process did great harm to each.

THE MOLOTOV–RIBBENTROP PACT

In the 1920s issues of foreign policy only occasionally intruded in the power struggle. The opposition, for example, blamed the Stalinist leadership for the failure of the Comintern's China policy; and Stalin attempted to depict his enemy Trotsky as an adventurer too willing to give risky support to the international revolutionary movement. In 1927 Stalin created a more or less artificial war scare which may have helped to justify radical actions. However, up to the mid 1930s the Soviet Union was not threatened with involvement in a large-scale war, and the Bolshevik leadership well understood that, because intervention was unlikely, it could safely concentrate on domestic matters.

The great change occurred as a result of Nazi victory in Germany. From this point on foreign policy could no longer be kept on the back burner. The goal of Stalin's foreign policy in the decade preceding the Second World War was simple and by no means reprehensible: he wanted to keep his country out of war. It might seem paradoxical that, at a time when he pursued a most adventurous domestic policy, in foreign affairs Stalin behaved with sensible moderation. The explanation is that he feared that the turmoil caused by his domestic policies made foreign conflict extremely risky, both for his country and for his personal rule. In this respect there was no parallel between Nazi Germany and the Stalinist USSR. A will to war was not a feature of Soviet communism. The Stalinists were extremists in their desire to remake Soviet society, not the map of Europe.

Before Hitler came to power and for some time afterward, the Soviet leadership paid little attention to fascism in general or to the Nazis in particular. Communists believed in historical laws and saw analogies everywhere. They regarded Hitler as a German Kornilov, a person who had attacked the existing rickety system from the right but had little chance of success. They saw the situation as rather promising: after the victory of the extreme right, the turn of the left would come, and German communists would once again have a chance to come to power. The Stalinists certainly had no objection to Hitler's oft-announced goal of undermining the Versailles order. After all, those who had made peace at Versailles had been bitterly hostile to Bolshevism and had done everything within their limited power to destroy it. Of course the leaders in Moscow were aware of the Nazis' anticommunist rhetoric, but they were convinced that at least for some time the Nazis would not have the means to carry out an aggressive policy in the east.

The international communist movement, the Comintern, by now entirely directed from Moscow, obviously underestimated the Nazi danger. Only that error could explain the suicidal policy of concentrating fire on the Western socialists. The Stalinists before 1933 never contemplated collaboration with the socialists. At a time when Stalin ruled over the Soviet party, and when he destroyed everyone with a modicum of independent thought within the Soviet Union, there could be no question of seeking alliance with people outside the country whom he regarded as equivalents to the Russian moderate socialists, the Mensheviks. Undoubtedly the ill-considered policy of the powerful German communist movement contributed to Hitler's success. At the same time, we should put Stalinist policy in context. Nazism was a new phenomenon, and few appreciated the danger it represented. Soviet policy was no more shortsighted than that of other political forces inside and outside Germany.

The Soviet leaders were among the first to recognize their mistake and change their policies. Nazi anti-Bolshevik rhetoric did not diminish but increased. The Soviet policymakers now feared that Hitler's anti-Bolshevism might have an ideological appeal to West European conservatives, and that Hitler would exploit it to the detriment of Soviet interests. The decisiveness, recklessness, and brutality that Hitler exhibited early in his rule convinced the Soviet leaders that he would stay in power.

This was an ironic turn of events. The great economic depression from an ideological point of view benefited the Stalinists, because now they could contrast the extraordinary building efforts in their own country with the destruction and despair in the capitalist world at the time of the great depression. The misery that the depression created, the Stalinists believed, would help bring world revolution closer. Marx's predictions were to be realized. But things did not quite turn out as the Bolsheviks had hoped. The great depression undermined international order, and the Soviet Union not only did not benefit but faced the danger of war. Given internal conditions, such a danger seemed to threaten its very existence. But what policy would be most likely to ensure peace? Stalin and his lieutenants were not so naive as to believe that a simple protestation of a desire for peace – in a world threatened by Hitler's aggressive designs – would lead to success.

Soon after Hitler's coming to power, Stalin reoriented Soviet foreign policy. Although the diplomatic corps of all segments of the Soviet bureaucracy was hardest hit by the purges, the Soviet Union still possessed able and devoted diplomats who carried out Stalin's orders with great skill. It should be pointed out, however, that Soviet diplomacy possessed some inherent advantages. In this highly centralized system, decisions could be reached quickly; there were no interminable debates, leaks, and hesitations. The makers of Soviet foreign policy did not have to be concerned about popular pressures. They did not even have to prepare their own population for the most dramatic shifts; they were in the position to change course at a moment's notice as they saw fit. Nikita S. Khrushchev, in his memoirs dictated in the 1960s, gave us an excellent illustration of how small the circle of foreign-policy makers was. In 1939 he was a member of the Politburo; nevertheless, he first learned of the Molotov–Ribbentrop pact by reading *Pravda*.

Incongruously, the Soviet Union, which had been a determined enemy of the Versailles order, now became one of its pillars. The Soviet Union sought allies in the Western world among the previously despised socialist and liberal political circles in order to protect the international status quo. This new policy was implemented at the same time that the Stalinist leadership was exterminating the last vestiges of opposition at home. Maxim Litvinov, the Soviet foreign commissar from 1930 to 1939, became a familiar figure in the international congresses, arguing eloquently and passionately for all sorts of good causes such as disarmament, collective security, and resistance to aggression. The enlightened policy of the Soviet Union, as articulated by Litvinov, especially when contrasted to Nazi aggression and Western pusil-lanimity, gained many friends for communism. The reorientation of policy included joining the previously despised League of Nations, changing the policy of the Comintern, and concluding a security treaty with France.

In 1935, at its last congress, the Comintern called for a "popular front," meaning collaboration among enemies of Nazism. This changed policy enabled French communist deputies in the parliament to vote for war credits. Stalin hoped that French rearmament combined with a Franco-Soviet treaty would restrain Hitler. The Soviet–French military agreement was inspired by the memory of that cornerstone of the pre-First World War diplomatic order, the Franco-Russian alliance, which had threatened Germany with a two-front war. However, unlike tsarist times, the actual terms of military cooperation, the precise agreements between the two general staffs, were not drawn up. Given the fact that as a result of the reconstruction of Poland, Germany and the Soviet Union had no common border, it was not clear how the Red Army could come to the aid of France "in the case of an unprovoked attack by another European state." Neither the French nor the Soviets envisaged at this point actual military cooperation, such as sharing war plans. The treaty was more a gesture than a military alliance.

Soviet policy, in its chief aim of restraining the Nazis and avoiding involvement in a major war, obviously did not succeed. However, the communist movement, and therefore the Soviet Union, gained a great deal of good will in Western public opinion by being able to depict itself as the most consistent and committed antifascist power. That Soviet policy did not succeed, and the Nazis were not restrained, was not Stalin's fault. It is questionable that even the wisest policy could have dissuaded Hitler from pursuing his aggression, and the policy of the Western governments certainly was not the wisest. The toleration by the democratic West of the Italian conquest of Ethiopia, the willingness of the British government to sign a naval agreement with Germany, and above all the French acceptance of the remilitarization of the Rhineland undermined whatever faith the Soviet leaders might have had in collective security.

In the summer of 1936 General Francisco Franco organized a rebellion against the Spanish republic, and the Western democracies were threatened with the establishment of yet another fascist regime in Europe. The Spanish Civil War, which lasted for three years, became the most bitterly contested event in Europe, one that divided international public opinion more strongly than any other. The Italians and the Germans gave open and substantial help to the rebellious Franco; the Western democracies, by contrast, pursued an ineffective and cowardly policy. The Soviet leaders acted cautiously: on the one hand, it was in Soviet interests to tie down the Germans in Western Europe, and they certainly did not want the Spanish Civil War to end with a quick fascist victory. As the power that claimed to be the most committed enemy of fascism, the Soviets could not afford to seem indifferent. On the other hand, the establishment of a communist government, which seemed just barely possible, might frighten the French especially but also the British, and lose them as possible allies against Germany. As a consequence, of all powers it was the Soviet Union that gave the most generous help to the Republican forces; but, on the other hand, the possibility of direct intervention on the scale of the Italian and German intervention was simply out of the question.

Participation in the Spanish Civil War, however covert and however indirect, presented the Stalinist leadership with another dilemma. The Republican side attracted support from left-leaning groups from all over the world. Trotskyists, Stalinists, anarchists, and socialists were supposed to be on the same side in this conflict. However, Stalinist fear, suspicion, and hatred of their Trotskyist and socialist opponents were so great that the communists carried out a veritable purge behind the lines, compromising the communist cause in the eyes of many. Unlike Western democratic countries, the Soviet Union did not allow voluntary recruitment for participating in the Spanish Civil War. On the other hand, it did send agents and journalists who played a major role in organizing the international communist forces. Moreover, those who returned from Spain were overwhelmingly likely to become victims of the purges.

The turning point in interwar diplomatic history was the Czechoslovak crisis of 1938. In Munich, Neville Chamberlain and Édouard Daladier accepted the dismemberment of Czechoslovakia. Britain – by this time one can hardly speak of an independent French policy – acquiesced to the destruction of the state that had been the cornerstone of the Versailles order. The consequences for democratic Europe were disastrous. It appeared that the bourgeois politicians of Europe were willing to buy peace at any price. Since the Soviet Union was excluded from the negotiations, even leaders less suspicious than Stalin had reason to think that the West wanted to turn Nazi aggression eastward. There were, in fact, politicians in Western governments who would have happily seen the two antidemocratic forces of Europe tear one another apart. The destruction of Czechoslovakia was a move that directly threatened Soviet security, and a step toward the Nazi–Soviet pact. The West lost the moral basis for objections to a Nazi–Soviet reconciliation: what the Stalinists did in 1939 was not essentially different from what the British and French had done a year before.

It is impossible to establish when the Soviet leaders first entertained the idea of finding a modus vivendi with Hitler. Very likely it occurred early, long before the Munich agreement. After all, the Soviet goal was not to destroy fascism, but to avoid involvement in a war. If the Nazis could be won over, so much the better. Good diplomats that the Soviets were, they understood that a one-sided policy aimed entirely against Germany would have lessened the USSR's value as an ally in the eyes of the British and French. As it was, the British and French had little regard for the Soviet Union as a possible ally, not because Stalin had carried out a murderous policy against his own people, but because they thought that the terror had wrecked havoc in the Red Army, and that consequently its fighting capacity was low.

It would be wrong to attribute supernatural powers to Stalin and believe that he accurately foresaw events. He was not planning for a Nazi–Soviet alliance but, as a good diplomat, he wanted to keep his options open. It should be recalled that almost all European powers – with some notable exceptions, such as Edvard Benes's Czechoslovakia – considered at one point or another the possibility of finding a modus vivendi with the Nazis.

Following Munich, the Soviet determination to achieve an agreement with Hitler became much stronger. Litvinov's removal in May 1939 and Viacheslav Molotov's appointment as foreign commissar were steps in this direction. Not only was Litvinov Jewish, but he had also come to be associated in the public mind with the policy of collective security. He was not the person to carry out the new policy. His removal was also meant as a signal to Hitler. There was yet another factor that favored a policy of accommodation with the Nazis. In the Far East, the Soviet Union was threatened with involvement in a war with Japan. Japanese aggression in China and especially their creation of a puppet state in Manchukuo called for an energetic Soviet response. In May 1939 serious fighting broke out on the Mongolian border. The Red Army gave a good account of itself, and thereby discouraged Japanese aggression against the Soviet Union. Nevertheless, the danger of a two-front war was real.

The Soviet Union received a diplomatic present: when Germany in the spring of 1939 destroyed the remnants of Czechoslovakia, and when Hitler started to make threatening noises concerning Poland and the Polish treatment of Germans in Danzig, it became obvious that concessions would not satisfy Hitler and that the next victim was to be Poland. The policy of

Chamberlain, appeasement, was a failure. The British response was to guarantee Polish borders. The goal was to restrain German aggression by announcing that, in the case of German attack on Poland, the British would declare war. From the Soviet point of view this was a marvelous development, for it meant there was no longer any danger of facing the Nazis alone: there was no way the Germans could attack the Soviet Union but by violating Polish territory. The British might have improved their position by making their commitment conditional on Soviet support. They did not do so, presumably because they had a low regard for the Soviet Union as an ally.

Soviet negotiations with Britain and France continued. The talks ultimately broke down because the Western allies could not guarantee that Romania and Poland would allow Soviet troops to pass through their territory. At the same time the Soviets let the Germans know, in subtle and not-so-subtle ways, that they were ready to improve relations. The goals of Soviet policy were understandable: by negotiating with the Germans, they improved their bargaining positions vis-à-vis the Western powers, and by negotiating with the British and the French they made Hitler understand that he faced the danger of a two-front war. It seems that the Soviet leadership up to the last minute did not choose its course, but simply kept its options open. At this point, both the Western allies and the Soviet Union found it in their interests to prolong negotiations.

The diplomatic game, which in the course of the previous months had moved at a very slow pace, became hectic from the middle of August. The German war plans called for an invasion of Poland on August 26, and the Soviets knew about it. The Germans needed to conclude an agreement before hostilities commenced, because they did not want to embark on a war against Poland without first knowing Soviet intentions. Joachim von Ribbentrop, Hitler's foreign minister, came to Moscow to sign a nonaggression pact with Molotov on August 23. Negotiations for this momentous diplomatic revolution had to be remarkably fast. Stalin offered a toast to the health of the Führer, "beloved by the German people." Ribbentrop, in turn, after his second trip to Moscow a month later, reported to the Führer that in Moscow he felt at home: it was like being among comrades. (Lenin might have concluded a treaty similar to this one, but he would have never offered a toast to Hitler.) The chain of events that led to the outbreak of the Second World War was set in motion: German troops crossed the Polish border on September 1, and two days later France and Britain declared war on Germany.

6

A Great and Patriotic War

1939–1941

Contrary to the impression Soviet diplomats wanted to create, the Molotov–Ribbentrop pact was more than a nonaggression treaty; Germany and the Soviet Union became de facto allies. A secret protocol was attached to the pact that delimited the future "spheres of influence" of the contracting parties, according to which the Soviet Union was to have a free hand in Finland, Bessarabia, Latvia, and Estonia. The protocol also established the precise line in Poland that was to divide German and Soviet occupation spheres. At the end of September, Ribbentrop returned to Moscow to modify the original division: Lithuania now fell in the Soviet zone, but the Wehrmacht occupied the Lublin district in Poland. Remarkably, as long as the Soviet Union lasted, Soviet spokesmen and historians denied that there was such a protocol despite all the available evidence.

Stalin concluded his pact with the Nazis because he believed that the British and French would live up to their commitment to Poland and embark on a large-scale European war that would tie down Germany for some time. Without such a war, German military presence at the newly drawn Soviet border was too frightening to contemplate. Indeed, the Western powers declared war on Germany on September 3, and the Second World War began. The Soviet Union resisted German pressure and waited until September 17, that is until the Polish forces were more or less destroyed, before the Red Army crossed the Polish border and came to occupy territories assigned to it. As a consequence, according to Soviet figures, the Red Army lost only 737 men in this mop-up operation. Stalin's fears that the German army might continue its victorious march into the Soviet Union were alleviated when the meeting of the two armies took place peacefully, and the fifth division of Poland was accomplished.

In view of what was to happen two years later, the sad fate of the large Jewish minority in the newly occupied region is particularly noteworthy. Germans attempted to push the Jewish population into Soviet-occupied territories, but the Red Army closed the border to Jews. Although both the Nazis and the Soviets were anxious to avoid confrontation, concerning this matter the two armies almost came into conflict. It was the cruelest of ironies: the Soviet authorities arrested a large number of Jews in Ukraine and Belorussia and exiled them to Central Asia; it was these Jews who were most likely to survive.

Now that the Versailles order had broken down, Stalin was quick to seize what territories he could without undue risk. In October 1939, after incorporating western Ukraine and western Belorussia, he pressured the Finns for territorial and strategic concessions. The demands were relatively moderate: the Soviet Union wanted Finland to cede territory northwest of Leningrad in order to make the defense of the city easier, and to grant in addition the right to lease the Hango peninsula, which controlled the entry to the Gulf of Finland, and Petsamo, an ice-free port in the Far North. In exchange, the Soviet Union was ready to cede thinly inhabited territory in Karelia. Stalin assumed that the Finns would understand that without German protection they had no hope of standing up to the vastly superior Red Army, and therefore would give in. But the Finns did not accept the Soviet ultimatum – they particularly objected to giving up Hango – and the Red Army attacked at the end of November 1939.

The war was a military and moral disaster for the Soviet Union. It soon became clear that the purges had exacted a high price: the leadership of the Red Army quickly proved itself incompetent, the morale of the troops was low, and the army was inadequately equipped. The transportation system was stretched to its limits, so that the entire country suffered shortages. Small Finland was able to resist the Red Army for three months, inflicting in the process dreadful losses. The Soviet Union did not publish figures concerning losses, and only now, after the collapse of the Soviet Union and the opening of the archives, do we know that in excess of 126,000 Red Army soldiers died, a figure more than six times higher than the Finnish losses. The war was also a moral defeat. It inflamed Western public opinion, already bitter as a consequence of the Molotov–Ribbentrop pact. The Soviet Union was expelled from the League of Nations and, as the war dragged on, the British and French even considered sending troops to help the Finns. But, perhaps more importantly, Soviet performance in this war increased the Germans' contempt for the fighting capacity of the Red Army, and thereby encouraged Hitler in his aggressive designs.

Stalin's thinking in concluding an alliance with Nazi Germany and thereby giving the aggressor a green light to start a major war was based on a faulty assumption. The Soviet leaders, recalling the not-too-distant past, took it for granted that the French army, the largest in Europe, was a major

Molotov and Ribbentrop in Berlin, 1940

force that would be able to fight the Germans to a standstill. It is hard to blame Stalin for this error: most of his contemporaries shared his view, and no one in August 1939 foresaw the moral and political collapse of France. Had Stalin's assumption been correct, the Soviet Union indeed would have greatly benefited from being left out of a European war. In reality, of course, France collapsed in six weeks, and the Germans lost fewer soldiers than the Soviets lost in the war against Finland.

The period 1939–41 formed an unusual interlude in Soviet history. Previous slogans were quickly abandoned and new ones introduced. At a time of European conflagration, of course, the Soviet Union was constantly in danger of being dragged into the war. It was, however, unclear for a long time on which side the Red Army would fight. Andrei Zhdanov, a member of the Politburo responsible for propaganda and ideology, addressed a conference of filmmakers in May 1941 and told them their task was to prepare the Soviet people for war and self-sacrifice.[1] It was clear from his speech that at this late date the Soviet leaders still did not know on which side they would fight, even if they assumed that they would sooner or later have to do so. The character of films that were made in this period reflected the change in emphasis. In the mid 1930s filmmakers were obsessed with internal subversion, and the plots of the majority of films turned on unmasking the saboteur. Now the domestic enemy disappeared from Soviet screens; the good Soviet citizens struggled against foreign, mostly British, spies.

The time was used for military preparations. Learning from the war against Finland, the Red Army improved officer training by preparing cadres for modern warfare, organized new infantry divisions, and increased the number of airborne troops. Despite the improvements, when the German attack came, the Soviet side was still gravely unprepared.

The Soviet leadership must have been in awe of the military accomplishments of the Wehrmacht. Germany's quick defeat of Poland, followed by its easy conquests of Denmark and Norway in 1940, and finally the defeat of the French army after only six weeks and the retreat of the British from the continent, filled the Soviet leadership with terror. Despite the territorial gains, the country now, for the first time, had a long common border with Nazi Germany and therefore was less secure than at any time since the rise of Hitler.

As Hitler won his easy victories, the Soviet Union used the opportunity to incorporate those territories assigned to it by the Molotov–Ribbentrop pact. Perhaps we need no explanation at all for Soviet expansionism. The Bolsheviks increasingly regarded themselves as legitimate successors of the tsarist state, and since – with the insignificant exception of northern Bukovina – the Red Army was entering territories that had been part of the defunct tsarist empire, bringing under their rule millions of human beings seemed to them a most natural development. Furthermore, the Stalinists wanted to avoid fighting, but they were not so naive as to believe that this was possible in the long run. They therefore regarded the new territories as buffers, regions that would help to protect the Soviet core. They imagined the future war on the basis of their experiences in the First World War and did not foresee *Blitzkrieg*. The Soviet Union put military pressure on the Baltic states, forcing them to accept incorporation in June and July 1940; the Red Army occupied Bessarabia at the same time, the only territorial loss the Soviet Union had not officially accepted at the end of the First World War, and used the opportunity to take northern Bukovina from Romania.

The Soviet system with all its horrors was quickly exported to the conquered territories. A horrifying picture emerges. The new authorities established themselves with the aid of bloody terror: they carried out mass murder and deportation; they suppressed the indigenous intelligentsia of the various captive nationalities; they struggled mercilessly against the manifestations of national self-consciousness; and they impoverished the population. No one in the occupied territories benefited. One wave of deportation followed another as the new authorities did everything within their power to exploit the wealth of the region for the benefit of Moscow. The incorporation of the Baltic states served as a model for the Soviet Union in the postwar era in setting up the East European satellite regimes.

In that rather strange period of German–Soviet alliance, the Soviet Union faithfully served the interests of its new and frightful ally. In the economic collaboration between the two countries the Germans got the better deal. At first the Soviet policymakers favored the Germans in order to encourage them to fight in the west; later, when the Wehrmacht exhibited its extraordinary power, the Soviet leaders feared to provoke them. Soviet aid to the Nazis took several different forms. The Soviet Union provided Germany with necessary raw material, including vitally important oil, tin, bauxite, and rubber, and with foodstuffs, primarily grain. The Nazis used Soviet territory for shipments from third countries and thereby evaded the British blockade. The Soviet Union allowed the Germans to build a naval base for submarines not far from Murmansk, a base used in the Norwegian campaign in 1940.

The Soviet shopping list consisted almost entirely of armaments: the Soviets asked for the latest planes, tanks, and ships. Ultimately not much was delivered. The Soviet Union received some blueprints, a battleship that was not fully equipped; but as time went on the Germans felt more secure and less dependent on their Soviet ally. Time and again they reneged on their delivery obligations, and ultimately the Soviet Union exported to Germany far more than it imported. As Hitler decided that the next object of his warlike attention would be the Soviet Union, German deliveries slowed to a trickle, while Stalin, afraid to provoke the Germans, scrupulously observed treaties. At the outbreak of the German–Soviet war in June 1941, Germany owed the Soviet Union 229 million Reichsmarks worth of goods.

Long before the Second World War, the Stalinist state, the child of the revolution, had betrayed most of the ideals for which the revolution had been fought. The Soviet Union transformed its citizens into accomplices who denounced themselves and others; the country became a place of terror, where no one was left to denounce the lies propagated by official propaganda. Among the many distasteful actions of the Stalinists – the false accusations for treason, the betrayal of friends – one particular event stands out. In 1940 approximately 800 Austrian and German communists, many of them Jewish, who had been languishing in Stalinist prisons were decently fed for a few weeks and given new clothes. It seems that even the Bolsheviks were ashamed of the physical condition of their prisoners. When these veterans of the communist movement and the Soviet prisons and camps looked presentable, they were herded over a bridge at Brest-Litovsk and handed over to the Nazis. It was ironic that the communists thus returned had a better chance for survival than those who stayed behind. Statistically speaking, life expectancy was better for political prisoners in Nazi than in Soviet camps.[2]

The international communist movement, which had been the great ideological enemy of the Nazis and Hitler's bete noire, now became a mouthpiece of German propaganda. The French Communist Party, for example, commenced a defeatist campaign, denouncing the war as an imperialist one. On occasion German warplanes dropped communist defeatist pamphlets over enemy territory. Of course, the propaganda line of the Soviet regime for domestic consumption also changed overnight. Molotov branded the British and French criminals for continuing the war against Germany under the "false flag of struggle for democracy." The anti-Nazi books and films disappeared immediately. *Professor Mamlook* and *The Oppenheimer Family*, the best anti-Nazi films, could no longer be shown. The very same half-Jewish Eisenstein, who in 1938 had made the bitterly anti-Nazi historical allegory *Aleksandr Nevskii* – which in the changed circumstances was immediately taken off the screen – in 1940 directed Wagner's *Valkyrie* in the Bolshoi Theater.

It is unlikely that the Soviet people were won over by the new propaganda campaign. Anti-Nazi propaganda had been too effective, and the Germans remained greatly unpopular. However, it was not public opinion that determined Soviet policy. Public opinion would come to matter only when the country became engaged in a life-and-death struggle.

WAR

It is difficult to form a picture of Stalin as a human being. He did not write down his thoughts and did not confide in others, so his actions were usually open to different interpretations. It is hard to find in the life of the dictator evidence of normal human emotions, such as love, loyalty, and friendship, or even such negative feelings as hatred and fear. On one occasion, however, in 1941, his behavior was so unusual that suddenly he became almost transparent: the tyrant was frightened.

Of the many treacherous surprise attacks of the twentieth century, none was less surprising than the Nazis' attack on the Soviet Union in June 1941, for everything in their history and ideology prepared them to take precisely that fateful step. The Nazis wanted war, and they ran out of enemies against whom they could use their magnificent fighting forces. Unlike Britain, the Soviet Union offered wonderful terrain for the large and quickly moving German forces. That Hitler would refrain from attacking his newfound ally because of a scrap of paper, signed in August 1939, was absurd on the face of it. It is not only the wisdom of hindsight that makes it clear that the Nazis would sooner or later attack the Soviet Union; farsighted contemporaries also expected the attack. The coming of that great struggle was overdetermined.

All through the second half of 1940, almost immediately after the great successes in Western Europe, Hitler began to consider his next major move. In December 1940 he issued his famous Barbarossa directive: the German army had to be ready for the invasion of the Soviet Union by May 15, 1941. The communist Soviet Union was to be defeated in five months. As it turned out, there were some matters that had to be taken care of, and the actual date was postponed a little over a month. Hitler well remembered the First World War. Britain had to be weakened to such an extent that no immediate danger of a two-front war would threaten Germany. Also, German power had to be solidified in Eastern Europe. The Germans now could count on Finnish friendship; their troops entered Romania and occupied Greece; and, when a popular uprising overthrew the pro-German government in Yugoslavia, the Nazis invaded the country.

The Soviet Union possessed the finest foreign intelligence network: it had agents everywhere, and the best of these people were ready to serve the communist cause for ideological reasons. The first reports concerning the planned invasion had arrived in Moscow already in the fall of 1940. In early 1941, Moscow received detailed information about Barbarossa, and in May its best agent, Richard Sorge, reported from Tokyo on the number of German divisions massed for the attack and gave the date for the outbreak of hostilities. British and American diplomats also warned Stalin. But even without this far-flung, well-organized network it is impossible that the Soviet leaders were not aware of the large-scale German troop movements, the ever-increasing overflights of Soviet territory, the delays in German deliveries. There were dozens of German border violations carried out for the purpose of reconnaissance.

How is one to explain the puzzling Soviet behavior? Why was the Red Army not placed on a war footing before the attack came? After all, in September 1939, when circumstances were far less threatening, the army was fully mobilized. Why were there no war plans drawn up when war seemed imminent to foreign observers? Why did Stalin deploy the bulk of his troops so close to the border as to make defense in depth difficult if the need for such a defense quickly arose? The ever-suspicious Stalin, who saw enemies and dangers everywhere, now seemed blind to the impending vast struggle and tragedy. One must look for a psychological explanation for Stalin's extraordinary behavior. The snake looked into the eyes of the mongoose, and the mongoose froze. Stalin had little faith in the ability of his army to stop the Germans. But, even if the Germans could be defeated, Stalin could not assume that his regime would survive. Would not the much-abused Soviet people use the opportunity to take revenge on their tormenter? He obviously well remembered the experience of the previous war, which had given an opportunity to the revolutionaries to bring down the tsarist regime.

The real Second World War, a struggle on a scale unparalleled, now began. In the following three years, until the invasion of Normandy, Germany was to suffer more than 90 percent of its casualties in this theater of the war. At the end of 1942 there were 193 German divisions fighting in the Soviet Union and 4 in North Africa. Even during the last year of the war, after the invasion of Normandy, the Red Army continued to face two-thirds of the German divisions.

The Germans, as predicted, struck at 4:15 a.m. on June 22. An army of 190 divisions, in excess of 4.5 million strong, 5,000 airplanes – these numbers included the armies of Germany's allies – were ready to defeat the Red Army. Although more than half of the Soviet army, almost 3 million men, were deployed near the western borders, at the critical junctions the invaders had considerable numerical, and above all technical, superiority. The Soviet army suffered dreadful blows: on the very first day of the war, 1,200 of its airplanes were destroyed, the vast majority of them on the ground, never having a chance to engage the enemy in combat. Railroad junctions and munitions depots were bombed. The high command was in disarray. On the evening of the invasion Marshal Semyon Timoshenko, the commissar of war, issued a nonsensical order to the Soviet armies: take the offensive, take the war into the territory of the enemy. The consequences were predictably disastrous: in these ill-planned actions the soldiers faced superior enemy fire and went to their almost-certain deaths. The explanation for this extraordinarily careless step must be that the Soviet leadership feared to fight the war on its own territory, for it distrusted its own people. The war – by all means, at whatever expense – had to be taken to enemy territory.

The clearest sign of disarray was Stalin's momentary loss of control. The dictator, who claimed credit for all achievements, now at the hour of the greatest crisis was incapable of addressing his people. Instead, the uninspiring Molotov informed the Soviet people eight hours after the invasion that the country was at war. Stalin retired to his dacha and for days saw no one; according to some reports he attempted to relieve his fear by drinking. But then, eleven days after the invasion, he collected himself and addressed the Soviet people in one of his most effective speeches.

It would be some time before the Soviet armed forces could put up serious and organized resistance. For the time being the German advance seemed unstoppable, and within three weeks all the Soviet conquests of 1939–41 period were lost. Hitler, always conscious of historical parallels, wanted to avoid Napoleon's mistake of marching with his army on Moscow without protecting his flanks. The German army would attack on three different lines: one group would occupy the Baltic states and take Leningrad; another would face the most powerful Soviet forces in the center and move against

Moscow; while a third would take Ukraine, move on to the northern Caucasus, take hold of Russia's most fertile lands, and occupy the oil fields of the Caucasus. On all fronts the Germans moved forward during the summer and fall. Hitler's plan for defeating the Soviet Union within a few months seemed to be succeeding.

The German northern army group under General Wilhelm von Leeb overran the Baltic states quickly, and on September 8 the Germans cut the last land link between Leningrad and Soviet-held territories. When Hitler decided not to take the city but to force it into submission by starvation, one of the most remarkable episodes of the Second World War commenced. Leningrad, a city of several million, was besieged for two and a half years, an unparalleled event in history. The suffering of the people of this city came to be emblematic of the experiences of the Soviet peoples during the war. The leadership could not be blamed for being unprepared for such a siege, because no one could have foreseen it. At first the food supplies were used liberally – indeed, food was sent out of the city during the summer – but the supplies were soon depleted, and starvation followed. People ate dead crows, dogs, and cats, and cooked soup from buttons made out of bone. In November 1941 the bread rations for dependants, office workers, and children under 12 was reduced to 125 grams. Factory workers received twice as much. The combined effect of the cold and starvation was that malnourished people collapsed on the street and froze.

Circumstances slightly improved when Lake Ladoga froze. On the dangerous ice road, constantly bombarded by the Germans, food could reach the city, and hundreds of thousands of people could be evacuated. By the end of 1942 the population of the city had been reduced to a little over 600,000. In the course of the siege more than 1 million civilians died in the city. Remarkably, here as elsewhere, the hold of the regime remained firm. During the first terrible months Leningrad munition factories continued to supply the Moscow front. One can only wonder why people endured the unendurable and did not revolt, did not overthrow the representatives of Soviet power. It must have been a combination of patriotism, fear instilled by the recent experience of bloody terror, and simple inertia. The party – whose chief, Andrei Zhdanov, continued to receive sausages and peaches delivered by airplane at the time of mass starvation – remained in control.

The German southern army group was also successful. Kiev fell in the middle of September 1941, after dreadful losses for the Red Army. The decisive battles, however, took place in the center. Arguably, the battle for Moscow at the end of 1941 was the decisive battle of the entire war. Mid October was the most threatening moment: the Red Army was disintegrating, and it was hard to see how the Germans could be prevented from taking Moscow. Government offices and embassies were being moved to Kuibyshev, and there was panic and looting in the city. Stalin himself may have left the capital at least for a short time, as contemporary rumors maintained. He was, however, certainly back in Moscow at the time of the decisive battles. On the anniversary of the October Revolution, in an underground subway station, he gave a defiant and powerful address to the Soviet peoples. The despair and fear were fully understandable: in the previous two years the German army had enjoyed victory after victory, and no force, neither West European nor Soviet, had been able to inflict a significant defeat upon it.

And then a miracle happened. The German army ran out of steam; and it had to stop the advance, regroup, and bring up fuel, munitions, and winter clothing through the enormously long and difficult lines of supply. The weather turned first colder and then very cold. In October the ground froze at night, and during the day the inadequate roads became an impassable sea of mud. November and December were desperately cold. It would be wrong, however, to attribute the German defeat only to bad weather and to deny the decisive role of the Soviet soldiers. However inadequate the leadership from the very beginning of the war, the soldiers often fought with desperate courage. Stalin threatened to hold soldiers' families hostage if they deserted or allowed themselves to be captured, but it is unlikely that these draconian and cruel measures (rarely enacted) were decisive. The soldiers were ready to defend the fatherland against an enemy whose barbarism was increasingly evident to all. If we give credit to the German army's superior leadership, discipline, and equipment for the quick advance during the summer and fall, we must then give credit for the great Soviet victory to the heroism and constancy of the soldiers of the Red Army, and to the improved leadership of the Soviet officer corps.

The momentary lull in the fighting enabled the most competent Soviet general, Georgii Zhukov, who had been entrusted with the defense of Moscow, to organize the resistance and bring reinforcements. The crucial reserves came from Siberia, where they had been facing the Japanese. The great Soviet diplomatic coup of 1941, a nonaggression pact with Japan, now bore fruit. Soviet intelligence agents reported that the Japanese were turning their aggressive attentions elsewhere. The Germans recommenced their advance, and at one point reached the outskirts of Moscow, but could go no further. On December 5, the Red Army successfully counterattacked and inflicted a defeat on the enemy. For the first time since Hitler came to power, the German army had suffered a major reverse. The front moved 150–200 miles further west, and the stability of the German front was in doubt.

Hitler might not have won the war, even if he had taken Moscow; but now his defeat was only a question of time. If the Soviet regime could survive the first moments of doubt, it was no longer in danger of disintegrating. Stalin was right when he said on November 6, "there will yet be celebration in our streets!" The battle for Moscow stopped the *Blitzkrieg*, the type of warfare in which the German army was undoubtedly superior. At the same time, however, the suffering of the Soviet people did not end – indeed, the worst was still ahead. In 1942 the Red Army suffered major defeats, and the great brutality of the occupiers imposed almost unendurable misery on the people. Stalin, in obvious despair at the time of the quick German advance, now fell victim to exaggerated optimism: after the great victory at Moscow, he ordered a counterattack on all fronts at a time when the Red Army had neither the reserves nor the supplies to support such a vast undertaking. The consequences were predictable. Within a couple of months, after dreadful losses on both sides, the attack petered out without reaching any of its strategic goals.

The weight of the German summer offensive was in the south, and German armies advanced as quickly as they had in the previous summer. On July 24 the Germans took Rostov, and by the middle of August they reached the outskirts of Stalingrad. At the same time they penetrated into the northern Caucasus. It was the steadfastness of the soldiers of the 62nd Army under General Vasilii Chuikov, defending each building in Stalingrad under appallingly difficult conditions, which brought the German advance to a halt. In mid November the defenders held only isolated outposts on the right bank of the Volga. The resistance of the 62nd Army enabled the Soviet command to bring up enough troops to organize a vast encircling movement, ultimately involving three Soviet fronts (as army groups were called in Soviet military parlance). Long after the end of the fighting for Stalingrad, this battle continued to symbolize Soviet heroism and courage. Ultimately the battle involved 2 million soldiers, about equally divided between the two sides.

The Soviet offensive began on November 19, and four days later the German Sixth Army, commanded by General Friedrich Paulus, was encircled. General Erich von Manstein, who was fighting in the northern Caucasus, was summoned to relieve Paulus but failed. From this point the destruction of the German Sixth Army, at the outset consisting of more than 300,000 soldiers, was a certainty. Hitler forbade surrender, and the Germans attempted to supply the army by airdrops, but this was obviously impossible; the besieged suffered torments similar to what the Red Army had suffered so often in the war. The end came on February 2, when Paulus, recently promoted to field marshal by Hitler, together with 24 generals and 90,000 soldiers, were taken prisoner. The Germans were forced to withdraw from the northern Caucasus to avoid being cut off.

What that magnificent victory meant both for the victors and for the defeated cannot be overestimated. Although the Nazi propaganda machine attempted to hide the magnitude of the disaster, the news could not be hidden, and for the first time in the war defeatist sentiment surfaced in Germany. By contrast, in the Soviet Union after the battle of Stalingrad, most people assumed that the ultimate victory was only a matter of time.

Of course, given the scale of the war, temporary setbacks were inevitable. The Soviet command was too optimistic following the great victory, and therefore was surprised at a German counteroffensive that succeeded in reoccupying Kharkov. In March 1943, at least temporarily, the Red Army

Soviet troops attacking during the Second World War

was again forced onto the defensive. In July 1943 the Germans attempted their last major offensive. This battle, the battle for Kursk, became the largest of the war in terms of the quantity of troops and armament; in fact it was the largest tank battle in history, involving 6,000 tanks. For the first time the Soviet forces had superiority both in numbers and in weaponry. The result of the vast battle was a great Soviet victory. Not only did the Germans fail to achieve their strategic objective, but their armies were shattered, never fully to recover.

From this point on the Soviet advance was continuous. In January 1944 the Red Army finally broke the siege of Leningrad. As a result of the winter and spring campaigns of 1944, the Red Army reached the previous borders of the Soviet Union almost everywhere. Meanwhile the quality of Soviet military leadership greatly improved. Whenever German resistance stiffened, the Red Army initiated offensive actions at different points on the vast front. In August 1944 the Soviet army stood outside Warsaw. The Romanians were compelled to switch sides. By the fall of 1944, in East Prussia, German civilians got a taste of their own medicine: now the war was being fought on German soil. In February 1945, Budapest was taken by the Red Army, and the last German soldier left Hungarian soil on April 4. American and Soviet troops met on the Elbe on April 24, and Soviet soldiers raised their flag over the Reichstag on May 1. On May 8 the representatives of Germany signed the document of surrender and the great war, at least in Europe, was over.

Aside from the heroism of the soldiers of the Red Army and their improved leadership, Soviet victory was made possible by the fact that the Soviet side could match the military hardware of the enemy. Although at the outbreak of the war there was no great numerical disproportion between the armaments of the two sides, the quality of the Soviet equipment was inferior. The mass production of the modern weaponry began under extraordinarily difficult circumstances. The Germans had overrun the most industrialized regions of the country. In light of the difficulties, Soviet economic accomplishments were nothing sort of miraculous. It turned out that the command economy, with all its faults, suited wartime conditions. The Soviet Union in a short time managed to mobilize the entire economy for the purpose of the war far more thoroughly than any other belligerent nation. By 1942–43 Soviet factories were producing more tanks and airplanes than their German counterparts.

The evacuation to Central Asia, the Ural mountains, and western Siberia of hundreds of small and large enterprises from occupied areas was a most impressive achievement. Ultimately, 10 million workers were moved eastward; this move was accomplished quickly so that in the reestablished factories the production of war materiel could recommence. It is difficult for us to imagine the conditions in which the newly resettled workers lived: there was a shortage of all necessities including housing.

The economic strategy of the great industrialization drive now bore fruit: the great stress on building heavy industry made it possible to convert the factories to military production. It was remarkable that gross industrial output (largely war materiel, of course) in 1944 surpassed prewar standards, despite the destruction caused by enemy occupation and bombardment. While during the last year of peace 15 percent of the national income had been devoted to war production, two years later the figure had risen to 55 percent.

There was a price to pay. As male workers were drafted, their places was taken in the factories by women. People worked under appalling conditions. The labor code of 1940 introduced harsh punishments for the violation of discipline. Now military discipline was fully introduced: people could not leave their jobs without permission, and overtime became compulsory. Total mobilization of the economy led to the depletion of the consumer goods sector. Even more painful for the Soviet people was the dreadful damage to agriculture and animal husbandry. In 1942 and 1943 the total grain harvest was only one-third of what it had been in prewar times. The consequences were predictable: food was in short supply, and clothing often unobtainable.

THE SOVIET PEOPLE AND THE WAR

The Second World War was the supreme test of the Soviet system. The economy passed that test: the industrial base, partially created during the great drive of the 1930s, was large enough ultimately to produce weapons in sufficient quantity and quality to match the German war materiel. It is more difficult to draw conclusions concerning the allegiance of the Soviet people to their political system. Although the Soviet Union defeated Nazi Germany, this fact alone did not demonstrate the commitment of the peoples of the Soviet Union to communism. On the basis of reports from defectors who chose to stay in the West after the war, we may draw some conclusions. Only a rather small minority of the peoples of the Soviet Union were devoted communists, people who fought for the maintenance of the Soviet system. Another minority, perhaps a somewhat larger one, were so hostile to Stalinism that they were willing to collaborate with the Nazis. The great majority were somewhere in between: they were willing to fight for their country and obey the communists in order to defeat a beastly enemy.

We should remember that in every country that came under Nazi occupation, without exception, the Germans found collaborators. The Soviet Union was a multinational empire in which only slightly over half of the population was Russian; and here the potential for collaboration was particularly great. In territories that had come under Stalinist rule between 1939 and 1941, the people remembered the brutal policies of sovietization, the terror and deportations carried out by the Stalinist regime. In Ukraine, in the Baltic states, in Belorussia, and in Bessarabia large segments of the population, perhaps even the majority at first, welcomed the Germans as liberators. The Germans also found allies among the indigenous people of the Caucasus and among the Cossacks, people who had felt particularly mistreated by the communist rulers. Given the potential, it is surprising how little the Nazis took advantage of the centrifugal force of the nationalisms of the non-Russians. On the basis of their racialist ideology, the Nazis made distinctions among the nationalities, and treated some better than others. Estonians and Georgians, for example, were relatively high on their scale, while Slavs and Armenians were low. They organized "national legions" from non-Russian and Cossack prisoners of war and sent most of these to the west, where they performed police duties.

The Germans also used collaborators as administrators in towns and villages and organized auxiliary detachments to carry out particularly distasteful tasks, such as shooting Jewish children. How many collaborators there were is impossible to establish and, of course, the degree and nature of collaboration varied; but it is fair to say that millions of Soviet citizens to some extent collaborated. General Andrei Vlasov, one of the heroes of the battles for Moscow, was captured by the Germans in the summer of 1942. An honest but politically inexperienced man, he was willing to have his name used by the enemies of his country, presumably because of his anti-Stalinist convictions. He became the leader of the largest Russian anti-Soviet movement; by the end of the war he commanded an army of more than 50,000 formed from prisoners of war. The Germans, given their ideology, distrusted this small Russian army, never equipped it properly, and did not use it in the war.

Some joined the Vlasov movement out of hatred of the Soviet regime, and others in order to escape the dreadful fate of Soviet prisoners of war in

Soviet civilians in the Second World War

German captivity, where approximately 3 million men died. It is therefore not clear to what extent the Vlasov movement can be used as an example of disaffection. At the end of the war, about 5 million Soviet citizens found themselves in the West as a result of having been prisoners of war or slave laborers, or voluntarily having joined the retreating Germans. Churchill and Roosevelt, who had signed agreements guaranteeing repatriation, never considered that people might not want to return to their homeland. At the end of the war hundreds of thousands had to be forced to return to the Soviet Union. Many of them were sent directly to concentration camps on their return.

The Soviet regime was saved by the fact that it faced an enemy which made it impossible for the people of the Soviet Union to accept defeat. They had to fight whether they believed in the existing system or not, because the Germans gave them no option. German policy in the occupied territories was based on a racialist ideology that considered the Slavs subhuman and treated them accordingly. According to this ideology, the Jews were not human at all, but vermin to be exterminated. The Germans followed a mad policy of destruction: they wanted to reduce Russians and Ukrainians to slavery and exploit the territories to benefit Germany. In order to bring this about, they wanted to destroy the intelligentsia physically. They wanted to create conditions in which many "natives" would die, and thereby create room for German colonization. When the Nazis exterminated villages in reprisal for partisan attacks they intended them to be repopulated by ethnic Germans. In the course of the war more than 4 million men and women were taken to Germany to work as slave laborers.

From the very outset the Nazis had a special policy for Jews and communists who fell into their hands: they killed them. The Nazis commenced their genocide immediately after the invasion. The invading armies were accompanied by "special groups of the SS," *Einsatzgruppen*, which rounded up and shot Jews. The German army thus became an accomplice in genocide. Within the first few months of the war a half-million were so murdered, and by the end of the war more than a million Soviet Jews had fallen victim to Nazi madness.

The Germans conducted very little propaganda, for offering anything to the Soviet people would have conflicted with their goals. Later, when it became clear that the war would not end quickly with a German victory, the invaders changed their approach. But even at this time German efforts were confused and contradictory. In any case, actions spoke louder than words. The population well understood what the invaders wanted and who they were. The Germans, having made little effort to appeal to the population when victorious, could not hope to do so in a period of defeat. One is tempted to pose a counterfactual question: what if Nazi policy had been more clever and the Germans had posed as liberators? The flaw in this perspective is that, had the Nazis not been so brutal, had they not been devoted to a mad ideology, they would have never commenced the war in the first place. The various aspects of Nazism could not be separated: daring, conviction of superiority, amorality, will to war and destruction, determination, and ruthlessness – all these had brought victory, and all ultimately brought defeat.

But, in June 1941, the Soviet leadership could not possibly have known the depth of Nazi criminality and political ineptitude. In the past the Soviet people had complied because they had no alternative: terror had eliminated all real and potential enemies. But would people now continue to obey? Stalin was immobilized for ten crucial days: he did not know how to address his subjects. When he finally did so on July 3, he did it most effectively and movingly. He addressed his listeners as brothers and sisters, and thereby foreshadowed the great change that was to take place in Soviet propaganda during the war years.

The might of German armies, enjoying victory after victory, was impressive. The enemy seemed unstoppable, and in the new circumstances it took some time for the Soviet propaganda machine to reorient itself and find its voice. However, decades of experience in mass mobilization and practice in various agitational methods all turned out to be useful. The themes of propaganda changed, but the instruments were already in place, ready to be used. Although the regime deemphasized ideology, the party as an institution retained its importance. It carried out a special recruitment drive during the war, making it easier for soldiers to enroll. It was assumed that identification with the regime would strengthen loyalty and raise the morale of the troops.

For the same reason, the Komsomol was also greatly expanded during the war: between 1940 and 1945 its membership grew from approximately 10 million to 15 million. The youth organization was especially useful for the regime when operating in occupied territories. The regime had greater faith in the young, those who had been educated entirely under a communist system. Indeed, Komsomol members were the most likely to join the partisan movement.

Nor should we forget another important Soviet institution, the NKVD. Propaganda and coercion, as before, went hand in hand. This leopard did not change its spots; terror did not abate during the war. Those who had lived under German occupation, or who had become prisoners of war and escaped, suffered the consequences of NKVD suspicion, and hundreds of thousands of them were arrested. The Soviet regime punished the families of deserters. A new phenomenon during the war was the punishment of entire nations: the Volga Germans were deported immediately at the outbreak of the war. In 1943 and 1944 it was the turn of the Crimean Tatars and Muslim minorities of the Caucasus: deported to Central Asia, they lived in the most inhuman conditions. The new element in this terror was its naked racism. Every member belonging to a certain minority group was punished, regardless of class status, past behavior, or achievements. Communist Party officials were deported as well as artists, peasants, and workers.

Despite the arrests, the number of prisoners in camps declined during the war. This happened partly because inmates were sent to the front in punishment battalions, where they fought in the most dangerous sectors. The morale and heroism of these battalions were impressive: most of the soldiers did not survive. The camps were also depopulated by the extraordinary death rates: approximately a quarter of the inmates died every year. People died because of mistreatment, overwork, and undernourishment.

In wartime nothing is more important than maintaining the morale and loyalty of the armed forces. In addressing this need the Soviet Union learned from decades of experience. At first, the regime reverted to the dual command system it had developed during a previous time of crisis, the civil war. From the regimental level up, political appointees supervised regular officers. They were responsible for the loyalty of the officers and at the same time directed the political education system. The abandonment of united command, however, harmed military efficiency; once the most dangerous first year had passed, the Stalinist leadership reestablished united command. This did not mean that the political officers had no further role to play. The network of commissars, supervised by the chief political administration of the army, survived. The commissars carried out propaganda among the troops: they organized lectures, discussed the daily press with the soldiers, and participated in organizing agitational trains that brought films and theater productions to the front.

Yet another network within the army functioned to ensure the loyalty of the troops – the network of security officers. Although these men wore military uniforms, they were entirely independent of the high command and reported directly to the NKVD. According to contemporary reports, these security officers were greatly disliked by regular officers.

Of course, it was much harder to control the partisan movement than the army. The German advance during the summer of 1941 was so sudden that the retreating Soviet forces did not have a chance to prepare for resistance in enemy-held territory, and the partisan movement began autonomously. One manifestation of the independence of the movement was that its propaganda, while necessarily coinciding with Soviet themes in most respects, had distinctive features. For example, Soviet propaganda never admitted past Soviet errors; but the partisans, especially in their oral approach to the population, could and did say that the errors of the past would be eliminated in a future and victorious Soviet Union.

The partisan movement had great significance: it tied down and harassed the Germans, and it projected Soviet presence in an area not under the regime's control. It was essential for the future that the population in the occupied areas receive the Soviet point of view and live with the expectation that the previous rulers would return. The best propaganda carried out by the partisans was propaganda by example. By their very existence they showed to the Soviet population that the power of the Germans was not limitless. By their willingness to accept martyrdom, they exposed the bestial nature of the Nazi occupiers. The Soviet regime, well aware of the value of this work, did not spare scarce resources. Planes dropped pamphlets distributed by partisan propagandists; the partisans obtained small presses that enabled them to spread information they received on short-wave radio; and they carried out oral agitation. As the movement grew, the leadership set up agitational sections consisting not only of experienced agitators, but also of singers and artists who gave performances.

In regions not under enemy occupation, every branch of art was pressed into service. Novelists described the heroism of the soldiers and civilians, musicians composed patriotic songs, and graphic artists drew posters that glorified the Red Army and the Soviet people and ridiculed the enemy. It is worthwhile to examine Soviet films made during the war, not for their artistic merit, but because these show most clearly the character of the propaganda. The leadership had a special appreciation for the role of cinema and film documentaries, and filmmaking came to be fully mobilized for the war effort. During the war Soviet directors made a total of seventy-eight films; only a handful did not deal directly or indirectly with the war. Documentaries made

Partisan warfare

a specially great impression on audiences, and documentary makers received all the support they needed. In the course of the war thousands of cameramen shot 3.5 million meters of film, thereby producing a remarkable chronicle of the war. These documentaries, unlike the German ones, did not shrink from depicting the suffering imposed on civilians.

At first the main task of Soviet propagandists was to puncture the Germans' image of invincibility in order to lessen the likelihood of collaboration. Soviet publicists overstated German losses, passed over Soviet defeats, and stressed the courageous resistance of the population. With the first important victory of the Red Army at Moscow in December 1941, the task of the propagandists became much easier. People hungered for good news. When newsreels of that important battle appeared in the theaters, people stood in line for tickets. Seeing German prisoners of war led through the streets of the capital was a wonderful experience for people who had suffered so many humiliating defeats.

The soldiers of the Red Army and the partisans went to fight for "motherland, for honor, for freedom and for Stalin." On this list, motherland was the first and most important. The heart of appeals to the people was Russian nationalism, a love for their native land and its traditions. The resurrection of Russian nationalism had preceded the war. Historians and publicists extolled the achievements of tsarist generals and statesmen, and by dwelling on the great figures of the past conveyed the message that their contemporaries had a high tradition to live up to. By showing past Russian successes they intended to convince the audience that Russia would once again prevail.

Soviet Marxist writers, scholars, and artists did not consider their praise of generals, tsars, aristocrats, and other "exploiters of the people" incongruous. Nor did they object to an un-Marxist hero worship. In their depiction it was individual courage and leadership that mattered above all. Long gone were the days of the 1920s, when these same people focused attention only on the "masses." To continue to do that in the age of Stalin would have been ludicrous. During the war, nationalism, love for the motherland, meant the willingness to accept sacrifice and even martyrdom for the sake of victory. Film directors and novelists depicted positive heroes; partisan stories, especially concerning female partisans, provided particularly good material. The courage, self-sacrifice, and strength of Soviet women, whether working at the factories or fighting the enemy with weapons, were favorite topics of Soviet authors. By showing the courage of women, the publicists conveyed the message that men could be expected to do no less. By depicting the Germans' mistreatment of women and children, they aroused hatred against a bestial enemy. The three best-known films about partisans each had a female protagonist. Interestingly, while the first two managed to escape death – saved at the last moment by partisans or by the Red Army – the third one, Zoia Kosmodemianskaia, about whom a film was made in 1944, died a martyr's death. In a period of victories, Soviet audiences no longer had to be spared from witnessing the execution of a partisan.

Russian nationalism was a powerful motivating force for resistance against the aggressor. At the same time, the encouragement of this nationalism was not without dangers. The half-hearted and contradictory Nazi attempts to exploit existing national hostilities and jealousies had to be countered. Soviet propagandists stressed the theme of friendship among the peoples of the union. Films would often depict a situation in which, for example, a Russian and Georgian soldier would undertake a dangerous reconnaissance mission. The success of the mission, indeed the survival of the soldiers, depended on their cooperation. At the end either the Georgian would save the life of the Russian or (more likely) vice versa. In order to harness the histories of the minorities for the Soviet cause, the film studios during the war produced one major epic for each important nationality. Some of these films projected the theme of the "friendship of peoples" into the past. A historical character, let us say the seventeenth-century Ukrainian Bogdan Khmelnitskii, would explain that the wellbeing and happiness of the Ukrainians depended on their close cooperation with their Russian brothers.

There was one nationality, however, that was conspicuous by its absence from Soviet propaganda. Publicists failed to mention that the Nazis had a special policy toward the Jews. Soviet publicists believed that denouncing anti-Semitism was not good propaganda for home consumption. Anti-Semitism was, of course, an essential ingredient of Nazi propaganda aimed at the Soviet peoples, and the Soviet propaganda apparatus wanted to give no opportunity to the Germans to describe them as pro-Jewish. Soviet propaganda simply ignored the matter. When, during the last year of the war, the Red Army liberated some of the death camps, the newsreels showing these events never mentioned the nationality of the victims. In this respect Soviet foreign and domestic propaganda differed. The Soviet leaders, like the Nazis, greatly overestimated the power of the international Jewry to influence the decisions of Western governments. The regime mobilized prominent Jews in order to attract help from abroad.

A corollary of the rebirth of old-fashioned Russian nationalism was the officially sponsored revival of pan-Slavism. In Soviet propaganda the theme of the solidarity of the working classes of the world was superseded by the theme of the solidarity of the Slavic peoples. In the summer of 1941 an all-Slavic committee was formed in Moscow. Soviet newspapers and films paid great attention to the exploits of Yugoslav, Czech, and Polish partisans. Official slogans proclaiming Slavic brotherhood comforted the Russians and convinced them that they were not alone against the brutal Teutons.

The mirror image of the heroic Slav was the bestial German. In the first confused days of the war the propagandists' picture of the enemy was unfocused. The Germans seemed not only cruel, but also silly and cowardly. However, this approach was soon abandoned. Not only did it conflict too obviously with reality, it did not help to inspire hatred and make people accept sacrifice. Instead, Soviet propaganda came to focus on the Germans' brutality, on their contempt for the Slavs, and on their far-reaching plans to enslave the conquered populations. At times Soviet accounts exaggerated German atrocities, but the population had suffered at the hands of the Germans and was predisposed to believe the worst. Indeed, German behavior was such that a simple and truthful description was enough. Reality was often so bad that propaganda could not surpass it. The propagandists did not make distinctions among Germans. There was no room in Soviet propaganda for the good German. This one-dimensional portrayal of the Germans did not change even when the Red Army was marching forward victoriously. Soviet propaganda even projected the wickedness of the Germans into the past in an almost racist fashion. A 1945 Soviet film, for example, depicted Volga Germans as determined enemies of Soviet power already in 1918. At a time when the descendants of these people had been deported from their homes, such a film was particularly reprehensible.

The stress on Russian nationalism was accompanied by a deemphasis on the revolutionary and communist nature of the regime. Once the life-and-death struggle against Nazism was under way, it was important to maintain national unity; this was clearly no time to talk about world revolution. Not only did internationalist communism make poor propaganda for home consumption, it would also have endangered the precious alliance with Great Britain and the United States. In 1943 the Soviet Union dissolved the Comintern. It also dropped "The Internationale" as its anthem and instead adopted a new one, with insipid music and text.

The propagandists had to draw a delicate line. On the one hand it was essential not to demoralize the communist activists by repudiating the past, but on the other it was self-evident that for the great bulk of the Russian people it was the defense of the motherland, not the defense of the communist system, that mattered. Soviet propagandists handled the task with skill. They depicted the country's past and future in such a way as to allow people of different political persuasions to draw different conclusions. Soviet newspapers, novels, and films repeatedly contrasted the happy life of the people before the war with the terrible present. The writers, however, remained vague about the nature of that happy life. The soldiers fought under the Red banner; they went to battle "for Stalin"; the Soviet people continued to celebrate holidays such as the anniversary of the October Revolution and May Day; they listened to unceasing glorification of the founder of the Soviet state, Lenin. And, of course, the leaders of the regime apologized for nothing.

A temporary abandonment of antireligious propaganda accompanied the deemphasis of communism. If tsars, generals, and aristocrats could be held up as examples to follow, there was no reason why churchmen should be excluded. The glorification of the Russian past helped the revival of the church. After all, the Orthodox Church was an inseparable part of Russian history. The motives for abandoning the persecution of the church are easy to see. The Soviet leaders wanted to prevent the Germans from posing as the defenders of religion, and they wanted to gain the good will of the democratic West; but, most importantly, they wanted the help of the church in the great national effort. The state allowed the printing of religious books; it reopened churches; Radio Moscow started to broadcast religious hours. The church responded warmly: the Orthodox leaders visited Stalin in the Kremlin and gave their blessing to the war effort.

The leaders of the regime well understood the hostility of the Russian people to antireligious policies and the necessity for concessions. They also knew that the overwhelming majority of the peasants deeply resented the collective farms. In this matter, however, it was far more difficult to retreat. Even if the creators of the system had been willing to sacrifice the collective farms, which is questionable, such a move in the short run would have led to enormous confusion. The Soviet leaders, good politicians that they were, well understood this weakness in their position. They braced themselves for an attack, because they assumed that the enemy would exploit their weakness. But the attack never came, for the Germans, instead of identifying themselves with the aspirations of the peasants, decided to exploit the collective farms for their own purposes. They, too, found it easier to compel the collectives to provide food than to force individual peasants. Partisan propaganda took advantage of the failure of the Germans. The partisans encouraged the belief that after the victorious conclusion of the war the farms would be dissolved. It is impossible to establish to what extent this aspect of partisan propaganda was centrally planned. Most likely the partisans used their independence to tell the peasants what the peasants wanted to hear. As the war was drawing to a victorious conclusion, the Russian people expected "good things" to happen, even if such expectations were unrealistic and sometimes even mutually exclusive.

WARTIME DIPLOMACY

The grand alliance of Great Britain, the United States, and the Soviet Union was of course created by necessity. Neither Churchill nor Roosevelt long hesitated: once the Red Army was fighting the Wehrmacht, the Soviet Union immediately became a worthwhile and desirable ally, deserving of help. On the very day of the German invasion, Churchill announced his intention to help; in July Roosevelt's special envoy, Harry Hopkins, came to Moscow to discuss American aid. During the war the Allies had no choice but to present to the outside world the appearance of comity and common purpose. Western public opinion came to regard the Soviet Union favorably, admiring the constancy of the Russian people and the military accomplishments of the Red Army. Old quarrels, memories of purges and terror, religious persecutions: all were forgotten, even if only temporarily. It could not have been otherwise: Western governments could not operate without public support. But even in governmental circles in Washington and London there may have been naive expectations that the Soviet Union had changed, that Stalin had become a conventional nationalist leader who had abandoned his revolutionary commitment.

Soviet policymakers did everything within their power to foster such an understanding. In 1943 Stalin dissolved the Comintern – by now only a shell of its formal self. The dissolution of course did not lessen Soviet influence over international communism. Stalin counseled the communist anti-Nazi underground movements in Yugoslavia and elsewhere to underplay their true ideological commitments. Soviet theaters played British and American films and newsreels, and the newspapers depicted the democratic West sympathetically. Undoubtedly, many Soviet people took pleasure in having democratic countries as allies and hoped that after the victorious conclusion of the war the Soviet Union would itself adopt democratic reforms.

In Stalin's suspicious mind, however, there was no question about the nature of this alliance: this was a temporary arrangement that the Soviet Union desperately needed. He and his comrades had an ambivalent attitude to the West. On the one hand, they had a healthy appreciation of the economic strength of the West, especially of the United States; but, on the other, we know from internal communications that they had contempt for what they perceived as weakness, softness, and cowardice. Soviet policy-makers wanted to limit contacts between their own citizens and Westerners. Such contacts, however, were inevitable: there were, for example, approximately 8,000 American and British sailors in Murmansk and Archangel in 1942. They had delivered war materiel, but their ships had been damaged by German submarines and could not immediately return. The local party leader in his report to Moscow described the Westerners as cowardly, made the absurd accusation that the sailors themselves were somehow responsible for the damage suffered by their ships, and reported that the Americans were buying Russian girls for chocolate bars and openly expressing contempt for the Soviet social and political system.[3]

The British and the Soviets signed a treaty already on July 13, 1941, in which the two sides obligated themselves not to initiate separate negotiations – much less a separate peace – with the enemy. The Soviet position greatly improved at the end of 1941 – the Japanese carried out their surprise attack on Pearl Harbor and Hitler, idiotically, declared war on the United States. Now that the Japanese were engaged in the Pacific, the danger of a two-front war had passed and troops from the Far East could be safely brought to Europe. And just as importantly, the United States became a full-fledged ally.

Even at the earliest stages of the newly forged alliance the two issues that were to dominate wartime diplomacy were already in evidence. One of these issues was what kind of military help the allies could give to the Red Army, and the other was the question of future borders of Poland and the future shape of Eastern Europe. During the dreadful summer of 1941, the Soviet regime was on the verge of collapse; it desperately needed and wanted fighting help. Stalin attempted to persuade the British to engage the Germans in Scandinavia, and at a most threatening moment of the war even asked that the British land troops in the Soviet Union in order to fight the Germans. The plan was utterly unrealistic, and the fact that Stalin nevertheless advanced it revealed his desperation. Having British soldiers on Soviet territory was dangerous, but it was better than the alternative – facing the Germans alone.

After the passage of the worst period, the bleak fall of 1941, the Soviet Union would never have tolerated a large number of foreign troops on its territory. Nevertheless, Stalin continued to demand fighting help, a demand motivated by the understandable desire to lessen Soviet losses. Furthermore, the Soviet leader was very much afraid that the West would come to an agreement with Hitler, leaving the Soviet Union to face the German army alone. Soviet diplomats believed that if large Western armies engaged the enemy in Europe, such a separate peace would be less likely. They constantly badgered the Allies to open a second front in Europe, preferably in France. Allied responses were vague and noncommittal. The Allied invasion of North Africa in the fall of 1942 did not appease the Soviet leaders, nor were they impressed by the landing in Sicily in the summer of 1943. These actions did not relieve the burden of having to face the German armies, for all practical purposes, alone. Stalin and his entourage managed to assume the moral high ground: they were carrying the major share of the burden. The majority of the Soviet people also felt that the Allies were not doing enough to give them fighting help. It is unlikely that many Soviet citizens at this desperate time remembered that not long before, between 1939 and 1941, the Red Army not only failed to help their future allies, but on the contrary aided the Nazis. It is unlikely that Soviet citizens understood that, if their country had had the option of staying out of the war, their leaders would certainly have used such an option. Memories were short.

After many postponements, the Allied invasion of northern France occurred at a time when the fighting strength of the German army had been broken. Although indubitably the Soviet army did most of the fighting, the Allies, in particular the Americans, provided generous and much-needed material help. It is difficult to say how important a component Western help was in Soviet victory, for we cannot easily separate aspects of Soviet performance. Unquestionably, the Soviets themselves produced the vast bulk of the war materiel and, therefore, it is likely that the Red Army would have withstood the German assault alone. After all, at the time of the greatest danger, in 1941, foreign help was not yet available. On the other hand, it also seems likely that the great successes, the Red Army's almost-uninterrupted series of offensives beginning in 1943, could not have been carried out without American help. The Red Army benefited most from the large number of trucks that were delivered; they greatly advanced the mobility of the army, and Soviet industry could not produce them in sufficient numbers. In addition, communications equipment, radar, and other items of technology made a difference in the performance of the Soviet troops. The suffering of the Soviet peoples was also somewhat alleviated by the delivery of foodstuffs. Of course, the Allies also benefited: had the war lasted longer, more British and American soldiers would have died.

At first the bulk of the material was delivered via the North Sea. This route, however, given the strength of the German submarine fleet, was exceedingly dangerous. Soon the British and the Soviets occupied Iran in a coordinated operation, and the bulk of military aid started to flow into the Soviet Union through the Persian Gulf. Given Soviet suspiciousness, even the delivery of aid was not a simple matter. The Soviets were so secretive during the war that they did not allow their American allies to make an objective evaluation of the performance of the weapons they were contributing. On one occasion, for example, the Americans, reasonably enough, wanted maps showing the location of Soviet airfields. The Soviets responded by saying that (a) there were so many airfields planes could easily find them without maps, (b) the country was flat, so any field could be used, and (c) there were no maps. Therefore, the donors, even at the time, could only guess how much their material aid had contributed. Undoubtedly Soviet preoccupation with secrecy hurt the war effort.

The two great and contentious issues of wartime diplomacy – when and where the second front should be established, and the future shape of Eastern Europe – were closely connected, much more closely than many contemporaries in the West have been willing to recognize. Allied diplomats spent a disproportionate amount of time on the question of Poland. The Allies, in particular the British, faced a dilemma. They had declared war on Germany in September 1939 in order to guarantee the territorial integrity of Poland. The Soviet government, Britain's new and crucially important ally, on the other hand, having declared the Nazi–Soviet pact null and void, was still unwilling to promise the return of territories taken in 1939.

Shortly after the outbreak of the Soviet–German war, the Soviet government and the exiled Polish government in London signed a treaty but postponed the resolution of the contentious issue of future borders between the two countries. In spite of the treaty, relations between the two governments were poor from the outset. The Soviet authorities mistreated Poles living in Soviet territories, and the Polish government-in-exile had good reason to question Stalin's trustworthiness. Nevertheless, a large share of the blame for the bad relations must be borne by the London Poles. Their fault was not that they did not "trust" Stalin – they had every reason not to – but that they did not understand the weakness of their position. They remained absolutely obstinate in their demand to reestablish the borders of 1939, even though their claim for the lost territories was dubious from the point of view of ethnicity and, more importantly, unenforceable without diplomatic support from their British and American patrons. By taking an unbending stand against the Soviet Union, they achieved the opposite of their goal. Stalin early on decided that the Poles would establish an anti-Soviet government if left to themselves, and was determined to prevent that at all costs.

The London Poles evinced an understandable interest in the fate of those who had been deported from Polish territories and in the fate of tens of thousands of soldiers captured by the Red Army in September 1939. With the reestablishment of diplomatic relations, the Soviet government allowed the formation of a small army on Soviet territory comprising ex-prisoners of war, under General Wladyslaw Anders, with the expectation that they would fight the common enemy. However, the Soviets never sufficiently equipped the Poles, either because they were unable or unwilling. Further, the Poles demanded a degree of autonomy that the Soviets were loath to concede; as a consequence, the army never saw action on the eastern front. The Soviet leadership finally allowed the Poles to leave the country in order to fight on the western front. This affair too left considerable bitterness on both sides.

The final break between the London Polish government and the Soviet government came as a result of the discovery of the Katyn massacres. The Germans announced in February 1943 that they had found the corpses of more than 4,000 Polish officers in the Katyn forest near Smolensk. The Germans put together an international commission that confirmed their allegation that the officers had been murdered in 1940, a year before the occupation of the district by the Germans. The Soviet government, of course, denied the accusation and blamed the Germans for the atrocity. The Poles, however, requested an investigation by the Red Cross. Relations between Stalin and the London Poles had been close to the breaking point before the Katyn affair, and now the Polish request to the Red Cross gave Stalin the opportunity he was looking for to break relations with their London government-in-exile.

The confirmed number of victims at Katyn was relatively small compared to the other atrocities carried out by Germans and Soviets, yet Katyn became a symbol of dreadful inhumanity. During the war and immediately afterwards, the Allies were compelled to accept the feeble Soviet explanation that the murders were carried out by the Germans. The Soviet authorities carried out a flimsy and transparently phony investigation, after the Red Army recaptured the Smolensk district in 1944: agents simply stuffed 1941 newspapers into the pockets of the uniforms of the corpses, purporting to show that the officers had been alive in 1941 and therefore could have been murdered only by the Nazis. Allied propaganda accepted this explanation. But what were the Allies to do? Should they have advertised to the world that their Soviet allies were hardly better than the Nazis and equally guilty of mass murder?

After the collapse of the Soviet Union and the opening of the archives, we have documentary proof that the mass shooting of the Polish officers was proposed by the head of the NKVD, Beria, who in his letter to Stalin gave no more justification for this atrocity than saying that the officers were enemies of the Soviet regime. Stalin, Molotov, Klement Voroshilov, Anastas Mikoian, Mikhail Kalinin, and Lazar Kaganovich all gave their approval.

Under Soviet patronage a so-called Union of Polish Patriots was formed, one that was willing to recognize the borders demanded by the Soviet Union. When the Red Army entered Poland, Stalin was in a commanding position: his union renamed itself the Committee of National Liberation and established itself in Polish territory in Lublin. The British and the Americans were tired of the intransigence of the London Poles; they considered them a nuisance that disturbed relations with their important ally, and in fact abandoned them.

In August 1944 the so-called Home Army, which owed its allegiance to the London Polish government, called for an uprising in Warsaw. The Home Army clearly had political motives: the Poles wanted to liberate their capital before the arrival of the Red Army. In the same way, also for political reasons, the Red Army gave no help to the insurgents. It was certainly in the interest of Stalin to see the destruction of the Polish anticommunist underground carried out by the Germans. Claiming that it was necessary to bring up reinforcements, the Red Army stopped at the outskirts of Warsaw and allowed the Germans to take brutal revenge on the Polish fighters. The uprising lasted for an amazingly long six weeks, while the inadequately equipped but heroic Poles held out against the regular German army. The Soviet Union not only gave no help, but refused landing rights to Allied planes that could have dropped supplies to the insurgents. The Soviets yielded only when it was obviously too late.

During the two great wartime conferences, at Tehran in 1943 and Yalta in January 1945, Roosevelt, Churchill, and Stalin spent a disproportionate amount of time and energy on the discussion of the Polish situation. The future of Eastern Europe was inextricably bound up with the resolution of this issue. This was because the Soviets were most unrelenting concerning Poland, and the Western Allies took a greater interest in it than in any other East European country. Yalta became the symbol of betrayal. The Allied leaders, especially Roosevelt, have been blamed for selling out the East Europeans, for being naive, for not foreseeing what kind of regimes the Soviets would establish in the occupied countries. These accusations miss the point: diplomacy had no chance against occupying armies. The Allies could have helped the East Europeans in only one way: they could have established a second front in 1943, or even better in 1942, so that the meetings of the Allied and Soviet armies would have taken place not in the center of Germany at the Elbe river, but further east. Of course, such a strategy would have required the sacrifice of hundreds of thousands of British and American soldiers. Understandably, neither the United States government nor the British were willing to make that sacrifice.

The Allies could have refused to recognize Soviet conquests. But it is unlikely that an open declaration of hostility would have improved Soviet behavior. On the contrary: the Soviet leaders, very much aware of the weaknesses of their country, would have found it necessary to make certain that no hostile government were allowed on their most sensitive western borders. A threat of military intervention would not have made much difference, for such a threat was not believable. Stalin knew as well as anyone that the West, completing one great war against a totalitarian state, was not in a political or psychological position to embark on another. Indeed, the Americans very much desired help against the Japanese, for they could not have foreseen that that war would also end quickly. At the end of the war in Europe, as far as the eastern half of the continent was concerned, the Soviets had the upper hand: their armies occupied it.

7

The Nadir: 1945–1953

THE ORIGINS OF THE COLD WAR

The dominant conflict during the forty-five years following the end of the Second World War was the hostility and competition between the Soviet Union and the West, in particular the United States. It is not surprising, therefore, that the origin of this conflict, the cold war, has occasioned an enormous and varied historiography. As is usually the case, the changes in approach of American historians occurred not because they learned new facts about the USSR, but because American politics, society, and public opinion changed. In the two decades following 1945, American historians were practically unanimous: the cold war was the fault of the Soviet Union. The Soviet Union, according to this view, was based on the explicit premise of spreading world revolution. Communism, like Nazism, was inherently expansionist, and therefore the West had no choice but to respond to Soviet threats. That response, such as building up military and economic power, the Marshall Plan, and the formation of NATO (North Atlantic Treaty Organization), was ultimately successful, and Soviet expansion was checked.

For Western scholars, the main evidence of Soviet expansionist designs was the creation of a system of satellites in Eastern Europe. These scholars believed that the Soviet leaders had a blueprint for world conquest in which the incorporation of Eastern Europe was merely the first step. They described a pattern: first, everywhere or almost everywhere in Eastern Europe, the communists created a genuine coalition government of antifascist parties. That initial step was followed by a second stage, the gradual emasculation of all noncommunist parties, accomplished by using crude pressure often involving the Red Army itself. At this stage the East European governments became sham coalitions; the format remained, but the independent leaders were removed one after another. Finally, in the third stage, all these countries ended up with openly communist regimes, and the coalition format was discarded.

At the time of the Vietnam War the American scholarly consensus broke down. A new generation of historians embarked on revisionism. According to the opinion of these mostly young scholars, the cold war was the consequence of the aggressive policies of the West, in particular of the United States. In the opinion of Gar Alperowitz, for example, the atomic bomb was dropped on Japan not in order to end the war but to frighten the Soviet Union and, in the view of Gabriel Kolko, Stalin's government was simply responding to American imperialist designs driven by economic interests. These revisionist historians paid little attention to the Soviet Union. They did not know the language, and they were not particularly interested in Soviet political culture. American archives were available and Soviet archives were not. It was possible therefore to find all sorts of ulterior motives to explain American policy and the Soviet Union could be portrayed as an object of policy, rather than an independent agent. The revisionists never fully dominated Western scholarship, and within a decade or two their anti-American, anticapitalist fury was largely spent. They may have made some contributions to the analysis of the formation of American policy, but they singularly failed in drawing a convincing picture of the origin of the cold war.

The outbreak of the cold war was overdetermined. That is, there were many reasons, given the nature of the two opposing camps, that the cooperation and friendship of wartime could not have continued long after the defeat of Germany. The Americans could not have lightly acquiesced to Soviet behavior in Eastern Europe. Given the nature of a more or less democratically controlled foreign policy, it is hardly conceivable that American policy could have been based on the sophisticated analysis of the diplomat and scholar George Kennan. Politicians could not easily have explained to their constituents that, while on the one hand the Stalinist Soviet Union was a murderous dictatorship, on the other it was not a threat to vital American interests, at least for the time being.

More significantly, no American concessions, such as the continuation of the lend-lease program that had been abruptly stopped, or even economic assistance in reconstruction, could have substantially modified Soviet behavior. Stalin and the Stalinists were morbidly suspicious. They had always felt that their rule was threatened, and now at the end of the war that threat seemed overwhelming. The country was destroyed, its economic power greatly diminished, its human resources almost exhausted, and social discipline had been unacceptably loosened.

The communist leaders correctly perceived that further contacts with the capitalist West were inherently subversive. The Stalinist response to the challenge was a furious attempt to reimpose order in the only way they knew: hundreds of thousands were sent to camps. It was considered essential to cut the Soviet peoples off from the rest of the world. The Soviet leaders did not need a war, and they dared not risk conquest if it implied the danger of war, but they above all could not tolerate friendly relations. The Stalinists depicted their country as surrounded by merciless enemies. The cold war suited their needs: it became a mobilization device that justified the harshest measures.

How can we characterize Soviet foreign policy of the period? How did the world in 1945 look from the perspective of Moscow? We can dismiss the proposition that Stalin had a considered plan for world conquest. First of all, the ideological passion for spreading world revolution had been abandoned long before. In any case, support for world revolution was dangerous, and Stalin's foreign policy, as compared to Khrushchev's, for example, was extremely cautious. He was, of course, willing to take advantage of opportunities to extend Soviet influence if that could be done without undue risk. But he dreaded situations that threatened his power. He made extraordinary, albeit futile, efforts to avoid being involved in the Second World War. During the war he cautioned the impetuous Marshal Josip Broz Tito; he abandoned the Greek communists to the British in 1944; he dissolved the Comintern in order not to endanger the grand alliance. The Soviet Union did not recognize the Chinese communists until they achieved their victory. In fact, the Stalinists were always very stingy in their support of indigenous revolutionary movements. Perhaps they foresaw that any movement that came to power on the basis of its own strength and effort would be unlikely to follow Soviet directives blindly, and would therefore be more trouble than it was worth.

As Stalin grew old, his mental abilities deteriorated and on occasion he made mistakes, such as underestimating Tito's strength and forcing Yugoslavia out of the Stalinist camp in 1948. Nevertheless, even in his old age he remained a subtle politician who by and large understood how far he could go. He had the great advantage that he did not have to worry about Soviet public opinion. Soviet foreign policy was thus capable of making sudden and abrupt changes that would have been inconceivable in the democratic world. He could evaluate the balance of forces, and never underestimated the significance of economic strength. Undoubtedly he was impressed by the atomic bomb, but he did not need a demonstration of nuclear weapons to have a healthy respect for American power. He knew that American productive capacity was hardly touched by the war at a time when his own country was in ruins. The Americans demobilized, but the Soviets demobilized even more quickly. They had no choice: the country could not have afforded the maintenance of wartime strength. The Stalinist leaders had neither the strength nor the desire to push the "boundaries of socialism" to the Atlantic Ocean, as some contemporary observers feared.

Even though Stalin was a capable politician, he did not have extraordinary foresight. No one foresaw the postwar status quo as it eventually emerged. The people in the Kremlin imagined the postwar situation on the basis of their previous experience. They expected that the Soviet Union would be a far more powerful and important player in world affairs than it had been, but they did not foresee a bipolar world; they expected that the struggle would be within each country for influence. In some countries, of course, they would have greater influence than the West, and vice versa, but the idea of the creation of hostile blocs has not yet arisen. They very much hoped, for example, for influence in Italy and France through the powerful communist parties there. At the same time they at least at the outset had no plans for setting up satellites.

The worldview of the Stalinist leadership was formed in the past and therefore was oriented toward Europe. It is not that these men paid no attention to Asia. They well remembered the Russo-Japanese war of 1904–05; of course they remembered the long border struggle during the 1930s against Japanese aggression; and they very much wanted to have bases on the Pacific. Their engagement in European affairs, especially in Eastern Europe, however, was of a different order. They continued to think of the primary importance of Germany, and very much worried about the revival of German militarism. The Soviet Union had the strength to project its power only to regions that were contiguous to its territory. In this sense the Soviet Union at the end of the Second World War was not yet truly a world power.

The Stalinist leaders had a minimum program: they wanted to prevent the reconstruction of the cordon sanitaire that had existed in the interwar period between themselves and Western Europe. At Versailles, French diplomacy had created a bloc of states that was to act as a counterweight against both resurgent Germany and Soviet Russia. The plan never really worked, because no combination of East European states could stand up to Nazi Germany. These states came to be potential and later real German allies and threatened Soviet security. Although not wanting hostile states on their border was a moderate goal, the consequences of Soviet policy were far from moderate. The problem was that the East European countries, especially Poland and Romania and to a lesser extent Hungary, could not be trusted from the Russian point of view. Soviet policymakers foresaw that, if these countries were allowed to form democratic governments, they would probably end up anti-Soviet. Thus a paradoxical situation was created: the more anti-Russian a people was, the weaker the communist party of an East European country, the more likely it was to fall under communist rule. By contrast, countries with little anti-Russian sentiment and strong communist parties, such as Finland and Czechoslovakia, had a chance of escaping Soviet domination.

Because of its size and location between Germany and the Soviet Union, from the Soviet point of view Poland was the most important country in Eastern Europe. Stalin was determined even when the war was far from decided that he would hold onto the acquired territories and would not allow the exiled government in London to return. The connection between the bitterly anti-Soviet prewar government and the London Poles was all too obvious. Poland's fate was the first to be decided: it was not going to be free and democratic. Stalin at Tehran and Yalta engineered Poland's move westward; it would be compensated for the lost eastern territories at the expense of Germany. From the Soviet point of view this solution had the advantage of not only weakening a future Germany, but also firmly tying Poland to the Soviet Union. It was assumed that no German government would long tolerate the loss of territories, and therefore that the Poles would have no alternative but seek Soviet protection.

The fate of Poland might be contrasted to that of Czechoslovakia. The Czech government in the interwar period was the only democratic one in Eastern Europe. Benes, the Czech foreign minister and later president, sought security for his country by attempting to bring the Soviet Union and the Western democratic governments together. The Czechs had a long history of friendly feelings for their brother Slavs the Russians, and Czechoslovakia possessed the only legal communist party in the interwar period. That party after the war emerged as the strongest, gathering 40 percent of the votes in the Czech lands and 30 percent in Slovakia. Ironically, the only country where an actual coup d'etat had to be carried out was Czechoslovakia in February 1948. This happened because in Czechoslovakia a genuine coalition survived until the world situation changed for the worse. Up to that point, it seemed that Czechoslovakia might share the fate of Finland and escape sovietization. It did not. By this time the lines in the cold war were sharply drawn, and the Soviet leaders could not afford a potential enemy in the center of Europe. Only Finland escaped sovietization. On the one hand, the Soviets were satisfied that Finland would not become a hostile base and, on the other, they feared that a communist Finland might push neutral Sweden into the arms of NATO.

How can we explain the obvious similarities in the sovietization of the satellites? As circumstances changed, so did Soviet policy. Surely the Soviets with the aid of the Red Army would have had an easier time setting up satellite regimes in 1945 than they did a couple of years later. Why did they not? It is remarkable that at certain times and places they went to considerable trouble to create coalitions. For example, we have the reminiscences of Wolfgang Leonhard, a young German communist who had spent the war years in Moscow. He and the other communists returned to Germany with instructions to help to organize the other non-Nazi, bourgeois parties to become respectable coalition partners.[1]

The Soviets feared Allied reaction. While they did not intend to continue friendly relations (which, by the way, were never very friendly on the Soviet side), they also did not want a Western Europe from which they were totally excluded. They must have calculated that an overly aggressive policy in Eastern Europe would ruin the chances for French and Italian communists to participate in their governments. The central feature of the 1945–48 period was the ever-sharpening definition of the two blocs. It became gradually clear that there could be no middle course. The last stage in this process was the Berlin blockade. Stalin hoped to squeeze the West out of Berlin, but the Americans responded forcefully and despite the logistical difficulties continued to supply the West Berliners. Following that event, the Soviet leadership accepted that it would influence only those regions it actually controlled.

The year 1948 was a turning point, the end of an era. In some ways it was a most gloomy period: end-of-the-war optimism had dissipated, and the cold war was in full force. On the other hand, the sharp division of Europe, an area by far the most important from the Soviet perspective, had achieved stability. The end of the Berlin blockade clearly established how far Soviet influence would go.

The Tito–Stalin break in the same year was also a consequence of the hardening line between the two camps. The Soviets in fact were presented with an alternative. They could control the East European satellites while giving them a modicum of autonomy, by allowing what was called at the time "different roads to socialism." Or they could impose absolute conformity, but in that case Yugoslavia, the only country that had played a role in its own liberation from Nazi rule, would have to be excluded. The Stalinists chose the second solution. Given the nature of the Stalinist regime in the postwar period, even slightly varying interpretations of Marxist dogma were simply unacceptable. What the Yugoslavs had in common with the Chinese was that they had established their communist regimes without the aid of the Red Army. It is of course not an accident that it was precisely these countries within their own camp that challenged Soviet authority.

From the point of view of the history of world communism the victory of the Chinese communists was incomparably more important than events in a medium-sized Balkan country. In China before Mao's victory the Soviet Union exercised extreme caution. Stalin would have been satisfied with a divided China or with a coalition regime. It is impossible to know whether the Soviets anticipated that communism in China might threaten their interests. Presumably they expected that the interwar situation in China would continue for the foreseeable future: it would remain weak and divided; the nationalists and the communists would continue fighting without either side being completely eliminated. They assumed that the Americans, traditionally interested in the Far East and in China in particular, would not allow a complete communist victory, and they did not consider China vital enough to challenge the Americans in this area. The Soviets waited to recognize the communist government until the complete victory of Mao's forces.

Soviet behavior at the time of the Korean War was also cautious. The Stalinists obviously miscalculated: they took it for granted that the Americans, who had allowed the conquest of China, would not respond forcefully to an affair that could be depicted as a civil war.[2] Once it became clear that this would not be a quick victory, the Soviet policymakers made sure to avoid a military conflict with the United States. The situation implied risks for the Soviet Union, and therefore Stalinist foreign policy was all the more cautious.

DEVASTATION AND RECONSTRUCTION

At the end of the war, many people in the West saw the Soviet Union, the country that had vanquished Hitler's Germany, as a mighty power, boundlessly ambitious and ready for new conquests. In fact, the country had been devastated beyond the imagination of Westerners, and the primary goal of the Stalinist leadership was not to push the borders of the Soviet Union to the Atlantic Ocean, but to reimpose discipline and order at home. This was not an easy task. In the territories conquered between 1939 and 1941, desperate guerrillas continued to fight against the troops of the NKVD and the Red Army for several years. Millions of citizens who had been exposed to foreign influences – and who therefore, from the paranoid Stalinist point of view, were not fully reliable – had to be reintegrated into Soviet society. Ideological orthodoxy that had been dangerously diluted during the war had to be reimposed. The collective farm system was in disarray. Even if the leadership had been bent on further conquests (it was not), under the circumstances it lacked the means. The war stretched the resources of the country to the furthest limits.

The human and material losses suffered by the Soviet Union were on a different scale from those inflicted on the other ex-belligerent countries. Even today, after the partial opening of the archives, the numbers are imprecise, but we may estimate that during the war 26–27 million Soviet citizens died. Among citizens of Ukraine and Belarus, the death rate was particularly high; after all, these were the districts where the fighting was the heaviest and German occupation had lasted longest. According to numbers published after the collapse of the Soviet Union, more than 8.5 million soldiers died on the battlefields.[3] Although there are no comparably exact figures, several million prisoners of war died in German camps, where they had been cruelly mistreated. The rest died as a result of enemy bombardment, starvation and cold, or mass executions carried out by the Nazis, or became victims of Stalinist terror and died in concentration camps or in places of exile. In addition, tens of thousands managed to escape forced repatriation and stayed in the West.

Even this extraordinarily high number of dead does not provide a complete picture of the demographic calamity. On the battlefield it was above all young men who died, and therefore in the immediate postwar years the working-age population in particular was reduced. The demographic imbalance between males and females that had begun at the time of the First World War, and had been exacerbated during famines (men are less able to endure starvation) and purges (which targeted men more than women), now reached extraordinary proportions. As late as 1951 there were 21 million more females than males in the Soviet population; and, according to the 1970 census, for every 620 men in the age group that served in the war (those born between 1916 and 1925) there were 1,000 women.[4] In other words, women had trouble finding husbands, mothers brought up their children without fathers, and the birth rate came to be depressed.

The Soviet people had experienced material deprivation before: the civil war and collectivization were both followed by famine. Subjectively, however, the post-Second World War period was perhaps the worst. People endured cold and hunger during the war, firmly believing that their misery was only temporary, and consoled themselves with visions of a richer and brighter future. But that better future was slow in coming. Farm equipment (25 percent of tractors) and animal herds (87 percent of hogs, 60 percent of horses) had been destroyed. In 1956 there were still fewer cows in the Soviet Union than there had been before the First World War in the Russian empire. In 1945 the output of agriculture was only 60 percent of what it had been before the war, and the overwhelmingly important grain output was less than half what it had been in 1940.[5] To the baneful consequences of the war a series of droughts were added, to produce a dreadful result. In 1946 the grain output was only a little over a third of what it had been in 1940. The peoples of the Soviet Union once again suffered a famine: the regions of the country that had been occupied by the Germans, and Ukraine in particular, were most hard hit. The regime, as in the 1930s, took no pity on the victims: not only did it fail to organize famine relief, but it covered up evidence of starvation, continued compulsory grain deliveries in the affected regions, and even exported grain. Indeed, how could the regime admit it could not feed its own people and at the same time claim to be a superpower, a state that had achieved socialism, an example for others to follow? Remarkably perhaps, the most shocking picture of misery comes from the memoirs of Nikita S. Khrushchev, who was at the time first secretary of the Ukrainian party organization. Reports came to him showing that people went mad of hunger and ate their own children. Corpses were discovered showing evidence that meat had been gnawed from the bones. If we are to believe Khrushchev, he was moved by these examples of suffering and pleaded with Stalin for help, but in vain.

It was under these extraordinarily difficult conditions that the task of economic reconstruction began. At the heart of the difficulties was the perennial problem sector of the economy, agriculture. After the ravages of collectivization there had been some improvement in the second half of the 1930s, largely because the regime allowed collective farm peasants to cultivate tiny private plots. But the improvements of the second five-year plan period were wiped out by the war. From the point of view of the regime there were two agricultural issues: how to increase production in order to provide the population with food, and how to reassert control over the villages. The party leaders pretended that the two goals were not only consistent, but in fact closely connected. The government was more successful in achieving the second goal than the first.

During the war discipline on the collective farms was substantially loosened. At least in some places, the peasants were able to expand their private plots at the expense of the collective, and the peasants grew what they wanted without state intervention. Indeed, some relatively few fortunate ones who lived near cities were able to take advantage of the shortage of food and sell their produce in the markets for high profits. During the war there had been rumors among the peasants, which the regime did nothing to contradict, that following victory the system of collective farms would be abolished. The government, however, following the disastrous harvest of 1946, issued a decree that compelled the peasants to return all lands that had previously belonged to the collectives, and reasserted the primary obligation of the collective farms to provide deliveries to the state. Not only were the collective farms not abolished, but between 1947 and 1949 the system was also extended to the Baltic states: the methods, the resistance, the consequences were the same as they had been in the previous decade in the rest of the country. In their desperation many Baltic peasants joined the guerrillas who were still fighting the Soviet state. The machine tractor stations, these outposts of the regime in the countryside, once again organized "political departments," which had the task of supervising the collective farms.

The peasantry was the mistreated stepchild of the Soviet regime. Conditions on the collective farms were deplorable. The majority of villages had no electricity, and hardly any of the peasant houses, most of them overcrowded shacks, had running water. During the war young men had been drafted from the villages into the army; many did not survive, and others, who did survive, showed no eagerness to return to the miserable conditions prevailing in the countryside. In any case the regime, constantly fearing subversion, had a policy of not allowing those who had been abroad to return to their villages. The Stalinists assumed that the returning soldiers or prisoners of war would be less likely to confide in strangers. Already in the 1930s people were overmotivated to leave the villages, but now the desire to escape became even greater. The consequence was that the labor force in the collective farms was a residue: disproportionately old, female, and ill educated. Combined with the shortage of investment in agriculture, and the low prices paid for agricultural products, it is understandable that productivity recovered very slowly. Not until the mid 1950s did Russia reach the per-acre productivity of 1913. The overall grain output in 1954 was still smaller than in 1913, and the per-acre productivity of 1963 was only a shade higher than in 1913.[6]

The decisions of the Soviet government were partially responsible for the slow recovery. Limiting private plots was occasioned by ideological rather than practical considerations. But, most importantly, the government continued to favor industry and was unwilling to pay the price that would have been necessary to increase farm production. The share of investment in agriculture, as long as Stalin was alive, remained pitifully low. The procurement prices the government paid for compulsory deliveries not only failed to pay for the cost of production, but on occasion did not even pay for the cost of transportation to the delivery points. Under the circumstances, incentives remained nonexistent. Just as before the war, the building of industry was based on the exploitation of the peasantry.

The Stalinist leadership hoped to improve agriculture without paying for the improvement. Constant reorganizations had always been a characteristic feature of the Soviet political system. Totalitarian Soviet society was never immobile. The desire to reorganize was based on the gap between high expectations and a reality that was not easy to mold. The leaders time and again thought they had found the right solution to their problems, that everything would work out fine, as ideology had promised. Needless to say, they were disappointed each time.

At first the regime put its faith in the so-called link system. That system, associated with the name of Andrei A. Andreev, the member of the Politburo responsible for agriculture, was introduced before the war. It meant that a few people (ranging from five to eight) assumed responsibility for cultivating a strip of land, and their income depended on their performance. The advantage of the system was that it offered some incentive to the workers, and in some aspects at least freed them from the constant intervention of the collective farm authorities. In the immediate postwar period the issue, much discussed in the press, was how suitable this form of organization was, especially for the most important product, grain. The MTSs understandably opposed the links, pointing out that they made the rational use of tractors more difficult.

The link system was also suspect for reasons of ideology: it smacked too much of individual enterprise and a return to private farming. Some even feared that the system undermined the very foundations of the collective farm. Perhaps if the system had led to a great increase in productivity, it would have been allowed to exist. But given the circumstances, it could not by itself solve the problems of the collective farms, and agriculture continued to languish.

The link system came to be repudiated, and with it its chief sponsor, Andreev. The new organization favored by the regime was the brigade, a much larger entity, sometimes including as many as 100 peasants. The brigade was built on assumptions that were the very antithesis of those on which the links were founded. This was the system associated with Nikita S. Khrushchev. Instead of making the working collectives smaller and therefore better connected with their work, the new system, adopted in 1950, aimed to make the collective farms larger. Soviet leaders had always assumed that giant size, both in industry and in agriculture, was superior and some-how more "modern." Furthermore, at a time when the regime found it difficult to establish control over the farms, the party and the government considered it easier to control a few big ones rather than many small ones. As a consequence of the new policy, the collective farms came to be amalgam-ated, and their number was thereby greatly reduced. The ultimate extension of the idea was to make peasants live like workers in apartment houses – in effect, in small cities. The peasants would have ceased to be peasants, and would have received higher income and some of the social benefits enjoyed by workers. This would be the realization of the age-old Marxist dream of eliminating the distinction between the town and the country.

Nothing came of this plan; indeed, it was explicitly repudiated in 1952 at the Nineteenth Party Congress. Society did not have the means to realize it, and furthermore, the party leaders understood that the peasants would resist the idea just as furiously as they had resisted collectivization – not so much because they hated to be parted from their villages, but because they would have lost their private plots, the economic mainstay of their existence.

Unlike agriculture, the recovery of industry was impressively quick. Aside from the many dreadful consequences of the war there was also something positive: as the Germans advanced, the Soviet authorities moved factories to the east. In the long run, the dispersal of factories benefited the country and contributed to industrialization of Siberia.

The industrial policy of the regime during the postwar years had the same features as it had during the great industrialization drive. The economy remained greatly overcentralized. As one would expect, the Stalinist leader-ship gave primary attention to the rebuilding of the producer goods segment of the economy, which by 1950, according to the unreliable Soviet figures, greatly surpassed prewar standards (although industries that produced con-sumer goods took much longer to rebuild). Even if we take into consider-ation the exaggerations built into Soviet statistics, it is still indisputable that the Stalinist methods worked, and that the speed of reconstruction was impressive.

The Soviet Union benefited from stripping industries from the defeated countries, primarily from eastern Germany, and to a lesser extent from the other countries of communist Eastern Europe. At the same time, the wealth that the Soviet Union thus acquired made up only a tiny fraction of its dreadful losses. Soviet economic achievements in the postwar period cannot be explained by pointing to the exploitation of the defeated.

Although the industrial working class did not suffer the abysmal poverty of the peasantry, standards of living in the cities did not catch up with low prewar standards for several years following the war. Immediately after the war the government eliminated the two-tiered price system for food, which meant a halt to government subsidies. In 1947 the government introduced a financial reform that devalued the ruble ten to one. The purpose of this move was to confiscate the money that some peasants had managed to accumulate and deposit in banks.

After 1948 there was a gradual improvement in living standards in the cities, but nevertheless people suffered from shortages of almost everything. The favored Soviet method for improving standards of living of urban inhabitants was a gradual lowering of food prices. The decision to lower prices repeatedly was made on political, rather than economic, grounds. After all, food remained in extremely short supply. The leaders rightly believed that lowering prices would make a greater positive impression than increased wages. The artificial changing of the price structure further worsened the position of the peasantry vis-à-vis the rest of the population.

The diet of the working classes was monotonous: it was largely limited during the winter to potatoes, cabbage, and bread. Clothing was of bad quality and so expensive that everything – coats, shoes, and shirts – had to last for a long time. The situation was most desperate in housing. The industrialization drive that had preceded the First World War created a proletariat that was poorly housed in the fast-growing cities. (In 1913, an urban family had 7 square meters per person of living space.) The Soviet authorities, bent on a breakneck pace of industrialization, badly neglected housing construction, and the situation was getting worse. The war demolished entire cities: Leningrad, Kiev, Stalingrad, and dozens of others were almost completely destroyed. Housing in the countryside was not spared: in 1945, 25 million people were left homeless. In the following two decades people in the cities lived in circumstances that are difficult to imagine. Six or seven families would share old apartments, most of them in buildings constructed before the First World War. Women had to wait their turn at the stove. There were instances when rooms were assigned to several families and there was not enough space for beds, so people had to sleep on mattresses on the floor. (Average living space per person in 1955 was still only 5.1 square meters. On average, even as late as 1958, 3.2 persons shared one room.) Communal living and utter lack of privacy were among the most characteristic features of Soviet life in those years.

POLITICAL CULTURE

The last years of Stalin were the darkest and gloomiest in all of Soviet history. Families mourned their dead, people lived in grinding poverty, and the Stalinists, instead of relaxing the oppressive features of the Soviet regime, further tightened the screws. "Traitor peoples" who had been deported during the war were not allowed to return, and the concentration camps filled up once again. People who had collaborated with the enemy, or were accused of collaborating, ex-prisoners of war, nationalists who had fought against Soviet power, in particular people who in the Baltic region and western Ukraine had resisted collectivization, and, just as in the 1930s, people who had committed no crimes by any definition but were accused of "anti-Soviet activities" were sentenced to years of servitude. At a time when those who lived in liberty suffered privations, people in the camps were still much worse off. Men and women weakened by malnutrition and mistreatment, working long days in labor camps, died by the hundreds of thousands. For the first time in Soviet history, the unendurable conditions on occasion resulted in riots and strikes in the camps, which were brutally suppressed.

Communist ideology had long been emptied of meaning, reduced to the repetition of meaningless phrases. Professional ideologists, people of undistinguished intellectual abilities, asserted that the country had already "achieved socialism" and now was building communism. The ideological nakedness of the regime was covered up by the creation of a surrogate ideology of hero worship, which now reached pagan proportions. The leader's pictures were everywhere, poets sang his praises, painters painted him, his name found its way into every book published, including cookbooks. From the very outset the Stalin cult differed in content and style from Hitler's cult. Hitler, as long as he was successful, loved to harangue the masses and see himself in newsreels; he was an actor. Stalin, by contrast, had little desire for such satisfaction. A pock-marked little man, speaking poor Russian, and an indifferent orator, he did not like to appear before audiences. After the war he gave only two speeches: one at the time of the election campaign in 1946 and the other at the Nineteenth Party Congress in 1952, when he spoke for five minutes. (He allowed his apparent successor, Georgii Malenkov, to give the main report.) He did not even like to appear in closeups on movie screens. On rare occasions when he did appear, the audience gasped in amazement: this was not the way they had imagined their leader. Instead, Stalin had an idealized image created for himself that bore little resemblance to the historical figure. This imaginary leader fit well into the world of Soviet propaganda, where equally imaginary happy peasants competed to produce more food for happy factory workers. It was grimly appropriate that a mythical leader should head a mythical society.

There is some evidence to show that, at least in the early stages of the Stalin cult, the dictator had an ironic attitude toward it. Isaac Babel, the great writer who became a victim of the terror, described an episode to a Hungarian friend. Babel and Gorky were visiting Stalin when the dictator's daughter Svetlana came in. Stalin said to her: "Tell the father of the peoples, the leader of the world proletariat, what you learned in the school today."[7]

During the Second World War agitators found it advantageous to underplay communism in their ideological appeals, but they did not deemphasize the role of the leader. On the contrary, the cult of Stalin as a surrogate ideology developed further. It was at this time that Stalin became a brilliant general. After all, during the war Soviet soldiers were being sent to battle "for the motherland and for Stalin." Films made during this period depicted Stalin as winning the war practically single-handedly. Stalin was depicted as the father of his people, the greatest philosopher, statesman, and so on. In order to get a flavor of the adulation it is necessary to quote at some length from contemporary writings. This one, chosen almost at random, by a contemporary film director named Otar Chiaureli, appeared in a film journal in 1947:

> Many Soviet artists saw Comrade Stalin frequently, had conversations with him, heard his voice, looked into his eyes, saw his warm smile, felt his handshake. In the simplicity of his words there is the wisdom of the ages; in his eyes there is the brightness of genius; in his gestures there is self-confidence; in his dealings with you there is the simplicity of a great human being. How to show in art the magnificence of this simplicity? Here in front of you is a person who comprehends with the profundity of a philosopher the complex organism of the universe, our world, the relationship of classes, societies, and states. In front of you is a person who comprehends the incomprehensible, who is a carrier of great ideas and the representative of the moving force of history. He calmly and thoughtfully converses with you, and in his appearance there is nothing extraordinary; he does not seem to differ from any Soviet person, worker, peasant, scholar, artist. For all of these people he is close, comprehensible – a family member. Involuntarily you begin to think that Stalin is more than a human being. This thought arises from the impossibility of comprehending that everything great is simple. Although your mind affirms that this is so, your feelings search for some sort of outward sign of greatness. No! In spite of everything, he is different from ordinary people even in appearance. I long looked at his hands, followed his every movement, wanted to preserve in my mind even the smallest details of his appearance, gestures, every line in his face, his expressions, his way of speaking. And all this time the thought did not leave me that unconsciously I wanted to "bring down to earth" the figure of this great man, to bring his figure into our everyday language. But that very moment I understood the grandiosity of his work and once again felt everything about him is extraordinary: his hands, his smile, his eyes. Please forgive me, my artist colleagues, but none of us has succeeded. None of the portraits of Stalin can be regarded as satisfactory. None of us artists succeeded in transmitting the warm glow in his eyes, the charm of his smile, the hidden, deep humor of his well-chosen words, those hardly noticeable details which belong only to him, which make up the figure, which is simple, but epic.[8]

Stalin came to be isolated from Soviet reality. He formed an imaginary picture of the world around him, largely on the basis of movies and newsreels made for him. He became the primary victim of Soviet propaganda: other Soviet citizens could evaluate the picture they got from newspapers and films against the world in which they actually lived, but Stalin believed what he wanted to believe. In a sense, then, the convinced communists who survived in camps and were saying to one another, "If Stalin only knew!" were correct: Stalin did not know what was happening in his own country.

At first he considered it politically advantageous to foster a personality cult, but in later years he came to acquire a faith in his own infallibility; it was impossible to contradict him on however minor an issue, however obvious his error. Milovan Djilas in his book reports on an incident when Stalin insisted that Holland was not part of "Benelux," and no one surrounding him had the courage to point out that the "ne" in the word denoted the Netherlands.

Politics – that is, the discussion of complex issues facing society – continued to be restricted to a narrow elite; the public saw only the faintest shadows of the disputes as they appeared in the newspapers. As in any society, decisions had to be made. Although economic decisionmaking was highly centralized, the issue still remained how much decentralization should be allowed. To what extent could the setting of prices, a kind of surrogate market mechanism, be allowed to function? To what extent should heavy industry be given priority over consumer goods? Should investments be made in the reconstruction of the old industrial base, or should more attention be given to areas that had been peripheral in the prewar period, such as the Far East and Central Asia? Should agriculture be administered by a single ministry or should different parts of it be administered separately? The conduct of foreign policy also, of course, presented pertinent issues for resolution.

Soviet society was totalitarian: no aspect of human life remained outside the presumed competence of the authorities, no autonomous organizations were allowed to exist, and fear governed the life of all, from the lowliest peasant to members of the Politburo. But of course that did not mean that this political system functioned like a well-oiled machine, that one man alone, namely Stalin, made all the decisions. On the contrary: totalitarian societies are never efficient. In this totalitarian society, properly constituted institutions were emasculated, and decisions were made in a haphazard fashion. Leaders competed for power – that is, for Stalin's favor – advocating different and often conflicting policies. It is impossible to say to what extent the disputes were genuine, occasioned by deeply held differences of opinion, and to what extent they were maneuverings, because most likely the protagonists themselves did not know it.

Stalin allowed his followers to become associated with a set of policies and, if those policies failed, the person responsible could be demoted or removed. He was never responsible for errors; he only claimed credit for successes. It is unclear whether Stalin consciously cultivated this style of leadership or whether, more likely, he was increasingly losing touch with the surrounding world.

During these years, the standards of political life declined even further than the already abysmally low standards of the 1930s. Stalin preferred to have mediocre people around him, people who presented no danger to him, no possible alternative to his rule. The people who surrounded Stalin and governed in his name were not a distinguished group. None of them showed great intellect or strength of character. People who had long been associated with him, who had supported him at every turn of past struggles, such as Molotov, Voroshilov, and Mikoian, were pushed into the background, and their places were taken by younger people such as Zhdanov, Beria, Malenkov, Khrushchev, and Nikolai Vosnesenskii. All of them were, of course, beneficiaries and architects of mass murder, and all served Stalin faithfully. Even now, when the archives are more or less open, it is difficult to form a picture of these people as individuals. They were singularly devoid of personality – with the exception of Khrushchev, who, after he assumed power and especially in retirement, revealed himself to be an original figure, altogether human in his strengths and failings.

We have only glimpses of how high politics worked during these years. Only a handful of first-hand accounts have come down to us written by people who had extensive contact with Stalin. One of the most valuable of these is Khrushchev's memoirs, published in the West after he lost power. Khrushchev, of course, had an ax to grind. He needed to justify himself both for working for Stalin and for denouncing him later. We have a few other descriptions: one from Stalin's daughter Svetlana, who rarely saw her father in these years; another, a remarkably insightful description from Djilas, the Yugoslav leader, who later repudiated communism; a third from Molotov, who at that particular time was not close to Stalin; and one from the well-known Soviet writer Konstantin Simonov, who seldom saw Stalin.[9]

Especially from Khrushchev's description, a horrifying picture emerges. In his last years Stalin suffered from a variety of illnesses and was only a shadow of his former self. He was mortally afraid of being assassinated and trusted no one. Each and every dish had to be tasted first by his guests before he would eat. Even the highest institutions of the regime, such as the Politburo, were reduced to insignificance, and major decisions were taken by an ever-changing and haphazard small group of advisers. Whoever were at the moment Stalin's favorites would be invited to long evening sessions in the Kremlin or to his dacha, where they would watch movies and between the reels would discuss governmental business. Stalin's main pleasure was to humiliate and embarrass those who were closest to him. He insisted that his entourage drink themselves insensible, and no one dared to refuse. Under the circumstances it is not surprising that cirrhosis of the liver was an occupational disease in the highest circles. Members of this all-male company were often forced to dance with each other – something for which they had no greater talent than they did for statesmanship.

The tenure and power of the handful people at the top at all times remained tenuous. In these years Molotov was not invited to spend his evenings with Stalin, and his Jewish wife was arrested; Kaganovich's brother was in a camp, and he himself, as a Jew at the time of the "anticosmopolitan" campaign, was barely tolerated; Zhdanov, who at the height of his power and influence between 1946 and 1948 was the most powerful leader after Stalin, died in mysterious circumstances in 1948, quite possibly murdered; Vosnesenskii was executed; Mikoian's son was for a time arrested; Khrushchev's influence and power declined when Ukraine suffered famine – he appealed to Stalin for help and regained his influence, perhaps because he seemed so innocuous; Malenkov in 1946 was sent to Uzbekistan, away from the center of power; Beria, the most sinister of Stalin's associates, the head of the secret police apparatus, was a particular object of Stalin's suspicions during the last months of the tyrant's life. In this strange world political fortunes could change from one moment to the next.

Immediately after the war, Zhdanov's star was on the rise. Malenkov's demotion was most likely the result of Zhdanov's influence, and his closest associates, Aleksei A. Kuznetsov and Vosnesenskii, received important assignments. Zhdanov's faction is described as "party revivalist," meaning that his policies aimed to bring back the ideological rigidity loosened during the war. He controlled the Leningrad party organization, and his power was partially based on the party as opposed to government machinery. Zhdanov also participated in the formulation of foreign policy and was primarily responsible for relations with foreign communist parties. However, shortly before his death in 1948 his influence ebbed, and the victors in this struggle behind the scenes were Malenkov and Beria. Malenkov, who after 1948 until Stalin's death seemed to be in the strongest position to inherit the leadership, based himself on the vast governmental bodies that oversaw the entire centralized economy. Those who considered him a liberal (as opposed to Zhdanov) saw him as a defender of technocrats, factory managers, and nonideological experts. After the defeat and death of Zhdanov, Malenkov moved quickly to solidify his position by carrying out the last major bloody purge aimed at the elite. Malenkov and Beria fabricated the so-called Leningrad affair. Zhdanov's most important followers – Vosnesenskii, one of the most able leaders, a member of the Politburo and a chief economist among the leaders; A. A. Kuznetsov, a secretary of the central committee; and P. S. Popkov, the Leningrad party secretary – were not only removed from their positions and arrested, but executed. Unlike the prewar years, they were spared a show trial, and the charges against them were never published.

The last years of Stalin had a nightmarish quality. There were periodic purges uncovering "conspiracies," and people expected even more bloodletting to come.

THE POLITICS OF CULTURE

The dark years between the end of the Second World War and Stalin's death present us with voluminous material, a veritable case study of a culture under limitless tyranny. In 1945 no one foresaw what was ahead. In the euphoria of victory many believed that the people had showed their commitment to the Soviet form of government and could therefore be trusted, that terror was not necessary to maintain stability. The leaders thought otherwise. During the war for tactical reasons they had allowed considerable laxity in ideological matters. Sometime in 1946, however, they decided that it was essential to restore communist ideology in its most dogmatic and narrow-minded form, and gradually tightened the screws.

Some Western historians have argued that this tightening was the consequence of the break with the West. It was necessary to mobilize the country to face a new enemy. More likely it was the other way around: the Stalinists, fearing social disintegration and aware of the great weaknesses of the regime, recognized that continued friendly relations with the West were too dangerous and subversive. They needed the cold war.

The major turning point occurred in August and September 1946, when a series of resolutions were published under the authority of the Central Committee of the Communist Party. The decision was made at the highest level – we cannot tell from archival sources how the decision was made or whether there were discussions or disagreements – that Soviet-style discipline had to be reimposed in all aspects of the life of the nation. This tightening was not limited to the intellectual sphere. During the same period the regulation concerning "strengthening discipline in the collective farms" was also published. The cumulative effect of the condemnations and brutal attacks on individual intellectuals was to further narrow the sphere of the permissible in the intellectual life of the nation. More and more topics were placed beyond legitimate discourse.

We do not know what role Andrei Zhdanov, the man responsible for ideology in the Politburo, played in the adoption of the new policies. But since he articulated them and was their most visible spokesman, the two years between 1946 and his death in August 1948 came to be called the Zhdanovshchina. It would be wrong to see him as the single author. As the "Yezhovshchina" was not Yezhov's creation, nor was the Zhdanovshchina Zhdanov's. The policies were Stalin's, even though, as chief ideologist, it was Zhdanov whose task it was to carry them out. The victims of Zhdanov's denunciations did not lose their lives, and after Zhdanov's fall and death in 1948 both the intellectual climate and the terror became worse. For this reason some historians describe Zhdanov as a moderate. But the changes occurred not because of the different personalities who temporarily seemed to possess Stalin's trust, for Stalin trusted no one. More likely, the changes occurred because of changed circumstances.

The best-known and indeed perhaps the most significant of the staged events was in literature. The method here as elsewhere was to choose examples for attack, thereby defining the limits of the permissible and conveying in the most concrete terms what was expected. The party chose two journals, *Zvezda* and *Leningrad*, and two prominent literary figures, the humorist Mikhail Zoshchenko and the great poet Anna Akhmatova, as object lessons. On August 15, 1946, Zhdanov delivered a speech to the leadership of the Leningrad party organization, followed by a day-long discussion in which the various dignitaries echoed Zhdanov's arguments and exercised self-criticism. The next day Zhdanov repeated his performance and participated in another meeting where he made more or less the same points to an organization of Leningrad writers. In his speeches he blamed the party leaders and writers for lack of vigilance. Party leaders and writers then heaped abuse on the unfortunate artists; in usual Soviet style, the leadership insisted on making everyone into an accomplice. One of the sad ironies of the situation was that within a few years all the leading figures of the Leningrad party organization who participated in this meeting themselves became victims of the so-called Leningrad affair.

Although this was more than an attack on two individual creative figures, and the intention was to redefine – that is, to further limit – the sphere of the permissible, the two figures were well chosen from the party's point of view. Zoshchenko, a brilliant satirist, had been criticized during the war for his strange (in Soviet circumstances) autobiographical work, *Before Sunrise* – it was called self-indulgent, Freudian, apolitical. Akhmatova, perhaps the greatest living poet, had always been only barely tolerated. It is correct to say, and this is of course to their credit, that the two figures stood outside the mainstream of Soviet literature. The journal *Leningrad* was closed down, and the editorial board of *Zvezda* was changed. Akhmatova and Zoshchenko were expelled from the Union of Writers.

It would not have been necessary to spend so much time on only two people. That the intention of the party was greater than merely condemning two writers became clear two weeks later, when the party condemned the repertoire of theaters as apolitical and containing too many second-rate Western plays. Over the next months it was the turn of the filmmakers. Once again, the method was the same. A Central Committee resolution, published on September 4, made an example of a mediocre film called *A Great Life*, by director L. Lukov. At the same time works of such luminaries of Soviet cinema as Grigorii Kozintsev, Leonid Trauberg, Vsevolod Pudovkin, and Sergei Eisenstein were attacked. It must be admitted that the Soviet treatment of intellectuals was egalitarian: the outstanding and the second-rate received the same abuse. A chief accusation against the artists was that they had paid "too much attention to personal problems" rather than to social issues. A Soviet artist was not to waste his time worrying about such personal matters as love, jealousy, or death. The other point made by the critics was that the artists painted too gloomy a picture of Soviet reality. Zoshchenko, in his story "The Adventures of an Ape," gave the impression that it was better to live in a cage in the zoo than in a Soviet city; and Lukov in his film came close to giving a realistic picture of the difficult material conditions of the Soviet people immediately after the war. Soviet artists, in other words, were expected to widen further the gap between the world as depicted by them and reality. The socialist realist artist was to see the germs of the beautiful future in the less-than-perfect present; the distinction between the "is" and the "ought" was to be abolished.

The consequences for Soviet art were devastating. The party micromanaged the writing of novels, and requirements changed all the time. Aleksandr Fadeev, for example, who had written about the heroic exploits of a group of young people during the war in a way that corresponded to contemporary requirements, had to rewrite his novel, *The Young Guard*. The writer now had to show that in fact the Communist Party played a major role in the leadership of the partisan movement. Filmmaking was almost obliterated. While in the late 1920s about 120 films were made annually in Soviet studios, during the last years under Stalin the situation became so difficult that no more than 4 or 5 films were completed each year. These films were so uniform and so lacking in artistic interest that even contemporary observers pointed out that dialog could easily be moved from one film into another without the audience noticing. Because Soviet cinemas had so few new films to show, they continued to exhibit some of the successful films made two decades earlier and, absurdly, showed captured films – so-called trophy films – that were recut and equipped with new subtitles to make them suitable for Soviet audiences. Most of these were mindless musicals without political content.

Given the character of the Soviet state, one can understand why the regime considered it essential to control down to the smallest details literature and cinema, which by their very nature were likely to carry ideological messages. It is harder to understand why such control needed to be extended to branches of art which did not carry any ostensible ideological message, such as music. The Soviet regime, however, did not tolerate the notion that there was anything outside its competence or, indeed, that experts, artists, scholars in any field whatever had any autonomy beyond the reach of the regime. The Central Committee of the party claimed that it could decide better than musicians which was a good opera and which was not, what was good music and what was not. In February 1948 the object of attention was Vano Muradeli's *The Great Friendship*, by all accounts a dreadful work by a third-rate composer. The occasion was used for once again denouncing "formalist" music, that is, the kind of music that an average listener, leaving the concert hall, could not hum on his way home. The musicians were criticized for producing "antipopulist," dissonant music without memorable melodies. Sergei Prokofiev and Dmitrii Shostakovich had the "honor" of being chosen as the primary representatives of formalism; neither international reputation nor past services to the regime protected an artist. For comparison, we should recall that the leaders of Nazi Germany also objected to modern "decadent" music; however, the boundaries were drawn even more narrowly in the Soviet

Union. Richard Strauss, a favorite of the Nazis, composed music that could not have been performed at the height of Stalinism.

In the Stalinist conception, Soviet art, music, literature, and cinema were based on different principles and were superior to anything produced in the West. The Stalinists extended this idea even to the sciences. In their view there was a bourgeois, reactionary science and a progressive, socialist science. According to their reasoning it was not the task of scientists to prove or disprove Marxist precepts, for their "truth" had been established, but – conversely – the correctness of scientific propositions depended on whether they could be reconciled with the most simple-minded pronouncements of vulgar Marxism. Since members of the Central Committee by definition were better Marxists than, let us say, physicists, the ultimate arbitrator of scientific work was the leadership of the Communist Party.

The social sciences suffered the most. The disciplines of sociology and political science did not exist, and the writing of modern history came to be so distorted that no worthwhile texts survive from this period. Stalin at the end of his life wrote a short pamphlet on economic issues and, oddly, took a special interest in linguistics. In his essay "Economic Problems of Socialism in the USSR," he made the rather unstartling observation that the laws of economics would continue to apply, and that the Soviet Union could go on building socialism even without the triumph of world revolution. In his essay on linguistics, he refuted the nonsensical theories associated with the linguist Nikolai Marr, according to which language, as part of the "superstructure," would change under communism, and all the people of the world would come to speak the same language, an amalgam of all languages. He proposed his own theory, just as nonsensical but more in tune with the spirit of the times: the language of socialism would be Russian.

Neither did the physical sciences escape. In Nazi Germany, Einstein's relativity theory was attacked as "Jewish" science; in the Soviet Union it was dismissed as bourgeois science. Nor could Marxist science accept the idea that the path of movement of subatomic particles was unpredictable: "electrons could not possess free will," announced the party secretaries. Despite the antiscientific and anti-intellectual pronouncements, Soviet physics, unlike biology, was not destroyed. In their everyday work the scientists could safely disregard the "theories" promulgated by the vulgar Marxists, because they were able to produce miracles – that is to say, nuclear weapons.

The situation was different in biology in general, and in genetics in particular. Soviet geneticists, who were among the most prominent scientists in their field in the 1920s, by the nature of their discipline could not produce miracles. As so often in the past, utopian solutions grew out of miserable realities. The Stalinists wanted to revamp backward, miserable agriculture, but were unwilling to pay the price of heavy investment. At a time when incremental solutions offered little comfort, many came to be attracted to the extraordinary, the supernatural. The path was open for a charlatan such as Trofim Lysenko.

The story of Lysenko is an important one, not only because of the great harm he did to Soviet agriculture and science, but also because his story is so revealing of the nature of the Stalinist regime. Lysenko first attracted some notice in the late 1920s. His achievement was "vernalization," which meant that after soaking and chilling the seeds – in order to "make them get used to the cold" – winter wheat was planted in the spring. This process was completely without scientific foundation and of course never produced verifiable results. Lysenko and his supporters based an enormous and entirely false superstructure on this half-baked idea. This was the time of "the great socialist transformation." The Stalinists proudly proclaimed that there were no "fortresses that the Bolsheviks could not storm." One of the fortresses that they stormed and demolished was genuine science. Lysenko managed to gain the approval of the authorities by clothing himself in Marxist garb, and was thus protected from normal scientific criticism. His "scientific theories," such as the Lamarckian belief that acquired character-istics could be transmitted, raised an issue central to Soviet science of the 1940s: the repudiation of the notion that there are any scientific principles independent of the nature of society.

By the mid 1930s Lysenko had accumulated enough power to destroy his opponents, and used this power mercilessly. One of the greatest Soviet scientists and Lysenko's main opponent, Nikolai I. Vavilov, fell victim to the purges. But the apogee of Lysenko's success and power came in the postwar world. At this point that debate on issues raised by Lysenko came to an end, and the topics of genes and heredity were placed beyond legitim-ate discussion. During the following years Lysenko's followers' nonsensical pronouncements could not be criticized. Soviet science now described genes as the creations of metaphysical, bourgeois, reactionary science. According to Lysenko and his followers, under unfavorable conditions wheat could metamorphose itself into weeds. Furthermore, if there were no genes, of course there could not be genetically caused illness, and Soviet medical science stopped looking for cures for those diseases.

During 1948 Zhdanov gradually lost some of his power; he died in August of that year, when his functions as chief ideologist were taken over by Mikhail Suslov. It is futile to try to guess the reasons for Zhdanov's diminishing influence. Some have speculated that he paid the price for not having taken an energetic enough position in support of Lysenko; others saw the cause of his fall in the changed Soviet policy toward Tito. Zhdanov was one of the architects of the Cominform, an organization in which Yugoslavia was to play a major role. But there is no need to search for any particular cause: no one could retain Stalin's favor for long. Being part of the top leadership was both a dangerous and an uncertain position.

Although Zhdanov's name came to symbolize the worst in the cultural policies of the regime, his death did not bring any improvement, but rather the contrary. In the Zhdanov era, people who were denounced lost their jobs and survived; after 1948 the terror became bloodier. This is not to imply, as some historians have done, that Zhdanov was a moderate in any meaningful sense; it is simply that the character of the Stalinist regime changed constantly. Most likely the deterioration was caused by Stalin's ever-increasing paranoia. The trends already in motion now accelerated. In the severely limited public sphere, the same few topics were repeated time and again: (1) "vigilance," fear of subversion from the West, (2) "anticosmopolitanism," and (3) a vastly overblown Russian nationalism.

These themes were closely connected, and all were introduced into Soviet ideology before the end of the war. Nationalism, which became a strong component of Soviet ideology in the late 1930s, had become a guiding principle during the struggle against the Nazis. Millions of Soviet citizens at that time acquired some acquaintance with the West and saw that life in Europe was better and the standard of living higher. These experiences undermined the claim that the Soviet Union was the most advanced and progressive society on the face of the earth. Soviet propagandists dealt with the problem with a sleight of hand: they greatly exaggerated Soviet and past Russian achievements. The campaign that reached full flowering in 1948 and 1949 emphasized anti-Semitism, more or less implicitly; insisted on the superiority of everything Russian, projecting this superiority into the past; and called for vigilance concerning contacts with the West.

In the development of anti-Semitism, oddly, the war against Hitler was a contributing factor. The leaders probably feared that Hitler's identification of Bolsheviks with Jews could be successful and had to be combated. Perhaps the Soviet leaders were influenced by Nazi propaganda. Whether Stalin in his early career successfully hid his anti-Semitism, or whether this prejudice developed later is unclear, but it is evident that gradually he removed almost all Jews from positions of power and influence. He very much objected to his daughter Svetlana marrying a Jew, and Svetlana later reported that her father made the crudest anti-Semitic remarks. The creation of Israel was a major factor contributing to the anti-Semitic policies of late Stalinism. It was not so much that a pro-Arab policy was considered superior, but rather that the creation of a Jewish state presented the danger of divided loyalties among Jews. Given the ambitions of a totalitarian state, such divided loyalties could not be tolerated; Jews could not be trusted.

During the last years of Stalin, anti-Semitism reached murderous proportions. Most of those who participated in the state-sponsored Jewish anti-fascist committee, which had the task of collecting money abroad during the war, were killed. The "doctors' plot," devised by Stalin during the last months of his life, was directed against doctors, almost all of them Jewish, who were accused of attempting to murder high government functionaries.

The government more or less openly discriminated against Jews, and many, though not all, were removed from scientific and educational institutions. Jews ceased to play significant roles in the party or in administration. The country was a hairbreadth away from the revival of pogroms, this time organized by the government.

"Rootless cosmopolitan" was frequently used as a synonym for Jew, but the vast and brutal anticosmopolitan campaign also had other goals: by overstating past Russian achievements it aimed to compensate for the Russian feeling of inferiority and backwardness, particularly among the millions who had come into contact with Europe during the war. Claiming credit for past achievements reached ludicrous extremes. According to Soviet publicists, all major scientific achievements of the nineteenth century were made by Russians. Russian philosophy of the nineteenth century had to be described as the most "advanced." Marx and Engels became honorary Russians. Such nonsense could be propagated because there was no one who could have pointed out the emptiness of the pretensions. According to the newly formulated ideology of the Stalinist publicists, the tsarist state was not to be blamed for suppressing small nations, or even for being the protector of the rich against the poor, but above all for being an incompetent defender of the national interest. Who would have dared to point out that the Bolsheviks in 1904 and 1905, during the war against Japan, had hoped for the victory of the enemy?

In order to block or at least limit subversive influences, the regime went to extraordinary lengths to prevent contacts with the outside world. Of course, no ordinary citizen could travel abroad, and no one was allowed to marry a foreign national. A film critic who wrote with admiration about the films of Charlie Chaplin (whose films at the time could not be shown in the United States because he was suspected of communist sympathies) was denounced for groveling before the West. The notion that science knew no borders was described as a reactionary, anti-Soviet idea. Soviet scientists who in the different atmosphere of the war had published with official permission in Western scientific journals were now punished and had to exercise self-criticism. Needless to say, it was not Western but Soviet science that suffered as a consequence.

8

The Age of Khrushchev

Stalin made such a profound impression that our image of Soviet history is largely determined by him. Just as Nazism is unimaginable without Hitler, so the Soviet form of communism is inconceivable without Stalin. The questions that have occupied – and divided – Western historians of the Soviet Union concerned the causes of Stalin's victory in the 1920s and the nature and extent of continuity from the era of Lenin to the era of Stalin. What was it in Marxism and Leninism that made the rise of a Stalin inevitable, as some historians think, or at least possible, as others are constrained to admit? Were there genuine alternatives to Stalin? Stalin's rule also presents us with many difficult issues: Why did the tyrant kill so many? How did the Soviet form of totalitarianism function? How much support did he receive from the people? After 1953 the central issue for the leaders and peoples of the USSR was how to deal with Stalin's monstrous legacy. It was obvious that the continued existence of the political system without Stalin was an impossibility, yet in 1953 neither the Soviet people nor the political elite could imagine a different government. For many years Soviet society groped for a new equilibrium, one that was not easily found.

KHRUSHCHEV'S VICTORY

Stalin suffered a stroke and after a brief illness died on March 5, 1953. His death must have brought relief to many who feared a new purge. His closest collaborators feared for their lives. Beria, in particular, saw himself in danger: there were signs that the suspicious Stalin was turning against him, and Beria was losing his grip on power. If we are to believe contemporary observers, such as Stalin's daughter Svetlana, and Khrushchev, Beria could hardly contain his joy at the demise of his master. Yet, as recently available documents concerning the public mood at the time testify, the most

Stalin's funeral: Kaganovich, Bulganin, Molotov, Malenkov, Beria

prominent emotion both among the leaders and among the common people was not relief but anxiety. People understood that an era had ended, but few could imagine their lives without Stalin. The uncertainty was frightening, and people – incredibly for the distant observer – genuinely mourned the tyrant's passing. Even many among those who had been victims of his vicious dictatorship wept, and the country was near mass hysteria.

The first days after Stalin's death seemed to justify the fears of those who believed that only he could guarantee order. The body was put on display at the House of the Trade Unions in the center of Moscow, and at four o'clock on the afternoon of March 6 the doors were opened. The organizers of the funeral attempted to choreograph the occasion with the same precision with which such events had always been staged in the Soviet Union, but this time they failed. In subfreezing temperatures, hundreds of thousands of

The people of Moscow mourning Stalin

Muscovites thronged to take their last look at the body. Beria brought reinforcements from Leningrad, but even his troops could not control the masses. We do not know the exact numbers, for such figures were not published in the Soviet press, but eyewitnesses spoke of hundreds of people crushed to death. Like an Egyptian pharaoh who had slaves buried along with him, Stalin compelled some of his people to accompany him to the other world.

Who could succeed a Stalin? It is a general characteristic of dictatorships that they are without an orderly succession system. The normal institutions of government fall into disuse, for they would be a limitation on absolute power. No one can be groomed as an heir apparent, for anyone lasting too long in that position would be suspected as a competitor to the dictator. Heir apparents therefore frequently change and often are physically eliminated. There is constant struggle behind the back of the seemingly all-powerful dictator, and when he disappears from the scene that struggle becomes sharper and visible to all.

The character of the Soviet system as it developed under Stalin demanded a single ruler. Nevertheless, the top leaders, those who had attended Stalin's miserable midnight dinners, called for "collective leadership"; it seemed impossible for any of them to fill Stalin's shoes. In any case, they wanted to prevent the rise of another dictator because they feared for their personal security; they had every reason to fear and distrust one another. They had had a great deal of practice in internal struggle, backstabbing, and hypocrisy.

The country was exhausted by war, terror, and poverty. The Stalinist state had paid little attention to the welfare of its citizens, and the state budgets composed during the last years of Stalin were in fact a continuation of a war economy. The people who had surrounded Stalin during the last years of his life, and from whom the top leadership would have to emerge, desired the establishment of a normality the like of which had not existed since the 1920s. All of them agreed that it was necessary to ameliorate terror and improve the standard of living of the people. They had not been so isolated as Stalin had been, and therefore were more aware of the weaknesses of the regime and the desperation of the peoples of the Soviet Union. Even from the point of view of their narrow self-interest, a continuing terror of which they were likely to be the first victims was obviously not desirable.

The new leaders saw the maintenance of order as their immediate task. They wanted to assure the Soviet people and the rest of the world that the country would carry on without Stalin. As an expression of their desire to make collective leadership a reality, they reduced the size of the recently expanded Presidium of the Central Committee (formerly and later called the Politburo) from twenty-five members to a more manageable ten. In the new regime this was to be the decisively important organ.

The Soviet people and world opinion saw Malenkov, Beria, and Molotov as the three most prominent leaders. Molotov had the longest record as a major figure in the party and, behind Stalin, was the best-known Soviet leader in the rest of the world. However, he was never a serious contender: Molotov had suffered an eclipse in power during the last years of Stalin and did not possess an adequate base of support. The other main contender was Beria, the head of the NKVD since 1938. He was perhaps the most able member of the top leadership, but undoubtedly the most monstrous. He understood that – as another Georgian and as head of the feared and hated terror organization – he could not, at least right away, assume the top job, and therefore suggested Malenkov for prime minister. In return he got complete control over the security organs, reuniting under his leadership the Ministry of the Interior and State Security.

Malenkov's position was the strongest. He was a rather colorless figure who had spent his life in the party bureaucracy. Like all the top leaders, he had been involved in many of the bloodiest purges of the regime, most recently and importantly in the so-called Leningrad affair, where he – with Beria's help – had had the followers of Zhdanov eliminated. That he was allowed to give the major report at the Nineteenth Party Congress in 1952 indicated his standing in the party. This is not to say that Stalin trusted him or accepted him as his successor. Still, since the old and infirm Stalin was incapable of giving a speech several hours in length, Malenkov got the job. We do not know the nature of the relationship between Beria and Malenkov – the evidence is contradictory – but it seemed at the time that they were allied, and that together they possessed ultimate power.

In retrospect it is clear that Malenkov made a mistake in choosing the premiership rather than assuming leadership of the party. We must recall, however, that Stalin had emasculated the party apparatus. The bloated ministries carried out the day-to-day business of government, most importantly running the economy. Under the circumstances the governmental organization appeared a better base of power than the seemingly moribund party.

Khrushchev was mentioned only in fifth place among the members of the Presidium; no one could have predicted that he would ultimately emerge victorious. But perhaps it was the seeming remoteness of his chances that smoothed his way. In some ways the situation was similar to that following Lenin's death: no one could see Stalin as Lenin's successor; therefore his competitors did not consider him dangerous. It is easy to understand why his competitors did not see in Khrushchev a future dictator. Like many of his colleagues, he came from a humble background. He had very little formal education, and as a young man had worked in a mine. An energetic and ambitious person, he benefited from the opportunities offered by the revolution, received education in party schools, and quickly rose to the highest levels of leadership in the 1930s, at a time when the old elite was eliminated.

Khrushchev differed from the other faceless functionaries of his generation inasmuch as he retained his earthy ways. Unlike the other members of the Politburo, he moved easily among the common people. Indeed, he sought them out; he could be imagined as one of them. One can only wonder how such a person could survive and flourish in a political atmosphere that demanded conformity. Khrushchev conformed only outwardly. For the historian it is difficult to form a picture of Stalin, and it is almost impossible to see the human being behind his actions, but the case of Khrushchev is altogether different. He remained the rather crude but intelligent and sly person that he always was. He proved himself to be a resourceful fighter, and an individual character.

Khrushchev as secretary of the Moscow party committee was entrusted with the organization of Stalin's funeral, but speeches were given only by the top three leaders. Although Khrushchev ranked only fifth in the Presidium, he was the only member of that body who also was a member of the secretariat. This double responsibility turned out to be a decisively important advantage. Through the secretariat, Khrushchev was able to revitalize the party, and in addition to build a power base for himself. Like Stalin three decades before, he gave party jobs to his followers, and their support soon enabled him to make his bid for supreme power.

The struggle for power and disagreements over policies came to be intertwined. Ironically, the most odious of the leading figures, Beria, was the one who wanted the most far-reaching reforms separating the current regime from its Stalinist past. These reforms concerned the lessening of terror, abandoning some grandiose and economically questionable Stalinist projects, and investing in the consumer sector of the economy, thereby raising the standard of living. The first sensational move came in less than a month after Stalin's death: the rehabilitation of the victims of the doctors' plot. An implicit attack on Stalinist terror, this was to be the first of a series of rehabilitations.

Khrushchev took a decisive step in his struggle for power by organizing a risky but successful plot against Beria. He prevailed because he had won over his fellow leaders in the Presidium, all of them terrified by the sinister chief of the political police. In addition, and very importantly, he had the support of the top leadership of the army. Marshal Zhukov personally arrested Beria at a meeting of the Presidium at the end of June. He carried out this task, as he later confessed, nervously but gladly. Ironically and fittingly, Beria was the last victim of a Stalinist-style purge. Needless to say, he fully deserved his fate; but nevertheless it is worth noting that he was punished not for his real crimes against millions – like his own victims, he was arrested on the basis of utterly fanciful and false accusations. The charges against him were spying against Bolshevik Russia as early as 1919, and working against the interests of the Soviet state ever since; working for the British secret service; and undermining Soviet collective agriculture. In December, Beria and six other KGB (Committee on State Security) leaders were executed. (According to some historians Beria was executed immediately after his arrest, and therefore his "trial," to put it mildly, was only a formality.) Although Malenkov was a participant in the anti-Beria plot, the removal of a powerful potential ally from the Presidium weakened him in the coming power struggle against Khrushchev.

Although the entire leadership agreed on the necessity of immediately improving the lives of the people, it was Malenkov who came to be associated with the new policies in the people's eyes. As premier it was he who enunciated these policies. Malenkov acquired a degree of popularity as a result of these reforms, but in the internal struggle Khrushchev was more successful, for he was the better politician. Malenkov's notion that the party and government hierarchies could be separated turned out to be unrealistic. Not only were these two organizations intertwined, but everywhere the party organizations turned out to be more powerful. At this time, just as in the 1920s, factional struggles were not decided by popularity among the common people, but by a narrow circle of the elite. Khrushchev's strength lay in his ability to use the revitalized party organization and his close relationship with the top leaders of the army. The generals were grateful to him for removing Beria, but above all they supported him because Malenkov's stress on the production of consumer goods seemed a dangerous policy to them. They regarded Khrushchev as a friend of what came to be called the military industrial complex.

After the disavowal of the doctors' plot, the victims of the so-called Leningrad affair were also rehabilitated, and this act was a further blow to

Malenkov's standing. Malenkov, as an heir apparent, had greater responsibility for this particular crime than Khrushchev. By the end of 1954, Khrushchev, firmly in control of the party organization, had eclipsed Malenkov, and in February 1955 Malenkov was forced to resign as premier – although he retained his seat on the Central Committee's Presidium. Khrushchev's friend and ally Nikolai Bulganin became prime minister. By this time it was clear to the rest of the world that Khrushchev was *primus inter pares*. The first act of the power struggle was over, and Khrushchev, unexpectedly, had emerged victorious.

DE-STALINIZATION

From the very outset the leaders of the new regime faced insoluble dilemmas: on the one hand, they neither could nor wanted to rule by Stalinist methods; on the other, they could not repudiate the past. These people, after all, had not been innocent bystanders but were heavily implicated in the crimes of the previous era. Stalinist institutions – such as the political police, prison camps, the one-party state, and the collective farms – continued to exist, and the new leaders did not even contemplate doing away with them. Most importantly, perhaps, the legitimacy of the regime was inextricably bound up with past policies. How could one admit that the majority of the people had never supported the revolution? How could one describe the terror that accompanied collectivization while retaining the fruit of that terror, the collective farm system? How could one insist on the monopoly of the party in the politics of the nation and at the same time recount openly the crimes committed in the name of that party? Post-Stalinist Soviet society was built on rotten foundations.

The party functionaries considered how the past was depicted extraordinarily important, because the legitimacy of the regime depended on the "correct" presentation of past events. As a consequence the writing of history was strictly supervised. The problems were delicate: it was not easy to find a reasonably consistent and authoritative interpretation and stick to it. In fact, evaluation of the Stalinist past in open discourse constantly changed, depending on the correlation of forces within the leadership. Books written by historians on some aspects of the Soviet past – such as the revolution, collectivization, the nature of terror, and foreign policy – were so misleading and written in such a stilted language as to be almost unreadable. Although several hundred such books were published each year, the vast majority of them remained unopened.

History writing was the voice of the Soviet regime and was therefore heavily controlled. By contrast, the work of artists could be left open to interpretation, could be regarded as something contingent. As a result, writers and filmmakers could get much closer to telling the truth. From the point of view of creative artists, the difficulty was that the line between what was permissible and what was not constantly changed. In one year a writer could achieve success for discussing an issue openly, but in the next a different writer saying more or less the same thing could get into serious trouble. Indeed, the single best indicator of the liberalism of the moment was the current state of the so-called Stalin problem. When writers were allowed to publish works about their past sufferings in the camps, that implied openness, reform, and liberalism; by contrast, when Stalin was at least partially rehabilitated and his "historic achievements" stressed, that suggested a turn to conservatism and increased repression.

Immediately after Stalin's death Soviet intellectual life experienced a period that came to be called, after a novella published by Ilia Ehrenburg in early 1954, the thaw. By the mid 1950s many of the old restrictions were lifted, and every component of Soviet culture benefited. Works produced by writers and film directors reasserted the significance of the individual, the reality of emotional life, thereby extending the private sphere. Artists turned to genuine issues and expressed themselves with passion. Since the Soviet system politicized all aspects of life and claimed credit for all achievements, a film or a novel that depicted the world more or less realistically and thus pointed to problems was inherently subversive. Vladimir Dudintsev's novel *Not by Bread Alone*, published in 1956, by its very title expressed the spirit of this new generation. Dudintsev attacked a soulless bureaucracy incapable of appreciating talent. Artists who had done interesting work in the distant past once again took advantage of the opportunity and returned to experimentation. The fine directors Sergei Iutkevich and Grigorii Kozintsev once again made films well worth watching, and the younger director Mikhail Kalatozov made *The Cranes Are Flying* in 1957, which had a stylistic exuberance that reminded viewers of the golden age of the Soviet cinema, the 1920s. From this time on among Soviet intellectuals one could distinguish between the friends and foes of change, and the Soviet Union ceased to be a totalitarian society.

The concept of de-Stalinization included a set of connected yet distinct policies. Initially it meant the rehabilitation of at least some of the victims and their return to Soviet society; but it also came to mean relatively greater openness in treating some historical issues, liberalization of economic policies, and at least a small degree of change in the political system. Usually, though not always, these different aspect of de-Stalinization proceeded hand in hand.

We may say that the process began even before Stalin's body was buried. By adopting the principle of collective leadership, the new leaders attempted implicitly to distance themselves from Stalin and his methods. Openly acknowledging that the doctors' plot was based on trumped-up charges had far-reaching implications: it was the first attack on a pillar of the Stalinist system, the political police, that had been the primary instrument of terror. In the three years following Stalin's death, however, only a few political prisoners were freed. At the same time, the new rulers gave a much more generous amnesty to common criminals. However, freeing even a small number produced some ferment: if some were found innocent, then why not others? After all, the methods by which the newly freed had been convicted were no different from the methods used in other cases.

The official approach to Stalin changed implicitly but markedly in the period from 1953 to 1956. A brief examination of the party newspaper, *Pravda*, for this period demonstrates the change. Stalin was still revered as the "continuer of Lenin's work," but the ludicrous excesses of his deification stopped, and politically sophisticated readers of newspapers noticed that his name appeared less frequently. Some daring authors even made some indirect criticisms of his rule. Within the leadership, for example in the plenum of the Central Committee, Stalinist policies even received modest but explicit criticisms as early as July 1953.

This was an unstable status quo. People were returning from the camps; cinema and literature were becoming freer; pressure was building for the repudiation of terror, and thereby of Stalin. At the same time Stalinist political institutions remained intact, and no one in the leadership had an untainted past. The great change, surely one of the pivotal events of Soviet history, occurred in February 1956 at the Twentieth Party Congress. Khrushchev, after being elected first secretary by the congress, gave a four-hour-long so-called secret speech. Although this speech was not published in the Soviet Union until 1989, it was not really secret. It was given in front of 1,500 delegates, among them some prominent foreign communists, and was almost immediately published abroad. In the following months party cells discussed it, and soon every politically conscious Soviet citizen knew more or less what Khrushchev had said at the party congress.

In his speech Khrushchev denounced Stalin's autocratic rule, his terror, and his falsification of history, and blamed him for the reverses the country had suffered at the outset of the Second World War. Of course, Khrushchev did not give a fair and reliable evaluation of Soviet history. In his description Stalin had departed from the correct path only in 1934, that is, at the time of the Kirov murder and the beginning of mass terror. Khrushchev accused Stalin of Kirov's murder, but did not hold him responsible for the terror connected with collectivization. He emphasized Stalin's communist victims, but not the murder of ordinary citizens who were caught in the machinery of terror. Although by implication he exculpated the chief victims of the purge trials, he did not explicitly rehabilitate them, and their names continued to be absent in discussions of the Soviet past. In "scholarly" articles, for example, describing the first steps of Soviet diplomacy, the name of the first commissar for foreign affairs, Trotsky, still could not be mentioned.

Nevertheless, it is undeniable that Khrushchev risked a great deal, both for himself and for his regime. By attacking Stalin's methods, Khrushchev undermined the very legitimacy of the Soviet system. Dangerous questions were inherent in Khrushchev's presentation. Why draw the line in 1934? Why rehabilitate some figures from the Soviet past but not others? What is one to say about a system in which such horrendous crimes could be committed?

One can only speculate about Khrushchev's motives. It seems likely that he genuinely intended to make a clean break with a past that he recognized as criminal. He realized that it was necessary to examine the past in order to move forward. At the same time the speech was a crucial move in his struggle for power. Khrushchev was a gambler, and probably believed that, however much he might suffer by the revelations, his competitors for power would be harmed more. Almost all the top leaders – Kaganovich, Malenkov, Molotov – were more directly involved than he, who in the darkest years of 1937–38 had been away from Moscow in the relative backwater of Kiev.

The consequences came quickly. After the speech it was impossible to keep most political prisoners in the camps any longer. The freeing of the innocent that had begun as a trickle in 1953 became a flood after the Twentieth Party Congress. Millions returned to their homes, demanding and in most cases receiving formal rehabilitation. These events were not publicized, but Soviet citizens could not help knowing about them. The return of so many of Stalin's victims to Soviet society made the Stalinist horrors visible to all.

Khrushchev dealt a major blow to the entire world communist movement. Communists in foreign countries, who had felt compelled to defend every Stalinist act and lie, now had the rug pulled out from under them. Thousands found their situation untenable and left the Communist Party. The consequences of Khrushchev's revelations were particularly harsh in the Soviet satellites. Here communist bosses who had committed crimes by copying Stalinist methods were still in power. On the one hand, they could not prevent the adoption of a new Soviet line coming from Moscow, but on the other they wanted to retain their posts. This contradiction resulted in revolutionary situations in Poland and Hungary in October 1956. In Poland bloodshed was narrowly avoided, but the Hungarians revolted, demonstrating for everyone to see that the communist regimes could be sustained only with the aid of Soviet troops. Many foreign communists who had not given up their commitment even after the admission of Stalin's crimes could not stand the spectacle of Soviet tanks crushing the revolution in Hungary and left the party.

The Stalin question came to be the dominant issue in the internal struggle within the leadership. The Central Committee resolution of June 1957, drawn up by conservative leaders such as Malenkov, Molotov, and Kaganovich, stemmed from the fear that Khrushchev had unleashed uncontrollable forces. While this resolution recognized some "mistakes" in Stalinist leadership during the last period of his rule, it maintained that Soviet achievements during this period outweighed the "mistakes." The resolution was a major step backward on the road toward greater freedom and openness. The ferment within the Soviet camp in the fall of 1956 proved to conservative forces that Khrushchev had damaged the Soviet cause. The attempt to remove him from office – an attempt that Khrushchev named the "antiparty" group, was the direct consequence of the secret speech. To his fellow leaders Khrushchev seemed a dangerous adventurist, and the Presidium voted eight to four to remove him from office. Khrushchev responded that, since he had been elected by the Central Committee, only that body had the right to remove him. Then, with the aid of his friends in the military including Marshal Zhukov, he hastily assembled the Central Committee, and there he prevailed. Khrushchev's enemies had miscalculated. They failed to appreciate that the process he had started could no longer be stopped. Khrushchev's policy line had supporters not merely among the Soviet population, which would not have had much political consequence, but also in the apparat where Khrushchev had placed supporters in crucial positions.

The attempt of the "antiparty" group was a first in Soviet history. It was the first time that the top policymaking body had formally attempted to remove a leader, and it was also unprecedented that the leader, insisting on observing formal rules, was able to retain his office. Furthermore, it was the first time that an opposition movement was politically defeated while coming to no physical harm. Malenkov became a plant manager in Kazakhstan, and Kaganovich was appointed director of a cement factory in the Ural mountains. Molotov, an ex-premier and ex-foreign minister, had to suffer the indignity of taking over the Soviet embassy in Ulan Bator, Mongolia. The following year, in March 1958, Khrushchev assumed the premiership in addition to leadership of the party. With the defeat of his enemies Khrushchev reached the apogee of his power. He never became the dictator Stalin had been; but the idea of collective leadership, enunciated only four years before, was now forgotten.

The most sustained attack on Stalin during Khrushchev's tenure in office took place at the Twenty-Second Party Congress in 1961. This time Khrushchev's speech, in which he broadened his attack, was given in a public forum. Now he explicitly held his ex-colleagues Malenkov, Molotov, Kaganovich, and Voroshilov responsible for crimes. Newspapers published documents above the signatures of these people demonstrating their involvement in the terror. The crowning moment in de-Stalinization occurred at this congress, when an old party member reported that Lenin had told her in a dream that he found it unpleasant to have Stalin as his companion in the mausoleum. Consequently – to be sure, only at night, with no public announcement – Stalin's body was reburied in the Kremlin wall, where other major figures of the communist movement had found their eternal rest. This was a considerable postmortem demotion.

AGRICULTURE

In economics, as in politics, Stalin left behind a disastrous legacy. The concentration on heavy industry and military preparedness had resulted in a highly unbalanced economy, and neglecting the production of consumer goods had caused dire poverty. In 1952, for example, Soviet factories produced barely one pair of shoes, and that of the flimsiest quality, per citizen. From the point of view of the average person, the improvement of the standard of living was perhaps the most significant aspect of de-Stalinization.

The new leaders immediately recognized that far-reaching changes were needed to make the system viable. They saw that at this politically dangerous moment they had to cement their position by introducing popular reforms. The imbalance in the economy had to be righted, and incentives had to be given to workers to raise productivity. Some of the reforms were necessitated by the needs of the moment and made little economic sense. The government paid higher prices to the collective farms for compulsory deliveries, increased wages in factories, and reduced pressure on the population to buy government bonds. At the same time it lowered food prices. Neither industry nor agriculture could satisfy the increased demand: lines in stores got longer, and frustrated consumers put further pressure on the state for an improved standard of living.

Khrushchev was a fervent believer in the superiority of the Soviet political and economic system. Like the founders of the Bolshevik regime, he saw in economic growth and modernization the justification and legitimization of the vast historic undertaking. Once safely installed in power, he was ready to challenge the rich Western nations, especially the most powerful, the United States. He had no doubt that societies and economies were infinitely malleable, and that the powerful regime he headed gave his country great advantages. All that was necessary was to find the right system, the right combination of incentives, coercion, and encouragement, and then the Soviet Union would flourish more than any country on earth. He was ready to try. He introduced one reform after another, some of them necessary and wise, some necessary but ill conceived, and some foolishly utopian and ultimately disastrous.

By far the most serious economic problem facing the nation was the state of agriculture – the always-neglected stepsister of heavy industry. How could one talk about improved standards of living when the population was on the verge of starvation? The memory of famines was still fresh. The demoralized, exploited peasants, deprived of investment that would have enabled them to modernize their farms and use machinery and fertilizers, were barely able to feed the population. The peasants were second-class citizens; unlike workers, they were not allowed to carry their own domestic passports, and therefore their freedom to travel depended on the good will of the chairman of the kolkhoz. Whoever had the opportunity to escape to the cities did so.

Khrushchev from the very beginning took a major role in agricultural reforms. He had been born into a peasant family; of all the major leaders of the Stalin era, he had the best understanding of the disastrous conditions of the countryside. He visited farms and, unlike other bureaucrats, moved easily among the peasants. As the leader of the Ukrainian party organization he had overseen the recovery of the countryside after the war, and had called Stalin's attention to the famine of 1947. On returning to Moscow, in a desperate attempt to lessen the distinction between peasants and workers, he sponsored the utopian idea of creating agricultural towns.

As leader of the USSR, Khrushchev spent a considerable portion of his time dealing with the problems of the countryside. He was a man of extraordinary energy, willing to try various methods to overcome backwardness. He was full of ideas. Any brief schematic description of the agrarian reforms would give a misleading picture, as it would give the appearance of systematic thinking and order in a process that in fact was haphazard. At times Khrushchev's government allowed the farms greater independence in deciding what to plant and how to carry out their work; on other occasions, the independence of the collective farms came to be further limited; at times the government encouraged peasants to take advantage of the private plots; at other times the entire system of private plots came under fire as "insufficiently socialist."

The first and most significant and necessary step was so obvious that one could hardly call it a reform. The government needed to reduce the great income inequality between workers and peasants. This was done by raising prices on products that the collective farms had been compelled to deliver to the state, and by lowering the tax that the peasants paid on profits from the sale of produce and domestic animals. In the following years several further reductions took place. Although only a tiny segment of the land under cultivation was affected, the policy led to rapid improvement, for it gave incentives to the peasants to increase their holdings of livestock and to produce more on their small plots. Increased investment in the production of fertilizers and agricultural machinery did not have such immediately beneficial results, but clearly was a necessary and wise step.

The slow and steady rise of total output and productivity was not enough for Khrushchev. He had far more ambitious plans. On his initiative the Soviet government decided to increase the availability of food, not by further improvement in productivity but by bringing new lands under cultivation. By definition this meant cultivating marginal lands where the climate was inclement or unreliable. In the course of the next two or three years, vast areas, mostly in Central Asia and southern Siberia, were brought under cultivation. All the newly cultivated regions lacked the necessary superstructure to make life reasonably comfortable, or even tolerable. In Soviet circumstances, of course, there could be no question of attracting people by offering them land and freedom. The government instead organized an

A Moscow subway station

elaborate campaign, largely among Komsomol youth, of persuading people to accept the inevitable hardships and move to these lands. During 1954 alone, 300,000 young people went east. This heroic large-scale undertaking, a mass mobilization calling on the population to sacrifice in the hope of a better future, was very much in the usual Soviet style. The campaign was similar to the campaigns of the 1930s, when the government persuaded, cajoled, and compelled young people to build cities, power plants, and steel mills in remote locations in Siberia.

How should we evaluate the success of the virgin lands program? The first harvest in 1954 was good, but the next year, a drought year, was disastrously poor in the virgin lands. The failure undermined Khrushchev's still-precarious position within the leadership. Fortunately for him, in 1956 the weather conditions were favorable in the newly cultivated areas, but not in European Russia, so he could argue that the newly cultivated lands had saved the country from starvation. After a few years, because of ecological problems, the average yield declined. It also became obvious that the grain produced in these lands, partly because of the cost of transportation, was several times more expensive than what was grown in the traditional grain-producing areas. The country paid a high price for the virgin lands program. Much of the new agricultural machinery produced by Soviet factories was sent to these regions, and therefore the much-needed mechanization of the traditional Russian village had to be further postponed. After a few years people started to return to European Russia, and a substantial portion of the newly cultivated lands had to be abandoned. Still it would be wrong to write off the virgin lands program as a mistake. Despite the errors of management and the vagaries of weather, the newly cultivated lands continued to make up a substantial portion (between one-third and one-half) of the total grain output of the country.

It is also difficult to give a simple verdict on the most significant agricultural reform of the Khrushchev era – the abolition of the machine tractor stations in 1958. When these stations were first established, at the time of collectivization, the regime could not have managed without them. The country possessed few tractors, and there was no other way to provide the newly established collective farms with mechanized labor. Furthermore, the Stalinist regime needed these outposts of the city in the still incompletely controlled countryside for political reasons. They acted as intermediaries between the regime and the peasantry, carrying out tasks of control and indoctrination. Although temporarily necessary, they were hardly an efficient way to deal with the problems of agriculture. The collective farms constantly had to negotiate with the MTSs regarding when and how the necessary work would be carried out. The kolkhozes could never be certain that the work would be accomplished on time. Divided responsibility was obviously harmful.

Khrushchev decided that both the collective farm system and the economy were strong enough to do away with this unnecessary division of responsibility. He may have been correct, but the reform was carried out hurriedly, without sufficient planning and preparation. Instead of taking several years, in which the farms could have accumulated enough capital to purchase the necessary machinery, the reform was completed within a single year. In the case of the largest collectives the problems were manageable: often a machine tractor station served a single kolkhoz, and under the circumstances it made good sense to consolidate them. The smaller and poorer collective farms, however, could not manage. Often they had to abandon building projects in the middle of construction, or assume crippling debts that deprived them of capital for years to come.

The abolition of the MTSs had other negative consequences. The workers were reluctant to become kolkhoz members, which meant not merely a reduction of income but also – even worse from their point of view – a reduction in status. The skilled and ambitious among them sought jobs in the cities, and the farms were left without enough people to take care of the machinery. The exodus produced increased waste. Machinery that could easily have been repaired stood idle, gathering rust. In the following years the kolkhozes were in no position to buy new machinery, and the overall output of the Soviet agricultural machine-making industry actually declined. In the mechanization of the Soviet countryside, the abolition of the MTSs represented a step backward, and it took a long time to catch up even with the previous low standards.

The large collective farms could cope with the new situation better, and this was yet another reason for Khrushchev to encourage the amalgamation of small kolkhozes into giant ones. However, one suspects the main reason was a communist belief that large size equaled modernity and progress. For a communist, and especially for Khrushchev, the larger farms also seemed more socialist than the small ones. Hand in hand with the process was the transformation of many collective farms into state farms. From the point of view of the individual peasant, working on a state farm meant having a more reliable income, but losing the option of keeping a private plot, which in some circumstances could be quite profitable. Generally, the large farms, whether collective or state farms, were better administered. However, the increased size of the farms further removed the individual peasant from the place where the decisions were made, thereby contributing to alienation.

Khrushchev paid particular attention to animal husbandry. The consumption of meat, milk, and eggs seemed to him the most reliable sign of material wellbeing. In order to prove, therefore, that the Soviet Union was going to be the richest country on earth, he had to raise output in meat and meat products. In 1957 he made a utopian, foolish, but somehow touching announcement that within a few years the Soviet Union would overtake the richest country on the face of the earth, the United States, in the production of meat, milk, and butter. The Soviet Union would not only be the most egalitarian society on earth, but also would provide its citizens with the highest standard of living.

Khrushchev's choice for the arena of competition was particularly unfortunate, for of all aspects of the economy it was animal husbandry that had suffered most in Soviet times as a result of collectivization and the Second World War. Khrushchev would have needed a miracle to achieve his goal, and miracles seldom happen. An incident that occurred in Riazan, hardly significant in itself, is symptomatic of the Soviet dilemma, approach, and ultimately tragedy. The party sent out a circular to the districts to pay increased attention to meat production. The first secretary of the Riazan district committee, a certain Larionov, committed his district to more than double its meat production in 1959. As was the custom in the Soviet Union, the achievement of one person, or at least in this instance the promise of achievement, served as a mobilization device for the entire nation. Larionov and his district received a great deal of national attention and honors, and other districts were instructed to follow the Riazan example. Indeed, quotas were raised, and promises of vastly increased output came from different parts of the country.

It is impossible to know if Larionov really believed that he could achieve this goal, or if he knew that he was participating in a rigged public relations effort. The realization must have come to him that by normal methods he could not possibly achieve his goal. He therefore compelled the collective farms to slaughter their animals, and made his agents buy animals in the surrounding districts – until the authorities in those districts discovered what Larionov was doing and resisted his efforts. His people used various subterfuges, such as buying meat in the shops and reselling to the state at vastly lower prices. Riazan's "accomplishments" were celebrated nationwide, and Larionov received medals and distinctions. He promised further increases for the following year, although the agriculture of the district was on the verge of collapse. When at the end of 1960 the scandal could not be covered up and Larionov's methods were investigated, the unfortunate man committed suicide.[1] At the time of Khrushchev's departure from the political arena in 1964, the nation's output in meat and meat products was lower than in 1959.

Khrushchev believed that the best animal feed was corn. He enthusiastically supported the expansion of the area devoted to growing corn from the beginning of his tenure. He embarked on the project of increasing meat production and, especially after his visit to the United States, became almost obsessed. Corn was planted in regions that were clearly unsuited for it, with obviously unfavorable consequences for Soviet agriculture. The planting of corn required much time, labor, and machinery, and the results were disappointing. Converting from other animal feeds made little sense given the climatic conditions, and after Khrushchev's removal from office the campaign was abandoned.

Unfortunately for Khrushchev, 1963 was a drought year, leading to such a shortage of bread that rationing had to be reintroduced. The agricultural failure was one of the contributing factors to Khrushchev's ultimate political defeat. This time, for the first time in Soviet history, the authorities decided to alleviate the suffering of the people by buying grain abroad. In the following decades such purchases became a regular occurrence.

INDUSTRY

During the Khrushchev era, as before, the industrial sector of the economy performed better than the ever-troubled agriculture sector. Despite serious problems, industrial growth continued to be impressive. The government made substantial investments both in national defense and in heavy industry, while raising the standard of living of the people of the Soviet Union. The performance of the economy allowed Khrushchev to believe that the future belonged to communism and to issue his foolish challenge to the capitalist West. "We will bury you," he said, meaning that his system would prove itself superior and win the economic competition. The rest of the world, seeing Soviet achievements, would inevitably follow the communist path.

The remarkable fact is that the impressive economic performance took place despite appalling inefficiencies and irrationalities. The problems were the consequence of the very nature of the highly centralized Soviet planned

economy, based at least partially on Marxist ideology. The problems, therefore, could not be resolved. Khrushchev, aware of some of the problems,
responded by constant attempts at reform and reorganization. Instead of
improving the situation, he sometimes made it worse by creating confusion.

The problems which retarded the normal development of industry
remained the same: the economy was overcentralized, and planners, in the
absence of a market and realistic prices, found it increasingly difficult to give
meaningful instructions. Methods that had found success when the economy
was reasonably simple worked less and less well. Since according to Marx
only human labor, not capital, produced value, planners had great difficulty
deciding how scarce capital should be allocated. On what basis, for example,
would a Marxist economist calculate whether it was better to build a capital-
intensive electrified railroad line or one that used steam engines? Since
interest on capital could not be calculated, capital came to be inefficiently
used and overcommitted.

The absence of a realistic price structure, due to the lack of a market
mechanism, was an even more serious problem. Since the simple measure of
producing profit could not be used, economists had to wrestle with the
problem of success indicators. They could find no other way of measuring
the performance of enterprises than their fulfillment of the plan. Since the
income (in the form of bonuses) and career of the factory manager, party
secretary, chief bookkeeper, chief engineer, and so forth depended on the
factory's fulfillment of the plan, they were overmotivated to meet specific
plan targets. It was in their interest to persuade the planners to set these goals
as low as possible. Furthermore, they avoided the introduction of any new
product and were suspicious of innovations that might produce uncertainty.
How the planning figures were expressed almost always gave the factory
managers irrational incentives. If, let us say, the plan of a factory that
produced nails was expressed in terms of weight, it was in the interest of
that factory to produce large and heavy ones. If the plan of a shoe factory
was expressed in terms of the number of shoes produced, the director of the
factory had an incentive to produce shoes of a smaller size.

The position of the planners was very difficult and, as the economy
became more complex and consumer demand increased, it became untenable. They made their calculations on the basis of past production, input/
output requirements, and political considerations, and were often under
pressure from powerful political forces. In order to avoid the irrationalities
built into a process that did not have the guidance of a market, the planners
had to give more and more precise instructions to the factories regarding
what was expected. The inevitable irrationalities of the system became most
evident and disturbing in the consumer sector. The factory manager who
was vitally interested in the fulfillment of the plan, because his bonus and his
career depended on it, had no great concern whether the shoes produced by
his workers could actually be sold in the shops. It was a sign of material

progress when, for the first time, stores had to face the problem of unsalable goods. Some of the consumer goods produced were of such shoddy quality that even the long-suffering Soviet consumers would not accept them.

In an article published in 1962, the economist Evsei Liberman came up with the daring idea that, at least as far as the production of consumer goods was concerned, the performance of the enterprises should be measured by profit. In other words, it was not enough to produce shoes: the shoes had to be of such quality that they could be sold. It was, however, impossible to divide the economy between light and heavy industry. Since a Soviet-type economy could not provide realistic prices for the raw material used in the consumer sector, the concept of profit continued to be more or less meaningless. Still, Liberman's idea was a good one, and Khrushchev and his successors experimented with this and similar reforms in the following decades.

Excessive centralization was built into the Soviet economy from the time of the Bolshevik Revolution. The branches of the economy were headed by ministries, and the ultimate coordinator of the economy was the Council of Ministers. But bureaucrats making their decisions in Moscow could not be aware of local conditions, and often they did not take advantage of geographical proximities and as a consequence gave irrational directions. A frequently cited example of such waste was the proverbial freighter belonging to one ministry that carried material up river, but returned empty, while another freighter, belonging to another ministry, carried material down river and made the return journey empty. Factories that depended on bureaucracies in Moscow sometimes had to acquire raw material from distant sources, even though the same material could have been acquired locally.

In 1957 Khrushchev introduced a revolutionary change. He abolished the economic ministries and in their place created more than 100 local economic councils, the so-called *sovnarkhozy*, each responsible for a district. He placed all enterprises within their territorial limits under them. Although Khrushchev had sound economic reasons for desiring decentralization, at the same time the move was also a maneuver in the political battle he was waging. At that time his opponents were still in control of the vast ministerial apparatus, and destroying them served his immediate political interests.

The establishment of the *sovnarkhozy* was a typical Khrushchevian reform: it grew out of a genuine need, but it was insufficiently considered and inadequately prepared, and ultimately created more problems than it solved. The local leaders did not and could not have had a national perspective, and therefore were in no position to establish priorities. The abolition of economic ministries did not diminish bureaucracy. Instead, decisions were handed over to generally less capable bureaucrats in the provinces, who felt unable to cope. Enterprises now could not count on raw material coming from a different district. National coordination fell to the State Planning Board, Gosplan, in Moscow, but this agency did not have the resources and power to enforce its decisions. Gradually committees were established, which functioned like the previously abolished ministries. The power and authority of the *sovnarkhozy* were gradually reduced, and after Khrushchev's removal they were abolished and the ministerial structure reestablished. It is fair to say that Khrushchev's attempt at reorganization made matters worse.

FOREIGN RELATIONS

The Stalinist worldview did not tolerate shades of gray. The Soviet Union had only friends and enemies: one could be either a servant, willing to follow every whim of the tyrant, or an enemy, to be opposed by all available means. In 1948, when the Yugoslav communists rebelled against Stalinist high-handedness and claimed a modicum of independence, Stalin excommunicated them from the bloc. Soviet propaganda attacked the Yugoslav leaders with a venom that surpassed even the extraordinarily vicious verbiage used against the worst enemies of communism such as Dulles, Churchill, and Truman. Stalin chose to have a smaller but monolithic bloc. Because he imposed a mind-numbing uniformity within his own country, it would have been inconsistent to allow people beyond the border to follow their own ideas and still call themselves communists. Stalinists, while they caused boundless misery to those who had the misfortune of living under them, nonetheless conducted foreign policy in a more or less predictable fashion and were generally averse to taking great risks. Soviet foreign-policy makers took an active interest only in regions that were contiguous to their empire. Given limited Soviet capabilities, it could hardly have been otherwise.

De-Stalinization in foreign affairs necessitated a thorough revision of an entire worldview. The new theoretical underpinning of foreign policy came to be called "peaceful coexistence." Khrushchev and his fellow leaders repudiated the longstanding Soviet belief that war was an inevitable consequence of the capitalist world order. Publicists went to a great deal of trouble to find proper quotations showing that a desire for peace had always been the cornerstone of Soviet foreign policy. Malenkov first, and later Khrushchev, openly acknowledged the obvious: a war between the nuclear powers had become unwinnable. Peaceful coexistence, however, did not mean that the Soviet Union would forever be satisfied with the existing correlation of powers. On the contrary: Khrushchev, the last Soviet leader with a boundless faith in the communist cause, took it for granted that the Soviet system would be victorious without war; its egalitarian ideology and economic successes would prove irresistible to the population of the world. Coexistence, therefore, meant both the plan to extend Soviet influence, and at the same time, perhaps paradoxically, a desire to lessen international tension to avoid the danger of conflagration.

The Soviet leaders took a new approach to all areas of the world. First of all, they attempted to find some kind of modus vivendi with the West, primarily with the preeminent capitalist power, the United States. Second, they were willing to reconsider the nature of Soviet control over international communism and to allow a degree of independence, a change that brought turbulence within a short time. Third, they took a far greater interest in the underdeveloped world, courting poor nonaligned countries and often using them to spread Soviet influence. A greatly increased military strength for the first time enabled the Soviet leaders to make the influence of their country felt everywhere in the world. By the end of the Khrushchev period the Soviet Union was participating in a vast chess game on a global scale. Aspects of Soviet foreign policy, of course, are distinguished only for descriptive and analytical purposes. In reality Soviet behavior in one part of the world greatly influenced Soviet opportunities and problems elsewhere.

Immediately following Stalin's death, the new rulers had much to worry about and were in no mood or position to risk any ambitious foreign ventures. But they well understood that, in the West, Stalin's death was perceived as a possible source of confusion and therefore weakness. It was essential both to ameliorate international tension and at the same time to convince possible adversaries that the Soviet Union was able and willing to defend its interests. Fortunately for them, the explosion of the first Soviet hydrogen bomb in August 1953 demonstrated the fact that the Soviet Union was now a major power.

Soviet leaders took concrete steps to show the world that they wanted to start a new era. First of all, they pressured their Chinese and Korean allies to end the stalemated war in Korea. In this respect the political interests of the new president of the United States, Dwight D. Eisenhower, and the new rulers in Moscow coincided. In Europe, the Soviet government decided to give up its bases in Finland, which had little military significance but could have become tools for pressuring Finland. From that time on, propagandists argued incessantly that, in contradistinction to the United States, the Soviet Union was peace-loving because it possessed no foreign bases. Perhaps the most significant Soviet concession was the acceptance of the Austrian state treaty in May 1955. At the end of the war Austria had come under four-power control. But, unlike in Germany, the Soviet Union never attempted to set up a satellite regime in Austria, which would have made the withdrawal of Soviet forces a great deal more difficult. We of course cannot know exactly what was going on in the minds of the Soviet leaders, but it is likely that acceptance of a non-Soviet-controlled but neutral Austria was primarily a signal to Germany. It was to whet the appetites of the Germans for a unified, independent, but neutral country.

For understandable reasons Soviet policymakers, barely a decade after the conclusion of the devastating war, were very much concerned about the revival of German military strength. The chief goal of Soviet policy in

Europe was the prevention of the rearmament of the Federal Republic as a part of NATO. But how could the Soviets prevent such a development? Propaganda, as always, was a useful tool; Moscow deployed the communist parties of Western Europe, most importantly among them the French party. The communists played on West European fears of revived German aggression, but propaganda alone was not enough. Soviet policymakers intimated that they were willing to sacrifice their East German comrades if the West was willing to accept a united but neutral Germany. From the point of view of Western politicians, sacrificing West Germany's contribution to NATO in exchange for the exclusion of the much smaller and weaker East Germany from the Soviet alliance system would have been a bad bargain, so Soviet intentions were never tested.

The situation in East Germany was becoming untenable. Four-power control over Berlin was a major obstacle in the process of legitimizing the East German regime. Berlin was an open door for the citizens of the east, and 3 million Germans simply took the subway and found themselves in the west. A Soviet-style regime could not tolerate giving its citizens the option of simply walking away. When Khrushchev finally recognized that his German policy had not succeeded – that he could not squeeze the Allies out of Berlin, and that a united, neutral Germany was an unattainable vision – he drew the necessary conclusions. In August 1961 he allowed the East German communist leadership to build a wall across the middle of Berlin, making further escapes impossible for all practical purposes. This solution led to much derision of international communism, but it is hard to imagine any other means of stabilizing the East German regime. This policy was ultimately vindicated when some years later East Germany was recognized as a member of the international community.

The rest of the Soviet bloc presented a different set of problems. The death of Stalin had the most immediate and far-reaching consequences in Hungary and Poland. Soviet high politics and politics in the satellites came to be intertwined. Imre Nagy, for example, a prominent Hungarian leader, was Malenkov's man in Budapest. In 1953 Nagy introduced a popular new program that increased investment in the production of consumer goods and allowed at least some of the victims of the terror to leave prison and concentration camps. However, when Malenkov lost his position in Moscow in 1955, Nagy was also forced to give up his position as premier, and Matyas Rakosi, perhaps the most hated Stalinist leader in Eastern Europe, regained control of the government.

Most but certainly not all the members of the ruling elites in the satellites welcomed the changes: diminished Soviet economic exploitation, repudiation of the terror, and a chance to grope for legitimacy by pursuing more popular policies. At the same time, the little Stalins – people who had compromised themselves by leading the bloody purges – were now exposed and found their positions undermined. Like the Stalinist leaders in

Moscow, Khrushchev's enemies, it was in their interest to resist the changes. But that put them in a paradoxical position: how could those whose power derived from the willingness to follow Moscow's instructions, suddenly, when the Soviet Union became somewhat more humane, begin to resist?

When Khrushchev had successfully elbowed out his fellow leaders and emerged on top, he decided to patch up the quarrel with Tito. After the violent Soviet denunciations of the Yugoslavs, bringing Tito back into the bloc was obviously a difficult and embarrassing matter. Khrushchev visited Belgrade, and in effect admitted past Soviet errors and blamed them all on Beria. Yugoslavia could never again be reduced to the level of a satellite; from this point on it was an ally that usually, but not always, supported Soviet positions in the international scene. That Tito was allowed to pursue his independent policies and still be recognized as a communist meant that other East European leaders would also have greater latitude. The seeds of polycentrism were now planted.

The reconciliation with Tito and the Twentieth Party Congress had significant effects everywhere in Eastern Europe. In Hungary and Poland the regimes teetered on the edge of collapse. The crisis became particularly severe in those two countries because of the disintegration of the leadership. In Poland the death of the Stalinist leader, Boleslaw Bierut, was followed by a struggle within the communist elite. Anticommunist forces among the working classes took advantage of the situation, with workers in the forefront of the struggle. In Poznan in June 1956, clashes occurred in the course of which dozens of people were killed. In October Poland was on the verge of revolution, and the party leadership was split on the question of how to deal with the crisis. Soviet leaders came to Warsaw to discuss the crisis and accepted Wladislaw Gomulka as first secretary. Since Gomulka had been excluded from the leadership in 1948, he possessed a degree of popularity. The Poles expected that Gomulka's leadership would mean the beginning of a new era, and the revolutionary wave subsided.

In Hungary events turned out differently: there members of the communist intelligentsia were the most active agents for change. Writers, poets, and scholars were searching for the new limits of freedom; in their writings and speeches they attempted to push the limits of the permissible. As would happen again in Prague in 1968 and in Moscow in 1989, permission to examine the past produced a momentary euphoria. But Rakosi, the old Stalinist leader who had successfully opposed the reformist course of Nagy, remained in power. An anomalous situation was created: courageous people ever more explicitly expressed their rage against past crimes, and yet those responsible for the very same crimes remained in power. The leadership gave ground only under pressure, and so slowly that it satisfied no one. Although Rakosi was forced out in July, the man who assumed his position, Erno Gero, was only slightly less reprehensible.

On October 23, university students organized a demonstration in support of the Poles. This was at a time when revolutionary changes were occurring in Poland. The demonstration almost immediately turned into a revolution. After only a few days of hesitation, the united Soviet leadership decided to suppress the revolution by force. Khrushchev and his comrades did not fear losing Hungary's contribution to the Soviet military alliance, which was in any case slight. Nor did they worry about the possible establishment of NATO bases in Hungary. However, they rightly believed that allowing Hungary to leave the alliance would have a devastating effect on the rest of the bloc. Nor could they tolerate a communist society ceasing to be communist: their ideology dictated that history move in the direction of communism – there could be no reverse course.

Difficult as Soviet problems with the East European "allies" were, worse was to come: relations with the other major communist power, China, gradually deteriorated. China was never a Soviet satellite: the Chinese communists had won power for themselves with minimal Soviet help, so the Soviets were never in a position to control Chinese policy. Nevertheless, in the 1950s the two major communist powers found a common interest in maintaining the appearance of "unshakable unity." Now, however, the Chinese had a series of complaints: they disliked the theory of peaceful coexistence, viewing it as a loss of revolutionary zeal in Moscow. They considered the denunciation of Stalin a dangerous precedent at a time of an ever-growing, insane cult of Chairman Mao Zedong. They blamed the Soviets for an unwillingness to share nuclear secrets with them. The Soviet leaders in turn were concerned by Mao's independent and aggressive policies. The appearance of a major and soon-to-be-nuclear power on their Asian border filled the leaders in Moscow with consternation. The disputes first took place behind closed doors. Then the two sides used proxies and an Aesopian language: the Chinese attacked Yugoslav "reformist" policies, and the Soviets reciprocated by attacking Albania, which was gradually becoming a Chinese satellite.

The Sino-Soviet split was a major setback for Khrushchev: now the Soviet Union had to compete for ideological leadership within the communist camp. Khrushchev was put on the defensive. The enemies of the Soviet Union would sooner or later exploit the open enmity, and the satellites would use the opportunity to increase their leverage. The Romanians went furthest: they soon started to pursue an independent foreign policy.

Khrushchev showed a great interest in the underdeveloped world. It would be idle to speculate whether an increased involvement in the policies of distant countries benefited the Soviet Union. The elite saw in the expansion of Soviet influence a sign that the future belonged to communism, and took pleasure and pride in this development. However, there was a price to pay. "Friends" were won over not by the power of communist ideology, but by the expectation of economic and military help. Such help was a great

Nixon, Eisenhower, and Khrushchev in the United States

additional burden on the Soviet economy, and Soviet involvement in trouble spots created the possibility of dangerous conflict with the West.

Khrushchev went out of his way to court the leaders of Asia and Africa. As relations with China deteriorated, Khrushchev successfully cultivated a relationship with India. France and Britain had been forced to retrench from their previously vast colonial empires, and they had left behind turbulent regions. The growth of Soviet influence was particularly strong in these most troubled areas. In the Middle East, the opening was provided by the creation of the state of Israel. Here, as elsewhere, Soviet foreign-policy makers encouraged nationalist movements to challenge and undermine the position of the West. In October 1956, Britain and France in a desperate and ill-considered move unsuccessfully attempted to prevent the nationalist Egyptian leader, Gamal Abdel Nasser, from nationalizing the Suez canal. Ridiculously, the Soviet Union, while suppressing the Hungarian revolution, posed as the defender of the underdog in the Middle East. Khrushchev threatened Western "imperialists" with missiles. The Soviet Union became ever more involved in Middle Eastern affairs, acquiring one client after another, each desirous of economic and military help. As long as American support for Israel was undiminished, the Soviet Union could count on having friends in the Middle East.

In time the Soviet Union came to sponsor almost all "liberation" movements around the world, and could do so without much cost to itself.

Although the Soviet Union never gained permanent friends in the under-developed world, Soviet help enabled the elites in these newly independent countries to take a more anti-Western stance than they would have otherwise.

Unlike Soviet involvement in the Middle East and Africa, where the advance took place without substantial risks, Soviet sponsorship of the Cuban revolutionary Fidel Castro turned out to be a dangerous business. In Stalin's time the Soviet Union took very little interest in Latin America. From the point of view of the Soviet leadership this was not a promising area – the continent had no powerful communist movement, and it was too close to the United States.

Although the Soviet Union had nothing to do with Castro's coming to power, nevertheless, soon after Castro's victorious march into Havana, US–Cuban relations quickly deteriorated. The socialist, antidemocratic, and anti-American policies of the young revolutionary leader were bound to alienate American policymakers. As Castro took steps against the middle class, and as some of his disenchanted followers came to the United States, the American attitude quickly solidified into hostility. American economic warfare and the threat of military intervention made the Cubans look for help where they could get it. After an American-sponsored invasion of the island failed, Cuba's move into the communist orbit was altogether predictable.

In 1962 Khrushchev embarked on his most dangerous foreign-policy venture: he placed intermediate-range missiles in Cuba, missiles capable of carrying nuclear warheads and thereby threatening the United States itself. Since the affair would quickly end, with great humiliation for the Soviet Union, the question has often been asked: why did the Soviet leader make this mistake? Obviously, he expected that the installation of the missiles could occur in secret and would confront the United States with a fait accompli. Since the Soviet Union was ringed by American bases, he assumed the Americans would be in no position to be indignant. We will never know his motives, but there are several possibilities. A prominent historian of Soviet foreign policy suggested that he intended to impress his Chinese comrades with his daring.[2] He may have wanted to ensure Cuban security by making an attack on the island impossibly costly. He may have regarded this move as a first step in increasing Soviet influence in the western hemisphere. Of course, these options were not mutually exclusive.

He obviously did not expect the strong American response, and willing-ness to take the gravest risk. The difference was that as of 1962 American missile strength and, more importantly, American logistical ability so near the American mainland were incomparably superior to Soviet strength. The Soviets were simply not capable of projecting strength to this distant part of the world. The Soviet backdown was humiliating for the country, and no doubt for Khrushchev personally, and surely contributed to his ultimate downfall. In the long run, however, the consequence was a commitment by the Soviet leadership to an increased military buildup.

KHRUSHCHEV'S DEFEAT

On October 14, 1964, the plenum of the Central Committee of the Communist Party of the Soviet Union freed N. S. Khrushchev from his state and party responsibilities, ostensibly at his own request, on account of his deteriorating health. This was the only successful palace coup in Soviet history. Obviously, Khrushchev's numerous opponents learned from the lessons of the abortive 1957 coup. They prepared their move carefully: they chose an occasion when the first secretary was away from the capital, gained the assent of almost all the top leaders, and made sure they observed all party rules and regulations.

The charges leveled against Khrushchev by Mikhail Suslov at the plenum – not published at the time – included mismanagement of the economy and "errors" in foreign policy. Neither the Cuban missile crisis nor the deterioration of relations with China was mentioned, presumably because on these major issues there were no differences within the leadership. One gets the impression that, although foreign-policy setbacks weakened Khrushchev's position, these were not the major reasons for his removal. The fact that the country had endured a couple of disastrously bad harvests was a great blow to him. He obviously failed to solve the most serious economic problem of the country – the inability of collectivized agriculture to provide cheap and plentiful food. His successors were not much more successful than he, and this implies that Khrushchev was not entirely at fault, that the problems were inherent in the system.

Khrushchev's opponents succeeded because he had managed to alienate large segments of the population, and most especially the political elite that really counted. Even if the common people had given him their support, it is doubtful this would have assured his political survival. Most of the charges against him were well founded: his constant changes in the administrative structure – they could hardly be called reforms – had created confusion and a sense of instability.

Nikita Khrushchev was the last Soviet leader with a firm belief in the superiority of Marxist-Leninist ideology. He never doubted the justice of his cause. Ironically, perhaps, it was the strength of his beliefs that was the source of much of his political troubles. Because he believed in the egalitarian promise of the revolution, he considered it his task to reduce inequality. He was well aware of the unseemly privileges of the elite: shopping in special stores for items otherwise unavailable, access to good apartments at a time of extraordinary shortage, connections that enabled them to send their children to the best and most prestigious schools. This elite, like most elites, was very successful in perpetuating itself.

Khrushchev attempted to narrow the ever-widening gap in the standard of living between the privileged and the rest of society. He made an effort to narrow wage differentials by raising the standard of living at the bottom of the social scale; collective farm peasants, unskilled workers, and pensioners benefited. The first secretary had a populist faith that the Soviet people could be mobilized against the vested interests of the bureaucracy. His ill-fated reform of destroying the ministerial structure of the economy and creating instead territorial organs, the *sovnarkhozy*, was conceived in this spirit. Not surprisingly, with his attacks on privilege and bureaucratic power he made himself unpopular among the politically powerful. However, the kind of mass participation he had in mind had little to do with pluralism or the genuine autonomy of social organizations. Mass mobilization, meaningless "voluntary" organizations, were of course not new in Soviet history. The practice of sending agitators to apartments to "explain" the issues in purposeless elections had been used before Khrushchev. But he made concerted efforts to revitalize the Komsomol and the trade unions.

Some of his ideas for mass mobilization were novel. Most significant of these was the *druzhina*, a "volunteer" people's militia, which was to help the authorities in maintaining order. These came to be one of the least attractive forms of social control and enforcement of conformity. The authorities used the *druzhiny* for combating "parasitism," and at times for harassing dissidents. The *druzhiny* often deteriorated into brawling bands, interfering with the lives of citizens.

From the point of view of the entrenched elite, Khrushchev's educational reforms were particularly distasteful. The Soviet Union was supposed to be a country of the working classes, yet it was obvious that the workers possessed little prestige. The elite was able to reproduce itself by sending their children to schools of higher education, which alone within the Soviet system promised jobs of high status. Khrushchev's worthy but utopian goal was to bring education and physical work closer together. Students and scholars from schools and universities were required to spend a day in a factory or farm and to learn a trade. The requirement was universally hated. On the one hand, specialists and scholars whose expertise was much needed spent useless hours on the factory floor or picking potatoes; on the other, the genuine workers considered it a waste of time to teach these uninterested and unmotivated students, who contributed practically nothing to the overall output.

A place at a university was a scarce commodity. Children of the intelligentsia, as everywhere, were in a good position to compete. By contrast, the working classes, and especially the collective farm peasantry, were greatly disadvantaged. In order to improve the chances of those who came from the lower classes, Khrushchev abolished tuition fees at institutions of higher

education and made financial aid dependent not only on academic performance but also on financial need. These steps, while well intentioned, were not
enough. Khrushchev took more radical measures. At first a certain number
of places were put aside for candidates with a few years of work experience;
they did not have to take competitive exams with students who had just
completed high school. Despite these attempts, the proportion of students
from disadvantaged backgrounds did not substantially rise. In 1958, therefore, the regime took a more drastic step. It required students, after the
completion of a compulsory eight-year course, to work in factories or farms
for three years. The law was increasingly circumvented: it was absurd for
talented young mathematicians, for example, to waste three valuable years
learning to be proletarians.

Khrushchev, a fervent communist, saw inefficiencies and irrationalities all
around him. It was the wide gap between reality and the promises of
ideology that inspired his ceaseless attempts at change. Under his rule the
conservative Soviet system was subjected to constant proposals for reform.
His fertile mind and willingness to experiment, and his courage in undertaking ambitious reforms, were the appealing aspects of his rule. Often his
reforms were hopeless because the problems he wanted to solve were essential features of the regime and therefore irremediable. But at other times he
could be fairly blamed for attempting to introduce reforms that were insufficiently considered and created more trouble than they were worth. Those
who accused him later of "hare-brained" schemes were not unjust.

Two of his reforms aimed at the party elite caused the greatest discontent
among those who mattered most politically. One of these aimed at preventing the ossification of the leadership and encouraging mobility within it. The
new rule required that one-third of the membership of the governing bodies,
both at the regional and the national levels, had to be replaced at each
election. The constant evaluations of the party secretaries at each level aimed
at improving work, but it created a sense of instability. Those whose jobs
were now subject to this scrutiny not surprisingly turned against the first
secretary.

His second reform of the party created even greater dissatisfaction. It was
a strange and ill-conceived idea: in 1962 Khrushchev decided to split party
committees at the local level into agricultural and industrial sections, each
substantially independent of the other. In this way it was thought that the
local leaders would have greater expertise over the area they were supposed
to supervise. But the unintended consequence of the reform was unfortunate:
the industrial sector freed itself from the burden of helping the agricultural
sector, producing further deterioration in the conditions of agriculture. This
was the first of Khrushchev's "reforms" to be rescinded on his removal
from power.

October 1964 marked the end of a period of relative optimism, a period
during which many people inside and outside the Soviet Union believed that

the flaws of the system could be remedied. Khrushchev, in spite of his unpromising background as Stalin's bloody henchman, his crudity, his lack of constancy, and his numerous poor judgments, deserved credit for alleviating the worst aspects of Stalinism. During his tenure the Soviet Union ceased to be totalitarian; his rule can be better characterized as authoritarian. Ultimately his failures showed that the problems he recognized were inherent in the system that he wanted to save. It is understandable that when another Soviet leader, Gorbachev, once again embarked on a course of significant reforms, he also attempted to rehabilitate Khrushchev's memory.

9

Real, Existing Socialism

The aftermath of the removal of Khrushchev in October 1964 bore distinct similarities to the power struggle that followed Stalin's death. Once again the newly installed leaders insisted that they would avoid "the cult of personality" – a fault for which they blamed Khrushchev – and institute "collective leadership," which they assured the peoples of the Soviet Union was the only appropriate form of government for a socialist country.

Leonid Brezhnev assumed the most important post, the first secretaryship of the central committee, and Aleksei Kosygin became premier while remaining a member of the Politburo. Nikolai Podgornyi took the chairmanship of the Supreme Soviet – in other words, he became the president of the USSR. Gradually, Brezhnev emerged as the supreme leader, and in appearance at least the Soviet Union once again had a single leader. While in the mid 1960s it was the premier – i.e., Kosygin – who met with important foreign leaders, as time went on Brezhnev more and more often assumed this role. It was Kosygin, for example, who met with Lyndon Johnson in Glassboro, New Jersey; but a few years later Brezhnev received Richard Nixon in Moscow.

Brezhnev gradually developed a modest personality cult: he had a city named after himself; collections of his boring, rambling speeches were published. Idealized pictures of him were plastered all over the enormous country, and schoolchildren learned about his "magnificent achievements" as leader at the time of the "great patriotic war." In reality, however, he was only *primus inter pares*. Lenin, Stalin, and even Khrushchev had had far-reaching ambitions to refashion the society over which they ruled. This almost-manic energy was missing in the Brezhnev era, and consequently the leadership style was different. The country was governed by consensus, and decisions were made by a remarkably stable oligarchy.

N. S. Khrushchev in retirement

All the prominent figures – Brezhnev, Kosygin, Podgornyi, and the chief guardian of ideology, Mikhail Suslov – were entirely products of the Soviet system who had made their careers in the party organization. None of them had experienced the 1917 revolution. They came from modest backgrounds, acquired some technical and political education in the 1920s, and made their careers in the 1930s at a time when there were many openings in the top leadership. In other words, they were the beneficiaries of the terror. These were people of the new Soviet middle class who shared the tastes and prejudices of this class.

The regime deteriorated into senescence. As time passed the leadership became increasingly conservative: turnover in important positions slowed down, and the incompetent were not removed. Brezhnev and his comrades saw in the process of liberalization above all a danger that change might lead to disintegration. During roughly the last five years of Brezhnev's life there were constant rumors of his failing health. When he did appear in public, his speech was slurred, and he made a pathetic impression. He had to be supported by aides when he walked. Indeed, his condition was so bad that his last appearance at a party congress could not be televised. His comrades in the Politburo, almost all of them as old as he, were also tired, unimaginative people. The Soviet leadership became the butt of jokes at home and abroad.

Publicists of the Brezhnev era described the political and social system of their country as "real, existing socialism." This phrase well described the difference between Khrushchev's and Brezhnev's Soviet Union. The new leaders felt uncomfortable with a utopian ideology, unconsciously realizing that the promise of a just and affluent society in the distant future had outlived its usefulness: people were tired of waiting. The publicists simply declared that "socialism" had arrived. The implication was that constant experimentation, mass mobilization, and exhortation for new and ambitious campaigns would largely be abandoned. The era was one of complacency and conservatism.

The institutions of the regime had not changed since Stalin's time. At the top of the formal hierarchy was the Supreme Soviet, a body "elected" by non-competitive voting; it met twice a year and simply accepted all the resolutions proposed. Not even the most naive person believed that this body was in fact a policymaking one. Membership in this body carried no responsibility and certainly no power. One meaningless election followed another: aside from national ones, there were also republican and district polls, all taking place at different times. These elections were preceded by meaningless campaigns which served only to promote the current policies of the regime.

The Soviet Union was burdened by an enormous bureaucracy: ministries proliferated, not only on the union level but also in the republics. The governmental structure became so very large because, aside from the tasks that any government had, it also controlled the entire economy of the nation. Each small branch of the economy had its own ministry, sometimes several ministries. In theory the party congress, which met every five years, elected a central committee and chose a Politburo of approximately fifteen people. Reality was otherwise. The system operated as a feudal hierarchy: when a new leader assumed office, he placed his own people in key positions, and they in turn selected their own subordinates. In the Brezhnev era the Politburo continued to evolve. The foreign minister, the head of the KGB, the minister of defense, and of course the premier, who stood at the top of the ministerial structure, were now all members of the Politburo. They were there, for all practical purposes, ex officio. It was on this level that conflicts were resolved and different interest groups fought for resources. The affairs of the nation were decided in secret because, although the Politburo met regularly and frequently, no protocols were published.

This was the golden age of the nomenklatura, an original Soviet concept. Its concrete meaning was a list of office holders who required approval by the relevant (national, republican, or provincial) party agencies. However, nomenklatura came to mean a political elite, which in this period included approximately half a million people. It was this group, rather than the vastly larger 19-million-member party, that ruled the country and enjoyed privileges. The elite had access to closed shops where goods unavailable anywhere else were found in abundance; and, at a time of great housing shortage, they had not only comfortable apartments but also weekend houses (dachas) in restricted areas. The nomenklatura itself was highly stratified: the most privileged among them were even able to travel on occasion to the West, returning with foreign goods that greatly added to their prestige. They were also able to send their children to schools where admittance was difficult. They enjoyed their positions not only because of their abundant privileges but also because of a new sense of security. Now they did not have to worry about the uncertainties of the Khrushchev era, to say nothing of the bloody threats of Stalin's Soviet Union.

Members of the nomenklatura resented Khrushchev because of his populist attacks on their privileges, and disapproved of his constant changes and ill-thought-out experiments. They wanted to enjoy their privileges in peace. To achieve that goal, they got rid of their unpredictable boss, and in Brezhnev they got what they wanted: he was their man. The anti-Khrushchev coup of 1964 achieved its goal. Not surprisingly, the first moves of the new leadership were to do away with precisely those reforms of Khrushchev that went contrary to the interests of the elite: the compulsory rotation of party positions, the division of the party into agricultural and industrial wings, and the educational reforms. The industrial ministries, the centers of bureaucracy ensconced in Moscow, regained their original powers.

No political system is free of corruption. However the Soviet Union in the Brezhnev era encouraged corruption to a fabulous extent. Political power could easily be turned into economic advantage, and the country was ruled by people who lacked a tradition of service. The members of the nomenklatura protected one another. Since these people had lost faith in the noble ideas of equality and freedom as essential features of the future communist society, there were no psychological obstacles to using their positions to achieve as much mundane personal gain as possible. But primarily corruption was widespread because the Soviet system did not tolerate openness, and journalists did not consider muckraking one of their tasks.

Corruption spread to the very highest levels, and very much involved Brezhnev's family. Like other communist bosses, such as Nicolae Ceausescu in Romania and Kim Il Sung in North Korea, the first secretary of the party placed his relatives in positions of leadership. It was widely known in Moscow that Brezhnev's daughter, Galina, with the help of her lover, a gypsy circus performer, had secreted large sums of money abroad. This was occurring at a time when her husband, General Yurii Churbanov, was first deputy minister of internal affairs, that is, the second most powerful person in the police.[1] Corruption was particularly odious in the Central Asian and Caucasian republics. Some party chiefs became millionaires who kept their wealth in dollars. One of them, a man in Uzbekistan, maintained a harem and a torture chamber. Such behavior on the part of the powerful of course greatly contributed to the demoralization that characterized this twilight period. It was a society in which cheating and bribe-taking were for all practical purposes universal.

In contrast to the utopian promises of the Khrushchev era, the publicists in this conservative period toned down their rhetoric: they stopped giving dates when the output of the Soviet economy would surpass that of the American. Since the Soviet regime collapsed shortly afterward, the era that preceded it is generally regarded as a period of missed opportunities and stagnation. In its own terms, however, the Brezhnev regime was not unsuccessful. The problem was, rather, that – in view of the decline of ideological commitment and the inability of the economy to live up to oft-repeated promises – the source of legitimacy, the main measurement of success, came to be military strength.

Only in retrospect are the signs of the beginning of disintegration obvious. At the time, the Soviet Union epitomized stability and order, and almost everyone assumed that the regime would continue for several more generations. The very fact that the Soviet system had survived for so long conferred on it a degree of legitimacy. Although seemingly the Soviet Union was the most stable society, governed by a conservative leadership, inevitably changes occurred. As urbanization continued, as more engineers, doctors, and scientists were trained, for the first time in history a sizable middle class developed. These people desired bourgeois comforts and wanted to be treated with dignity.

The eighteen-year-long Brezhnev era was full of paradoxes. It was a time when the Soviet Union achieved its greatest international success: it became a world power, second to none. But it was also a time of wasted opportunities, a time when the country's economic decline, now seemingly inevitable, commenced. It was a period of much-desired stability and tranquility, certainly the quietest in the country's troubled twentieth-century history. In light of subsequent developments Brezhnev's era came to be described as a time of stagnation, yet most people of Russia today look back on it with nostalgia.

THE ECONOMY

The loss of idealism, the ever-present corruption, and the deterioration and aimlessness of the leadership were factors that led to the disintegration of the Soviet system. However, none of these factors was as important as the failure of the economy. It was this failure that shook the confidence of the leaders in the system and ultimately persuaded them that changes were needed. The decline in economic performance mattered so much because the communist elite had come to base the legitimacy of the regime on the belief that planned economies by their very nature were superior to the chaos of the market. Stalin took the first step in this direction. He promised his listeners not a just and egalitarian society, but a well-functioning economy. Khrushchev in a rather crude fashion equated communism with a degree of economic well-being: in his view communism would come when the citizens did not have to pay for streetcar tickets and apartments.

This method of legitimization worked for some time. People inside and outside the Soviet Union were impressed by the performance of an economy based on central planning, and many accepted that this method of organizing the economy was the wave of the future. But, of course, the argument had power only as long as the economy functioned satisfactorily – that is, as long as it was able to satisfy the extraordinary requirements of the military, a prerequisite of an ambitious foreign policy, and at the same time to improve the standard of living of the population. In this respect the best years of the Soviet regime were from the death of Stalin until the mid 1970s – from the time the government started to pay attention to the neglected needs of the consumer, to the moment when the economy began to run out of steam. However, methods that had worked at least reasonably well in an earlier period, when the economy was a great deal simpler, ultimately ceased to work.

The new leaders of 1964 wanted to undo some of the acts of Khrushchev that they – not without reason – considered unwise, but they did not intend to change direction completely or to stop economic reforms. Although the constant campaigns and extravagant promises of immediate abundance were abandoned, there was no complete break with the Khrushchev period. Just as in the previous era, the leaders were determined to continue to raise the standard of living. How exactly this was to be brought about, however, was subject to debate. Premier Kosygin stressed the need to increase the production of consumer goods, while Brezhnev considered the primary task to be the improvement of the overall output of agriculture.

Since Brezhnev and his colleagues were unable or unwilling to accept the obvious fact that the source of weakness in Soviet agriculture was structural and therefore could not be remedied without abandoning the entire collective-farm system, they experimented with incremental change and placed their hope in increased investment. Indeed, investment kept growing during the Brezhnev period, but without achieving the much desired breakthrough. Although overall output substantially increased, and even productivity improved, agriculture continued to be the major problem for economic planners. An increased standard of living (including that of collective-farm peasants) meant that people wanted to eat better. As a result, the demand for meat and milk products increased faster than Soviet agriculture could supply. The solution was to buy grain regularly from abroad, mostly from the United States. Foreign grain freed Soviet products for animal feed. The government used its precious supply of convertible currency to improve the diet of the people. Although the people ate better than during the dreadful years of late Stalinism, shortages did not disappear; on the contrary, they became ever more troublesome. That the state possessed the necessary supply of convertible currency was the consequence of fortuitous circumstances: the Soviet Union, the largest producer of oil in the world, benefited from the rise in oil prices following the 1973 war in the Middle East. The inflow of convertible currency postponed the crisis that was bound to follow.

In concrete terms, increased investment in agriculture meant a willingness to pay higher prices for agricultural products to the collective farms. The planners assumed that these material incentives would encourage the peasants to produce more. In addition, as a result of Brezhnev's program, the country expanded industries that provided the farms with fertilizer and machinery. Khrushchev for ideological reasons had imposed various limitations on the private plots of the collective-farm peasants. Now, in this less ideological age, these restrictions were loosened. However, investment in agriculture had to come at the expense of consumer goods production and investment in further economic growth. Only the defense industries were spared; in fact, resources continued to be lavished on them.

For the first time since the beginning of the industrialization drive, agriculture came to be subsidized by the Soviet state. The higher prices paid by the state were not passed on to the consumer; the government budget absorbed the difference. For example, in the early 1980s the government paid to the collective farms almost double what the stores charged retail customers. As time passed the weight of this subsidy increased, and ultimately agricultural subsidies took up one-quarter of the Soviet budget. This was an ironic development: the Soviet Union devoted a larger share of total investment to agriculture than any major industrial country, and was still unable to provide the population with a satisfactory diet.

Pouring in money could not make up for past errors: the Soviet Union had destroyed the best and most ambitious farmers, killed incentives, and motivated people to leave the countryside for the cities, where life was more tolerable. In comparison with other industrial countries, the Soviet Union had a far larger share of the population living in the countryside, but there was still a constant labor shortage because of extremely low productivity in the agricultural sector. This problem was dealt with in a ridiculously inefficient way: time and again in the fall, schools, universities, and even scientific institutions sent people to harvest potatoes. The Soviet economy, which had been built on the exploitation of the agricultural sector to benefit future growth, now was compelled to pay the price for past decisions. Brezhnev and his colleagues sacrificed the prospect of future growth for current consumption. They were not visionaries.

Kosygin, who as prime minister was responsible for the economy, introduced reforms in the industrial sector, but these were no more successful than the agricultural reforms. The pace of growth of the Soviet economy slowed, and the gap between the advanced economies of the West and especially the fast-growing economies of Southeast Asia continued to widen. The situation was especially worrisome in the case of the most strategically important and most technologically advanced branches of industry. Methods that had produced impressive growth in the past did not work any longer. The increase in productivity that had resulted from urbanization – i.e., transforming peasants into workers – did not pertain any longer, and planning became increasingly inefficient as the economy became more complex. Furthermore, from the 1970s onward the Soviet Union suffered from a labor shortage. The chief cause of the shortage was low productivity: there were too many idle hands in factories, and managers had no incentive to fire them. There were also still far too many people engaged in agriculture (over a quarter of the labor force). As birth rates declined in European Russia (as opposed to Central Asia, where birth rates remained high), new factories had trouble finding workers. The Soviet Union proved incapable of moving from extensive to intensive growth, from labor-intensive to capital-intensive methods. It could not take advantage of labor-saving mechanization because of its technological backwardness.

Although Kosygin attempted to give greater independence to the factory managers, he also wanted to retain centralized planning directed from Moscow. The industrial ministries regained the power that Khrushchev had taken away from them. However, Kosygin's reforms were far too modest and did not touch the real sources of weakness. In spite of the increased autonomy of the factory managers, the basic situation remained: the primary interest of the manager was to fulfill the plan, and these plans were less and less able to keep up with an ever more sophisticated economy. It was in the interest of the factory management to keep the specified plan figures as low as possible. Doing too well in one year implied that the planning figures would be raised for the next period. The introduction of new products – indeed, innovation of any kind – went contrary to the immediate interests of the factory management, and therefore was likely to be resisted.

The Liberman reforms (introducing profit calculations in the evaluation of the performance of factories that produced consumer goods) created new economic irrationalities. As long as prices were not set by supply and demand, the calculation of profits did not just remain an irrational exercise but, worse, often provided the wrong incentives. The factory manager had no incentive to lower the cost of production. There was an excessive demand for capital, and the economic system proved incapable of allocating it rationally. Since no interest had to be paid on capital, there was no incentive to keep inventories small. The factory manager never knew whether raw material would be available when needed and therefore attempted to keep as much on hand as possible. When the choice arose between quantity and

quality, managers always opted for quantity, since that was easier to measure and was more likely to be rewarded by bonuses.

Giving greater power to factory directors, centralizing and decentralizing,
and introducing "improved" planning by use of computers ultimately made
little difference. Meaningful changes would have endangered the political
system, and the reformers did not have the will to push through such
reforms. The political elite resisted, and at the same time there was no strong
constituency for change. Although the Soviet people in the long run would
have benefited, in the short run significant economic reforms would have
meant the loss of job security for millions, the demand for greater work
discipline, and a temporary fall in the standard of living resulting from the
withdrawal of wasteful subsidies.

By the end of the Brezhnev period it became clear that genuine economic
reform – i.e., the creation of a system in which prices reflected the pressures
of supply and demand – could not be reconciled with the Soviet system of
planning on which the political power of the party was based. The priorities,
the thinking of Soviet leaders on economic questions, had of course greatly
changed since the time of Stalin. The structure of the economy, however,
remained impervious to change. Ultimately the reforming zeal petered out.

Economic stagnation ended the slow but steady rise in the standard of
living to which the citizens had become accustomed. Wages continued to
rise, but that increase was not accompanied by a greater availability of food
or consumer goods. The consequences were predictable: consumers had
nothing to spend their money on, and so savings increased; and the gap
between official prices and free-market/black-market prices widened. Social
distinction was achieved not by income differences so much as by access to
goods not easily available. The Liberman reforms stressed material, as
opposed to ideological, incentives. Such an approach might have made
economic sense, but the inevitable consequence was an increase in social
inequality – i.e., an abandonment of Khrushchev's egalitarian policies.

The black market, the so-called second economy, came to flourish as never
before. The attitude of the regime was ambivalent. On the one hand, by
definition the second economy violated the law and the ideological assumptions on which the regime was based. On the other, the second economy
fulfilled a necessary function: it smoothed over the difficulties that the
planned, highly centralized, and therefore rigid system created. Taking
energetic steps to stifle the underground economy would have made consumer dissatisfaction even worse.

DISSENT

Dissent is a difficult concept to define. In pluralist societies one cannot talk
about dissent, since by definition a multiplicity of views can be freely

expressed. On the other hand, in the most repressive societies there also can be no dissent, because, as the history of the twentieth century demonstrates, modern totalitarian states can succeed in repressing the expression of all unorthodox political ideas. A minimum degree of freedom is necessary for a situation in which even friends would dare to share their opinions. The concept of dissent, therefore, makes sense only in a twilight zone between freedom and unfreedom, where on the one hand political alternatives cannot be freely formulated and expressed but, on the other, repression is not so overwhelming as to make it impossible for some courageous individuals to express their views.

Soviet dissenters did not form and did not even aim to form a movement of political opposition. They did not plan to take over the government and did not offer an alternative set of policies. They did not agree with one another concerning the large political issues of the day, and they came to object to official policies for a wide variety of reasons. The heterogeneity of this small group became ever more obvious. Yet this group had something in common: its members were courageous people who were willing to accept considerable risks for principles in which they believed. They represented a moral voice, and their willingness to accept persecution showed that the Soviet regime was hypocritical and did not live up to its own ideals. Their behavior demonstrated that it was possible to "live in truth," as the great Czech dissident Vaclav Havel put it.

Dissent arose gradually in the Khrushchev period – that is, at a time when the Soviet Union ceased to be a totalitarian state. One factor was the amelioration of terror, and another was the ever-increasing contact with the advanced capitalist countries. Soviet propagandists were correct when they maintained that the West was a subversive force, though not of course in the way that they believed or pretended to believe. The number of Soviet visitors to the West remained pitifully small, but movies, novels, and especially radio did penetrate and made an impression. By the 1970s even simple Soviet citizens who fully accepted the existing social and political order knew well that people in the West enjoyed a much higher standard of living. The West provided the country with grain, and Soviet citizens believed that absolutely everything made in the West was superior to domestic products. Even Western films that showed the plight of the unemployed were impressive for Soviet audiences. They could not help but notice that even the unemployed lived better than they did.

But perhaps the most important source of dissent was the gradually diminishing power of ideology. The ubiquitous and silly slogans on the walls were never taken seriously by most people, but still there were many who believed that the country was in fact building a better, more rational and just society. But in the Brezhnev era the ideological promise began to ring hollow. Newspapers and orators at meetings spoke one language, but people spoke differently at home. At first very few, but gradually more and more men and women with integrity found such behavior intolerable. For them it was often not so much a desire to remake society (few had illusions about their power to do so) but a certain self-regard that made it impossible to go on lying – lying about the nature of society in which they lived and lying about the past of their country.

The year 1956 was a pivotal one. Khrushchev's "secret speech" filled many with hope and enthusiasm, and a conviction that a new era would come into being. After all, the first secretary himself had called for an honest examination of the nation's past. In the first blush of enthusiasm a great deal of truth was spoken. Inevitably, in the aftermath of a more or less open discussion of Stalin's crimes and after the return of tens of thousands of innocent people from concentration camps, ideas would be expressed that went beyond the officially approved views. Writers were struggling to find the limits of the permissible, but those limits were difficult to find, for Khrushchev's regime was rather unpredictable. Some individuals honestly believed that their ideas might meet with governmental approval. Since Khrushchev's personality was mercurial and circumstances were constantly changing, it was often hard to know what was permitted and what was not. Many people inadvertently found themselves in trouble.

The authorities were terrified by the visible effects of openness: the almost revolution in Poland and a full-fledged revolution in Hungary. The Pasternak affair mirrored the mood of the moment. Boris Pasternak, one of the greatest twentieth-century poets, wrote his novel *Doctor Zhivago* at a time when it could not possibly have been printed. He had, however, submitted the manuscript to Soviet publishing houses in 1956, in the year of the Twentieth Party Congress, obviously believing that his profoundly anti-communist novel could be published in the new era. Pasternak later gave his manuscript to the Italian left-wing publishing house Feltrinelli, which brought out the book in 1957.

Although there was no law against a Soviet author publishing abroad, Pasternak was subjected to an officially inspired and furious campaign. When in the following year he received the Nobel Prize for his work, the denunciation became extraordinarily shrill. Most of the best-known figures of the literary world participated in this shameful affair. Pasternak, in order to avoid expulsion from his native land, was forced to renounce the prize, and to exercise a cleverly phrased and ambiguous self-criticism.

But this was not the Stalinist regime any longer. On the one hand, the memory of terror was fresh enough to convince some prominent members of the intelligentsia that they had no choice but to participate in the vicious campaign; but on the other hand Pasternak was not arrested and even retained his dacha in Peredelkino, the village of dachas for privileged artists. At this time there were people who, at least in private, dared to express support for Pasternak. When Pasternak died in 1960, many who believed that the authorities had driven him to his grave gathered in the cemetery in silent support of the anti-Stalinist cause. This was the first post-Stalin political demonstration. The dissident movement, a small group of courageous intellectuals, was slowly coming into being.

While the events in Poland and Hungary in 1956 frightened the Soviet elite, and convinced them that even limited freedom of expression was a dangerous matter, the brutal repression of the Hungarian revolution created soul-searching and dismay among a small number of students, writers, artists, and scientists. The majority of these people considered themselves good communists and desired nothing more than to return to the so-called Leninist norms (though they no doubt misunderstood those "Leninist norms").

The dissidents began to spread their ideas by typescripts produced in many carbon copies. The writings passed from hand to hand, sometimes reaching thousands of people. In this way *samizdat* (self-publishing) was born. This form of "publishing" became a regular part of the life of a large part of at least the urban intelligentsia. In the early stages of the cold war the United States established a set of radio stations in Munich, West Germany, in order to broadcast news and entertainment to communist Eastern Europe. The station that broadcast in Russian, Radio Liberty, made available to Soviet audiences Pasternak's entire long novel. This particular form of "publishing" was called *tamizdat* (published elsewhere). The songs of dissenter bards such as Aleksandr Galich, Bulat Okudzhava, and Vladimir Vysotskii were spread by passing audio tapes from hand to hand. Of these, Vysotskii was by far the most popular, although his songs were not as bitterly biting as those of the other two.

In the course of the second wave of the anti-Stalin campaign in 1962, Khrushchev personally intervened in order to allow the publication of Aleksandr Solzhenitsyn's novella *A Day in the Life of Ivan Denisovich*. This work was a subtle but unequivocal denunciation of Stalinist terror, perhaps the most daring work published up to that time in a Soviet journal. But at more or less the same time, people got into trouble for relatively trivial offenses, such as having in their possession some typewritten pages from Pasternak's novel in English. While the author of that book was not arrested – for the arrest of Pasternak would have caused an international scandal, further harming the standing of the Soviet Union – the unknown and therefore unprotected reader could spend years in a labor camp for such an offense.

In this respect the Brezhnev era was substantially different. There continued to be periods of relaxation and periods of more intense repression, but by and large the regime became more predictable. The authorities wanted to end the de-Stalinization process initiated by Khrushchev, which seemed too dangerous to them. As we now know from archival documents, the Politburo in 1969 even considered a partial rehabilitation of Stalin. But without the use of bloody terror it was impossible to return to the silence of an earlier period. It is not even clear whether on balance the Brezhnev period was more repressive than the Khrushchev era. Those who went to prison or camps were genuine martyrs, because they chose their fate: they accepted suffering for committing acts that their conscience dictated. They knew the risks, and yet they acted courageously. Perhaps the turning point in the history of the dissident movement occurred in 1965 with the arrests of two writers, Yulii Daniel and Andrei Siniavskii.

Daniel was not a well-known author, but Siniavskii, a respected literary critic, was. He had published works in the West under the pseudonym Abram Tertz and acquired a considerable reputation, reviving the tradition of satire and fantasy altogether missing from socialist realist literature. In February 1966, for the first time, the Soviet regime put a prominent writer in the block and organized an open trial. Siniavskii and Daniel were tried not for any underground subversive acts, but for published works. Since there had never been a political trial in the Soviet Union in which the accused were not found guilty, the verdicts were not surprising: Siniavskii was sentenced to seven years and Daniel to five for "spreading anti-Soviet propaganda."

From the point of view of the regime, however, this judicial persecution badly backfired, and the authorities never committed this mistake again. The news of the trial brought ill repute and even ridicule to the regime abroad, and even some Western communists found it necessary to distance themselves from the Soviet regime. More importantly, instead of frightening potential dissidents into silence, it gave them a platform to organize. It was only from this time forward that one can talk about a self-conscious movement of courageous and mutually supportive individuals. Dissidents compiled a record of the trial, spread it among themselves, and even sent it to the authorities. By undermining the monopoly of the regime in spreading information, and by acting openly, the dissenters attacked the regime at a vulnerable point. When the organizers were arrested, that action spawned further protests.

The principles and tactics of the dissenters grew out of the situation in which they found themselves. First, they decided to act as openly as was possible under Soviet circumstances. Second, they made the point repeatedly: the regime was not observing its own announced principles. The dissenters were willing to accept a great risk by maintaining connects with foreign journalists and letting them know about what was happening. Their protests, and Soviet responses, were published in Western newspapers, and more importantly broadcast over Western radio stations, and in this way penetrated into the Soviet Union itself.

The crowning achievement of the dissenters was the publication of the purposely modestly titled *Chronicle of Current Events*. This *samizdat* publication, beginning in 1968, went from hand to hand, typed and retyped with so many carbons that at times it was hardly legible. It simply described arrests and searches of apartments for compromising materials, wisely refraining from comments. In most instances comments were unnecessary, for the regime was self-evidently hypocritical. The always-anonymous editors were periodically arrested, but others took their place. That this publication could survive – with shorter or longer gaps – for approximately a decade, showed how much the Soviet Union had changed. However faintly, one could see in the dissident movement the emergence of public opinion, the gradual opening of the public sphere.

Like the Daniel–Siniavskii trial, the Soviet intervention in Czechoslovakia in 1968, which was aimed at suppressing intellectual and political ferment, had a contradictory impact. On the one hand, it inspired fear in the conservative, unimaginative leadership that could see only threat in change and that was increasingly concerned about the power of ideas. On the other hand, some Soviet citizens found the repression by the Red Army shameful and appalling, and had the courage to protest it openly, thereby practically courting arrest. The impact of the invasion of Czechoslovakia on Soviet public opinion was considerably greater than the bloodier repression of the Hungarian revolution eleven years before. The country had changed; public opinion had evolved.

In 1975 Western and Soviet diplomats signed the Helsinki accords. Soviet diplomats considered it a great success that the West recognized the existing territorial status quo in Europe. In exchange for this Western concession, the Soviet Union committed itself "to observe human rights." At the time this concession from the Soviet side seemed a minor one. However, the dissenters took advantage of it and established "Helsinki watch committees," which monitored Soviet behavior.

The regime fought back. Although the difference between the Stalin and Brezhnev eras was vast, the Soviet Union in the 1960s and 1970s remained a repressive society. Dissenters were called into the offices of the KGB, where agents tried to reason with them and persuade them to mend their ways. The agents let them know that the Soviet state possessed powerful instruments to enforce its will. The recalcitrant lost their jobs and were sent to prison or labor camps. A particularly gruesome method, increasingly used by the KGB, was to declare dissenters mentally ill. From the point of view of the state, locking up dissenters in mental hospitals was a clever strategy because it saved the authorities from having to observe legal niceties. Furthermore, sending opponents to mental institutions conveyed the message that only lunatics would oppose the just and powerful Soviet system.

The two giants of the dissident movement were Aleksandr Solzhenitsyn and Andrei Sakharov. Solzhenitsyn acquired his reputation when Khrushchev, as noted above, allowed him to publish his novella *A Day in the Life of Ivan Denisovich*. Although after his success he was able to publish a few other novellas, his semiautobiographical novels *Cancer Ward* and *First Circle* could not be published in the Soviet Union, and so were published abroad. As he became unpublishable in Brezhnev's Soviet Union,

Solzhenitsyn acquired an ever-greater reputation both at home and abroad. In the mid 1970s he was working on a most ambitious work, the history of concentration camps in the Soviet Union, *The Gulag Archipelago*. When the KGB discovered his manuscript, Solzhenitsyn instructed his foreign contacts to print the first volume. For this offense in 1974 he was put on an airplane and against his will flown to Germany.

In time, Solzhenitsyn's views evolved. While his early writings could be construed as a liberal-democratic criticism of totalitarianism, in his later works he claimed to find the solution to his country's ills in religion and a return to traditional Russian values, which did not include the Western concept of democracy. Living in the West, he did not become an admirer of Western institutions; on the contrary, he came to deplore much that we associate with modernity. While Solzhenitsyn was considered a neo-Slavophile, the other great dissenter always remained within the democratic, liberal camp. Andrei Sakharov, one of the country's best-known and greatest physicists, a man who for his contributions to the development of nuclear weapons had come to enjoy all the privileges and benefits that the Soviet regime could bestow, became a defender of the unjustly persecuted. For his defense of liberal, democratic, and humanitarian values, he willingly accepted persecution and exile into the provincial city of Gorkii.

In retrospect the question emerges: how important a contribution did the dissidents make to the ultimate collapse of the Soviet regime? On the one hand, one would like to believe that these courageous and often lonely opponents of the regime played a major role. They pointed out the failures, weaknesses, and injustices of the system, when the chances of their success seemed remote. On the other hand, many historians argue that the small group of dissenters remained ineffective, that not only did they fail to make an impression on the vast majority of workers and peasants, but even the intelligentsia to the very end remained basically conformist and therefore loyal. It is impossible to deny that a Sakharov or a Solzhenitsyn found few supporters among ordinary citizens. At the same time, it would be a mistake to write off the role of the dissidents altogether. They did change the character of the Soviet Union. Even loyal members of the party, indeed even high-ranking officials, read Pasternak and Solzhenitsyn and others, and the fact that the unsayable was said made an impression.

Furthermore, the line between open dissent and tolerated opposition was not always sharp. After all, at least for a while Solzhenitsyn was able to publish. Other important figures, such as the historian Roy Medvedev, who considered himself a Leninist, could not have their writings published but nevertheless were tolerated and managed to stay out of prison. (Many assumed that Medvedev had supporters in the leadership of the party.) Writers and filmmakers in the age of Brezhnev were able to publish novels and make movies in which the attack on the fundamental assumptions of the regime was barely disguised. For example, the excellent writer Yurii

Trifonov published novels in which the Soviet regime from the very beginning was shown to have corrupted people, and Valentin Rasputin in his writings celebrated village life and implied that Soviet modernization destroyed traditional values. These and other writers enjoyed far greater freedom of expression than those who attempted to make explicitly political statements. Interestingly, much of the best of Soviet art in this twilight period of the regime came to be almost openly subversive of the fundamental claims and assumptions of the regime. The dissidents by their resistance to lies and injustice pushed the limits of tolerance further. In post-Soviet days, the memory of these courageous individuals serves the cause of democracy in Russia.

NATIONALITIES

At a time of intense repression, the expression of nationalist sentiments was impossible. That allowed many to think that the Soviet Union was solving the nationality problem and was in the process of creating a new, Soviet identity. Indeed, there were people in the Soviet Union who considered themselves Soviet patriots. Others saw themselves as, let us say, both Georgian and Soviet, taking pride in their heritage but also in the power and accomplishments of the state of their citizenship. Khrushchev was among those who believed that a Soviet patriotism was indeed being born and, as a convinced communist, underestimated the power of nationalist sentiment.

Early in his tenure Khrushchev had to deal with the consequences of one of Stalin's worst crimes: the deportation of entire nations. The clamor of these unfortunate people to return to their native lands increased and this was a difficult situation to remedy. Allowing people to return was bound to lead to personal and ethnic conflicts that the state would have trouble handling. The property of the victims had been confiscated, and their houses occupied by others. When the Chechen, Ingush, Karachai, and Balkar were allowed to return to the Caucasus in 1957, they encountered hostility from the local Russians, and ethnic clashes took place in 1958 in Groznyi, the capital of the region.

The Crimean Tatars (as opposed to the Tatars of Kazan, who had a different history and culture) had also lost their homeland as a consequence of Stalin's declaring them a "traitor people." In Crimea their autonomous republic had been eliminated and their places of residence given to Russians and Ukrainians. Neither the Khrushchev nor the Brezhnev government was able and willing to redress this particular historical wrong. In order to mark the third centenary of Ukraine joining Russia, in 1954 Khrushchev detached Crimea from the Russian Federation and gave it to Ukraine. To allow the Tatars to return would have caused trouble with the Ukrainians. The Tatars demonstrated peacefully, collected signatures, and appealed to world public opinion. An important segment of the dissident movement, most important among them General Petr Grigorenko, championed their cause. The authorities responded predictably: they arrested hundreds of activists.

The German minority was also a nation without a homeland. The approximately 1.8 million Germans in the Soviet Union were the descendants of colonists brought to Russia by Catherine in the eighteenth century who had settled in the Volga region. At least until the Second World War these people to a remarkable extent retained their culture and language. During the interwar period they enjoyed the benefits of an autonomous republic, but immediately after Hitler's attack they were deported – not as a punishment, but as a prophylactic measure. In the 1960s, like the Crimean Tatars, they received amnesty, but their autonomous republic was not recreated. They enjoyed a great advantage over the Tatars, however: the Federal Republic of Germany took an interest in their fate, and Germany was a significant trading partner whose good will mattered. As a result, the fate of the Volga Germans came to be connected with the status of Soviet–West German relations. As a consequence of socialist Chancellor Willy Brandt's *Ostpolitik*, which resulted in much improved relations of Germany with the Soviet bloc, in the Brezhnev era tens of thousands of Germans managed to emigrate to West Germany.

The third "nation" without a territory were the Jews. (On the passport that every Soviet citizen had to carry, the fifth entry was nationality, and Jewishness counted according to Soviet understanding as a nationality.) It is difficult to measure the strength of popular anti-Semitism, but we may assume that it continued to exist after the Bolshevik Revolution in more or less the same form as before. The attitude of the authorities to the Jews, however, varied. During the 1920s the government attacked the Jewish religion as it attacked all other religions, but it cannot be said that it treated Jews any worse than others. Jews became victims of the purges out of proportion to their numbers, but largely as a consequence of the fact that they were overrepresented in precisely those groups that suffered most during the Stalinist terror: people who had relatives abroad, the intelligentsia, and party leaders.

It is only after the Second World War, during Stalin's last years, that Soviet policy could be characterized as more or less explicitly anti-Semitic. During the Khrushchev and Brezhnev eras, overt anti-Semitism was toned down, but undoubtedly the ruling elite shared the anti-Semitism of the Russian and Ukrainian peoples. Consequently, Jews were often discriminated against in receiving promotions or admission to universities, though it must be added that Jews continued to be overrepresented both in the party and in the intelligentsia. The 1967 war in which Israel managed to defeat its Arab enemies raised Jewish pride, but also increased the governmental struggle against "Zionism," which inevitably had an anti-Semitic component. The continued presence of anti-Semitism and the rise of Jewish consciousness resulted in a desire on the part of many Jews to leave the Soviet Union. In an age of relaxed international tensions, and largely as a consequence of US pressure, some Jews were allowed to emigrate. How many left in any given year was largely the measure of the status of US–Soviet relations. By the time of Brezhnev's death, some 300,000 Jews had left, mostly for Israel and the United States.

In the 1970s and 1980s observers of the Soviet Union took it for granted that the existing social and political system would survive for a long time. There was a general agreement among these observers that if there was a dangerous weakness of the regime, it was the nationality question. Cycles of liberalization, in which a degree of cultural and political autonomy was allowed, were followed by cycles of repression. It was necessary to find a delicate balance: the Soviet state was by its very nature essentially a central-izing one; on the other hand the leaders believed that allowing a modicum of autonomy would actually strengthen the system by satisfying the demands of the moderates. The recovery of national histories included a particular danger: many of these histories might have been construed as a struggle against past Russian imperialism.

The injustice and the consequent hostilities done to the smaller national-ities did not endanger the stability of the state. From the point of view of the regime, far more dangerous were the budding nationalist movements in Ukraine, the Baltic republics, and in the three Caucasian republics: Armenia, Azerbaijan, and Georgia. Although the nationalist movements had not yet developed in the Central Asian republics, the emergence of militant Islam in Iran, just beyond the Soviet border, frightened the leadership in Moscow.

Ukrainians made up the largest minority. From the mid 1960s some members of the Ukrainian intelligentsia began to oppose russification openly. As a consequence, Viacheslav Chornovil, Valentin Moroz, and Ivan Dziuba, among others, were arrested and spent years in camps for "nation-alist agitation." The arrests did not stop the spread of the movement, and even the party hierarchy came to be infected. Petr Shelest lost his job as first secretary of the Ukrainian party organization in 1972 for taking Ukrainian interests too much to heart. The Ukrainians believed, perhaps wrongly, that the union exploited their native land and that they got less, economically speaking, than they gave.

No one, of course, at this time thought of independence. The nationalists demanded respect for the economic interests of the nation, and above all promotion of the national culture and language. They insisted that the republic give preference to the Ukrainian language over Russian. Contrary to Soviet expectations, the use of the national languages actually increased rather than decreased.

Aside from Ukraine, the Baltic states, especially Lithuania, concerned policymakers in Moscow. The Latvians and Estonians were largely Protest-ant, but the Lithuanians were Catholic, and the Lithuanian church played a central role in the self-definition of the nation. From Moscow's point of view the mutual reinforcement of religious and nationalist sentiments was especially worrisome. The three Baltic states, forcibly reincorporated in 1940 after twenty-two years of independence by the infamous Molotov–Ribbentrop pact, were economically the most advanced republics. The fact that in this period the standard of living in Estonia and Latvia was appreciably higher than in the rest of the Soviet Union did not, however, satisfy these peoples. They compared themselves to the Scandinavians: the gap between the standard of living of their republics and the Scandinavians had greatly widened since the introduction of Soviet rule. The memory of independent statehood was fresh, and the Baltic peoples resented the Russians more than other minorities did. Some intellectuals in these states went further than the Ukrainians and expressed hope for the reestablishment of independent states.

In the Brezhnev period the awful uniformity imposed by Stalinism on the entire vast country began to change. The Baltic, Caucasian, and Central Asian states regained at least some of their original cultural characteristics. Estonia, for example, came to be a far more tolerant place for modern art than the rest of the Soviet Union. The same trends appeared in Georgia and Armenia as in the Baltic region. The ferment among Georgian intellectuals was especially noticeable. Armenia was the most ethnically homogeneous of the Soviet republics, but perhaps it was Georgia that managed to preserve its culture and way of life best. The response of the Soviet state to resurgent nationalism was familiar: many of the prominent dissidents were arrested.

By contrast, Central Asia was only a potential problem. In the Soviet period this region went through a vast transformation. The degree of industrialization that took place, however, was largely the work of Russians and Ukrainians who moved into the region, some of them forcibly, but most of them voluntarily. It is likely that the Soviet leaders in Moscow worried about the potential problems of Islam. Soviet values and mores were least successful in penetrating this ancient civilization. Then there was a demographic problem. Population growth in European Russia had slowed to such an extent that the Soviet leadership had to be concerned about the shortage of labor, but such a slowdown did not occur in Muslim societies. As a consequence, the percentage of Central Asians within the Soviet population constantly grew. Soviet policymakers evidently worried that their army would soon be disproportionately made up of young Muslim men.

In the twilight period of the Soviet regime, in the Brezhnev era, nationalist passions did not diminish, and a supranational Soviet identity did not come into being. Theorists who had expected that modernization, urbanization, and large-scale population movements would undermine the foundations of nationalism turned out to be wrong. The very factors that they imagined would create a Soviet identity in fact furthered nationalist causes: universal literacy, mass mobilization, and above all the movements of millions of people within the borders of the Soviet Union. Russians and Ukrainians moving into Central Asia or into the Baltic states did not simply melt into a Soviet people. On the contrary, their very presence created a desire among natives to get rid of outsiders. People in their home republics became aware of their national identity in opposition to outsiders. It was not Stalinist or post-Stalinist repressive policies that created nationalisms; it was the very fact of modernization, factors inherent in living in the modern world. The fact that nationalism was becoming an ever-stronger force among the peoples of the Soviet Union did not, however, mean that the collapse of the system was caused by seething nationalist passions.

THE SOVIET PARADOX

Soviet standing in world affairs was not based on ideological appeal, but on military strength. At the end of the Brezhnev era, when the Soviet economy ceased to perform well and the political system was troubled, the Soviet Union possessed an influence in the international arena that neither it nor its predecessor, imperial Russia, had ever before achieved.[2]

At the time, American intelligence estimated Soviet military spending as 15 percent of GNP. Later, Eduard Shevardnadze, Gorbachev's foreign minister, who was presumably in a position to know, said that the country had spent approximately a quarter of its GNP on the military. We will never know the exact figure, but it is now clear that the Soviet leaders spent an extraordinary proportion of the country's resources building up its military strength. If Shevardnadze was correct, the proportional burden on the Soviet economy was five times greater than that on the US economy. But even this high figure is somewhat misleading: in an economy of scarcity, most of the much-needed resources were used for ultimately nonproductive purposes, and the most able and best-educated people worked for the military industrial complex.

It would be simple-minded to attribute the collapse of the Soviet experiment entirely, or even largely, to heavy military investment; however, it stands to reason that such a policy was a contributing factor. The question arises: why these heavy investments? Undoubtedly the Soviet leaders perceived threats. The lesson of the Cuban missile crisis was that the Soviet Union was not yet a global power, one able to project its strength anywhere in the world. As relations with China deteriorated, the leaders were concerned for the security of the extremely long border between the two countries. The Soviet leaders considered the East European satellites the first line of defense of the fatherland, and this region was obviously insecure. The politicians in Moscow understood that the communist regimes there depended on the presence of the Red Army. Yet it is obvious, at least in retrospect, that the military buildup went beyond the needs of simple

Ford and Brezhnev

defense. After all, Brezhnev and his colleagues did not need a powerful army to keep Poles, Hungarians, and Czechs in line, and it was highly likely that the United States could be deterred by the Soviet nuclear arsenal.

We must look for psychological explanations. The Soviet leaders were insecure. One could easily read between the lines of their statements: they craved respect, and above all they wanted to be treated by the Americans as equals. It was obviously easier to achieve prestige by building up military strength than by creating a modern, vibrant economy able to meet the needs of the people. During the early decades a major source of strength of Soviet foreign policy had been its ideological appeal; but in the age of "real, existing socialism," an assertive foreign policy could be based only on military power. Brezhnev and his comrades built up a vast military colossus in order to acquire prestige, respect, and legitimacy. This policy was not unsuccessful. Not only did members of the Politburo enjoyed the prestige that came with the leadership of a superpower, but many if not all the citizens of the Soviet Union probably took some satisfaction in the military power of their country. In purely military terms, in terms of influence in world affairs, a Soviet citizen could legitimately think that the direction of change favored his system, and that the future was on the side of his regime. Such a belief was an important legitimizing force.

Relations between the two superpowers were of paramount importance for Soviet policymakers. Soviet spokesmen advocated a policy of peaceful coexistence and relaxation of tensions. This relaxation, however, from the

Soviet point of view, did not mean that the Soviet Union would not make further efforts to extend its influence by supporting "wars of national liberation" or take advantage of the problems faced by the West. Indeed, the temptation was irresistible: the United States in the late 1960s and early 1970s was torn apart by the Vietnam War and later by the Watergate affair. The Soviet goal was to continue the expansion of Soviet influence and at the same time lessen the danger of war. As the enemies of détente in the West never failed to point out, the relaxation of tensions allowed the Soviet Union to achieve its greatest success in the international arena.

Improved Chinese–American relations also compelled Soviet policy-makers to find a modus vivendi with the United States, for they were concerned that their two enemies might come to an agreement at their expense. It was important for them that President Nixon and his chief foreign-policy adviser, Henry Kissinger, after their remarkable trip to China in 1971, also traveled to the Soviet Union. But perhaps the most important reason for pursuing the policy of détente was the desire to get access to Western technology and credits. Western technology has always been an important factor even in the earliest stages of Soviet industrialization; in an age of vast technological expansion, access to this technology was essential.

The time was ripe. Western policymakers, especially Nixon and Kissinger, thought in terms of *Realpolitik*: they assumed that since communist ideology was a visibly spent force, the Soviet Union had ceased to be a political entity governed by ideology. They saw it as an expansionist power, but neverthe-less a participant in the global balance of power, a state among others – in a word, a fit partner for negotiations. In particular, Nixon and Kissinger hoped to gain Soviet help in settling the Vietnam War. From the Western point of view the purpose of détente was to lessen the danger of war, of course, but also to tie the Soviet world to the Western economies and thereby to encourage more restrained and responsible behavior. Rightly or wrongly, many in the West believed that the integration of Soviet-style economies into the world economy would give leverage to the developed countries. Ironic-ally, Western businessmen who overestimated the possibility of commercial benefits for themselves from such contacts became the most enthusiastic promoters of détente.

In 1972 American and Soviet negotiators signed the SALT (Strategic Arms Limitation Treaty) agreement, which in effect legitimized the existing bal-ance of nuclear forces. Almost immediately the two sides entered negoti-ations for SALT II, a treaty that would have resulted in an actual reduction of the number of weapons. The Soviet Union also enthusiastically joined the US effort to prevent nuclear proliferation, because it was in the Soviet interest to prevent Germany and China from acquiring nuclear weapons.

In 1975 European and American diplomats gathered in Helsinki for a European "security conference." On this occasion the contracting parties signed three sets of treaties; the first dealt with political and diplomatic issues. It was this section that included the famous paragraph in which the signatories promised to respect "human rights," such as freedom of thought and religion. From the Soviet point of view, the paragraph that really mattered was the one in which the participants recognized the existing borders in Europe as inviolable. Soviet diplomacy had worked for this goal for a long time. It meant a formal recognition of borders regarded as only temporary since the 1945 Potsdam conference. At the time this was regarded as a major Soviet gain. However, it had been clear for a long time that the West had not the slightest intention of changing these borders in any case, and it is therefore hard to see this as a major concession.

The second set of agreements concerned economics, scientific exchanges, and trade relations. Undoubtedly these agreements were far more important for the Soviet side, which hoped to gain credits and access to advanced technology. In the third set of treaties the Soviet side gave concessions: it accepted the obligation of allowing the reunification of families and in general improved and extended international contacts. Few people at the time believed that outside powers would be able to ensure that the Soviet side lived up to its commitments. Nevertheless, the vague obligation to "observe human rights" accepted by Soviet diplomats in Helsinki turned out to be a powerful weapon in the hands of dissidents, who time and again embarrassed the regime by pointing to international treaty obligations.

In retrospect it is unclear who got a better deal in Helsinki. It was, of course, an advantage to have the gains of the Second World War fully and officially recognized, and the Soviet Union undoubtedly needed extended economic contacts with the West. However, as the Soviet leaders realized, these ties were dangerous. The West was inherently subversive, because the vision of Western affluence undermined the Soviet regime.

The Helsinki agreements made little difference on the international chess board. In every trouble spot in the world the Soviet Union and the West supported opposite sides; the path of détente was not smooth. It would happen, as it did in Ethiopia and Somalia, that two sides in the dispute actually changed sponsors in mid course of a conflict. In most of these conflicts, save the Middle East, Soviet involvement, while expensive in terms of resources, was not such as to risk military confrontation with the United States. When it came to actual fighting, the Soviets preferred to use a proxy; their Cuban allies in fact participated in several civil wars in Africa. The desire to be a superpower and to have worldwide influence was not cheap. As so many powers before and since have found, such participation rarely gains genuine allies or brings material benefits. Third world countries and movements within them managed to use the great powers at least as much as they were used by them.

The Middle East was different. Here American commitment to the state of Israel was so great that Soviet support for the other side created a most dangerous situation. In the 1973 war leaders in Moscow faced a dilemma:

on the one hand, another military defeat of the Arab states, armed by Soviet weapons, might fatally weaken Soviet influence in the Middle East; but, on the other, an Arab victory would bring American intervention and the danger of a Soviet–American confrontation. After the initial Egyptian victories, achieved by surprise, the tide of battle quickly turned and the Israeli armies moved forward victoriously. At this point the goal of Soviet diplomacy was to conclude an armistice as soon as possible.

Although Soviet arms and training methods proved inferior, and the Soviet Union did not emerge from the crisis with increased respect among its Arab clients, nevertheless the conflict had beneficial consequences for the Soviet Union. The skyrocketing price of oil weakened Western economies and benefited the Soviet Union, the world's largest oil producer. Further, the 1973 war weakened Western unity, because Western Europe was unwilling to follow the pro-Israeli American policy.

Ironically, following the Second World War, Soviet soldiers fired in anger only at citizens of other communist countries. The promise that in a world of classless societies wars would become impossible turned out to be as utopian as many other Marxist predictions. In fact, Soviet policymakers had no greater problem than how to deal with a bellicose communist China. The Chinese became competitors in the struggle for ideological supremacy within the communist camp, and the dispute allowed Soviet satellites to maneuver between the two communist giants. Chinese denunciation of Soviet policy as revisionist was damaging because it was true: Moscow had long since abandoned the cause of international revolution.

The hostile relations between the two major communist powers differed from US–Soviet relations. Presumably there was much in Western and particularly US policy that surprised the men in the Kremlin, but nevertheless the two sides came to know one another fairly well, and the Soviet leaders did not really expect the Americans to embark on an action that would have unforeseeable consequences. By contrast, Chinese policy in the age of Mao's "cultural revolution" seemed altogether unpredictable and, from the Soviet point of view, highly dangerous. Mao's statement that the country could afford to sacrifice the lives of hundreds of millions of its citizens could not altogether be regarded as a bluff in the age of the cultural revolution, at a time when millions went on rampages, waving the "little red book" of Chairman Mao's largely infantile sayings. Soviet strategy was to make it clear to the Chinese – and not only with words, but with actions – that the Soviet Union was ready to defend its borders and interests. The consequence was a protracted border war along the Amur river for the possession of insignificant islands. While the majority of the Soviet people may have been ambivalent about the West, they had unmitigated dislike verging on racist hatred for the Chinese. The hard line taken by the leaders against China was undoubtedly popular.

The bloc was disintegrating; the awful uniformity imposed by the Stalinist Soviet Union gradually lifted. The direction taken by individual satellites depended on past tradition and political culture, but also on the accident of personalities. Yugoslavia never again became a satellite; Albania was taking advantage of the Sino-Soviet split and preferred to have a distant sponsor; Romania's Ceausescu, who started out as a reformer, became the worst tyrant but exhibited increasing independence from the Soviet Union in foreign policy; in the Balkans, only Bulgaria remained unfailingly loyal. Moscow had the most trouble with the East Central European satellites; and these were considered most important, from both an economic and a strategic point of view.

The German "Democratic Republic," as East Germany was called, functioned surprisingly well. A reasonably high standard of living, combined with an efficient repressive machinery, assured stability. The Hungarians also found an acceptable compromise with the communist regime of Janos Kadar. The man who came to power with the help of Soviet tanks that suppressed the Hungarian revolution amazingly managed to convince his countrymen that his brand of liberalism was the best they could get under the circumstances. He allowed a degree of free public discussion and criticism and used the slogan, "those who are not against us are with us." Most significantly, he introduced economic reforms that for a while at least brought a degree of prosperity. In the 1960s and 1970s, Hungary was the most livable country in the Communist bloc, or as was said at the time: "Hungary was the gayest barrack in the camp of socialism."

In the Brezhnev era the Czechoslovaks were the first to challenge the communist regime. Arguably, other countries in the region had needed thoroughgoing social and political changes after 1945 and therefore to some extent benefited from the communist revolution. A country that had maintained a decent democratic regime until 1938, when it was betrayed by the Western Allies, and that had an advanced economy needed no such revolution. Communist methods of organizing the economy had caused only harm.

By the early 1960s it was clear that the Czech economy was in trouble and that much-needed reforms necessitated a relaxation of political controls. However, the neo-Stalinist Antonin Novotny was in power and would give no concessions. The nationality question also added an explosive element. Although economically the Slovaks benefited from being part of the Czechoslovak state, they felt themselves discriminated against by the richer and better-educated Czechs. They well remembered that their leadership, accused of "bourgeois nationalism," had been particularly hard hit in the purges of the late Stalin period. The demands for de-Stalinization, for economic reforms, and for increased Slovak autonomy proved too strong for Novotny to resist. When the Soviet leaders did not come to his aid, in December 1967 he was forced to give up the leadership of the party.

Alexander Dubcek, a Slovak who became first secretary on Novotny's removal, was a leader in the mold of Imre Nagy and Gorbachev – that is, a convinced communist who believed that it was possible to do better within the existing system. However, when things got out of hand he refused to turn against his own people. The spring and early summer of 1968 was a period of euphoria in Prague. Courageous individuals spoke increasingly openly and honestly, overcoming inhibitions instilled by two decades of terror. For a while it seemed that socialism would not be merely a promise in the distant future, that its humanistic potential would be immediately realized. Maybe, after all, the promise of socialism was not altogether empty. Maybe it was possible to build a society that combined freedom and social justice, and thereby to construct "socialism with a human face." This was the last flicker of the communist ideological flame. Events within a communist country, if only for a historical moment, could still inspire enthusiasm beyond the boundaries of the camp.

The Czechoslovaks had learned from the Hungarian experience and were extremely careful not to provoke Soviet intervention. They continued to speak of "the leading role of the party," whatever that meant under the circumstances, and did not aim to return nationalized property to the previous owners. Most importantly, they continued to toe the Soviet line in foreign policy. Nevertheless, in August 1968, after repeated warnings, Soviet troops invaded the country and ended this experiment of "socialism with a human face." The military operation was carried out with impressive efficiency, and there was little resistance against the occupiers. The politics of the operation, however, was clumsy. For some time the Soviet authorities could not find a Czechoslovak Kadar, a party leader of standing who would take responsibility for having invited the Soviet intervention.

The fact that Moscow was willing to tolerate Ceausescu in Romania, a man who followed a much more independent line than Dubcek, indicates that Soviet concerns were not with foreign policy. Their fear, perhaps well justified, was that the communist system was disintegrating in Czechoslovakia, that this would have an inevitable effect on the rest of Eastern Europe, and that ultimately the reformist spirit might infect the Soviet Union itself. In view of what happened a couple of decades later, such fears cannot be dismissed as altogether unrealistic. The Soviets justified this particular brutal action by the "Brezhnev doctrine." Soviet spokesmen maintained that the "victory of socialism" was irreversible, and therefore it was the duty of other "socialist" countries to protect it wherever it was under siege. This articulation may have been novel, but the policy, of course, was not. Ultimately, under Gustav Husak (another Slovak) in the 1970s and 1980s, Czechoslovakia became the most repressive communist state in East Central Europe.

In Czechoslovakia by brutal oppression, in Hungary by a mixture of concessions and repression, the Soviet-sponsored regimes achieved equilibrium. In Poland, by contrast, that stabilization never took place. The consequences of the Polish October of 1956 were long-lasting: a semi-independent Catholic Church survived, agriculture was never recollectivized, and a degree of freedom of the press and travel to the West were allowed. Most importantly, perhaps, the lesson that Polish workers drew from the extraordinary events of 1956 was that they could put pressure on the government by demonstrating. It was soon evident that the hero of 1956, Gomulka, had no vision of a post-Stalinist Poland. When in 1970 the government attempted to raise food prices, a confrontation with workers in the streets forced Gomulka out of office. A regime that gave concessions not out of strength, like Kadar in Hungary, but out of weakness, proved itself particularly vulnerable to further attacks.

Gomulka's successor, Edward Gierek, was successful at first. He attracted foreign investment, and his easygoing style was more congenial to the average Pole than that of the severe and puritanical Gomulka. But then success turned to failure. The government did not use the foreign loans wisely. Instead of investing in the modernization of the economy, the loans were used to maintain consumption standards, because the regime desperately wanted to preserve stability. When Western economies floundered following the oil crisis of 1973, these markets came to be closed to Polish products. Consequently, the country could not repay the loans and came to be heavily burdened by an ever-growing foreign debt. In 1976, when the government once again attempted to raise food prices, demonstrations followed and the government had to back down. It was an ironic situation: a tyrannical communist regime was unable to make economic changes that any democratic regime could easily have made.

The disturbances that started in the summer of 1980 at first seemed to repeat the old pattern. However, within a short time the most deadly challenge to the Soviet system developed. The Hungarian revolution was too brief for the anti-Soviet coalition to break down: reform communists and anticommunists fought together. In Czechoslovakia in 1968 reform communists were in the foreground, and the working classes were hardly involved. In Poland, by contrast, the moving force was the working class. The workers formed a labor union which they appropriately but provocatively named "Solidarity." The organization soon became much more than a labor union. The entire country came to be united not to reform the regime, but to repudiate it altogether. The country enjoyed an extraordinary sense of unity: workers, farmers, and intellectuals joined the noncommunist Solidarity movement. The party disintegrated, and the pretense that communist Poland was a workers' state was forever demolished.

For a while the Soviet leaders and the Polish communists hesitated, but after the passage of more than a year they decided to act. The denouement came in December 1981. This time the operation was carried out by the Poles themselves; and from a purely technical point of view, the job was done impressively well: the military cut communications and arrested Solidarity activists quickly, making resistance impossible. However, for the first time communist forces utterly failed in the second stage of normalization. The military action against the united Polish nation succeeded only because

Demonstration in Moscow in the days of Brezhnev

the Soviet army stood behind the oppressors, and it was better that the repression be carried out by Poles than by hated Russians. Poland in the 1980s came to be a running sore in the side of communism: here was a regime where the economy was in a shambles, the population sullen, the political system unreformed and unreformable, and the machinery of repression hesitant.

If at the end of the Brezhnev period Soviet foreign-policy makers attempted to evaluate their successes and failures, they must have come up with a mixed evaluation. Within the bloc, the failures outweighed the successes. Although the rhetoric of the Sino-Soviet conflict moderated somewhat, and the danger of military conflict ameliorated, no genuine normalization of relations could take place. Regional interests in Southeast Asia, and a Russian dislike of the Chinese which can fairly be characterized as racist, continued to stand in the way of improved relations. Eastern Europe became a drain on Soviet resources. Worst of all, the Soviet leaders allowed themselves carelessly and stupidly to be drawn into an Afghan civil war in 1979, placing themselves in an unwinnable situation. That war not only inflicted casualties; it also acted as a brake on improved relations with the West.

The election of a Republican administration in the United States ended détente and led to a new arms race that the Soviet Union could ill afford. Soviet diplomacy initiated a campaign aimed at blocking the deployment of American middle-range missiles in Europe. Although this campaign had some successes in separating the United States from its European allies, ultimately it failed to block deployment. The revolution in Iran in 1979 weakened Western standing in the Middle East; however, that revolution did not ambiguously advance Soviet interests. The Soviet Union expended much-needed resources to influence events and gain allies in different parts of the world. On occasion some of those responsible for the formulation of foreign policy must have asked themselves: was it all worth it?

Failed Reforms

INTERREGNUM

Stalin's death created a temporary panic; Khrushchev's removal from office surprised most people; but Brezhnev's death in 1982 had been anticipated, and even eagerly awaited by many. Leonid Brezhnev had suffered a stroke in 1975, and by the time of his death he was obviously infirm and increasingly senile. Soviet citizens and foreigners saw this unimpressive, old, tired man as the symbol of the country he headed. It was a regime that had run out of new ideas.

The power struggle that brought Yurii Andropov to the top had been decided even before Brezhnev's death. The decisive moment was Andropov's move from the KGB to the secretariat of the Central Committee. Even in the Soviet Union of the 1980s it would have been unseemly to go directly from the political police to the head of the empire. When Andropov took over Suslov's job – the latter had just died – it was clear that he was well positioned in the power struggle. He was somewhat younger than the other members of the geriatric Politburo, and clearly more energetic and intelligent. (The average age of the members of the Politburo at the time of Brezhnev's death was 71.) He had achieved his first major distinction at the time of the Hungarian revolution of 1956, when he was the Soviet ambassador to Budapest. His sly and duplicitous behavior won the admiration of his senior colleagues. In that crucial time in Budapest he came in touch with the top leaders of the party and called attention to himself. Soon he was made head of the department of the Central Committee that handled relations with the other communist countries. From this post he was moved to the powerful position of head of the KGB, and in 1973 became a member of the Politburo. Andropov was thus the first top Soviet leader who had spent a substantial part of his career in service of the political police.

In that most important post Andropov showed himself to be a smart, ruthless figure in struggling against subversion – i.e., against the dissident movement. It is interesting, therefore, that on his ascension to the top position he was regarded not only within but even outside the Soviet Union, at least in some circles, as a reformer, a moderate, and indeed a liberal. It is of course absurd to see a man partially responsible for the bloody repression of the Hungarian revolution, a determined and ruthless enemy of the dissident movement, as a liberal in any meaningful sense. It is not surprising, however, that as an intelligent man he understood that the country needed reforms of some kind. Indeed, his intimate knowledge of the ideas of the dissidents probably made him more open-minded than most of his colleagues. In a similar vein, we now know that in 1953 it was the unspeakable Beria, another chief of the terror machine, who had advocated the most thoroughgoing reforms.

It was not difficult to appear more competent than Brezhnev. In fact, however, Andropov's proposed solutions to the country's problems were superficial; presumably he saw no need for systemic reforms. Andropov advocated enforcing labor discipline in the factories and initiated a struggle against corruption. He stayed in office too short a time to realize how profound the problems were; his tenure lasted only fifteen months, and during most of this period he was incapacitated by illness. It is at least conceivable, though unlikely, that had he stayed in office he might have followed the same path as Gorbachev.

The details of the complex political struggles that took place within the highest leadership are not altogether clear, but it is obvious that there was a faction more conscious of the failings of the system and therefore more willing to experiment with reforms, a sort of reformist party, and another group of old men for whom reforms seemed dangerous. Matters had to be settled by compromise. While the seemingly more daring Andropov received the top job, the number two man remained Brezhnev's closest associate, Konstantin Chernenko. When Andropov died in February 1984, Chernenko was elected first secretary; but this time the relatively youthful Mikhail Gorbachev, Andropov's protégé, was made second in command. The 73-year-old Chernenko was surely the least intelligent, capable, and charismatic of all the Soviet leaders. His achievements were minimal – he owed his eminent position entirely to his closeness to Brezhnev. In that feudal political system, Chernenko's political star rose in conjunction with that of his friend and mentor.

Chernenko failed to put his stamp on the political system. Most of the time he was not in charge because he was ill. In the absence of the ailing general secretary, Gorbachev often chaired Politburo meetings, thereby acquiring experience in areas where formerly he had had little. One might say that the most important political development during Chernenko's brief tenure was the increase in Gorbachev's stature. Gorbachev traveled abroad and made a good impression on Western leaders, among them Margaret Thatcher. She uttered the famous phrase: "Gorbachev is a man with whom we can do business." This trip to London was a significant event in Gorbachev's rise to

Nevskii prospekt in Leningrad

power, for not only did he give a good account of himself, but for the first time he appeared on television in the West, and more importantly at home. He proved himself to be a natural television personality: he exhibited poise and also a curious kind of warmth for a Soviet leader. Gorbachev appeared in London with his wife, Raisa, a stylish and well-educated woman. This was an extraordinary change: at the time of Andropov's death, the US State Department did not even know whether the Soviet leader had a wife.[1]

When Chernenko died, the Politburo was determined to prevent the embarrassment of having yet another ailing leader. They wanted to select a general secretary who was young and vigorous, and Gorbachev was the obvious choice. There was no doubt a struggle behind the scenes; some of the leaders were more favorably inclined toward initiating reforms than others. However, it would be a mistake to think of the top leadership as neatly divided between the friends and opponents of reform. Most of the leaders were ambivalent. None could have completely failed to see the seriousness of the problems that the Soviet Union faced, but all must have been somewhat afraid of the risks inherent in experimentation.

"ACCELERATION"

Russian and Soviet history has always been characterized by alternating stasis and reform. After the quiet period of Brezhnev and the two short-lived regimes of Andropov and Chernenko, the country was on the threshold of a time of rapid changes. The newly elected general secretary, Gorbachev, may have imagined himself an Alexander II, the "tsar-liberator," who with a series of reforms transformed the tsarist system, and perhaps extended its life span by fifty years. Politicians, statesmen, and revolutionaries never actually accomplish what they set out to do, so it is not surprising that the Soviet leader achieved something very different than he would have liked. No one, including Gorbachev, could have foreseen the magnitude of the changes the country was embarking on.

Brezhnev and Chernenko were conservative men, faceless representatives of the Soviet bureaucracy. It is hard to see them as individuals; their background and upbringing hardly mattered, for they did not put their own stamp on Soviet society. Gorbachev, by contrast, belongs to the category of Stalin and Khrushchev, leaders who embarked on their tasks with a desire to introduce change. It is safe to say that had Gorbachev not emerged victorious in the power struggle, or had he been a different person, the fate of the Soviet Union would have been different. Who Gorbachev was, how his worldview developed, and how he saw his tasks are therefore matters of historical significance.

Intelligent as he undoubtedly was, and aware of the seriousness of the problems, it is highly unlikely that even he appreciated the depth of the crisis in which his country found itself. In this respect he was similar to two other figures of recent communist history, the Hungarian Imre Nagy and the Slovak Alexander Dubcek. Like them he initiated a process. When matters got out of hand, when the process went too far or in the wrong direction, he was presented with a choice of brutal repression or acquiescence. In these circumstances, as Nagy and Dubcek had done before him, Gorbachev almost always made the morally correct choice.

How could the Soviet system produce a man like Gorbachev? This question is based on the false assumption that the Soviet regime had indeed succeeded in creating "the new socialist human being" – faceless bureaucrats without individuality, without the ability to think for themselves. Human beings turned out to be much less malleable than some hoped or than others feared. Most likely there were hundreds if not thousands of middle-level party and governmental figures who, while echoing the official line, could see perfectly clearly that the Soviet Union was approaching a crisis. It is true, however, that since the political system rewarded conformity, the real Stalin, the real Khrushchev, and indeed the real Gorbachev could emerge only after they achieved supreme power.

Gorbachev was born in the fertile Stavropol region of south Russia in 1931. His paternal grandfather was a victim of the antikulak campaign that accompanied collectivization. He was deported and allowed to return only years later. To what extent the experience of his grandfather played a role in Gorbachev's political development is impossible to say. Being a convinced supporter of the system while at the same time having a close relative who was a victim of terror was not unusual. Most of the Stalinist leaders had relatives in camps, and nonetheless they continued to serve the "master." Gorbachev's close colleague and later an opponent of his reforms, Yegor Ligachev, also had victims of Stalinist terror in his family, yet remained fundamentally conservative.

Gorbachev had received a much better education than leaders of the previous generation. Unlike most other leaders, who had technical educations, Gorbachev studied law and took a correspondence course in agricultural economics. He came to intellectual maturity in the post-Stalin era: as a student in Moscow, he witnessed the intellectual and political ferment of the period. It is an interesting coincidence that one of his friends at the university was Zdenek Mlynar, later an architect of the Prague spring.

Gorbachev's rise within the hierarchy was typical of a successful member of the apparat. First he achieved distinction in the Komsomol organization and found powerful supporters who recognized his talent and ambition. Then at a relatively early age he was promoted to the powerful position of first secretary of the party organization of the Stavropol district. Since this district was a favorite vacation place for members of the party hierarchy, the young politician quickly acquired important contacts. Gorbachev also gained first-hand experience with the Achilles heel of Soviet economics, agriculture. He proved himself an adept, imaginative, and flexible organizer, and as a consequence achieved remarkable jumps in his career: in 1978 he was brought to Moscow as a secretary of the central committee, in the next year he became a candidate member of the Politburo, and in 1980 he became a full member of that body. Gorbachev, a relatively young, vigorous, and articulate man, was clearly different from his predecessors. Unlike them, but much like Khrushchev, he was not afraid to appear in different parts of the country, mingling with the common folk and listening to their problems.

After Gorbachev became general secretary, a change in the style of leadership was immediately evident. The difficulties the Soviet Union faced were considerable, and the new leader had to start out in several directions at once: he had to reinvigorate the party and governmental apparatus, institute reforms that would improve the sluggish economy, and in order to gain time ameliorate the hostility with the West, in particular with the United States. Like Soviet leaders before him, he consolidated his power by bringing his own followers into the highest levels of the government and of the party. Since the Brezhnev regime had turned into a gerontocracy, where the political system operated under the slogan "stability of cadres" and the goal was to ensure as much security for high officials as possible, the average age of the leadership had risen to ridiculously high levels. Under the circumstances, the change of personnel was not only the result of Gorbachev's desire to consolidate power, but also the natural consequence of the long-postponed house-cleaning. He removed those who had been in office too long and were very old, and those who had been his rivals. The 80-year-old conservative prime minister Nikolai Tikhonov went into long-overdue retirement, and his place was taken by Nikolai Ryzhkov, who soon also joined the Politburo. Andrei Gromyko, who had the distinction of being the longest-serving foreign minister of a major power, was eased out of his job. But, because he had supported Gorbachev's appointment, he was rewarded with the largely honorary post of president. Grigorii Romanov, the first secretary of the Leningrad party organization, a rather unsavory character who had been Gorbachev's chief rival, was now removed from the Politburo. Viktor Grishin, another possible alternative to Gorbachev who headed the Moscow organization, lost that post in 1986.

Had Gorbachev been a radical reformer in 1985, he would have appointed like-minded people to positions of power. In fact, the new appointees were a remarkably heterogeneous group. They included Viktor Chebrikov, the head of the KGB, who for his early support of Gorbachev received a seat on the Politburo. Ligachev, an Andropov associate, was also made a Politburo member. Soon these two politicians came to be leaders of the conservative forces within the top leadership. On the other hand, a close associate of Gorbachev – Eduard Shevardnadze, the chief of the Georgian party organization – took Gromyko's job in the foreign ministry; and Boris Yeltsin, a maverick already in the dull age of Brezhnev, became first secretary of the crucial Moscow organization. Aleksandr Yakovlev, the future theorist of *perestroika* and the most consistent liberal in the new top leadership, became a member of the Politburo in 1987. As a long-time ambassador to Canada, where he had been "exiled" for his liberal views, he had a better knowledge of the West than other members of the Politburo. (While in Canada, naturally, he had never voiced his heterodox views.) This leadership could not long remain united.

At the same time Gorbachev carried out much-needed purges in the provinces. Middle-level leadership, heavily compromised by corruption, needed renewal. This change hit especially hard in the Central Asian republics, where corruption had been notoriously widespread. The removal of some corrupt figures from republican leadership, however, contributed to the development of nationalist feelings. For example, the removal of a Kazakh as head of the republic party organization in 1986, and the substitution of an ethnic Russian, resulted in riots in Alma Ata. Evidently, many in the Caucasus and in Central Asia believed that it was better to be ruled by their own scoundrels than by the Russians. In retrospect Gorbachev came to regard placing a Russian at the head of the Kazakh organization as one of his greatest errors, a sign that he did not understand the power of nationalism.

The first and most important task was to improve the performance of the economy. The peoples of the Soviet Union in the era of Khrushchev and during the first decade of Brezhnev's rule became accustomed to a slow and gradual, but nonetheless meaningful, improvement in their standard of living. Deteriorating economic performance brought such improvements to an end. Gorbachev rightly feared that there would be a political price to pay. Furthermore, Soviet standing in world affairs depended on the level of military spending, which in turn depended on the health of the economy.

Gorbachev reported later that as he rose within the hierarchy he acquired an ever-clearer understanding of the weaknesses of Soviet society, and above all of the problems of the economy. He understood far better than his predecessors that his country was falling behind precisely in the most advanced branches of the economy, and he knew the dangers implied by technological backwardness. He regarded narrowing that gap between the Soviet Union and the advanced West as one of his most important tasks. His first reforms, however, did not touch the essential elements of the system: as Andropov had before him, he called for increased discipline, improved quality, and decentralization in decisionmaking. In order to improve quality the government created a new bureaucracy and introduced evaluators and controllers in factories, whose task was to reject faulty products. This simplistic way of dealing with a complex problem created only dissatisfaction on the factory floor. Increased discipline meant that people had to work harder for the same amount of money. Gorbachev failed to win over the working class. He did not understand that reforms were unlikely to produce immediate results – but on the contrary in order to improve the economy sacrifices first had to be made. Such a position, however, was difficult to sell to the Soviet people, for they had heard such requests often enough in the past, and the glorious future never seemed to arrive.

The struggle against overcentralization was well within the Soviet tradition: both Khrushchev and Kosygin had attempted to give greater freedom to factory directors. The directors' hidden incentives, however, often encouraged them to go against the interests of the national economy. The directors, for example, preferred to spend money on their wage fund and invested too little in new technologies that would have been essential for economic growth. Investments in new technologies were inevitably risky and unlikely to bring the immediate results on which their bonuses depended.

The idea that the regime should altogether abandon centralized control over the economy remained unthinkable, something contrary to the new leaders' concept of socialism. A genuine market economy would have had obvious and far-reaching political consequences. Gorbachev and his comrades were determined to carry out changes within the system; but it was the system itself that was the source of the trouble. The changes, instead of improving the situation, undermined the existing centrally planned and centrally controlled economy. The sad and paradoxical result of the attempt at reform was that the growth rate further declined and the gap between the advanced economies of the West and the Soviet economy widened. Gorbachev's achievement in the first period of reforms was a negative one: it became increasingly obvious that, within the system, major improvements were not possible.

Almost immediately after coming to power, in May 1985, the new general secretary embarked on his first campaign, the war against alcoholism. This campaign, which perhaps made the most immediate impression on the Soviet people was in line with the economic reforms and very much in the spirit of Andropov. The problem was real and obvious: alcoholism was the long-standing curse of Russian and Soviet societies, a problem that was getting worse and worse. Alcoholism was a major cause of the decline in life expectancy, increasing infant mortality, crime, and of course the deplorably low labor productivity. Discipline had to be improved: people were drinking too much.

The campaign started with a barrage of temperance propaganda. At official functions the serving of alcoholic drinks was abandoned – which may or may not have made an impression on the general populace, but certainly created opportunities for making jokes at the expense of the general secretary. The government made greater efforts to enforce the law against home brew, raised the price of vodka, limited distribution by cutting the number of outlets, and limited the times during which alcohol could be sold. The campaign was carried out in a crude way: the attack was made not only on vodka but also on all alcoholic beverages, including wine. As a consequence some age-old vineyards in the Caucasus were cut down, which hardly helped to alleviate alcoholism.

There was a price to pay. Although alcohol consumption declined (it is difficult to measure exactly how much, for home brew continued to be produced and that, by definition, escaped the statisticians), the campaign was hugely unpopular. Alcoholics did not stop being alcoholics overnight, and little effort was made to cure them. Not surprisingly, those who needed alcohol in their desperation drank anything that contained it, and the number of people hospitalized for drinking poison increased greatly. The increased production of home brew (*samogon*) created a shortage of sugar, which then had to be rationed. Further, the campaign was expensive. Revenues from vodka were an important part of the state budget; when a larger share was produced by home brew, the treasury suffered.

Gorbachev had the misfortune of taking office when relations with the West were poor. At the end of the 1970s and the beginning of the 1980s the cold war revived: Soviet intervention in Afghanistan, the repression in Poland in 1981 (to be sure, carried out by the Poles themselves), the placement of SS-20 missiles in operations that threatened Western Europe, and finally the shooting down of Korean Airlines flight 007 in 1983 all resulted in strong Western responses. Because of the Soviet intervention in Afghanistan, the Carter administration refused to ask the Senate to ratify an earlier arms control agreement. When the Reagan administration came into office the Americans began using a bellicose language that had not been heard in

international affairs since the days of Stalin and Dulles and, more importantly, they matched words with action. They gained the agreement of
Europeans to place middle-range missiles on their soil, matched the Soviet
SS-20s, and embarked on a long-range military buildup that included the
Strategic Defense Initiative (SDI). The Soviet leaders felt threatened; the vast
military buildup achieved at the cost of great sacrifice did not, after all, bring
security. American words and actions convinced the Soviet leadership that
they were facing a dangerous and unpredictable enemy. Andropov's
response was to pursue an assertive and aggressive policy in order not to
show weakness.

Although Gorbachev's primary interest was in domestic policy – i.e., a
revival of the troubled economy – his earliest and most significant achievement was the reorientation of Soviet foreign policy. His priorities necessitated a new course based on a desire to ameliorate tensions with the West,
and in particular with the United States. Since the economic reforms made
the reduction of military expenditures inevitable, a calmer international
atmosphere was in the interest of the Soviet Union. Furthermore, as noted,
improved relations with advanced industrial countries were a precondition
for acquiring Western technology and credits. It became evident that the
West was prosperous and successful and that in the modern world the Soviet
Union could avoid participating in the world economy only at its peril. Most
likely Gorbachev was sincere when he spoke at the very outset of his tenure
of his desire to enable the Soviet Union to reenter what he memorably called
"our common European home."

To give Soviet foreign policy a new direction and a new face, Gorbachev
chose a new team; the foreign-policy establishment was shaken up more than
any other branch of the leadership. Military men now had a smaller role to
play in the formulation of policy. Shevardnadze, the new foreign minister,
had been first secretary of the Georgian party and had no foreign-policy
experience. Another close adviser, Anatoly Dobrynin, did have a great deal
of foreign-policy experience – he had been ambassador to Washington for
decades – but he had little standing within the top leadership within the
party. Perhaps the most influential adviser was Aleksandr Yakovlev, a man
with an intimate knowledge of the West and a genuine liberal. Gorbachev
also replaced most of the key ambassadors.

The new course required a new ideological base and an altogether different style for, in diplomacy, words mattered. Soviet leaders since 1917 had
regarded international affairs as an aspect of class struggle and had taken for
granted the inevitability of conflict. They recognized that on occasion they
had to give concessions to their enemies, but assumed that the interests of
capitalists and socialists were eternally in conflict, that whatever damaged
the interests of one system benefited the other. Given this background,
Gorbachev's talking about general human values that transcended class
interests was revolutionary. The general secretary considered the greatest

danger to his country not an unprovoked attack by the capitalist West, but nuclear war itself. His phrase "our common European home" meant that the two systems could work together for their common benefit.

The government was now presented with a difficult choice: the country could further improve its international prestige by investing more in military hardware, but only at the expense of undermining the economic base essential for future expansion, or it could, at least temporarily, retrench. It is worth noting that previous governments, going back to tsarist times, had faced the same dilemma. The new line in foreign policy meant an acceptance of the second solution: the Soviet government reduced involvement in distant parts of the world and attempted to revive détente. The confident assumption that upheavals in third world countries would ultimately benefit Soviet interests turned out to be false. Soviet assistance to "revolutionary" regimes around the world cost too much and brought few benefits. Gorbachev created a veritable diplomatic revolution. Unlike the economy, which remained impervious to his attempts to change it, the diplomatic scene was quickly transformed. Age-old assumptions that the leaders and propagandists of the two systems held concerning one another came to be abandoned within a short time. The changes were almost entirely the consequence of Soviet retrenchment: Soviet troops were withdrawn from Afghanistan in 1989, and Soviet support for "national liberation movements" around the world was gradually eliminated, leading to the end of civil wars in Angola and Ethiopia and to the undermining of the economic health of the Castro regime in Cuba.

Soviet and American diplomats during the previous two decades had expended enormous efforts trying to achieve meaningful arms control. The arms control negotiations, however, had been largely fruitless because the strategic needs of the two powers were different. Now the situation changed. After a gap of six years, two summits took place in a relatively short time. Gorbachev and Reagan met in Geneva in the fall of 1985 and then in October 1986 in Reykjavik. Although no concrete agreements were reached on either occasion, these were important meetings, especially the second one. The negotiations were genuine and the issues breathtakingly ambitious, such as the elimination by the two sides of nuclear weapons. Gorbachev showed himself to be an open-minded and intelligent negotiator, though he failed to persuade Reagan to abandon SDI, something that the Soviet Union at this point obviously could not match. In 1987 the important INF treaty was signed, which eliminated intermediate-range nuclear weapons from Europe. In this area also, the Soviet leaders were ready to accept positions that their predecessors had resisted: Gorbachev was willing to withdraw intermediate-range ballistic missiles behind the Ural mountains and thereby in effect to accept the American position.

The point has been made primarily by conservative American commentators that it was Reagan's military buildup that forced the Soviet Union into bankruptcy and drove home the conclusion to the new leaders that they would never catch up with the Americans, and that as a consequence Reagan's policies were primarily responsible for the collapse of the Soviet Union. One may acknowledge that American technological superiority and seemingly inexhaustible economic resources gave pause to the Soviet leaders and may have been one of the reasons for their changing course. Moreover, the recognition of inferiority made them look all the harder for changes within the system and thereby created a crisis which the Soviet Union did not survive. Ironically, the conservative position is based on a gross underestimation of the problems faced by the Soviet regime. Had the Americans pursued the most moderate and timid policies, the Soviet system still could not have been successful in the circumstances prevailing at the end of the twentieth century. Reagan did not defeat the communists; the communists defeated themselves.

GLASNOST'

The decisive step in the transformation (and ultimate demise) of the Soviet system was not the timid attempt to reform the economy, or even international initiatives that aimed to define the Soviet role in the world more modestly, and therefore more in line with available resources, but the introduction of openness in discussing the past as well as the problems facing contemporary society. The term *glasnost'* was chosen deliberately over freedom of the press, freedom of thought, or freedom of conscience. The history of the concept goes back to the nineteenth century, when Slavophile intellectuals advocated not Western-style intellectual freedom in a democratic society, but openness in discussing public affairs. The Slavophiles wanted to allow the Russian people to voice their concerns, but at the same time did not want to limit the power of the autocrat. Gorbachev and his comrades understood the term as "constructive" criticism, that is, the voices of people who took the existence and superiority of the Soviet system for granted.

Why did Gorbachev not merely allow *glasnost'* but even encourage it? We can only guess his motives. There is no reason to doubt that Gorbachev regarded a certain degree of intellectual freedom as valuable in itself. After all, he really meant to return to what he thought were the "Leninist norms," which did include a greater degree of openness and honesty than the Soviet people had experienced in the Stalinist and even post-Stalinist years. But also fairly early he must have realized that his economic reforms were not succeeding. In order to deal with the problems, they first had to be realistically discussed and evaluated. Also, by opening previously forbidden subjects, such as the nature and extent of Stalinist repression, Gorbachev was hoping to find allies among the intelligentsia in his struggle against a conservative and entrenched bureaucracy.

The Chernobyl disaster in April 1986, so far the worst nuclear accident in human history, may have been the most significant turning point. The disaster was caused by shoddy construction and inadequate safety measures; but habitual, congenital Soviet-style secrecy contributed to the magnitude of the tragedy. When the accident occurred, the authorities attempted to suppress relevant information as much as possible, which of course made dealing with the dreadful consequences more difficult. In any case, the scale of the disaster and its international implications made concealment impossible. Allowing the news to dribble out slowly, telling the world the entire story only after the passage of some time, came to be a source of embarrassment, very much contrary to the image that Gorbachev hoped to convey.

In December 1986 Gorbachev had a telephone conversation with Andrei Sakharov, the great Soviet scientist and human rights advocate, who had been confined in exile to Gorkii, a provincial city closed to foreigners. Following this telephone call, Sakharov was allowed to return to Moscow. The return of this most admired dissident had great symbolic significance. It conveyed to reformers and liberals not only that this regime would deal with opponents differently than had previous regimes, but also that the great physicist had been right all along. Gorbachev hoped to gain the support of people like Sakharov, and to a great extent he succeeded, at least temporarily.

The years 1987 and 1988 were wonderful years of increasing freedom. Gradually *glasnost'* was transformed into freedom of speech. The phenomenon was similar to what happened in Hungary in 1956 and in Czechoslovakia in 1968. When intellectuals were allowed to speak more openly, they came to compete with one another in matters of courage, each attempting to push the limits of the permissible a little further. What seemed unthinkable at a given moment became commonplace a few months later. The taboos fell one after another, creating a heady atmosphere, a sense of excitement that can be compared to nothing else in Russian history.

The organizations of the creative intelligentsia, most prominently among them the Union of Writers and the Union of Cinematographers, were transformed. As a result of internal struggles, new leaderships came to the fore, and the party made no attempt to interfere. The new leadership of the Union of Cinematographers that came to power in May 1987 began by showing previously made films that had been banned from distribution. Outstanding among these was Tengis Abuladze's *Repentance*, a film made in 1984 in Georgia under the protection of Shevardnadze. This passionate and moving denunciation of dictatorship and terror was also a bitter attack on the generation that wanted to cover up the crimes, which seemed incapable of facing the truth.

The excitement in literature was caused not so much by new works that discussed current problems, but by the publication of books unavailable to Soviet readers in the past. Gorbachev and his associates not only allowed but encouraged the takeover of at least some of the journals by liberal editors. Authors who had enjoyed worldwide reputations, such as Nabokov, Brodskii, and Pasternak, for the first time became available to Russian readers. The accumulated great works of the past, and the bitterly anti-Stalinist works written for the desk drawer by writers such as Anatolii Rybakov (*Children of the Arbat*) and Vasilii Grossman (*Life and Fate*), had greater appeal than the writings of contemporaries. The readership of the literary journals, so-called thick journals, that published these authors vastly increased. People who had been hungry for honesty and truth for so long now could not get enough. Writers and intellectuals complained that they could not do their work because they spent all their time reading.

Ever since the death of Stalin, prominent writers such as Grossman, Vasilii Aksenov, Yurii Trifonov, and Andrei Siniavskii – sometimes in their published works, but more often in what could not be printed in the Soviet Union – had clearly showed that the entire system was rotten. They conveyed the impression to their readers that nothing from Soviet civilization was worth saving, that the line from Lenin to the present was straight. Explicitly or implicitly these writers found their models for a better society in the liberal West. Other writers, also well known – for example, Valentin Rasputin, Aleksandr Solzhenitsyn, Vladimir Soloukhin, and Viktor Astafev – though taking just as adversarial a stance and repudiating the Soviet past just as passionately, professed at the same time to find the medicine for Russia's current ailments in the distant past.

For the time being, as in revolutionary times, there seemed to be national unity at least as far as opposition to the neo-Stalinist system was concerned. In retrospect, we know that there never was such a unity, but the defenders of the old regime at least temporarily were silenced. The reformers, perhaps naively, believed that once the truth was revealed the old order that had been based on lies could never be reconstructed. Indeed, the Gorbachev reforms made an irreversible change. To be sure, in Hungary and in Czechoslovakia it had been possible to step back into communism, but a foreign army had to do the repressing. It is conceivable that, if Gorbachev at this point had become alarmed by the changes, he might have stopped them by the use of force. His greatest achievement therefore was something negative: he never carried out the clampdown that would have been necessary to return to the status quo ante, at a time when that was still possible. Evidently that would have gone contrary to his morality, to his convictions, to his ideas concerning socialism or communism.

In societies where alternatives cannot be articulated, whether because they are repressed or because people cannot easily envisage them, the crucial issues are discussed under the guise of historical debates. When people talked about the period of the NEP, a time of relative economic and cultural freedom, they wanted to argue either that the system that had existed in the 1920s could be used today as a model, or that the Soviet system never had a successful liberal period and therefore the possibility of a "market socialism" or "socialism with a human face" was remote. Many publicists wrote with great admiration of the last able tsarist statesman, Peter Stolypin. The point of reviving the memory of Stolypin was to argue that the imperial regime could have reformed itself; if Stolypin had not been killed and the war had not occurred, tsarist Russia would have survived. According to this view, the revolution and all the sufferings that followed from it were unnecessary. The Soviet regime was simply an unfortunate historical accident.

How history was handled had the greatest possible contemporary significance, and therefore historians should have had a particularly important role to play, but in fact they were never in the forefront. This is understandable given the nature of the profession. The Soviet political system had placed different and heavier limitations on historians than on creative writers, who could express themselves at least obliquely. Historians had the unpleasant task of legitimizing an illegitimate order through their writings. With omissions, outright lies, and conscious misinterpretations they created an ideological superstructure without which the Soviet state could not have existed. Under such circumstances the Soviet historical profession by and large did not attract the best people. Most historians were either genuine believers, careerists of various types, or simply not very bright.

The debates that took place among historians in the early *glasnost'* period – and there were many conferences and round tables – represented significant advances in the direction of producing more reasonable discussions of controversial turning points. These debates were often passionate, but for outsiders it was often difficult to understand the underlying causes, for the participants did not disagree on fundamental matters. By 1986 and 1987 there were no defenders of Stalin left – although Lenin remained the fount of all wisdom. There was surprisingly little finger-pointing. One might have expected that those who had been fiercely attacked for their heterodoxy and intellectual courage might harbor some resentment against their colleagues, but this did not happen. Maybe the participants in the debates understood that the genius of the Soviet regime resided in its ability to make everyone, or at least almost everyone, an accomplice. It was best not to look at the past behavior of colleagues too closely. If people were held responsible for past errors of judgment or cowardice, an entire generation would have to be silenced. It is fair to say that historians remained much more timid than writers and filmmakers.

The debates among historians, writers, and filmmakers signaled the birth of civil society. Beyond transforming existing institutions, making them genuine and autonomous, organizations grew up that were independent of the state from their inception. Of course, such organizations had existed before: dissidents had created support circles, but these were strictly underground organizations. Now when a demonstration took place in Moscow people were not severely punished. The voluntary groups were still required to register and find a "sponsoring institution," but in fact they were more or less left alone. In 1987 and 1988 thousands of them came into being, and their representatives even held a meeting in Moscow. Most of these groups had no political goals, they were simply associations of people, mostly young, who were interested in sports or music of a certain type. Others did have quasipolitical agendas, such as the protection of the environment or preservation of historic buildings. The appearance of these associations changed the face of Soviet society.

Precisely because they were independent of the state, the associations represented different interests and different social and political ideologies. The civic association, Memorial, was a creation of the liberal intelligentsia. It aimed to commemorate the victims of Stalinist terror; and, by drawing attention to the crimes of the Stalinist era, it was making a political statement relevant to the present. Members put up plaques in memory of the victims, publicized past horrors, and dug up mass graves. The group, which started out in Moscow in 1988, soon spread to the rest of the country, where local chapters were formed.

Not surprisingly, not all of these associations stood for the creation of a decent democratic society. In contrast to Memorial, Pamiat' (Memory) which appeared on the scene in 1987, had the ostensible purpose of protecting the environment and historically important monuments, but soon turned into an extremist Russian nationalist organization, with an increasingly explicit anti-Semitic program. Of course, it would have been odd if, once people were allowed to speak, all of them uttered only humane, democratic, and decent sentiments. Freedom to speak meant just that: freedom to express all opinions, including hateful ones. The anti-Semitic views that now came to the surface had obviously existed before, except that they could not have been expressed so openly. Members of Pamiat' propagated their views largely in the form of small broadsheets and pamphlets sold on street corners. Extraordinary venom appeared in these publication, with charges against Jews that had not been heard since the days of Hitler. At the moment of the creation of civil society, the future ideological divisions were already present.

PERESTROIKA

Perestroika means rebuilding or restructuring. The concept came to be used to describe all the changes taking place in the Gorbachev period. Gorbachev and his associates were ambivalent: on the one hand they increasingly well understood the seriousness of the problems faced by society and therefore the inevitability of change but, on the other, they continued to have faith in the superiority of their political and social system. As a consequence, they were looking for a middle way: they wanted to retain a planned, state-owned economy but marry it to the advantages of the market; they wanted to improve public life by allowing people to speak the truth, but only from the point of view of communist convictions; they wanted to restructure politics by "democratizing" it but at the same time maintain the "guiding" role of the party. The idea of squaring the circle, of finding a middle way between capitalism and communism, was the regime's last attempt to realize a utopian theory.

From ambivalence followed contradictory policies: Gorbachev realized that many members of the apparat were obstacles to reform, since they feared for their privileges, but he still could not imagine a political system in which the party was not in the position of control. Gorbachev wanted to "democratize" a party whose very essence was the opposite of democracy. In his search for a middle way he was sometimes inclined to give his ear to his conservative colleagues and sometimes to the liberals. Such maneuvering was always difficult, and in the end became impossible: the gap between conservatives and liberals became too wide.

Democratic politics means the possibility of alternative solutions to the problems facing society and the resolution of the resulting conflicts in an open sphere. Democratization arose from two different sources. One was a conscious decision on the part of the new leadership. As the economic reforms were not succeeding, at least partially because of the resistance of conservative forces, Gorbachev found it necessary to experiment with new institutional structures. The second source was unforeseen and undesired. It was inevitable that Gorbachev's reforms, primarily what came under the term *glasnost'*, would create opposition within the party leadership and within the nomenklatura, which felt its position threatened. As the friends and foes of reform struggled against one another, this contest came out in the open for the first time since the establishment of the Stalinist system, becoming visible to a fascinated Soviet audience. The sharpening of political struggles within the party, institutional innovations, and the deepening of *glasnost'* reinforced one another.

In 1987 Gorbachev attempted to introduce a reform into the political system very similar to the one Khrushchev had tried a generation before: he proposed term limits on people in leading positions – though, significantly, not at the very top. Gorbachev succeeded where Khrushchev had failed. Perhaps the most significant difference between the two eras was that during the 1960s there was a widely held belief that, though the economy needed reforms, the system as a whole was still functioning better than the economies of the capitalist world. Furthermore, as a result of greatly improved communications, the influence of the West in the 1980s was much more palpable and therefore a large segment of the elite had gradually accepted that changes were inevitable. Even those who attacked Gorbachev from the right and feared the consequences of what they perceived as his radicalism admitted that at least some of the reforms were necessary.

The most prominent among the conservatives were Yegor Ligachev, Viktor Chebrikov, and Vladimir Kriuchkov, who had inherited Chebrikov's job at the KGB. Aleksandr Yakovlev and Shevardnadze were Gorbachev's closest comrades. Boris Yeltsin, the head of the Moscow party organization, was consistently more radical than Gorbachev. What separated the two groups was not simply a struggle for power, but genuine differences in ideology and outlook. Although the conservatives recognized that after the stasis of the Brezhnev era something needed to be done, they did not propose a new ideology. The bitterness of the struggle between the two groups came into the open in the fall of 1987, when at the meeting of the Central Committee Yeltsin explicitly attacked Ligachev and the conservatives. This move led to Yeltsin's temporary eclipse: he was dismissed from his post and subjected to old-style Soviet attacks in the newspapers.

However, the conservatives overreached themselves. In the spring of 1988 an obscure Leningrad teacher of chemistry, Nina Andreeva, sent a letter to the newspaper *Sovetskaia Rossiia* in which she forcefully argued the antireform position. She in fact reiterated all the conservative slogans: the Stalinist era was "complex"; although errors were made it was wrong to concentrate only on the negative aspects of Soviet history and forget about the "glorious pages"; the class struggle was continuing; and the West was always a hostile and subversive force. The letter, whether in fact written by her or someone else in the leadership using her as a tool (as was rumored at the time), expressed the position of the frightened apparat. The publication of Andreeva's piece caused great consternation among liberals. The fact that such a letter could be published in a major Soviet newspaper indicated to them that powerful people stood behind Andreeva, and that her letter might be the first shot in the war staged by resurgent conservative forces. This time the attack was beaten back: ten days after the publication of the letter the editors of *Sovetskaia Rossiia* were forced to admit that they made a political error in publishing Andreeva's views. It was characteristic, however, that in this new and more open era Andreeva then formed a society called Unity for Leninism and Communistic Ideals which aimed to remove Gorbachev from office.

Although Gorbachev never gave up completely on the Communist Party, he recognized that the apparat was a brake on reform. He took a momentous step: he decided to create a real legislature and build up the government machinery as a counterweight to the conservative party leadership. In March 1989 competitive elections were held for an elected assembly that was to conduct meaningful debates concerning genuine issues facing society. Preparations for the elections, the elections themselves, and then the debates within the assembly were the most significant steps in the process of "democratization."

The elections generated considerable interest. In order to be elected, candidates had to formulate their platforms, and for the first time since

November 1917 the Soviet people were presented with alternatives. Ultimately 2,884 candidates contested 1,500 seats (750 were reserved for institutions). In 384 constituencies, just as in Soviet times, there were only single candidates. Remarkably, while some of the leading figures of the Soviet era were reelected, many of them, including figures such as regional secretaries and party chiefs of cities, were defeated. The new legislature included representatives of social organizations – such as the Communist Party, the Academy of Sciences, and the Union of Writers – and representatives from districts, nominated by groups of electors. Some organizations, such as the Communist Party, for example, nominated only as many candidates as there were seats assigned for them. Elsewhere, there were multiple candidacies. The institution that emerged from these reforms was complex, and obviously the result of compromises. Gorbachev wanted "democratization," but at the same time preferred to protect the "leading role of the party." The Congress of People's Deputies had 2,250 members, obviously an unwieldy assembly. After convening, this congress chose a smaller assembly of 542 deputies, which was to have more frequent and businesslike meetings. In 1990, in an election in which there was only token opposition, the Congress of People's Deputies elected Gorbachev president of the republic, a newly created post.

The idea of presidential government was a major departure in Soviet constitutional history. The congress accepted the notion that the government would be headed by a popularly elected president. However, given the extraordinary circumstances and the power vacuum that was developing, Gorbachev was elected not by the people as a whole but by the congress. In retrospect, this decision was obviously an error: Gorbachev could have greatly increased the legitimacy of his office had he chosen to stand for popular election. On paper, Gorbachev was acquiring increasing power; in reality, however, since the institutions of government were functioning less and less well, his newly acquired powers meant little. Clearly, previous general secretaries of the Central Committee of the Communist Party, who in theory had fewer powers, in fact were much more powerful.

Gorbachev's political reforms brought forth a key question: what should the role of the party be in a democratic society? What should the relation of the party and the state be? Gorbachev wanted to retain his position in the party and at the same time be the elected president. Could the party retain its function as "guiding force" and at the same time be accountable and required to observe the law? Could the party be transformed to play an altogether different role than it had ever played before, a role that remained undefined by Gorbachev? The purpose of Gorbachev's political reforms was always to mobilize forces against those whom he considered responsible for stagnation.

The elections for the central legislature were duplicated in the republics. The republics were allowed to go their own way to a certain extent, and different republics chose different constitutional forms. The centralized character of the state was eroding, and as a consequence nationalist sentiments were increasing.

Everything seemed open. Competitive elections implied the articulation of different political directions and the creation of not necessarily different political parties, but certainly platforms. Such developments went contrary to the idea of the one-party state led by the apparat. Some of the prominent figures of the Communist Party decided to quit: Yeltsin and Gavriil Popov, the newly elected mayor of Moscow and an economist were among those who resigned. Politicians formed rudimentary political organizations. These multiplied like mushrooms after the rain, though each was only loosely organized and had few members. The Soviet people were clearly experimenting with political forms.

THE COLLAPSE OF THE OUTER DEFENSES OF THE EMPIRE

Of all the remarkable things that happened in Eastern Europe after 1985, none was more surprising than the decision of Gorbachev and his advisers to allow the collapse of the East European satellites. Eastern Europe did not just slowly slip out of Soviet hands: Gorbachev signaled time and again that the Soviet Union would not interfere. The dissidents, in particular in Poland, Czechoslovakia, and Hungary, were courageous people, who by their behavior greatly contributed to the loss of legitimacy of these regimes, but they could not have successfully resisted tanks. In any case, their movement was not new; what was new was the announced unwillingness of the Soviet tanks to move.

Gorbachev believed in the possibility of reforming communism in the Soviet Union and in Eastern Europe. He did not appreciate how little legitimacy these regimes possessed, and therefore overestimated their independent strength. The problem that the Soviet leaders faced in 1989, as they had in the past, going back to 1945, was the absence of a middle road. These regimes were installed primarily because of the justified assumption of the Stalinist leadership that the East European countries left to themselves – most clearly Hungary, Poland, and Romania – would end up with anticommunist regimes. The only way to prevent such a development was to deprive people of the right to self-determination. The fundamental problem never changed.

During the period of *perestroika*, Gorbachev supported those leaders who advocated change, and for a time in East Germany, Romania, and Czechoslovakia, he became a symbol of reform. He used his decisive influence to get rid of the leader of the Bulgarian party, Todor Zhivkov. Gorbachev, appearing in Berlin in 1989 to great public acclaim, said, "Life punishes those who delay," thereby undermining the position of Erich Honecker, the hardline chief of the party, which quickly led to his removal. This was a paradoxical situation that could not long last: the head of an occupying power came to stand for liberty. The Soviet leader took a major step toward the disintegration of the German Democratic Republic by letting it be known that the Soviet Union had no objection to the Hungarians opening the border to East German citizens. The communist regime ultimately collapsed because the security forces did not carry out orders to shoot, because they knew that Soviet forces were instructed not to interfere under any circumstances. The symbolic end of the cold war came when East Berliners tore down the wall that separated East and West.

The change in Poland and Hungary was quasilegal: the ruling parties in effect allowed themselves to be voted out of office, and thereby perhaps prepared the soil for their reappearance at a different time, under different circumstances and under a different name. In Czechoslovakia and East Germany the old-style leadership did not so easily give way and therefore had to be removed by bloodless revolutions. Only the most odious dictatorship of all, in Romania, had to be overthrown by force.

Although Gorbachev at the outset did not foresee the full consequences of his actions, there was a moment when it became obvious that the process had gone further than he had wished. At that point the choice was to retain Soviet dominance by the use of brutal force or allow the disintegration of the empire. Gorbachev once again made the morally correct decision. His thinking may also have been influenced by the fact that maintaining the empire was expensive, and the Soviet Union could not any longer bear the cost of being a superpower. The Soviet leader wished to give primary attention to the economic, political, social, and even cultural regeneration of his own country. At least for the time being, domestic policy considerations had to outweigh the claims of foreign policy. Ending the cold war seemed like a necessary price to pay for Western credits and access to technology – that is, for joining the modern economic community.

Most likely the Soviet party chief's thinking went beyond the calculations of economic costs and gains. He genuinely wanted his country to rejoin the Western world, "our common European home," as he liked to put it. The great paradox of the October Revolution was that the Bolsheviks, who were anxious to Westernize the country and had little respect for Russian culture, in fact set their country on a path that cut it off from the Western world. Gorbachev was a Westernizer, who understood that being part of the European community meant more than economic reforms; it also meant the acceptance of European standards of behavior. European civilization has always been pluralist, and the price of joining was acceptance of this pluralism.

The consequences of allowing the communist regimes to be overthrown were profound. Gorbachev's strategy was risky because it was likely to alienate a significant component of the power structure, the generals and admirals. They could not be expected to approve the loss of what must have seemed to them the East European shield. In fact, the withdrawal from Eastern Europe put the Red Army at a great military disadvantage, and within a short time reduced the Soviet Union to the role of passive bystander.

Nor could the conservatives within the party leadership support such a strategy. The retreat contributed to the delegitimization of the Soviet regime itself. The loathing of the East Europeans for their regimes showed that time was not on the side of communism, that there was in fact no inevitable march toward a glorious communist future, as had always been assumed. Marxists had always derived great power from their belief that the future was predictable, that history was going in their direction. Shevardnadze in his remarkably frank speech to the Twenty-Eighth Party Congress admitted that the communist regimes in Eastern Europe could be saved only by the use of force. He went on to draw an explicit parallel between the dissatisfaction of Soviet conservatives about retreat from Europe and attacks by Joseph McCarthy and his followers on the US government for the loss of China.

Indeed, infection came from Eastern Europe. Now that Gorbachev's government had given the East Europeans the right to self-determination, how could they deny it to the peoples of the Soviet Union? Why should the Hungarians be allowed to have a system of their own choice, but not the Lithuanians – or the Russians, for that matter?

AUGUST 1991

On August 19, 1991, the premier, the vice president, and the head of the KGB, among others – all Gorbachev appointees – formed a "state committee on the state of emergency," which assumed all governmental powers, banned strikes and demonstrations, and introduced censorship – that is to say, they staged a coup d'etat. The conspirators were ludicrously inept, lacking both charisma and political sense. Beyond a dislike of Gorbachev's reforms and a desire for a return to the defunct Soviet order, they had no political program. Worst of all from their point of view, they took no serious measures to disarm the opposition. Within two days the coup had failed.

The putschists accomplished the opposite of what they had intended: by their actions they demonstrated that there was no force behind them, and that the old order could not be reconstructed. Their press conference, in which they allowed themselves to be ridiculed and showed themselves to be helpless, drunken, and fearful men, was a demonstration of the bankruptcy of the old order. Although the regime managed to hang on for four more months, this ill-considered conspiracy was the real end of the Soviet era.

1991: The people pull down the statue of Dzerzhinskii in front of the Lubianka

Historical analogies should not be carried too far. Nevertheless, it is remarkable how similar the putsch of August 1991 was to one attempted exactly seventy-four years before by General Lavr Kornilov. The general, like his successors, was a clumsy conspirator who had no ability to evaluate the forces supporting him, who took no steps to prepare his move but simply assumed that old ingrained habits of obedience would suffice. Also, like his successors, he had such hatred for the changes around him that he was certain that others must share his attitude. Kornilov rebelled against the man who had brought him to power, Prime Minister Aleksandr Kerensky, but then and later it was suspected that in fact he had acted in concert with the premier. Similarly, the putschists of 1991 kept the president under house arrest, but many believed that they were in fact carrying out Gorbachev's wishes. The two unsuccessful coup attempts frame Soviet history: the Soviet order ended as it had begun.

Yeltsin and Khasbulatov in the days of the putsch, August 1991

Neither the 1917 nor the 1991 putsch failed because it met strong opposition. They failed because the country was descending into anarchy and no political movement was able to marshal sufficient force; the weak struggled against the weaker. Gorbachev had assumed various important-sounding titles and thereby aroused concern among those who feared he was becoming a dictator, but in reality the country was suffering not from too much power in the hands of one man, but from the absence of all authority and the collapse of institutions. There were three interrelated crises that Gorbachev's government could not solve, and their combined impact led to anarchy and ultimate collapse: the ever-worsening condition of the economy, the decay of political institutions, and the centrifugal forces of nationalism in this multinational union.

Had the economic reforms improved the standard of living for the majority of the people, the other issues might have been resolved, but the problems of the economy proved intractable. Once again, the Soviet Union faced an unparalleled situation. The East Europeans had somewhat similar problems, though they were not nearly so severe: they started out with a higher standard of living; there was greater consensus on the need to move toward a market economy; and, since the Soviet system in Eastern Europe had existed for a shorter period, the principles of the market were less alien and less frightening to most people.

August 1991: Gorbachev returning from Crimea

Although Gorbachev and his advisers made numerous mistakes, the severity of the problems was not the consequence of their errors but the unenviable heritage of the Soviet regime. It is hard to imagine a course of action that would have eased the centrally directed economy into a market-oriented one without pain for the majority of people. There could be no meaningful economic reform without the workers accepting greater discipline, higher unemployment, and higher prices for those products the state had previously generously subsidized.

The source of Gorbachev's errors is easy to comprehend. He knew what he wanted: he wanted to combine what seemed to him the best in socialism, in which he had believed all his life, with the undoubted efficiency of the market. In human terms, the desire to have the best of both worlds is fully understandable. There were millions in the Soviet Union and Eastern Europe who shared this attitude. Gorbachev believed that there was a historical example for such an economic and social system, devised by Lenin himself, a man whom he continued to admire. He wanted to return to what had existed in the 1920s, the mixed economy of the NEP, a system in which a fundamentally centralized, state-owned economy coexisted with private, mainly small-scale enterprises that catered primarily to consumers. It was far easier to create a centralized economy – though that too was by no means easy, and cost a great deal of suffering – than to create a market economy. Furthermore, the world economy had profoundly changed since the 1920s; the degree of isolation from the world market that was possible then was possible no longer. The search for the third way was a search for utopia.

The source of one of the major economic problems of the transition period, inflation, obviously went back to the era of Brezhnev, when the Soviet Union had no realistic state budget. How was one to determine, for example, the value of military hardware that Soviet factories produced in abundance? In an economy of shortages, distribution was arranged not by bidding up prices, but by standing in line for products in short supply. Budget deficits were hidden, and the Soviet leaders paid little attention to this matter. Money accumulated in the hands of the citizens, who had nothing to spend it on.

Freeing prices, even if only in a segment of the economy, made the hidden inflation immediately visible. Too much money was chasing too few goods. The Soviet government was also unlucky: the fall of oil prices in the world market, a major Soviet export item, was a blow to the budget, and so was the immense cost of the Chernobyl disaster and the Armenian earthquake. Some of the reforms, however well intentioned, made matters worse. It was, for example, worthwhile to struggle against alcoholism. However, a substantial part of the Soviet budget was based on income from the sale of vodka, and now that income was drastically cut. The Soviet Union needed to import modern technology, but of course the imports had to be paid for. The increasing assertion of autonomy on the part of the republics meant that they were reluctant to send all of their tax revenues to Moscow. The government dealt with the problem the only way it knew how: by printing more money. The conditions for hyperinflation were created in the last years of the Gorbachev era.

Gorbachev experimented with half-measures. He tried the remedy that all previous reformers had tried: decentralization. Giving greater power to factory managers to determine their own product mix and wage scales in the absence of a real market led only to more problems, however. The factory management, lacking incentives to provide consumers with goods, preferred to work for the state, which was a predictable buyer. Moreover, the managers in their competition for labor bid up wages, knowing that the state would not allow the factory to go bankrupt but would in the last resort bail them out. These so-called soft budgetary constraints were yet another major contributing factor to galloping inflation.

Gorbachev's government after 1988 allowed and even encouraged the formation of cooperatives, which had a proper Leninist pedigree, and these came to play significant roles in some segments of the economy, especially in the economically better developed parts of the country – the Baltic republics, Moscow, and Leningrad. But if cooperative restaurants in Moscow and Leningrad made it easier to get a decent meal, albeit at a high price, they did little to remedy the fundamental problems of the economy.

Even in the best of circumstances, even if the leadership had been fully committed to moving as quickly as possible to a market-oriented economy, the conditions necessary for the transformation could not be created overnight. It was not enough to allow small traders and cooperatives to operate. It was also necessary to have a functioning distribution system, modern banking, including the Soviet equivalent of the US Federal Reserve, and trained and competent people to operate these institutions. It was necessary to have a legal system that could adjudicate contracts in a fair and predictable way.

Gorbachev's timid reforms not only did not bring about the desired results, but made matters worse. The reforms brought greater shortages to the Soviet people, a decline in productivity and production, inflation, and a black market controlled by criminals. The signs of deterioration were ever more visible. Liberal politicians and economists were telling Gorbachev that the way out of the crisis was to introduce more radical reforms. However, he knew that there was no constituency supporting such reforms, and indeed that the opponents of abandoning the foundations of the Soviet system were powerful, numerous, and well organized. Beginning in late 1989 his leadership became hesitant and erratic. He temporized, at one time supporting the reformers but then, a short time later, withdrawing his support. He became increasingly isolated.

One commission followed another, one economic plan was drawn up after another, and Gorbachev was unwilling to commit himself. The first of these plans was prepared by a large commission headed by the liberal economist, Leonid Abalkin, in late 1989. This was the first systematic project aimed at overhauling the entire economy rather than further experimenting with piecemeal solutions. This plan envisaged definite stages the Soviet economy would pass through to a genuine market economy. Abalkin promised gradual price liberalization, the sale of some state-owned property, the introduction of a stock exchange, and, most important, the closing down of unprofitable factories. The plan pleased neither the conservatives, who did not like the principles on which it was based, nor the liberals, who believed it did not go far enough.

At this point Gorbachev's cautious premier, Nikolai Ryzhkov, produced a more moderate variant that left out the closing down of unprofitable enterprises and retained the power of central planners. This was no reform at all. At the same time another economist, Nikolai Petrakov, presented a plan with Gorbachev's encouragement that would have taken the country to a market economy faster than Abalkin's.

As Gorbachev equivocated, the more radical economists, headed by Grigori Yavlinskii, worked out a reform plan that could be characterized as Polish-type shock therapy. Yavlinskii's project was followed by an even more elaborate plan by the team headed by Stanislav Shatalin. It aimed to create an economy based on market principles within five hundred days.

The plan envisaged the privatization of enterprises, the freeing of prices, and movement toward a convertible ruble. It also aimed to decentralize the Soviet economy by giving taxation powers and control over natural resources to the republics. The government raised the prices of essential items, including bread, as a move toward a more realistic price structure, and this alienated a large segment of the Soviet people. Aside from that single act, the government did nothing to realize any of the reform plans. Gorbachev had neither the strength nor the inclination to give the reformers his full support. The old economic system was falling apart, and there was nothing to take its place.

The failure of the economic reforms had far-reaching political consequences. As so often in Russian and Soviet history, the initiative for political reforms came from above. It was particularly ironic that the goal of these reforms was to introduce a degree of democracy into the political process. What followed was not the conscious pulling down of a regime hated by its citizens – a revolution from below – but a disintegration. The majority of the Soviet people never supported the principles on which Gorbachev's policies were based. Aside from a segment of the intelligentsia, *perestroika* never had a large constituency. As a consequence, Soviet politics in the Gorbachev era was not on firm ground.

At the heart of the Soviet political system was the Communist Party. Gorbachev did not aim to do away with it, and he had no intention of introducing a multiparty system. On the other hand, he wanted to democratize the party, an organization whose very essence was undemocratic. By democratization he meant a more or less open discussion of alternative policies, and elections of party functionaries. This attempt was bound to fail, for a Leninist party by definition cannot be democratic. As multicandidate elections were being held for the national legislature, no such elections took place within the party. Instead of being democratized, that mighty organization was falling apart. It not only failed to attract new members, but its membership precipitously declined. The party lost its unity – its leaders openly fought each other – and lost its purpose. In the new environment, its ideology, goals, and functions became confused. Most importantly, as a consequence of *glasnost'* the party stood accused of the bloody crimes of the past. Those who remained members were demoralized by the changes taking place around them. The so-called transmission belts – mass organizations through which the party extended its reach into Soviet society, such as the youth organization, the Komsomol – were hit even harder.

By 1990 the political situation in the Soviet Union had become highly volatile. The gap constantly widened between those who believed that the solution was to be found in ever more radical reforms and the dismantling of political and economic institutions, and those who saw in the recent changes the source of their troubles. This division existed among the peoples of the Soviet Union, and it found an expression in the conflict at the top of the political hierarchy. The struggle among the leaders was not merely about personalities, but for the highest stakes, for principles in which the protagonists deeply believed.

The Gorbachev era was over at the end of 1990. From this point on, Gorbachev had no new ideas for reform. He was a spent force. In reorganizing the political system, just as in matters of economics, he temporized. The danger of spreading disorder – indeed, the possibility of civil war – brought him closer to the conservatives, and he adjusted his policies accordingly. On the one hand, he did not want to go further in reforming away the Soviet system; on the other, he wanted to protect his reforms but did not know how to restore stability. His personnel appointments clearly indicated a shift toward the opponents of radical reforms. He brought into power a group of old-style, hardline party functionaries, hoping to protect himself from a conservative rebellion. He appointed Gennadii Yanaev vice president, Boris Pugo minister of the interior, and Valentin Pavlov premier. Within a short time, all three would be among those who attempted in August 1991 to overthrow the reformist regime of Gorbachev. By contrast, the articulate and vigorous defender of *perestroika*, Eduard Shevardnadze, resigned in December 1990. Like other liberals, he feared the possibility of dictatorship and lost confidence in the ability of Gorbachev to protect the reforms.

Boris Yeltsin came to be the standard bearer of the reformists. He had been dropped from the top leadership of the party and had openly clashed with the conservative Yegor Ligachev, and these facts may have contributed to his growing popularity. In March 1991 his conservative opponents attempted to get rid of him as head of the elected Russian parliament. He outmaneuvered them by creating the office of the president of the Russian Republic, and stood for the election to the presidency of Russia in June 1991. He won a respectable 57 percent of the vote and thereby acquired a degree of legitimacy that no other politician in the country had ever possessed. The election of the charismatic Yeltsin, who had officially left the party and thereby his communist past behind, was a warning for the conservatives. He succeeded in creating for himself a new power base. Under his leadership the Russian Republic of the Soviet Union was acquiring increasing autonomy.

As the Soviet Union was disintegrating, Yeltsin's position in relation to Gorbachev became increasingly strong. Yeltsin had charisma and a common touch that his rival obviously did not possess. It is not that Gorbachev was afraid to go among the people, but that he always seemed to be lecturing them. By contrast, the Russian people saw Yeltsin as a simple man, one of their own. They saw him as an opponent of Gorbachev, whom many already blamed for their troubles and for the spreading disorder. Unlike Gorbachev, Yeltsin had a clear-cut program: he was ready to jettison the union, the old political system, and above all the Communist Party, and to experiment with further economic reforms. The confrontation between the two men and their different policies was increasingly sharp.

It was inevitable that, at a time when all Soviet political institutions and economic policies were open for discussion, the questions of the relationship between the union and the republics and between Russians and non-Russians would also be raised. Even at the time when the Soviet Union seemed unshakably strong, both domestic and foreign observers regarded the nationality question as the Achilles heel of the empire. Yet the multinational state did not unravel by itself. It fell apart for other reasons; the struggle of the national minorities for autonomy or independence was only the last straw. The situation was remarkably similar to the time of the 1917 revolution and civil war. People suddenly discovered their national identities, and nationalists ceased to be afraid of the repressive power of the state.

In Stalin's time the Soviet Union was totalitarian. After his death it evolved into an authoritarian state. Politicians in totalitarian and authoritarian states are inevitably centralizers; centralization follows from their ideology and from their concept of politics. Under the circumstances there could be no genuine autonomy for the republics, and the right to secede, included in the constitution, was obviously a myth. Nevertheless, within the admittedly narrow limits set by the centralizing policies of the elite, Soviet nationality policies were often (though not always) enlightened, and not altogether unsuccessful. As a result, there were people in the Soviet Union who considered themselves Soviet patriots. It was not so much Soviet repression and humiliation of nationalist feelings, but the very processes of industrialization, education, and improved means of communication – i.e., modernization – that helped the growth of nationalisms. People discovered their national identities in contradistinction to others. Mixing, closer acquaintance with others, even intermarriage, not only failed to undermine nationalism, but these facts of modern life actually encouraged its growth.

The success and power of the Soviet state were the justifications for its existence. As long as the power of the state was convincingly strong, nationalism was driven underground. *Glasnost'* allowed the articulation of nationalist sentiments. Suddenly non-Russians – and, perhaps strangely, Russians – came to see themselves as victims, oppressed and exploited by the union.

The disorders that erupted were not always directed against the Soviet state itself. In Central Asia people who had lived in close proximity to one another for some time in the new era of freedom became bitter enemies. The Meskhetians (Muslims settled in Central Asia by Stalin at the time of the Second World War) were massacred by Uzbeks in 1989. The Kyrgyz in turn attacked the Uzbek minority in their republic, and hundreds were killed. The situation was even more volatile in the Caucasus, which with its extraordinary variety of small nations is virtually an ethnographic museum. Abkhazians, who made up only 18 percent of the population of their region within Georgia, wanted a greater degree of autonomy. The Georgian nationalists not only resisted, but wanted to abolish the autonomous status of Abkhazia.

In April 1989 Georgian nationalists demonstrated in Tbilisi, and Soviet troops were called in to disperse the demonstrators. The troops, unused to dealing with peaceful demonstrators, killed nineteen people and wounded hundreds, even thousands. This was the first major bloodletting committed by Soviet soldiers in the Gorbachev era. It created a shock to the entire union, a fear that this act was the harbinger of worse massacres to come. It embarrassed the president and greatly contributed to the growth of Georgian secessionist sentiment.

The longest and bloodiest fighting took place in Azerbaijan. Within that republic an autonomous region, Nagornyi Karabakh, contained an overwhelmingly Armenian population. The history of the relationship between the Muslim Azeris and Christian Armenians included a great deal of bitterness. The Armenians saw in the Azeris the brothers of Turks, who had massacred their ancestors by the hundreds of thousands. In Soviet times, within their nominally autonomous region, they felt discriminated against by their Muslim overlords. In January 1988 disorders broke out in Stepanakert, the capital of the region. The Armenians demanded the return of Karabakh to "the mother country." The Azeris responded by a massacre of the Armenians in other parts of the republic. The worst pogrom took place in Sumgait, where ninety people were killed and hundreds were wounded. Soon Armenia and Azerbaijan were for all practical purposes at war, and hundreds of thousands of Armenians and Azeris were fleeing for their lives.

The Armenians hoped that Moscow would support them in their effort to change the status of Nagornyi Karabakh, but Gorbachev's government did not want any changes of internal borders, for the understandable reason that if internal borders came to be renegotiated then all existing borders would be in doubt, since ethnicity and borders rarely coincided. Moscow's inability to guarantee satisfaction to either side greatly contributed to the secessionist feelings in the two republics, in particular in Armenia, where the nationalists suspected Moscow of siding with their enemy. A government increasingly incapable of guaranteeing civil peace lost respect, and people came to believe that it did not deserve support, or even survival.

The desire to leave the union greatly varied from region to region. It was the strongest in the three Baltic republics. Estonians, Latvians, and Lithuanians had desired separation from the outset of Gorbachev's introduction of *glasnost'*. Among these Baltic peoples the memory of twenty years of interwar statehood was very much alive. They resented the great influx of Russians and Ukrainians into their republics and looked down on them. They feared russification, and believed that Stalin and the Stalinists had wanted to eliminate them as nations, which explained for them one of the most horrendous Soviet crimes, the deportation of hundreds of thousands from their republics to Siberia. Without a doubt the vast majority of the citizens, including Russian residents, would have left the union if given a choice. They believed that as independent countries they could rejoin Europe and quickly achieve a higher standard of living. In these republics the nationalist sentiment became so strong that even the communist parties were not immune. When it became possible, they detached themselves from the Communist Party of the Soviet Union. The party disintegrated earlier than the union itself.

In March 1990 Lithuania declared independence unilaterally. For a time Gorbachev managed to avoid a bloody confrontation by using economic means to pressure and persuade the Lithuanians to suspend secession temporarily. But the determination of the three republics ultimately to achieve independence did not diminish. In January 1991 conservative forces attempted to "restore order" and reestablish Soviet rule in Lithuania. The Lithuanians resisted the Red Army, and fourteen people died.

It is not clear how strong the desire for independence was in the rest of the Soviet Union. People in Central Asia may have resented Moscow's interference and the growing influx of Russians and Ukrainians, who in some parts of the region came to make up majorities, but independence movements there were weak. Perhaps the political leadership understood that these republics had been benefiting from economic subsidies from the center, that the economies were too intertwined, that Central Asians could not afford an exodus of the Russians. Nationalist sentiment was strong among the Romanians in Moldavia. The Romanians resented crude attempts at russification, one of which was to require that their Romance language be written in the Cyrillic alphabet. Ukraine was a divided country. The western part of the republic had come under Soviet rule only after the Second World War, and there nationalist sentiment was very strong. In the east, and in Crimea, where the majority were Russians, Ukrainian nationalism had relatively little appeal.

The position of Russia within the Soviet Union had always been anomalous. It was by far the largest republic, containing half the population of the union, yet when in 1945 the Soviet Union was given two extra seats in the General Assembly of the United Nations neither of these was given to the Russian Republic. Everyone evidently assumed that since the Soviet Union was an extension of Russia, that republic did not need an extra seat. Perhaps for the first time in the Gorbachev era many Russian nationalists came to perceive the existence of the Soviet Union not as a glorious achievement, but as a burden on Russians. Indeed, it was true that Russia was subsidizing the poorer regions of the Soviet Union. These nationalists wanted to preserve ties with the two other Slavic republics, Ukraine and Belorussia, and to retain control over areas in Central Asia where Russians made up the majority of the population but had little interest in the rest of the union.

For Yeltsin, the presidency of the Russian Republic became a power base. He established contact with representatives of other republics and took a much more tolerant view of the nationalist aspirations of the minorities. He openly deplored the bloodletting in Vilnius in January 1991. Under Yeltsin's leadership Russia began to act independently of the Soviet government, behaving as if Russia really was just one of the republics. This development, more than any other, led to the dissolution of the union.

Gorbachev and his advisers underestimated the significance of the power of contending nationalisms. They believed in the claims of Soviet propaganda that the socialist system had succeeded in overcoming nationalist hatreds. Nevertheless, from the height of the period of *perestroika* in 1989, Gorbachev's government ever more insistently discussed the need for a new constitutional framework that would redefine the relationship of the republics to one another. After many discussions concerning various issues – such as whether the laws of the republics would supersede the laws of the union, and economic relations within the union – a draft treaty was published at the end of 1990. Like much else in Soviet political life at the time, how the plan would be executed was not made explicit. The treaty called for a sovereign, federal, democratic state, as a voluntary union of republics with equal rights, each left to determine its own social and political structure to a remarkable degree. Much of the governmental power and responsibility would have devolved to the republics, and the union would have retained responsibility only for defense and foreign policy. Other crucial issues, including economic relations, were to be decided by negotiation between the center and the republics.

To give legitimacy to the new arrangement, the voters were asked this oddly phrased question in a March 1991 plebiscite: "Do you consider it necessary to preserve the Union of Soviet Socialist Republics as a renewed federation of equal sovereign republics in which the human rights and freedoms of every nationality will be fully guaranteed?" There were so many different issues mentioned in this one sentence that it was impossible to give a meaningful yes or no response. People with different political views chose to draw different conclusions from the results.

As an expression of their desire for complete independence, Estonia, Latvia, Lithuania, Moldavia, Georgia, and Armenia declined to participate in the plebiscite. Some other republics added additional questions and raised additional issues that further muddied the results. (It was on this occasion that Yeltsin created for himself the presidency of the Russian Republic.) The question was loaded and the phrasing ambiguous, but the results could not legitimately be portrayed as a passionate desire on the part of the majority of the citizens of the Soviet Union to break up the union. Over three-quarters of voters (80 percent of the eligible citizens) answered the question affirmatively.

The results of the plebiscite enabled Gorbachev to claim that the peoples of the Soviet Union wanted continued association. The form of the renewed association would have been the "Union of Soviet Sovereign Republics." Gorbachev planned the formal signing of a treaty with the representatives of nine republics to take place in Moscow on August 20. The opponents of reform, fearing the destruction of the Soviet Union as they knew it, staged their coup a day before, for the explicit purpose of preventing the treaty. They succeeded, but only at the expense of delivering the fatal blow to the union they had hoped to save.

THE LAST DAYS OF THE UNION

Our most enduring image of the confused days of August 19–21, 1991, is Yeltsin standing on top of a tank in front of the White House, the seat of the Russian government, defying his enemies. His courageous gesture provided a wonderful contrast to the confused men who, for a moment, thought that they were in charge. It was Yeltsin's finest moment. He was the hero of the hour, surrounded by people just as courageous as he was, people who refused to be frightened into accepting a return to the Soviet past.

Although the putschists intended to reverse Gorbachev's reforms – the introduction of market economics, the new union treaty, and the "democratization of the party" – they were not hostile to the president as a person. Indeed, it is likely that at least at the outset they had hoped to win him over to their cause. But the president, who was vacationing with his family in Crimea when the coup took place, did not go along with the conspirators and was placed under house arrest. The real enemy of the putschists was Yeltsin and his democratic followers. Consequently, when the putsch failed, it was Yeltsin and not Gorbachev who was the victor. Gorbachev may not have immediately understood it, but when he returned to Moscow he came back to a city that was Yeltsin's.

The people of Moscow (much less the rest of Russia) did not rise up against the reactionaries; it was only a small percentage of the citizens, mostly better-educated and middle-aged, who gathered around Yeltsin in the crucial hours. The workers and the young stayed away. Some expected the coup to succeed, and most were indifferent. The Soviet people were not used to playing active roles in the politics of their country. Nevertheless, immediately after the failure of the coup there was something of a carnival atmosphere in Moscow, as if a storm had cleared the air. There was an expectation of the beginning of a new era, and at least for a moment the defenders of the old order were silenced. The leaders of the coup, the general staff of the Soviet regime, were arrested, and Boris Pugo, the most intelligent of them, committed suicide. National unity, however, was only apparent: different people had different ideas concerning the future of the nation, and these differences were bound to surface soon.

Had the coup not taken place, it is almost certain that the disintegration of the union, the further deterioration of the economy, the demise of the old political system would have occurred in any case. No force could have stopped the centrifugal tendencies, and no one had a recipe for a quick and painless recovery of the economy. At the same time, the coup obviously greatly accelerated these processes. Yeltsin immediately banned the Communist Party in the Russian Republic and suspended the publication of the party's newspaper, *Pravda*. Gorbachev on his return to Moscow was compelled to resign as general secretary of the Communist Party. This move was followed within days by the suspension of the activities of the party within the entire union, and the seizure of its assets. The Komsomol dissolved itself. The one-party state, as created in 1917, was no more. The republics one after another declared their independence. The Baltic states were the first, and soon all others followed suit. When Ukraine, the largest after Russia did so – on condition that the majority of the citizens approved a referendum – the Soviet Union in fact ceased to exist. The Russian Federation took over one after another the functions of the Soviet government.

Gorbachev was in the curious position of being president of a state that no longer existed. He did everything within his power to save as much unity for the future organization as possible, but he did not have a strong hand. Yeltsin has been blamed for contributing to the disintegration of the Soviet Union. It has been argued that this was for him the most convenient way to get rid of Gorbachev, by doing away with the state of which Gorbachev was still president. It is true that by this time there was a great deal of hostility and bitter personal dislike between the two leaders. Indeed, Yeltsin believed that it would be easier to introduce economic reforms and thereby lift Russia out of the crisis, if the country was not burdened by having to support the other republics. But it is not clear how the Soviet Union could have remained in existence if all its constituent units had declared independence, and there was no force to keep them in line.

During the last months of 1991 the leaders of the newly independent republics searched for a new kind of relationship between the ex-components of the Soviet state. They presumably understood that the breakup of the extraordinarily centralized Soviet economy would have painful consequences. On December 1, 90 percent of the people of Ukraine voted for independence. The lopsided nature of the vote indicated that even the great majority of the Russians living within the republic had voted affirmatively. After this vote there was no possibility of saving even a loose union of states. The presidents of Russia, Ukraine, and Belarus met on December 8 to dissolve the Soviet Union formally and establish in its place a genuinely voluntary Commonwealth of Independent States (CIS), which the other ex-republics were invited to join. On December 21, in Alma Ata, eight other ex-republics joined this newly created and ill-defined entity. Only the three Baltic republics and Georgia decided to stay away altogether.

This new entity had such vaguely defined powers and responsibilities that it was almost meaningless. It had no common parliament, army, currency, or foreign policy, and two of its states, Armenia and Azerbaijan, were at war with one another. All CIS members sought membership in the United Nations, and Russia assumed the seat of the Soviet Union in the Security Council. Despite the economic chaos created by independence, the new states went their own way. However, they had many things in common: inflation, declining economic production, political confusion, and ethnic strife.

Leap into the Unknown

In the course of the twentieth century the Russians time and again found themselves in situations for which there was no precedent. After the astounding Bolshevik victory in 1917, the revolutionary leaders were as surprised by their success as everyone else. Their ideology had not prepared them for the problems they had to face, and the building of the Soviet state turned out to be a vast improvisation. In 1992, on the ruins of communism, the Russians were attempting to build a political system suitable for a European state at the very end of the twentieth century and to create a market economy. To be sure, there were other countries in Eastern Europe that also had to struggle with the heritage of communism, but none had problems as serious as the Russians. The size of the country, the heterogeneity of the population, and the relative lack of democratic traditions and civil society exacerbated the problems facing Russia.

The situation in which the country found itself was oddly similar to that in 1917. Once again the stasis of a conservative old regime was challenged by a period of liberalization, leading to descent into anarchy. The period of anarchy was brought to a conclusion not by a genuine revolution of determined rebels supported by a majority of the people, but by the disintegration of the old regime. In 1917, the country had also experienced vast and traumatic social, political, and economic transformations. Tsarism, like the communist regime, was not brought down by its enemies but rather collapsed on its own; the principles on which it had been based suddenly appeared hopelessly anachronistic. The February Revolution was followed by a brief illusion of national unity. Very soon afterward, however, it turned out that, in fact, people had different and contradictory expectations. It was impossible to rule the country on the basis of democratic and liberal principles because consensus on fundamental issues was missing. In 1917, just as in 1991–92, the collapse of the center unleashed an extraordinary flourishing of nationalisms. The center could neither suppress nor satisfy the newfound nationalisms of the many minorities.

There is an intriguing parallel between the Lavr Kornilov putsch of August 1917 and the August putsch of 1991: both were ludicrously mishandled. The putschists in both instances imagined that they had popular support behind them, without trying to create such support. They did not even attempt to find out what kind of political forces might help them. They naively expected that the people, following old habits, would simply obey, and that therefore all that was necessary was to give some vague instructions to soldiers to show force. On both occasions the heads of the government – Aleksandr Kerensky and Mikhail Gorbachev – were suspected of collusion, and both lost power within months. Kerensky had appointed Kornilov a short time before the mutiny, hoping that the general would restore order. Gorbachev, attempting to balance competing political forces, had chosen the insignificant Gennadii Yanaev as his deputy. Yanaev's colleagues considered Dmitrii Yazov, the head of the army, like Kornilov, a courageous but rather stupid man. Boris Pugo and Sergei Akhromeev, like General Aleksandr Krymov who had led Kornilov's troops against Petrograd seventy-four years before, committed suicide in the wake of their failure. Most significantly, perhaps, both putsches showed that there was no popular support for a return to the old regime. The consequences of the ill-considered mutinies were the same: the government remained isolated and helpless, alienated from those who wanted to "deepen the revolution" as well as from those who thought that the changes had already gone too far. Gorbachev's government, like Kerensky's, lost the ability to govern or even influence events. The actions of the frightened conservatives, instead of bringing stability, drove the last nails in the coffin of the old regime.

There was, however, a fundamental difference between 1917 and 1991 that we ought not to overlook. The Russian Revolution was followed by a three-year-long civil war that claimed millions of victims. Fortunately, to the surprise of many, the Soviet regime went quietly into oblivion.

SHOCK THERAPY

Where should the great transformation begin? Yeltsin and his advisers understood that the Soviet Union failed because it could not create and manage a modern economy. The political obstacles to carrying out radical reforms at least temporarily disappeared and, thanks to Gorbachev's policies for alleviating tensions, the international environment was unthreatening. Economic problems had to be tackled immediately.

Unlike the cautious Gorbachev, Yeltsin listened to economists, foremost among them Yegor Gaidar, who believed in what came to be called "shock therapy." The changes that these people were willing to introduce were every bit as revolutionary as what had happened in 1917 or at the time of collectivization. The principle of the radical economists was simple: the old regime had to be destroyed at once and unrestricted capitalism had to be introduced. Just like the Bolsheviks in 1917, they were guided by an ideology, in this case that of unfettered capitalism. They saw that the half-measures introduced during the Gorbachev era had brought no positive results. They understood that the radical steps they proposed would cause social pain and therefore political danger in the short run, but they believed that there was no alternative. Russia was in a crisis: the Soviet-type economy could function only as long as there was a coercive regime in power. Once that collapsed, anarchy threatened. The government was once again in danger of not being able to feed the cities. Since the government could not use coercion, the peasants saw no need to sell their products for an increasingly worthless currency when there was nothing to buy in the shops in any case. It was ironic that sixty years earlier the government had responded to its inability to provide bread for the cities by suspending the market mechanism at the heart of the NEP. Now the reaction to the same problem was an attempt to reintroduce the market by making prices realistic. As collectivization was driven by an ideology, so was the introduction of shock therapy. Both produced foreseeable misery in the short run in hopes of great improvement in the future.

It strengthened the resolve of the reformers that shock therapy seemed to be working in another postcommunist country, Poland. However, Russia's difficulties were of a different order of magnitude: the old centralized system based on state ownership and central planning had ceased to function and there was nothing to take its place. The Soviet Union had had a highly centralized economy: in many cases a product had been produced in only one factory and now that factory might be beyond the newly drawn borders. The close economic ties between the Soviet Union and the rest of Eastern Europe were broken. What the Soviet Union could acquire in the past from the satellites in a barter system now had to be paid for with convertible currency. The newly independent republics started to print rubles, and Russia was in danger of being flooded with worthless money. The success of economic stabilization necessitated breaking up the ruble zone. In this period of transformation the country had neither a functioning banking system nor a convertible currency.

Just as importantly, Russia lacked a reliable system of commercial law and judiciary that could enforce contracts. Factory directors who had operated in a very different economic system could hardly be expected to understand the principles of the market and to act accordingly from one day to the next. Perhaps understandably, as human beings everywhere, the directors were above all interested in serving their own interests, and whenever possible they took advantage of opportunities to enrich themselves. But most damaging for the cause of reform, unlike in the countries of East Central Europe and the newly independent Baltic states, there was no broad consensus in favor of thoroughgoing change. Public opinion surveys at the time showed that the majority of Russians had a negative attitude toward private property.

What did shock therapy mean in practice? The average person first noticed the freeing of prices, in other words an enormous increase in the cost of everything. A few exceptions remained: the price of bread and transport, at least for a short time, remained controlled, that is, subsidized. (Already in March 1992, under pressure from conservatives, the government abandoned plans to free the domestic price of oil, which was about 1 percent of the world market price. This concession later allowed extraordinary corruption: some well-connected domestic oil traders bought and resold domestic oil on the world market and made fabulous profits.) In the Soviet era, prices had been officially and therefore artificially set and bore little relation to the cost of production. The distribution of scarce goods had been resolved not by adjusting prices but by constant shortages, which had required ordinary citizens to stand in line for scarce goods. At the end of the Gorbachev era, shops often stood empty. Since there was little to buy that customers actually wanted, even people with modest incomes had substantial savings. The immediate and foreseeable consequence of freeing prices was a steep and sudden inflation: a great deal of accumulated money chased too few available goods. Within a year prices rose 2,600 percent. Inflation eliminated savings. Old people on pensions were particularly hard hit; those who had saved for their old age and kept their money under a mattress rather than in a Soviet bank were financially wiped out practically overnight. On the other hand, those who had opportunities could benefit handsomely. The minor social revolution caused by inflation turned many Russians against the reformers.

Another part of shock therapy was a half-hearted attempt at withdrawing support from enterprises that were still owned by the state. According to the principles of market economics, the vast majority of factories operated at a loss. If the government wanted to eliminate the deficit and build a realistic budget, it could no longer afford to subsidize inefficient enterprises. A realistic budget was essential to make the currency convertible and thereby enable Russia to participate in the world economy and attract much-needed foreign investment. However, to implement the plans fully would have meant shutting down thousands of factories, creating an army of unemployed. Yeltsin recoiled from the consequences, and therefore, in this matter, Gaidar did not fully prevail.

At the heart of shock therapy was privatization. The state had to get out of the business of running the economy. But how to accomplish this in a country where people did not have the capital and there were no managers capable of operating in the new system? Another fundamental problem was the impossibility of appraising national property fairly. Privatization was an enormously complex, difficult, and drawn-out process that went through several stages. The goal of the government was not for the state to receive fair compensation for the factories and mines, which was considered impossible, but rather to create efficient enterprises and a shareholder society. The government achieved neither goal. The process lacked transparency, corruption was rife, and privatization understandably and justifiably did not inspire confidence among the Russian people.

Gaidar's initial solution was to give every citizen a voucher worth 10,000 rubles, at that time approximately $22, to enable them to buy stocks for that value. The intention was to make Russian citizens shareowners, that is, propertyowners with an immediate financial interest in running enterprises. Often the workers invested their vouchers in the company where they worked. The vouchers provided yet another opportunity to make money dishonestly. Enterprising people advertised in newspapers, promising great returns on investment based on vouchers, and set up pyramid schemes to take advantage of the gullible. Some succeeded in collecting millions and then escaping from Russia. The scandals that followed, discussed at length in newspapers, further undermined the faith of Russians in the economic reforms. Soon the shares lost even their small face value and were traded in the streets for a pittance.

No privatization has ever been without corruption. Even in Britain in the days of Margaret Thatcher, when state-owned companies were privatized, insiders or people with useful contacts unfairly benefited. In the Russian case the possibilities were infinitely greater, and therefore so was corruption. Those who had the opportunity could take control of enterprises for private gain. Instead of running the enterprises for the possibility of some future profit, the new owners, who could not be confident of their property rights, attempted to benefit as quickly as possible, often by selling the assets of the enterprises they had acquired. In theory, the workers who had stocks in the companies where they worked could have exercised oversight over the management, but in reality that almost never happened. One of the schemes factory managers concocted was to get government loans to pay their workers but, given the extraordinary inflation, they immediately turned the rubles into dollars. Then, weeks later, they bought back cheaper rubles with which they paid their workers overdue and worthless wages, pocketing large sums themselves. The unfairness and criminality inherent in this system were undermining the already-meager respect for the processes of democratization and economic change. The national wealth quickly came to be concentrated in a very few hands. This was harmful not only from a political and social point of view but also from the point of view of economics. Because of the highly concentrated wealth, neither a modern stock market nor a functioning banking system could develop.[1]

The second stage of privatization, which took place in 1995–96, was even more rife with corruption than the first. The state desperately needed money, so it entered into a relationship with groups of oligarchs in the banking and raw material sections of the economy.[2] This entailed shares of large enterprises that were still owned by the state being given as collateral in exchange for loans that were never expected to be repaid. In this way groups of rich people came into possession of even greater wealth. Political power, influence, and wealth came to be even more intertwined.

One would think that privatization in agriculture would be easier. Given the resistance of peasants to collectivization sixty years earlier, it seemed reasonable to expect that once the peasants were given the opportunity to cultivate their own land they would enthusiastically take advantage of it. It did not turn out this way. Although there were no more legal obstacles for private ownership of land, the peasants were reluctant to buy land at a time when agriculture was increasingly unprofitable, given the cheap Western imports and gradually increasing energy costs. Agriculture, the neglected stepchild of Soviet industry, did not become more productive. On the contrary, in the 1990s, the crucial grain harvest fell by almost half, and the situation was even worse in the output of milk and meat.[3] As a result of the reforms, the gap in the standard of living between people living in the countryside and those in the major cities further widened.

In contrast to Russia, land reform was highly successful in China. Perhaps because the Chinese peasants had been even poorer and more miserable than the Russians, they embraced privatization with enthusiasm, and the greatly increased agricultural productivity became the basis of the Chinese "economic miracle."

The Russian reforms could not achieve their goal; a functioning market-driven economy remained elusive. The necessary restructuring did not take place, and factories continued to demand and receive subsidies. Given the precarious nature of the Russian economy, the newly rich found it better and safer to keep their money abroad. When investment capital was urgently needed, far more money left the country than was received in foreign investment. Nor did the country become a society of small propertyowners. The reformers had imagined that shareowners would become partisans of the new state, based on a capitalist economy. In this they were disappointed. Russia did not become a society of small capitalists.

A NEW CONSTITUTION

Economics and politics are always intertwined, nowhere more so than in the Soviet Union or in post-Soviet Russia. A new state apparatus had to be created on the ruins of the defunct Soviet Union, and this was every bit as difficult as making the market economy function. The success of the market economy depended on a functioning state, and conversely the political reforms were endangered by the misery created by the economic reforms.

The problem of both economic and political transformation and their relative lack of success was the same: there was no constituency demanding them. The Russians craved neither private enterprise nor the doing away with the Soviet system and everything that entailed. The great changes that occurred took place with little public involvement.

Nevertheless, the transformation was real. Gaidar's reforms demolished the basis of the Soviet system. Whatever problems and dangers Russia would face in the future, a return to the Soviet system was out of the question.

Regular, free, and more or less fair elections took place, registering the public mood; Russians could freely travel abroad; civil liberties came to be better protected than in the Soviet era; and freedom of expression and freedom of religion were not merely meaningless phrases. Russian newspapers expressed a variety of points of view, some of which were worth reading. What did not change, however, was the conviction of most Russians that they had no control over their own fate. Their confidence in the major institutions of society, such as the police, the courts, the parliament, and the president, not only did not improve in the 1990s, but further declined.

It was inevitable that survivors from the Soviet nomenklatura would continue to dominate politics. Where else would the personnel for the rejuvenated democratic state come from? Ambitious people, who had made themselves prominent in the Soviet era, were well placed to take advantage of the new opportunities. With the exception of a handful of dissenters, most prominent figures of the 1990s had compromised themselves by their association with the old regime, but that did not seem to matter. The dissenters, courageous people as they were, by and large proved themselves incapable of participating in the rough and tumble of politics in a confused, almost anarchic era. The talents and personality traits that were needed to resist the Soviet state were very different from the ability to become actors in politics. In the central government, but even more on the local level, the same people remained in their posts, although they may have had different job titles. The holdovers inevitably brought with them a mentality that was not appropriate in a democratic state.

Yeltsin himself was a product of the Soviet world and as such did not think in terms of legitimacy based on popular approval. He made no effort to create a political organization, a party, that would be his support in difficult political battles. An autocratic strain in his mentality almost immediately manifested itself. The populism that had won him followers in the late Soviet era was not helpful in a leader who was responsible for governing a big and varied country. At the outset he arrogated to himself enormous, almost dictatorial powers. In addition to being president, he was able to select members of the cabinet. In November 1991 the congress gave him the power to implement reform by decree (although the Supreme Soviet could rescind the decree by a two-thirds' majority). Yeltsin was an impulsive politician who in moments of crisis could gauge the public mood, but he preferred to operate in the background. He had no long-term strategy or vision of a post-Soviet democratic Russia. As a product of an autocratic system, he did not understand the necessity of compromise and political give-and-take. To be sure, he was willing to give concessions when he was forced to, but that was not the same as a commitment to democratic governance.

That the unpopular economic reforms would create a backlash was inevitable. Not only pro-communist papers, but also respected economists who had advised Gorbachev, such as Nikolai Petrakov and Stanislav Shatalin, predicted catastrophe. But the dangerous opposition to the Yeltsin–Gaidar policies was concentrated in the parliament, the State Duma. According to the rather cumbersome Soviet constitutional system, the large Duma, with more than 1,000 deputies, elected a Supreme Soviet of 252 members. Since the Duma was rarely in session, the real political force was the Supreme Soviet. That legislature had been elected in 1990, when the Communist Party, at least in theory, was still the dominant political force: 86 percent of the deputies had been party members.[4] The assembly was an amorphous, ill-organized body that contained no political parties to impose discipline on its members. The lack of parties gave the speaker especially great influence. After Yeltsin's election as president of the Russian Republic, his place as speaker was taken by his protégé, an ethnic Chechen, Ruslan Khasbulatov. It was Khasbulatov and another previous Yeltsin ally, his vice president Aleksandr Rutskoi, who became the vocal leaders of the opposition.

The mood in the parliament became increasingly hostile to the president. Previously distinct groups – such as communists, who disliked the economic reforms; nationalists, who resented the dissolution of the union and the greatly diminished role of Russia in world affairs; and democrats, who came to oppose the government because of its autocratic ways – formed an unofficial coalition based on their dislike of Yeltsin and his shock therapy.

In retrospect it is clear that Yeltsin, at the height of his popularity in the first months after the August 1991 coup, should have called for new elections. Although the opposition to the reforms was organizing and was able to stage large demonstrations in Moscow, Yeltsin's popularity was still such as to be able to call together an assembly much more favorable to his policies. This would have been the time for Yeltsin to create a strong political base. He could have gained the support and confidence of the past democratic opposition by consulting with them, but he did not do so. Not calling elections, alienating genuine democrats, and not creating a base of support for his policies when that was still possible were Yeltsin's greatest political errors. His political capital, his popularity, was gradually eroding due to frequent drunkenness, unpredictability, and his high-handed treatment of his associates.

Yeltsin's political course became erratic. He fired some of his reformist ministers as a concession to the parliament and included in his new cabinet ministers who were not committed to reform. Foremost among these was Viktor Chernomyrdin, a representative of the oil industry, and Viktor Gerashchenko, the head of the national bank whose policy of continuing to issue subsidies to factory managers was contrary to the principles of economic reform as envisaged by Gaidar. The consequence of Gerashchenko's profligate spending was the government's inability to keep inflation in check. Inflation necessitated high interest rates, which made economic recovery more difficult.

Yeltsin was willing to give concessions as far as economic reforms were concerned, but he resisted limitations on his powers. The parliament wanted him to resign as head of the government and name someone who would be responsible to the legislature. Khasbulatov's goal was to restrict Yeltsin's power and gain control over the cabinet and thus over governmental policies. As so often happens, issues of personality, that is, struggle for power, and genuine differences concerning policies came to be intertwined to such an extent that the participants in the struggle themselves could not separate them. In theory the issue was whether Russia would become a parliamentary republic, like most West European countries, or a presidential one, like France and the United States. In reality, it was a struggle for power.

In their claim of legitimacy both sides had profound weaknesses. On the one hand it was an understandable desire on the part of the parliament to want to curtail the power of the chief executive, especially given Russia's history and Yeltsin's personality. On the other hand, Khasbulatov and Rutskoi, the two leaders of the anti-Yeltsin camp, were hardly convinced or convincing democrats: Khasbulatov was manipulative and devious and Rutskoi a man of limited intelligence with little understanding of politics. They spoke in the name of an institution whose legitimacy was very much in question, since it had been created in 1990, under very different circumstances, on the basis of a constitution that went back to the era of Brezhnev and had been amended hundreds of times. Many exceptionally unattractive figures, including pathological anti-Semites and admirers of Hitler, were among the vocal opponents of Yeltsin's policies, giving the congress an even worse image.

Drawing up a new constitution became the most contentious issue. The parliament resisted adopting a new constitution because the deputies understood that if the assembly was dissolved and new elections held, they would have little chance of returning to office. The deputies had been receiving generous compensation and were reluctant to lose it. The weakness of Yeltsin's position was that, in order to call a referendum to pass a new constitution, he needed the permission of the congress, whose tenure would not run out until 1995. A constitution could be created only by nonconstitutional means. It was clear that, while the conflict could be postponed with

various maneuvers, the two sides were so far apart in their political programs that an ultimate struggle for supremacy would sooner or later occur.

The struggle became ever sharper. The congress, which according to the
still-existing constitution regarded itself as the supreme power in the land,
forced Yeltsin to dismiss Gaidar in December 1992. In March 1993 the
congress stripped Yeltsin of his emergency powers and attempted to impeach
him. Although a majority of deputies voted to impeach, Yeltsin prevailed
because the constitution required a two-thirds' majority. After the failure of
the impeachment effort, the congress finally agreed to a referendum to ask
the voters whether they approved of the policies of the president. The results
were by no means a ringing endorsement of the reforms; nevertheless, they
demonstrated that the public preferred Yeltsin to the parliament, and the
partisans of the president could correctly interpret the vote as a victory.

It may have been a political victory for Yeltsin, but the constitutional
issues, that is, drafting a new constitution and holding elections, remained
unresolved because of the low participation rate of the voters. The struggle
over economic policies continued, with the congress putting one obstacle
after another in front of the reformers, challenging almost every move of the
government. It was an impossible situation; the government and the legislature pursued different policies and issued contradictory orders and regulations. Russia was in a crisis.

The resolution, when it came, was bloody. In a televised address to the
nation on September 21, 1993, Yeltsin issued an order dissolving the Duma.
He coupled the order for dissolution with the promise of a new constitution
and elections, not only for a new parliament but also for president. This
promise enabled his followers to argue that, although Yeltsin might have
acted unconstitutionally, the promise of new elections could not be considered antidemocratic.

This was the most dangerous moment in post-Soviet history. The parliament's response was predictable: the delegates impeached Yeltsin and swore
in Aleksandr Rutskoi as acting president on the very day of Yeltsin's
announcement. In effect, they called for civil war. They promised to punish
severely those who sided with the impeached president and readied themselves for battle, but they overestimated their forces. The army remained
neutral, and therefore the delegates could count on the active support only of
small bands of unreconstructed communists and extreme nationalists. Khasbulatov and Rutskoi overplayed their hands: the call for a general strike was
not answered. Life in Moscow and in the provinces continued more or less
undisturbed. The members of the liberal intelligentsia, the descendants of the
dissidents, either sided with Yeltsin or blamed both sides for the crisis. Even
Chernomyrdin, the congress's choice for premier, at the crucial moment
supported President Yeltsin.

The government forces successfully blockaded the White House (the
parliament building) and were planning to wait out the besieged delegates.

The denouement came on October 3, almost two weeks after the beginning of the crisis.[5] When the followers of Khasbulatov and Rutskoi attempted to take over the television station and the Kremlin, government troops responded, bombarding and ultimately occupying the White House. We have no reliable estimate of the number of victims: official Russian figures underestimated them, and the partisans of the defunct parliament overestimated them. Probably several hundred people died and thousands were wounded.

MISERY

National income started to fall during the last years of the Soviet era, and Gorbachev's reforms were unable to stop the decline. However, the really steep drop occurred in the 1990s. In the course of that decade, gross domestic product fell by almost half, and national income correspondingly plummeted. There is no parallel in history for such a decline in peacetime. Every branch of the economy suffered, but production of consumer goods fell particularly drastically because of foreign competition. Instead of domestically made products, kiosks, which sprouted like mushrooms in the major cities, sold mostly foreign-made products. From whisky and beer to shirts and gloves, the Russians were buying foreign goods, often of dubious quality, rather than what was made in their own country.

Incomes fell by one-third, which in concrete terms meant that the population was less well fed, clothed, and housed at the end of the decade than at the beginning. In 1998 Russian GDP was only 55 percent of what it had been in 1989. In 1999 a quarter of Russians lived under the very minimally defined subsistence level.[6] It should be pointed out that the official figures may have overstated the magnitude of the decline: they did not take into account – and could not have done – the very large "second economy." People made great and usually successful attempts to hide their incomes in order to avoid taxation. But even if we allow for the economic activity that was not included in the statistics, there can be no doubt concerning the seriousness of the deterioration. Income statistics may be not fully reliable, but data concerning consumption also show a deterioration of life in Russia: the sale of consumer goods, such as television sets and refrigerators, and of high-quality food products, such as milk and meat, substantially declined.

Russia is an enormous country, and statistics concerning average income do not take into account the fact that the standard of living in Moscow and St. Petersburg, but especially Moscow, was far higher than in the rest of the country. Much of the newly acquired wealth was to be found in the two capitals, whereas the regions and cities in Siberia and the Far North that had been developed out of strategic consideration during Soviet times suffered especially badly. In the past people had moved to these regions because the state had offered better wages and salaries there than in the rest of the country; without such incentives, those who could afford to leave did so, leaving behind a despoiled environment; abandoned factories, mines, and buildings; and urban settings that lacked the most basic services.

It is possible to argue that in the long run Russia would benefit from what occurred in the economic sphere in the 1990s, and that the Soviet economy was unreformable so that a thorough transformation, however painful, was necessary. It is, however, indisputable that, for the Russians who had to live through this period, the reforms brought extraordinary suffering, misery, and a deterioration of their quality of life in almost every aspect. The enormous decline in the output of farms and factories had obvious and immediate consequences. At least a million people lost their jobs. The situation was probably even worse because official statistics underestimated the number of unemployed. On the one hand, the state was barely able to support those out of a job, so there was little incentive to register as unemployed; on the other hand, the factories had reason to keep as many people as possible on their rolls to decrease their tax obligation and demand larger subsidies. The workers who did have jobs sometimes did not receive wages for months. At other times factories compensated their workers with products from the workplace. There are recorded instances of workers receiving toilet paper in lieu of a salary.

Pensioners were particularly hard hit. The state either could not pay them at all or paid such pitifully small sums at a time of great inflation that old people were threatened with starvation. Cityscapes changed: in the streets of the major cities old people were peddling their often-meager possessions in order to feed themselves. The homeless set themselves up at subway and railroad stations.

The state came to be impoverished because it was often unable to collect taxes from inefficient factories. The government also lacked functioning machinery for enforcement; it was easy to avoid paying the government what was due. The poverty of the state restricted the ability of the government to support the arts and sciences. Intellectuals, who had played a role in undermining the legitimacy of the Soviet system, were among the prime victims of the changes. Artists and scientists, in order to escape poverty, left Russia; some were able to find suitable employment abroad, but others became taxi drivers or manual workers. Their departure impoverished intellectual life, and the loss of first-rate scientists will undoubtedly have unfortunate consequences in the long run.

For the average citizen the spread of crime and the deterioration of the health-care system were more important and more visible problems. There was no money to equip hospitals with medicine and modern machinery or to pay doctors decently. Hospitals were neglected to such an extent that they could not even maintain elementary sanitary standards. Partially as a result of the collapse of the health-care system, male life expectancy between

1990 and 1995 declined from 63.8 to 58 years. (By the end of the decade it had risen slightly to 59.7.) At 74, female life expectancy was below Western levels, but not as bleak; in fact, the gap between male and female life expectancy in Russia was the greatest in the world. Men were also more likely to harm themselves. The extraordinary decline in life expectancy was the consequence of a combination of the ghastly legacy of Soviet environmental pollution, alcoholism, the high suicide rate, accidents, the deterioration in diet, and the spread of tuberculosis and HIV. Not only were mortality rates extraordinarily high, but birth rates remained extremely low: in the 1990s there were 170 deaths for every 100 births. Because of the high death rate and low birth rate, Russia saw a population decline that was unprecedented in peacetime. At one point, Russian health authorities reported that only a third of children younger than 18 could be considered healthy.

In spite of the influx of ethnic Russians from the ex-Soviet republics, primarily from Central Asia and the Caucasian republics, the size of the population has been plunging. Between 1992 and 2002 the population of Russia declined from 148 million to 144 million.[7] All authorities agree that this decline is certain to continue, and the great and seemingly inevitable diminution of the working-age population is bound to have serious and negative consequences for the recovery of the economy and for the country's military strength.

Lack of funds to pay decent salaries to the police and judiciary is not the only explanation for the flourishing of organized and unorganized crime, but it was certainly a factor. As in other aspects of post-Soviet life, the deterioration started in the late 1980s and greatly accelerated during Yeltsin's tenure. All forms of criminal activity increased, especially violent crime and theft of state and private property. During the first half of the 1990s youth crime rose particularly sharply. The deterioration was clearly connected with other social ills, such as unemployment, homelessness, and increased drug use. In the Soviet era, of course, weapons had been kept out of the hands of civilians, and the sudden availability of weapons, mostly from ex-military personnel, made violence more lethal.

A disturbing feature of the new post-Soviet world was the emergence of organized crime. Violent crimes, that is, murders, were often the work of groups fighting for territory. Because business people did not trust the police and the courts, they were compelled to pay for protection. The line between legitimate and illegitimate business became tenuous. Criminals gained control over banking, which had particularly pernicious consequences: entrepreneurs were able to borrow money only at usurious rates. These banks also engaged in money-laundering. The Russian mafia had ties with similar groups all over the world, providing help to one another.[8]

As was to be expected, those who were prosecuted and ultimately imprisoned came from the lowest levels of society. Law enforcement officers were unable to uncover contract killings. Most of the murders of politicians, journalists, and other well-known figures were never solved, and the perpetrators never punished. The inability of the police to solve these high-profile cases contributed to a general sense among the population of being unprotected. Violence against journalists attempting to expose corruption was particularly disturbing, and the culprits were almost never found. The public was correct to suspect that powerful people were protecting the killers.

The Soviet Union had not been exactly a classless society. Some people, those who had access to scarce goods, had lived much better than others. But in the 1990s Russia suddenly moved from a reasonably egalitarian society to one where the gap between rich and poor was wider than in any country in Western Europe. It was to be expected that in the new era income inequalities would widen; this happened in all postcommunist societies. It was the sharp contrast between the sudden accumulation of enormous wealth by a very few and the vast increase of poverty and misery among the population at large that made the Russian situation particularly unattractive. At the end of the decade 1.5 percent of the population owned two-thirds of the national wealth.[9] The new billionaires, who made their fortunes by exploiting Russia's natural resources, exhibited little social conscience or interest in investing in the future of their native land. For example, Roman Abramovich, the richest man in Russia, bought a British soccer club for millions instead of building factories in his homeland. Many of the very rich preferred to live abroad. Poverty was more difficult to bear, as poor Russians could not help but notice that some of their compatriots were living very well indeed. Stores catering to some of the world's richest individuals appeared in the center of Moscow and, to a somewhat lesser extent, in St. Petersburg. Luxury car dealerships did very well, and there was no shortage of designer clothes shops of the kind found in Paris, New York, London, and Rome.

The end result of the social-political transformation of the 1990s was that Russia came to be ruled by a combination of crime syndicates, corrupt bureaucrats, and oligarchs who had acquired great economic and therefore political power.

THE END OF THE YELTSIN ERA

In December 1993 the Russians voted for a new constitution and a new legislature. The ground rules for the adoption of the constitution specified that at least 50 percent of eligible voters had to vote. Although the government claimed that 54 percent voted, there are suspicions that the results were falsified and fewer than 50 percent voted, in which case the constitution was adopted illegally. The voters elected two houses of parliament. The autonomous republics and Russia's eighty-nine provinces were represented in the upper house, which came to be dominated by the regional elites. This house was also more supportive of the president than the lower house, which was elected according to a combined system: half of the delegates were elected directly in their districts; the other half were distributed among the parties according to their share of the vote, stipulating a minimum 5 percent of support.

The newly adopted constitution transformed Russia into a presidential republic. The balance of power shifted decisively from the Duma to the president. The Russians obviously preferred Yeltsin to the dispersed parliament, but it was difficult to interpret the results of the parliamentary elections as a ringing endorsement of his policies. The main spokesman for the parties of economic reform and the best-known reformist figure, Yegor Gaidar, lacked charisma and was very unpopular. For those who wanted to push the economic reforms and privatization further, the composition of the new parliament was not reassuring. The reformists did not do as well in the elections as they might have, at least partly because Yeltsin considered himself to be above the political fray and did not campaign for those who had supported him in the past. He was interested only in the vote for the constitution, and he kept aloof from the reformist parties during the campaign.

The partisans of the president had a slight majority in the new parliament, and the new assembly proved to be more docile than the old one. However, joining the communists in opposition to Yeltsin was a new party led by Vladimir Zhirinovskii, a buffoon and a demagogue, and it did very well. This party, ludicrously misnamed the Liberal Democratic Party of Russia, was in fact a nationalist and populist organization; it captured almost a quarter of the vote and became the largest party in the new parliament. The strength of Zhirinovskii's party and that of the communists demonstrated the continued power of the opposition. Indeed, the new government, once again headed by Chernomyrdin, was the least reform-minded of all previous post-Soviet governments.

In the next parliamentary election, which took place in 1995, the fundamental correlation of forces did not change much, although the communists became the largest party, taking votes away from Zhirinovskii's party. The weak parliament, which needed a two-thirds' majority in both houses to overturn presidential decrees, could not effectively oppose Yeltsin. Although the parliament was by no means supportive of the government, compared to the previous period, political peace temporarily prevailed.

The constitution gave enormous powers to the president, and some Russians understandably feared the reappearance of autocracy. However, Russia remained a weak state, continuing to have trouble collecting taxes and controlling street crime, to say nothing about confronting organized crime. A manifestation of this weakness was the inability of the central government to enforce its will against the leaders of the provinces, who at times failed to deliver tax revenues to the federal budget. Although governors were elected, officials from the Soviet era had overwhelming advantages in these elections, and they did not let power slip from their hands. Once elected, they could do as they pleased, for there was very little oversight and very little transparency. The weakness of the state was caused by the lack of mediating institutions between the government and individual citizens, such as strong political parties, voluntary societies, and procedures enabling mass participation in the political process.

After his victory, it seemed Yeltsin had lost his way. He suffered from bouts of depression. He had always drunk too much, but his drinking became an growing problem and a source of embarrassment for the country. He repeatedly made a spectacle of himself at international gatherings. On one famous occasion, obviously drunk, he took the baton from the conductor of a Berlin police orchestra and attempted to conduct. The world press published the picture, much to the embarrassment of Russians. Yeltsin was also ill: he had a serious heart condition. In his first years in office he gave decisive support to those who aimed to introduce market reforms. Whether this was the right thing to do and whether the reforms were carried out in the best way are issues very much in dispute. But it is unquestionable that Yeltsin was a decisive force behind the reformers, who could not have done what they did without his support. After the great and bloody crisis of September and October 1993 he stopped his direct and immediate involvement in the economic life of the country. Once he had a great deal of constitutional power, he did not seem to know what to do with it; his political course became increasingly erratic. He surrounded himself with favorites, among them the highly unpopular Anatolii Chubais, one of the people responsible for carrying out privatization and suspected of corruption. The other significant person near him was a rather unsavory character, Aleksandr Korzhakov, his bodyguard, who controlled access to the president. However, the only person in whom Yeltsin had unquestioned confidence was his daughter, Tatiana, who in these years acted as a vice president. Russia once again was governed by a group of unelected people, those who were close to the president.

The impoverishment of the population continued; real incomes fell further. Under the circumstances it was understandable that Yeltsin's popularity plummeted. Elections for president were scheduled to take place in June 1996. A poll conducted in January 1996 found that Yeltsin had the support of only 10 percent of the voters. It seemed inevitable that he would lose the election. Some of his partisans, most importantly Korzhakov, attempted to persuade him to offer concessions to the communists, his strongest opponents, by taking them into the government and reversing some of the economic reforms of the early period. The communists, in exchange, would agree to postpone or annul the elections.

Russia once again was on the verge of a crisis. The postponement of the elections would have meant an admission of failure of the democratic experiment. But the only viable alternative to Yeltsin was Gennadii Zyuganov and his Communist Party. It was Yeltsin's good fortune, but a misfortune of Russian democracy, that a strong Communist Party dominated the opposition, preempting the formation of a democratic opposition. The communists promised a return to the principles of the Soviet era. Nationalists, who above all bemoaned the loss of the country's great power status and regarded not only Yeltsin but also Gorbachev as traitors, supported them. As long as Yeltsin could depict the contest as between himself and those who wanted to return to the Soviet era, he had a good chance of winning.

The fight to keep his job seemed to have helped him to regain his energy and involvement. First, he had to refurbish his tarnished image. In order to give the impression that he was active and vigorous, he campaigned incessantly. He stopped drinking, lost excess weight in order to appear healthier, and attempted to demonstrate to the voters that he was well and still had the necessary energy for the job. He went to amusing lengths to exhibit his vitality. On occasion he danced in front of audiences. In addition, he had the advantage of incumbency, and therefore could make popular moves, such as raising pensions, firing officials he held responsible for unpopular policies, and promising to take steps to end the war against the Chechens. Very importantly he ultimately triumphed because he had a great deal more money to spend than his opponents. State-run television favored him by allocating far more time to him than to the other candidates. Crucial to his reelection victory was the support of the so-called oligarchs, a handful of the richest people, the main beneficiaries of the privatization scheme, including the heads of banks, oil companies, and other large corporations. As mentioned earlier, the arrangement was referred to as "loans for shares." This meant that the oligarchs financed the reelection campaign and in exchange received shares in companies still owned by the state. The violation of the most elementary principles of democracy must have been obvious to all. It was described at the time as an exchange of unaccountable wealth for unaccountable political power. It was the best example in post-Soviet history of the corrupt interrelationship of wealth and political power.

Yeltsin and the oligarchs needed one another. A communist victory was a threat to those who had recently acquired their wealth under dubious circumstances. The liberal Moscow intelligentsia, who had every reason to dislike Yeltsin, also ultimately had no choice but to support him. Even Yeltsin's bitterest Western critics could not convincingly argue that Zyuganov, supported by anti-Semitic and quasifascist demagogues, would be more likely to strengthen the fragile Russian democracy than Yeltsin. The results of the presidential election of 1996 demonstrated again that, when the choice was between a return to the Soviet system and the reforms, which is how Yeltsin defined the terms of the election, the people would choose Yeltsin's course.

In the first round, Yeltsin received a slight plurality over Zyuganov; in the second round, with 69 percent of the electorate voting, Yeltsin received 54 percent to Zyuganov's 40 percent. The playing field was anything but even; the president had overwhelming advantages against the rather hapless communist leader. Nevertheless, it would be wrong to argue that Zyuganov would have won had the election not been tainted. The results demonstrated the wide gap between two Russias: Yeltsin overwhelmingly won the vote of the young and city dwellers; Zyuganov's support came from pensioners and villagers, who were the great losers in the transformation of society.

After the election, the reality of Yeltsin's condition became obvious: he was a sick man. He underwent bypass surgery and was away from his presidential duties for months. Chernomyrdin served five years as premier; he was the longest-serving premier in post-Soviet history. During Yeltsin's illness, it was Chernomyrdin who provided a degree of stability. His term in office ended in March 1998, when Yeltsin dismissed him, ostensibly to speed up economic reforms, but probably to prevent Chernomyrdin from becoming too powerful. Chernomyrdin's departure was followed by a prime ministerial leapfrog: between March 1998 and August 1999 the country had five prime ministers. The 35-year-old Sergei Kirienko, a liberal, was resisted by the Duma and was voted down twice. But when the Duma was presented with the choice of accepting him or facing new elections, he was confirmed. Kirienko had the misfortune of being in office when the price of Russia's main export, oil, was dropping in the world market, leading to a disastrous budget deficit. Russia defaulted on its debt, and the ruble had to be devalued. Kirienko, unfairly, had to take the blame and was dismissed after just five months in office.

In this crisis situation Yeltsin chose Yevgenii Primakov to follow Kirienko. Primakov had good relations with the Duma, and he brought communists into the government. Unlike Kirienko, he had independent standing and a constituency behind him, and therefore he was regarded as a possible successor to Yeltsin. During his short term in office, Russia experienced a division of powers within the executive branch, which is why the president soon dismissed him. This disturbed the Duma to such an extent that it again attempted to impeach the president but failed, not reaching the necessary two-thirds' majority. The next premier, Sergei Stepashin, lasted only three months in office. Following him came the last premier during Yeltsin's tenure, Vladimir Putin.

CHECHNYA

The dissolution of the once-mighty Soviet Union took place remarkably peacefully. However, even after 1991, the most important successor state, the Russian Federation, remained a multinational empire, and therefore the possibility of further disintegration remained a worrisome problem. The effort to stop this process came to be focused on a small region in the Caucasus, Chechnya. The problem of dealing with the Chechens' desire for independence has continued to be a troublesome and unresolved issue throughout post-Soviet history.

The relationship between Russians and Chechens has been troubled since the two nations came into contact with one another. In the course of the nineteenth century, Muslim Chechens resisted Russian attempts to subdue them even more fiercely than did other small nations. Brutal Russian behavior, such as destruction of villages and deportations, only strengthened Chechen hostility and drove many of them to join the insurgent army of Imam Shamil, the most prominent, almost legendary Dagestani Muslim resistance leader. In February 1944 the Russians gave the Chechens more reason to hate them. In a particularly reprehensible move, Stalin deported all of them, including communist functionaries, to Central Asia and declared them to be a "traitor people." A quarter of the victims died as a result of the deportation and the harsh conditions of exile. In 1957 Khrushchev allowed the Chechens to return to their homeland, but their attempt to reclaim what had belonged to them resulted in conflict with those who had moved into their houses and taken their property. Further bitterness ensued. In view of these events it is not surprising that, among the small nations of the new Russian state, it was the Chechens who were most determined to gain independence.

According to the last Soviet census there were about 1.2 million Chechens living in the "autonomous" Chechen–Ingush republic within the Russian Federation. In November 1991 the Chechen leader, Dzhokhar Dudaev, declared his country independent. Dudaev, a former general in the Soviet army, became the leader of the most determined nationalists. He succeeded in establishing himself by violent means as the ruler of his small country and turned Chechnya into a lawless enclave, a threat to the surrounding territories.

After years of neglect (during which Moscow's involvement was limited to attempting to dislodge Dudaev by subversion), Yeltsin decided to take action. The Russians had legitimate concerns: they feared that Chechen separatism might spread to the Caucasus and other minority regions, including Tatarstan, Bashkortostan, and Dagestan, which also have large Muslim populations. Russia was also concerned about losing oil revenue, as the pipeline from the Caspian fields to the terminus of Novorossisk runs through Chechnya. The timing of Yeltsin's decision may have been influenced by a need to respond to the nationalist rhetoric in the Duma, in particular to Zhirinovskii.

Yeltsin ordered the invasion without consulting the Duma, and in December 1994, 40,000 Russian soldiers, assisted by tank columns, entered Chechnya. The campaign was a disaster; the Russians underestimated the determination of the Chechens, who, though greatly outnumbered, resisted fiercely. The Russian army gave a very poor account of itself. The soldiers were ill disciplined, often drunk or on drugs, demoralized, and incompetently led. In spite of their overwhelming numbers and far superior equipment, it took the Russians weeks to capture the capital, Groznyi, and this "victory" was by no means the end of resistance. The war became even bloodier; the rebels established themselves in the mountains and initiated guerrilla warfare. The response of the Russians was abominable: the soldiers killed civilians indiscriminately, looted, and raped. They tortured captured Chechen fighters, demolished entire villages, and executed people without trial. Tens of thousands of civilians, both Chechens and ethnic Russians, died, and the country was turned into a wasteland. In a particularly egregious instance, in the town of Samashki, in April 1995, the Russian soldiers slaughtered 250 men, women, and children by throwing grenades into basements where they were hiding. The Chechens reciprocated in kind. In June of the same year, Chechen warriors attacked the Russian town Budyonnovsk, killing police officers and taking 2,000 patients in a hospital as hostages. To ensure the survival of the hostages, the Russians were forced into humiliating negotiations with the guerrillas. Although both sides committed atrocities, the Russian soldiers, with the greater firepower, killed most of the civilians.

The cost of the war was high. The prestige of the Russian army suffered a major blow; both domestic and international opinion decried the brutalities committed by the Russians. International condemnation was universal, and the war was so unpopular at home that Yeltsin, preparing for his reelection in 1996, was compelled to take steps to stop it. Television news brought the war into the homes of Russians, and many of them recoiled at what they saw. In this instance the free media had a major and constructive role to play. One day people listened to a government statement that Groznyi would not be bombed and the next day the television news showed how bombs had devastated the Chechen capital. It was obvious to everyone: the government was lying about the nature of the war. Multinational Russia could not afford the deepening of hostilities among the nationalities. Nationalist jingoist voices, which accompanied the war, contributed to the alienation of the Muslim minorities living in different parts of the country. The expense of the war contributed to a budgetary crisis, leading to increased inflation.

The war in Chechnya was a major reason for the final alienation of the democrats from Yeltsin. Sergei Kovalev, a courageous civil rights activist, resigned his chairmanship of the Human Rights Commission, and in January 1996 Gaidar resigned from the Presidential Council in order to express his opposition to the war.

Although the Russians managed to kill Dudaev, the war was not going well for them; they failed to put down the insurgency. They were forced to sign an agreement with the new Chechen leader, Aslan Maskhadov, in which they promised aid for reconstruction but left the ultimate fate of Chechnya unresolved. The Russian army withdrew in defeat, without having accomplished its announced goal.

Unfortunately, the anarchy within the now functionally independent state did not abate. Although Maskhadov was elected president in January 1997 in a free election, he failed to impose order. Criminal activities, in particular kidnapping for money, became daily occurrences. Also, radical Islam established a foothold. Extremists, such as Salman Raduev and Shamil Basaev, were unreconciled, did not recognize Maskhadov's authority, continued their involvement in kidnapping Russians and foreigners, and undermined the president's authority.

There were two competing visions for Chechnya's future. The moderate Maskhadov, at least at this time, envisaged a functionally independent Chechnya in close economic and political cooperation with Moscow. In contrast, the radicals did not recoil from the idea of provoking a war with Russia, in expectation that the small Muslim minorities in the Caucasus and Dagestan would join in an Islamic state whose viability would be assured by its size and oil wealth. Attacked by the radicals and not receiving support from Moscow, Maskhadov's position became untenable. He was repeatedly forced to give concessions to the radicals, such as the introduction of *sharia* as the basis of Chechen law, but these concessions only emboldened the radicals.

In 1999 both the Chechens and the Russians were preparing to resume the conflict. Maskhadov, having not received the promised reconstruction aid from Russia, was unable to control the radicals, who continued to raid Russian territory and kidnap Russians and other foreigners. When radical Chechens invaded Dagestan in August 1999, the Russian government was able to portray the war as defensive. Russians saw that the issue was no longer the independence of Chechnya, but rather the desire of radical Chechens to establish a large Muslim state, and that would lead to the disintegration of the Russian Federation. When in September a series of unexplained apartment house bombings took place in Moscow and other cities, Russian public opinion quickly assumed that it was the Chechens carrying the war to Russia. The bombings had far-reaching effects on Russian public opinion regarding mobilizing for war. This time the war was popular. Putin's promise to take drastic action and his nationalist rhetoric greatly contributed to his popularity and helped him win the election in the following year.

The Second Chechen War turned out to be a series of tragedies. Any attempt to set up in Chechnya a functioning administration headed by pro-Russian elements was bound to fail. A Russian journalist correctly called Chechnya "a small corner of hell."[10] In this destroyed country, there were no legitimate jobs; instead banditry, counterfeiting, money-laundering, and kidnapping for money or political goals flourished. Under the circumstances, radical Islam had an increasing appeal. Chechen Islamic warriors carried out attacks, including suicide attacks, in places of their choice beyond the borders of their own little country. People willing to die for their beliefs took hostages, which, as a result of inept Russian responses, led to hundreds of victims. In the course of this war Russians came to demonize all Chechens, and the Chechens came to be united in their hatred of Russians. There is no end in sight. Russian public opinion would be willing to see Chechnya as an independent state, but the vast majority of people believe that this region will not be brought under the authority of Moscow for a long time to come.

PUTIN

Vladimir Putin became president of Russia in 2000 because Yeltsin chose him to be his successor. No one in the spring of 1999 could have predicted this development, because the future president was almost entirely unknown in the country and had no independent constituency. Most likely it was because he was Yeltsin's creation – and owed everything to him – that the infirm president anointed him.

It is to Putin that we now turn. Did Russia during Putin's first two terms retreat into Soviet-style autocracy? Year after year the president increased his power at the expense of the oligarchs who dared to challenge him. He also reduced the autonomy of Russia's provinces. More significantly, perhaps, from the point of view of the development of democratic politics, he took steps to lessen the role of an independent media. In Russia, as elsewhere in the modern world, television is the most important source of news for the great majority of people. Compared to the Yeltsin era, the situation seriously deteriorated. As the Kremlin succeeded in taking over big businesses, it used its newly acquired power to control television networks, where criticism of the president disappeared and independent candidates do not receive a hearing at election time. The situation in the printed media was not as dire, but here also the multiplicity of views that could be found in the early 1990s was no more by the end of Putin's second term. Members of the oligarchy who were not supporters of the president were deprived of their newspapers by legal or illegal means. Nevertheless, what had become most discouraging about the political scene was not so much Putin's attempt to amass more power, but the attitude of the Russian people. Poll after poll demonstrated that the Russian people approved when the president took action against his political opponents. Such antidemocratic action has not lessened his popularity, but rather increased it. The same polls show that the great majority of Russians do not believe that they live in a democratic country, and they are not much bothered by this. "If everything is going well," they see no need for an opposition.

Illiberal Democracy

Although the immediate economic and social consequences of the collapse of the seventy-year-old Soviet Union were negative and painful, nonetheless the early 1990s were a time of optimism. Most, though not all, observers took it for granted that after a difficult period of transition Russia would find the way back to Europe and build a democratic polity and a modern capitalist economy. This transformation in the none-too-distant future would bring a better life for all. After the passage of almost a quarter of a century such hopes appear to be remarkably naive. Were the 1990s in reality a missed decade? Were Yeltsin and his foreign and domestic advisers responsible for the missed opportunities? Or were the chances always slim that in a very short time Russia would become a democratic market economy, complete with those institutions that such a political and economic system required? In retrospect it is fair to say that most observers agreed with the second view. The transformation of the ex-communist countries in Eastern Europe was a much easier undertaking than repairing the damage that seventy-four years of Soviet rule had done to the heartland of communism. The task of creating social, economic, and political institutions that are necessary for the functioning of a modern liberal democratic state turned out to be very difficult. In the course of 1990s the regime that is associated with the name of Yeltsin succeeded in destroying the Soviet regime forever. There can be no return to that particular past. That was an achievement, but there was a high price to pay in terms of human misery that was imposed on the Russian people.

With the departure of Yeltsin, whose last years in office were an embarrassment for his fellow nationals, it seemed once again that positive changes that would improve the lives of the Russian people would be introduced. Indeed, with the arrival of the new millennium a different political system came into existence. This was to be the era of Putin.

THE NEW PRESIDENT

After his confrontation with the elected parliament in 1993, Yeltsin legally or illegally succeeded in transforming the country from a parliamentary system into a presidential regime, in which the head of the country accumulated vast powers. Yeltsin, because of his background and character, was never able to exercise all the available powers. However, his successor, an altogether different person with a different past, started out with enormous advantages. He possessed ambition and energy.

Putin became president of Russia for no other reason than that Yeltsin chose him. It is a much-debated topic why Yeltsin made this choice. None of the explanations seem altogether convincing. The reason frequently given is that Yeltsin chose Putin because the younger man promised impunity to him and his family for various wrongdoings during his years in office. There is no evidence that such a deal was struck, and there is no reason to think that other candidates might not have agreed to such terms.[1] Nor is there proof that Putin was the choice of the oligarchs who surrounded the increasingly incapacitated president. Probably we have to be satisfied with the notion that this choice was a whim and the ex-president could easily have chosen someone else. Putin was an accidental president, unlike his predecessors whose rise to ultimate power was predictable and who, therefore, came into office better prepared.

Vladimir Vladimirovich Putin was born in 1952 in Leningrad. When he assumed the presidency he was only 48 years old. Possibly his relative youth may have appealed to Yeltsin in selecting him as his successor. He came from rather humble beginnings. Although he had a grandfather who had cooked for Stalin, Putin's parents were by no means part of the nomenklatura. Young Putin did attend university and studied law, but he was a man without intellectual pretensions. It is a debated question to what extent his past explains his character, policies, and behavior. The single most relevant fact in his biography was that he had worked for the KGB for most of his adult life before assuming a political role. It is not only that he worked for the KGB, but that occupation, more than any other, appealed to him even as a young man. According to his own statement he had wanted to join even as a schoolboy and indeed was able to do so after graduating from university.[2] First he worked in counterintelligence and later was sent to Dresden, East Germany, where he served for five years. There he worked in cooperation with the East German political police, the Stasi. As a consequence of his stay abroad, he acquired a better sense of life in Europe than most Soviet people and learned to speak German fluently. The fact that he served in an East German city, and not in Berlin, demonstrates that he was not very high in the hierarchy. One can only speculate whether his work for the KGB instilled in him a worldview according to which in a political universe there were friends and enemies, and that people could not be trusted.

At the time of the collapse of the Soviet Union he retired from service as a lieutenant colonel. We can only guess how the collapse of the regime that he had faithfully served affected him. His political career started on his return to Leningrad, his native city, where he first worked in the international department of the university. The Leningrad connection continued to play a role in his subsequent career, for later he took people as his trusted associates from this city. On his return to Leningrad, he reestablished contact with his former professor in law school, Anatolii Sobchak, who was the first democratically elected mayor of the city and was regarded, at least for some time, as one of the prominent leaders of the liberal wing of the political spectrum. Probably Sobchak chose Putin as an associate because he remembered him as a diligent but not brilliant student and because he was one of the few people who had some experience working abroad. Knowledge of the outside world, however superficial, was a significant qualification at a time of great domestic change.

Putin was entrusted with foreign trade relations as deputy mayor. This job on the one hand involved him in activities that gave him enormous possibilities for corrupt dealings and, on the other, in the course of the 1990s, obliged him frequently to travel to the West, primarily to Germany and Finland. In 1996 he worked for the reelection of his mentor, Sobchak, and when that effort failed he moved to Moscow, where he became deputy head of the presidential property management department. This was another position where the possibilities for corruption were great. A significant step in his rise to power came in 1998 when Yeltsin appointed him head of the FSB (Federal Security Service), the successor to the KGB. Of course, holdovers from the KGB dominated the FSB, and it was remarkable that a person who had a relatively low rank in the hierarchy would get the top job. But perhaps it was precisely his low rank that was the reason that Yeltsin chose him. He did not have to carry so much of the burden for the past. It is probable that people close to Yeltsin knew Putin from his St. Petersburg days and recommended him to the president.

In August 1999 Yeltsin named Putin as the new prime minister. His choice was not merely a new head of government, but a successor. Putin perhaps appeared to Yeltsin to be a reformist and at the same time a man who was willing, in view of his KGB background, to use a strong arm against his opponents.

Yeltsin and his advisers prepared the soil for Putin's election, which was to take place in 2000. Control over television enabled people in power to manipulate public opinion and destroy the reputation of the other contenders, such as the mayor of Moscow, Yurii Luzhkov, and former premier, Yevgenii Primakov. On December 31, 1999, Yeltsin surprised the country and the rest of the world: in a television address to the nation he announced his resignation. According to the 1993 constitution, in case of the incapacitation or resignation of the president, the prime minister automatically becomes acting president.

Just as in the days of Brezhnev and Chernenko, under Yeltsin Russia once again was led by a man who had passed his prime, who was ill and no longer in control of events. In spite of his obvious incapacity to head the government, the timing of his resignation was a disservice to the cause of Russia's democratic development. His resignation made Putin acting president a few months before the elections and thereby greatly increased his chances of winning. Russian politics had become democratic in the sense that elections for parliament and for president take place regularly and predictably. However, the electoral contests never take place on an even playing field where several alternatives for national policies are presented to the voters who then have the opportunity to choose. Putin acquired a degree of popularity by taking strong measures against the rebels in the north Caucasus, Chechnya.

Putin as acting president brought the date of the election several months forward and thereby further increased his own chances since his opponents had less time to campaign. The support of the main television channel, owned by the oligarch Boris Berezovskii, played a significant role, although at this point Putin did not have a monopoly of media support. He managed to win the presidency on March 26, 2000, in the first ballot by getting 53 percent of the votes, i.e., 40 million votes. He was too new on the political scene to have a genuine, large following; on the other hand, it is unlikely that there was another candidate with greater popular support. It was hardly an even playing field, given Putin's advantages. On the other hand, it is far from obvious that he stole the election from some other person who would have been the people's favorite.

With his election a new era began. After the great upheavals of the previous decade people desired stability, and to a large extent the new administration was able to provide it. The new president was a vigorous, fairly young man and in his vitality the diametrical opposite of his predecessor, which must have contributed to his popularity. In an interesting duality he was at once the candidate of the establishment, which made him president, who promised stability rather than change, and at same time the opposite of the mercurial and at least at one time charismatic Yeltsin.

Although assuming the presidency of Russia was a difficult task, given the destruction and anarchy that the Yeltsin era produced, nevertheless in many ways Putin was fortunate. Unlike his predecessor, he did not have to compete with a well-organized opposition. The Yeltsin constitution gave him considerable powers and, again unlike his predecessor, he knew how to use them. Also, after the crisis produced by the default of 1998 the economy stabilized and the rising price of oil, Russia's major export, enabled the president to improve the budget and keep inflation under control. The economy was showing modest growth.

Putin did not want to change some of the fundamental characteristics of the post-Soviet state and others he could not change. He assured the beneficiaries of the privatization program that he would not undo it. Unlike

Yeltsin, whose ideology was anticommunism, Putin was a synthesizer. Although he distanced himself from many features of the Soviet past, and paid lip service to the idea of democracy, at the same time he realized that the seventy-four years of communist history could not be eradicated from the national memory. He decided not to dwell on the crimes of the Stalin era or hold people responsible for them. In a remarkably symbolic decision, he was willing to incorporate Soviet symbols, such as the music (but not the words) of the Soviet anthem. He allowed Lenin to remain in his mausoleum. He put up a plaque honoring Yurii Andropov, an ex-head of the KGB, and at the same time put flowers on the grave of Andrei Sakharov, the great human rights activists, and a victim of the former KGB chief whom Putin continued to admire and honor.

Putin's first tenure in office (2000–04) must be regarded as a success, even though in retrospect one can already detect some of the most unattractive aspects of what we think of as the Putin system. To some extent the new government was fortunate: the price of oil rose on the world market, and oil exports provided approximately 50 percent of the revenues for the state budget. Putin, and his first premier, Mikhail Kasyanov, pursued neoliberal economic policies, ones that Western liberal economists approved of. They closed down some of the outdated factories. The government reformed the tax code, lowering taxes on businesses and introduced a single social tax to finance pensions and medical insurance. It also introduced a new labor code, which liberalized labor markets. The devaluation of the ruble, a consequence of the 1998 default, made Russian goods cheaper on the world market. At the time there was every reason to believe that Russia indeed was on the road to a Western-type capitalist economy and that Putin could claim credit for the small economic boom. The economic success attracted foreign capital, and foreign investors greatly benefited from the extraordinary rise in the Russian stock market. At that time observers regarded the president of Russia as a Westernizer. The principles that Putin's government followed – i.e., the continuation of economic reform and liberalization, combined with preserving a large role for the state apparatus – were broadly popular.

The economy grew between 6 and 7 percent during the first decade of the century. This transformation after the misery of the previous decade was a source of optimism. The improvement of the standard of living at least for a large segment of the population was impressive. Unemployment went down from 12.9 percent to 6.3 percent.[3] Unquestionably the rise on the world market primarily of oil, but also of other raw materials that Russian exported, made the boom possible. But there was more going on than good fortune in the world economy that enabled Russia, a major exporter of raw materials, to profit. The impressive rise in the standard of living, and the great improvement in the state budget took place in spite of the extraordinary corruption and considerable waste of resources. For the first years of the century once again there were reasons to be optimistic that Russia would be able to overcome the experiences of the years of Soviet rule. Russia might be able to join Gorbachev's "common European home." GDP per capita, which stood at $5,951 in 1999, rose to $20,276 in 2008.[4] Then, however, Russia was particularly hard hit by the worldwide economic downturn, which greatly reduced the national income from the export of such raw materials as iron, oil, and aluminum.

THE PUTIN SYSTEM

Very early in Putin's presidency the future outlines of a newly created autocratic regime could already be discerned. The observation of Russian historians that their country oscillates between periods of anarchy and autocracy seemed to be demonstrated once again. In Yeltsin's years in office the government allowed considerable freedom of expression and social organization, and it pursued a pacific and conciliatory foreign policy. However, the reforms brought enormous suffering along with economic and demographic collapse. From the outset it was evident that Putin would do anything in his power to battle any organization, political, economic, or social, that might appear to limit his authority. In concrete terms this meant that the new regime greatly limited freedom of political discourse by taking control of the mass media; it meant the reduction of local autonomy; and it meant destroying the political power of the oligarchs. It should have been evident from the outset that, although Putin considered Russia to be part of Europe and envisaged close relations with West European countries, nevertheless he was establishing what came to be called "illiberal democracy," i.e., maintaining the outward forms, such as having elections regularly scheduled, political parties, and a functioning, but ultimately powerless legislature.[5] To the extent that illiberal democracy can be regarded as a consistent ideology, its central feature is that the state has a dominant role to play in the lives of the citizens, protecting them from what the leaders consider harmful ideas and detrimental influences from abroad.

Putin believed that for Russian economic growth and modernization the Asian examples, such as Singapore, South Korea, and China, were more relevant than those of Western democracies. However, unlike Lee Kuan Yew's Singapore, Putin's Russia evolved as greatly compromised by a high level of corruption. Unlike the successful Asian countries, Russia did not become thoroughly incorporated into the world economy; in other words, it failed to develop a diverse and modern economy. If we define democracy as a political system in which the population is presented with clearly articulated sets of choices to deal with issues inevitably existing in any society, then Russia has never been democratic, and Putin never intended to introduce genuine democracy.

The increased power of the state against society was the dominant feature of the new regime. Putin emerged as an autocrat inasmuch as no credible alternative leader could appear on the new political scene. Indeed, in none of the elections that took place after 2000 did Putin, or his favored candidate in 2008, Dmitrii Medvedev, have a chance of losing. By gaining control of the significant parts of the media, by making it impossible for groups that would oppose him to organize, he has dominated the political scene ever since he assumed power. The main political party, United Russia, became one with the state, and elections served no purpose other than legitimization. United Russia had branches in the rest of the country, and the state apparatus and the party to a large extent came to be fused. According to the ideology of the party, Russia did not need other parties to represent various social groups and interests. Similar to the notions of corporatism, in theory this party could reconcile within itself competing interest groups. Yeltsin's stance was that he, as president, stood above political parties. Putin, by contrast, although not a party member, nevertheless had identified himself with United Russia. The political process thereby came to be neutered. Although the number of political parties in the decade after 2000 diminished by two and thereby the parties were expected to become stronger, in reality they never managed to present a genuine opposition. In the 2007 election only seven parties competed and only four received enough support to be able to participate in the Duma.[6] The parties never acquired prestige, and interest and public involvement remained dismally low. We may conclude that no more than perhaps a tenth of the population supports a genuinely liberal project, that is, one fundamentally compatible with Western values. The elections of 2004 and 2008 were managed processes, and there was never any doubt of the outcome. Forms were observed and elections were carried out, as required by the constitution; however, the real political struggle, to the extent that it existed, took place behind closed doors. Elections could be better described as plebiscites, inasmuch as no genuine alternatives were proposed. Democratic forces, to the extent that they existed at all, were manipulated into powerlessness. To a certain degree, this was the fault of the putative opposition as they were unable to unify and present an attractive program corresponding to the needs and public mood of the moment. However, more importantly, their failure was the consequence of the manipulation of the process by the forces of the government, dominated by a single charismatic leader.

The kind of political system that thereby came into existence was by no means unique. On occasion the system is described as "managed democracy." In Europe, Turkey and Hungary come closest to Putin's political system. These are countries with weak traditions of liberalism, fragile civil societies, and a lack of well-developed political parties. The leaders of autocratic regimes rightly feel that they are under threat from the advanced West. The enlightened elite regard the West as an example to follow. The members of this group hope and on occasion succeed in receiving help from advanced and rich Western counties, above all, from the United States. The

West by its very nature is subversive. The response to such a threat is an emphasis on national historical traditions, uniqueness, imagined spiritual values, and social conservatism. Putin's rhetoric repeatedly contends that it is a matter of self-respect for Russians to maintain their own institutions. The ever-increasing personalization of power is characteristic of illiberal democracies that grow into autocracies. In the Russian case, the state came to be more and more identified with Putin.

While members of a Western-oriented and liberal section of the population, concentrated mostly in Moscow and St. Petersburg, dislike the autocratic form of government under which they are compelled to live, the majority of the Russian people do not feel that the state plays too great a role in their lives. Among the majority of Russians there has been little demand for far- reaching, revolutionary changes. The Putin system brought predictability and order. Nationalism, social conservatism, and respect for the church found an echo among the people. Putin's Russia is not totalitarian. Not only are democratic forms observed, but independent voices on occasion can also be heard. However, regimes, at least so far, have been able to keep these voices under strict control and only now and again find it necessary to jail and at times kill an opponent.

A notorious murder case was the assassination of the courageous journalist, Anna Politkovskaia, in October 2006. She had denounced the increasing authoritarianism of the Putin government, protested against violations of human rights, and taken a particular interest in the workings of the criminal regime of Akhmed Kadyrov in Chechnya. Before the murder she had received death threats. It is possible, indeed likely, that Putin did not directly order the murder; nevertheless his regime was responsible for creating an atmosphere in which such events could take place and remain unpunished. Although Politkovskaia's killing attracted the greatest indignation around the world, dozens of other journalists were also killed during the Putin era, many of them in the Caucasus in connection with the Chechen wars. Russia has been one of the most dangerous places for journalists. Usually the murderers were not found, and those who were found were frequently cleared after judicial proceedings. The autocratic regime maintained its rule on occasion by assassinating some particularly bothersome commentator or creating phony charges against political opponents and quasilegally jailing them, such as happened to Khodorkovskii. Like other autocratic regimes, the Putin government drew a line between acceptable criticisms and acts for which people were punished.

Putin never governed alone. He surrounded himself with people of similar background and ideology, many of whom had served in the KGB, the political police in the defunct Soviet empire. The Russian word to describe these people is *siloviki*, which is derived from the word strength, *sila*. These men, and they were all male, have played increasingly significant roles in Russian politics. As a good politician Putin managed to maintain a balance among competing forces, such as the relatively liberal intelligentsia, the *siloviki*, conservative nationalists, and business interests.

Many of the characteristics of the Putin system must be the consequence of the Soviet experience. In the Soviet system, in a country of constant short-ages, desirable goods were made available through personal contacts, a network of connections and patronage. In the era of Yeltsin at a time of enormously high incidence of crime, protection rackets flourished. This changed in the Putin era: protection came to be nationalized. This meant that state agencies, the police, and units of the army came to fulfill this role. People learned the rules of the game, what could be done, and what was beyond the acceptable. Those who attempted to go beyond the not clearly defined limits were punished by a corrupt legal system that has been willing to do what the regime expects. It is a system that is based on loyalty and on being an insider whose errors could be forgiven and overlooked. The system is a hindrance to economic modernization, it does not respect property rights and legal constraints, and it operates an economy of kickbacks. Remarkably, even within these limiting factors the economy continued to function and most of the time produced economic growth.[7]

The regime succeeded in bringing stability, but at the expense of concentrating power in the center. It meant undermining the independent judiciary, and thereby failing to prevent corruption at every level. It meant that the involvement of the citizenry in the government remained limited.

Putin made successful efforts to increase the powers of the central government against the provinces. The assertion of the principle of federalism was one of the attractive elements in Yeltsin's constitution. The problem was that the 1993 constitution did not spell out precisely the powers of the federal government in relation to the provinces. The vagueness allowed regions to go their own way, pursuing separate policies and defy Moscow. What came into being was called "segmented regionalism." Different regions claimed and exercised different degrees of autonomy: Chechnya, for example, asserted complete independence; Tatarstan became an autonomous minis-tate within the Russian Federation. A particularly contentious matter was tax-collecting: different regions passed different percentages of their tax revenues to the center. Some localities, rich in raw materials, conducted their own economic – indeed, even their own foreign – policy. At the time of the Kosovo war, for example, largely Muslim Tatarstan threatened to send volunteers in support of the Albanians if Russia intervened on the side of the Serbs.[8] Local constitutions often contradicted the federal one; on occa-sion Yeltsin had to negotiate treaties with the regions, which created inequal-ity among them. The unity of the state was in danger.

Local control looked better on paper than it was in reality. Instead of regional autonomy, local autocrats introduced undemocratic governance: more corrupt, more unaccountable than the central government. Some of the governors were flamboyantly corrupt. In the Primorskii krai, for example,

Mikhail Nadrazenko became an autocrat, who time and again defied Moscow and set himself up as a full-fledged ruler. Corruption here reached fabulous proportions: businesspeople would be notified that legal procedures were to be initiated against them; the were told *sotto voce*, however, that it could all be resolved by large sums of money, usually paid in dollars.

Against this background Putin made major and ultimately successful attempts to increase presidential powers against Russia's eighty-nine provinces. Such attempts can be regarded as an expression of the increase of authoritarian trends in current Russian politics, or as necessary steps to overcome the anarchy of the Yeltsin era. Putin's argument for strengthening federal powers was that in a modern state equal citizenship was taken for granted, while the existing system established different entities in which citizens were treated differently. Federal law had to apply equally everywhere.

Putin's first move was to establish seven large federal districts hierarchically in between the provinces and the central government. The heads of these districts were presidential appointees, and thereby the president was able to strengthen his control over the local units. The task of these appointees was to oversee the work of federal agencies in the localities and observe that federal decisions were faithfully carried out everywhere. Putin's next step in centralization was to remove the governors from the upper chamber of the parliament and substitute appointees of the governors and legislatures, thereby making it more difficult for governors to aspire to a national role. Finally, at the end of 2004 he abolished elections for governor altogether and instead appointed them (subject to approval by the local legislatures). The immediate consequence of the reform was confusion. The situation was reminiscent of the days of Khrushchev: the vast, overcentralized Soviet Union did not make sensible economic decisions. But then it turned out that decentralization introduced its own inefficiencies and irrationalities. Now it is difficult to establish the proper division of the authority of the local government and central power.

Since the Duma is a powerless institution, what mattered in politics were elections to the presidency, which took place at regular intervals and which became increasingly *pro forma*, since there were no doubts concerning the ultimate outcome. Although Putin's approval ratings have always been extremely high, no credible alternatives were allowed to appear on the political scene. Autocracy means that the current holder of power wins elections not by cheating, but by making it impossible that an alternative center of power could appear.

When in the not-too-distant past observers spoke of the victory of the democratic Western form of government and society against the communist East, what they had in mind was a particular set of developments. These were democratic institutions including elections that would take place regularly; competing centers of power, such as an independent judiciary; the rule of law; and private property that would come to dominate the economy.

With regard to these institutions, Putin's Russia moved in the wrong direction. On the other hand, those of us who took it for granted that economic developments can take place only if the process of democratization also advances may have been mistaken.

SOCIETY

Current statistics show that Russia's standing among the hierarchy of nations according to per capita income is not particularly low. The country is considerably ahead of Ukraine and Belarus, but also ahead of such European countries as Romania and Bulgaria. Russian per capita income is comparable to that of Argentina, and much higher than that of Turkey and Brazil. Since the painful 1990s, the standard of living has increased substantially for the average citizen, at least in the cities and in the countryside immediately surrounding them. Russia became a consumer society, and consumer goods became widely available. However, the statistics mask great regional and social variations. The collapse of the Soviet Union, as was to be expected, increased differentiation. Predictably, inequality greatly increased at the time of privatization when a few people became suddenly extremely rich while others lost their livelihood. According to 2012 figures, the top 1 percent of the population owned 71 percent of personal wealth. Even more remarkably, 110 people owned 35 percent of household wealth.[9] The degree of economic inequality greatly surpassed that not only of European, but also of modernizing Asian countries. The level of Russian inequality is comparable to that of the United States.

It is difficult to talk about social classes in contemporary Russia. The few fabulously rich people could not well be described as forming a social class. They are overwhelmingly likely to be the beneficiaries of the existing political order. According to estimates, the middle classes make up 15–25 percent of the population.[10] This group includes intellectuals, entrepreneurs, professionals, and a very large percentage of people who work for the bloated state machine. This middle class can be regarded as such in terms of material wellbeing and education but, because of its composition and lack of ideological unity, it has not so far provided sufficient support for building a liberal political order. Whatever opposition is likely to emerge in the future would come from these circles. Unlike during Soviet times, those who dislike authoritarian political order now have the opportunity to leave the country for the democratic West. In the course of the Russian civil war approximately 2 million people left the country. By contrast, in the period 2013–14 close to 4 million left, and these were the best-educated and most enterprising part of the population.[11] However, in spite of emigration and a low birth rate, the size of the population increased because of immigration from ex-Soviet states.

In the Putin era, the lives of the city dwellers were most affected by the great social and economic changes that were taking place. After very successful early years of this period, the Russian economy, and therefore the wellbeing of the Russian people, experienced a major setback as a consequence of the world economic downturn in 2008. After a 7 percent yearly growth from 2000–07, in 2009 the overall output declined 8 percent from its 2008 point. The economy was heavily dependent on the export of raw materials, especially oil, and therefore suffered disproportionally as a consequence of the decline of world demand. Unemployment rose and wages fell. Often enterprises, instead of firing workers, reduced their hours and wages. After an impressive rise of standard of living and increased expectations, the crisis produced great disappointment. Russian industry has suffered from low labor productivity, meager investment as compared to that of other industrializing countries, and relatively expensive labor, i.e., wages growing faster than productivity. Because of the low birth rate of the previous decades, the Russian population is relatively old, which has put pressure on the pension system and made investment in economic growth more difficult. At the end of Medvedev's presidency the economy had recovered fairly well and unemployment had fallen. As compared to the rest of Europe, where the currency crisis created economic problems, Russia was doing fairly well. Before the Ukrainian crisis and the Western sanctions there were reasons for optimism. The government had substantial foreign currency reserves, and the city population had a high saving rate, which made Western business see Russia as a possible market for consumer goods, electronics in particular. Given the size and variations in this enormous country, it is not surprising that the scale of economic recovery varied. Some regions in Asia were left behind, continuing to endure high unemployment. Many of the one-industry towns built in the Stalin era suffered particular hardship, and some have been abandoned.

Even during the Soviet regime there had been a great difference between life in the major cities, primarily in Moscow and Leningrad, and the impoverished countryside. The countryside has been resistant to change, and as a result the gap between modern enclaves and people who live in distant parts of the country, which lack the necessary infrastructure, ever widens. Russian villages are in trouble; small-scale family agriculture has no future in Russia. Large tracts of land are abandoned. The vastness of Russia, which is thinly populated, meant that, given the lack of infrastructure, marketing agricultural products was difficult or impossible. Russia has always been unfortunate because of climate and quality of the soil, and its agriculture has always been far less productive than that of more fortunate countries. Throughout its history, Russia's agriculture has rarely produced much surplus. In the current situation, individual farmers are not be able to compete with large-scale agriculture. However, there is a difference between faraway provinces and areas surrounding the major industrial cities, where farmers are close to markets and have a chance of making a decent income. The closer the fields are to the major cities, in particular, Moscow and St. Petersburg, the more productive they are. They attract investors because they are able to reach markets.

Today peasants are reluctant to leave the unproductive collective farms, and these are simply a means to channel funds from the state to individual peasants; almost without exception the collective farms operate at a loss. A consequence of Soviet policies of industrialization was that people had been overmotivated to leave the village and seek their fortune in the ever-growing cities. But of course, it was not a cross-section of the peasantry that moved into cities. Those who were left behind were the less ambitious, the old, and those who had suffered from some sort of disadvantage. Under the circumstances, demoralization has reached extreme proportions where stealing and binge-drinking are simply taken for granted, and there seems to be no way to redress the problem. In regions where the population is not ethnically Russian, but Tatar, for example, agriculture is still surviving on land which is no better than that cultivated by Russians. In fact foreigners are playing an increasingly important role in agriculture. People from Central Asia and China are populating the Russian countryside. Profitable agrobusiness is also largely in the hands of foreigners.[12]

CHECHNYA UNDER THE PUTIN REGIME

Chechnya has been and still is one of the most backward and poorest regions of the defunct Soviet Union and of the current Russian Federation. It is a land where the memory of the past is still alive. Chechens boast a history of resisting Russian encroachments in the nineteenth century and also recall the sufferings imposed on them by Stalinist repression at the time of the Second World War. Chechnya has been deeply affected by extremist Muslim ideology of the Sunni variety. For all these reasons Russian leaders in the post-Soviet world have had trouble in establishing security and stability. The First and Second Chechen Wars in the 1990s caused extraordinary destruction and further deepened misery. In the fighting, both sides committed atrocities not seen since the Second World War. Even in these troubled times the population, because of the high birth rate, is disproportionately young. In a destroyed economy, the young have problems in finding jobs. The lack of economic prospects has created outmigration and has also contributed to the appeal of an extremist religious ideology.

The second war in 1999–2000 was popular among Russians. The Chechens were blamed for carrying out acts of terror outside their own republic. Although there has been conjecture that they were blamed for some acts for which they were in fact not responsible, it cannot be denied that Chechen extremists did carry out acts of terror against innocent civilians. This enabled the Russian administration and Putin in particular to describe Russian actions as counterterrorism. Chechnya, in fact, played a large role in Putin becoming president. At a time when Russian public opinion turned against the Chechens, Putin promised and implemented a hardline policy against them. In October 1999, at considerable risk to himself, he traveled to the troubled region. By April 2000, the Russian army, which had learned from the mistakes of previous fighting, recaptured the capital, Groznyi. Putin came to office as a wartime president.

Putin articulated the need to respond forcefully to acts of terror. In addition, he warned that if the rebels were not defeated Muslin extremism would spread to other Muslim districts in the Caucasus, in particular to Dagestan. He also saw the danger that other areas of the Russian Federation, such as Tatarstan, would be affected.[13] Putin, fortunately for his regime, succeeded in finding an ideal Chechen collaborator, Akhmed Kadyrov. Kadyrov had fought on the Chechen side in the first conflict, but decided to change sides, evidently because of his fear of extremist elements in the anti-Russian camp. Undoubtedly, the end of the Second Chechen War and the consequent stabilization had much to do with the personal relations established between Akhmed Kadyrov and Putin. In June 2000 Putin appointed Kadyrov as head of an interim administration. In March 2003 a referendum was held in Chechnya, which approved a new constitution. How democratic the election was and how reliable the figures were – officially 97 percent voted in favor – could be disputed. However, this referendum provided a degree of legitimacy to a regime that had been imposed from Moscow, and made possible a degree of reconstruction and even stability. Kadyrov was duly elected president in October 2003.[14] The new president received considerable autonomy from Moscow, although the previous decade of lawlessness had discredited the fight for complete independence. The republic received tax benefits and control over domestic energy resources. Putin had mnaged to establish a fairly reliable viceroy in the troublesome republic, but in May 2004 Kadyrov was assassinated. The assassination threatened the return of chaos and violence. Fortunately, in a new, more or less uncontested election, once again organized by Moscow, Alu Alkhanov, an army officer who had fought on the Russian side in the First Chechen War, was elected by a comfortable majority. Three years later Putin dismissed Alkhanov and appointed Ramzan Kadyrov, the son of Akhmed, as interim president. (Alkhanov was rewarded with a job in Moscow.)

In spite of the beginning of stabilization in the war-torn region, Chechnya remained a place where terrorists were able to organize. In 2002, 40 Chechen Islamists broke into a musical theater in Moscow and held 900 people hostage for 3 days. The authorities stormed the building and killed the terrorists, but 130 hostages also lost their lives. The single worst act of terror Russia has experienced since the Second World War took place in September

2004 in the Ossetian town of Beslan, when Chechen and Ingush separatists, under the command of Shamil Basaev, captured a school and took approximately 1,100 people hostage. The terrorists demanded the recognition of the independence of Chechnya and the withdrawal of Russian forces from the republic. Russian security forces stormed the building. During this episode, between 300 and 400 people died, mostly children. Basaev managed to escape and was killed in an antiterrorist operation in 2006. In another incident, in 2010 two female bombers detonated bombs in a Moscow metro station killing thirty-nine people.

In the course of the wars of the 1990s Chechnya suffered extraordinary destruction. According to some estimates, approximately 220,000 people died.[15] (The 2010 census reported a population of approximately 1,270,000.) The reconstruction has been based on the cooperation between Putin in Moscow and Ramzan Kadyrov in Groznyi; it has come at great expense from the federal budget, but evidently for political reasons it was considered to be an advantageous investment. Putin explicitly justified the disproportionate investment in Chechnya by saying that the republic must develop its own industrial base in order to offer people jobs, thereby making it unnecessary for the citizens to leave their place of birth and inundate Russian cities.[16] The generous treatment of the devastated region caused some disagreement among Russian politicians and ordinary citizens, who resented the investment being made at their expense.

Putin considered this a worthwhile price to pay for relative peace in the troubled region. The threat of further disintegration of the Russian state was, for the time being, suspended. The Russian army no longer had to play a police role in the republic. Ramzan Kadyrov, on the other hand, achieved a degree of sovereignty. Only 30 years old when he came to office, the younger Kadyrov established a nepotistic and authoritarian state. The success of Kadyrov and Putin bringing peace to this volatile region is only relative. Since the former came to office, fewer civilians are being killed than before. However, this is a place where human rights abuses occur every day, where there are assassinations, where the president orders the executions of his opponents, where people disappear and torture is routine. Kadyrov has built himself an extraordinary personality cult. At the same time, he claims to be a good Muslim, an upholder of *sharia* law, and also a passionate partisan of his patron, Putin, and an enthusiastic supporter of whatever policy the Russian president attempts.

Under Ramzan Kadyrov, Chechnya has developed into a political entity to which no other part of Russia can be compared. On the one hand, Putin's government allows the young autocrat to do generally anything he wants at home. He uses federal money at his whim. Groznyi has been reconstructed with modern buildings, luxury boutiques, and high-rise apartment blocks; it even boasts an avenue named after President Putin. It has a functioning airport and has reputedly the largest mosque in Europe, named after

Ramzan's father, Akhmed. It is still a lawless place, but the number of civilian victims of terror is much smaller than it was a decade or two ago.

On the other hand, instead of a population threatened by a separatist, terrorist movement, Kadyrov has created a police state. Remarkably, contrary to the Russian constitution, Kadyrov was able to introduce Islamic law in his fiefdom. This means strict enforcement on laws against alcohol, a compulsory dress code for women, the encouragement of polygamy, and nonpunishment for "honor" killings. Chechnya now lives in a different world than the rest of the country. Although among young people unemployment remains high, compelling many to leave, the economic boom has produced a layer of newly rich people – at least among Kadyrov's friends.

The current state of Chechnya is built on the remarkable personal relations between the presidents of Russia and Chechnya. Chechnya is not subject to decisions made by the government in Moscow. At one point Kadyrov ordered the security forces to shoot at Russian troops if they entered the territory of the republic without his permission. He answers only to Putin himself. In this remarkable arrangement Kadyrov has been able to pursue policies profoundly different than what is acceptable in the rest of Russia; at the same time no one is a more devoted supporter of the Russian president in domestic and foreign affairs than Kadyrov. It is very likely that the Russian government has been using Chechen personnel in order to get rid of troublesome opponents.

CORRUPTION

Some observers consider corruption as a defining feature of Putin's regime and describe it as "kleptocracy."[17] Large-scale illegalities began at the time of the initiation of privatization in 1991. In retrospect, it is difficult to see how the enormous, but outdated Soviet economy could have been fairly privatized. How could each individual citizen receive an appropriate share from the sales of state property? In the entirely new economic and political environment, there were no laws that corresponded to the needs of the moment. Wealthy individuals, commonly referred to as oligarchs, have played major roles in the government ever since, and set policies in defense of their private interests. They successfully enriched themselves by despoiling the wealth of the nation. They fought and frequently betrayed one another. It is unlikely that they cared a great deal about the future of their country. They chose to live a lifestyle that was wildly inappropriate in their impoverished environment. Some of the richest people on earth lived ostentatiously in a poor country. They did not hesitate to move much of their wealth abroad, at a time when the country desperately needed investment. They understood that only getting their money out of the country could guarantee safety.

An extraordinary event of open, almost advertised corruption was the case of loans for shares. In 1996, when Yeltsin's reelection prospects seemed grim, a group of new millionaires offered much-needed money for the reelection campaign, and in exchange they received greatly undervalued shares in Russia's most valuable industrial enterprises. The shares were to be distributed in open bidding. However the affair was obviously rigged. People close to Yeltsin – that is, the people who were to benefit – selected the participants. The shares were supposed to be collateral for repayment, but it was obvious that the state would not be able to repay the loans. The oligarchs, who had already made a great deal of money at a time of the beginning of privatization, now doubled and trebled their wealth. This was a breathtaking act of corruption: the oligarchs – who had every reason to fear a Communist Party victory and therefore very much desired Yeltsin's reelection – also managed to benefit financially.

Putin's most significant struggle in establishing his more or less unlimited authority was against the oligarchs. They were a remarkable and not very attractive group of people who did not hesitate to circumvent laws. Most of them had been moderately successful in the Soviet era, and none had been a prominent dissenter. In the new era of the 1990s, different personality types distinguished themselves more than the courageous and idealistic dissenters. In the 1990s the most prominent among the oligarchs was Boris Berezovskii, who became rich by setting up car dealerships, then moved into buying a television channel and, of course, oil, where the most money could be made. Vladimir Gusinskii made his fortune in banking and also created a media empire. Vladimir Potanin came from a prominent communist family and in the 1990s succeeded in taking control of several banks. Mikhail Fridman enriched himself in the export and import business. Aleksandr Smolenskii started out in construction, but made his money in banking. Roman Abramovich also made his enormous fortune in the oil business. With the addition of Mikhail Khodorkovskii, these most prominent oligarchs of the 1990s came to play a dominant role in politics. Five of the seven richest men of the era were Jewish or at least half-Jewish. In a country where anti-Semitism is still common, this made Putin's task of purging them easier when he decided to turn against them.

Corruption was already deeply ingrained in the political system when Putin became president. Business and government were intertwined: businesspeople gave bribes to politicians for receiving licenses and preferential treatment, and politicians then invested their ill-gotten gains into business. Corruption reached the highest levels of government. Various interest groups struggled against one another, and in the process they revealed detailed charges, likely to be true, in the newspapers. Allegations were made against previous prime ministers, Viktor Chernomyrdin, Sergei Kirienko, and Viktor Kasyanov, and against important political figures such as Anatolii Chubais, who had a significant role in devising methods of privatization. Not surprisingly, all the major beneficiaries of the privatization process were shown to be corrupt, among them Berezovskii, Khodorkovskii, and Abramovich. The course of privatization – the stealing of state property – undermined the faith of the Russian people in Western-style capitalism. They had very little faith in such institutions to begin with. The way the market economy was introduced in Russia was not the way the democratic opposition in the Soviet regime had desired and envisaged. In this indirect sense the oligarchs could be held responsible for the coming autocracy of the Putin era.

One may approve the new president taking on some of the powerful figures, rightly accused of corruption, especially when one remembers that some of these same people had eased Putin's path to power. On the other hand, when he did so, it was always for his own political purposes. Khodorkovskii was justly accused of tax evasion when he made the "mistake" of showing political ambitions; Kasyanov was accused of getting hold of a valuable dacha by corrupt means when he showed interest in running for president in 2008 and attempted to unite the anti-Putin forces. Getting rid of some politically inconvenient people was not the same as fighting corruption in business and politics.

From the point of view of the president, confronting members of the oligarchy was a win–win situation. Not only did he manage to get rid of some inconvenient people as possible opposition to his own power, but at the same also increased his own popularity among the people. Opinion surveys demonstrated that people almost invariably took the side of the government, no matter how flimsy the case against a prominent businessperson or how obvious the political motivation behind the legal maneuvers. On the one hand, the Russians approved of a strong government; on the other, they were deeply suspicious of business. They would not draw a sharp line between legitimate business activity and cheating: from their point of view all business activity was suspicious. According to recent polls, two-thirds of Russians considered all businesspeople cheats. People accepted the pronouncements of Putin and his successor, Medvedev, that they had attempted to get rid of corruption, but at the same time remained convinced that corruption could not be defeated.

Putin's struggle against the oligarchs began immediately after he became president. Those who thought they could act as they did in the Yeltsin era, and use their financial power to influence policies, were disappointed. The first two men to be destroyed as political forces were Boris Berezovskii and Vladimir Gusinskii. They had considerable political power because of their control of major media outlets. They had the temerity to question and attack the new president's policies. Even worse, Gusinskii's television channel made fun of Putin. The kind of regime Putin had in mind was not reconcilable with ridiculing the president. The two oligarchs lost their holdings in television channels and newspapers, and criminal charges were brought against them for financial wrongdoings in the past. Within a year both Gusinskii and Berezovskii were out of the country. Gusinskii spent a few days in jail and was released only when he ceded a large number of shares in his companies. Putin demonstrated that people of great wealth would not be able to pursue policies different from his own. A fundamental issue was the control of the media. Putin would not allow an independent media that could influence public opinion against his policies. There was never any doubt that the criminal charges against these two men were entirely politically motivated as a reprisal for opposing the president in one form or another.

The case against another oligarch, Mikhail Khodorkovskii, initiated in 2003, was different. Khodorkovskii, similarly to other newly rich people, had already started his commercial ventures in the Gorbachev era. He opened a private café in 1987 and started to import computers. As with some other businesspeople in that era, becoming involved in business did not mean a rejection of the Soviet order *in toto*.[18] Khodorkovskii's behavior in the Yeltsin era from the point of view of legality and morality was no different from the other newly fabulously rich men. He was engaged in various financial industrial ventures and at the same time worked in government jobs. Again like other oligarchs in the Yeltsin era, Khodorkovskii combined a number of different functions. He was engaged in banking and the oil industry, as well as buying up enterprises and at the same time holding government offices. As he himself said at the time, "politics is the most lucrative business in Russia and it will be that way forever."[19] Yukos, an oil company that possessed Russia's largest share of oil reserves, came into existence in 1993. By the end of the decade Khodorkovskii had acquired dominant influence in the company. His methods of doing so were as shady and as disreputable as those of the other oligarchs. He did not hesitate to rob the shareholders of his company.

He was a beneficiary of that great steal, the loans-for-shares scheme. For a relatively small sum of money he managed to acquire oil reserves that within a few years made him the richest person in the new Russia. In October 2003 he was arrested for tax fraud and tax evasion. Unquestionably the real reason for his arrest was that he dared to take an anti-Putin stance in politics by giving financial support to parties that opposed the president's policies and programs. Perhaps even more importantly, the government, i.e., people close to Putin, intended to take charge of the extremely large and profitable oil company for their own purposes. The Khodorkovskii case was different from the other actions that the Putin government instituted against troublesome oligarchs. For one thing, the amount of money at stake was vastly larger. Khodorkovskii in 2003 was the richest person in Russia and the sixteenth-richest in the world. This wealth, the size of the company, and the value of the oil reserves allowed Khodorkovskii to act as a head of state, who negotiated not only with foreign companies, but also with foreign countries.[20] The removal of Khodorkovskii allowed Putin and his friends in one fell swoop to take control over a large share of the country's most valuable natural resources.

Second, it was different because of the harsh treatment he received. He was alone among the oligarchs to become something of a martyr. In 2005 he was sentenced to nine years in prison. In 2010 his sentence was extended for another two years; however, he received amnesty in 2013. But, third and most significantly, Khodorkovskii's case was different from that of the other oligarchs inasmuch as there were signs that he, unlike the other men who had become rich in the previous decade, was willing to recognize that in the new situation different behavior was necessary, and was determined not only to oppose the president, but also to attempt to govern his enormous company on a Western model of transparency. Khodorkovskii's challenge to the existing regime was greater than that of Berezovskii, for one example. Berezovskii and Gusinskii merely challenged aspects of Putin's policies. By contrast, Khodorkovskii, however implicitly, proposed a different kind of Russia. We must accept that Khodorkovskii, who had achieved his wildest ambitions to become the richest man in the country, genuinely assumed a degree of social responsibility. We must accept that he intended to run his enormous company on a Western model of transparency. Probably this economic model of a capitalist economy, observing the necessary preconditions, would have been more productive than the one in which the government continued to play a dominant role.

The consequences of Khodorkovskii's arrest were that some Western investors lost confidence in making investments in Russia. However, fortunately for the Putin regime, it was a time when the economy was doing remarkably well, at least partly because of the greatly increased oil price on the world markets as compared to the 1990s. Khodorkovskii's company, Yukos, was destroyed. It was presented with an extraordinarily large tax obligation that it could not pay; the company was therefore declared bankrupt, and its assets were taken over by a government-owned company for a fraction of their value. Although the company was publicly traded, the government owned the majority of the shares, and it was administered by people personally close to the president. The profits from running the company came to be a major contributor to the government budget. Out of the remnants of Khodorkovskii's empire, a powerful state-owned oil company, Rosneft, was created. It is most likely that a state-owned company could not operate with the same degree of efficiency as one owned by Khodorkovskii. On the one hand he presented a genuine and major challenge to Putin's state; on the other, taking away Khodorkovskii's enormous fortune, represented by Yukos, was an proposition that Putin and his comrades could not resist. The means of charging him with violations of laws were present.

The arrest of Khodorkovskii can be regarded as a turning point in post-Soviet history. With it the nature of corruption changed. During the era of

Yeltsin, the newly rich had possessed considerable political power and could impose their will on a weak regime. Now, in the relations between the oligarchs and the state, the president set the terms. To join the small group of tycoons, it was not enough not to oppose the policies of the regime. The oligarchs and the regime came to be one. Most, but not all, of those who were the most successful in the 1990s disappeared from the scene. A new group of tycoons took their places. This small group of extremely wealthy people came to be formed through the patronage of the president. This cohort, morally speaking, was an even less attractive group than the one it had replaced. These are people who have been personally close to Putin: some were childhood friends, such as his former judo partner, Boris Romanovich Rotenberg, and his brother, Arkadii. The brothers had become fabulously wealthy as a result of Putin placing them at the head of companies in the natural gas and oil business, in addition to construction and banking. In one particularly notorious instance, Boris Rotenberg gained a $5 billion contract outside the regular bidding at the time of the Sochi Olympics. Other members of the group emerged from Putin's acquaintances when he worked in St. Petersburg. Still others had been his comrades in his days of serving in the KGB. Yurii Kovalchuk, the head of Bank Rossiia, reputedly has been Putin's personal banker. Gennadii Timchenko, the 62nd-richest man in the world, who made his money by founding an investment group that has had interests in many areas of the economy, became the head of Rosneft. It is reputed, though not substantiated, that Putin himself has accumulated great wealth.

Corruption and autocracy have been interconnected. A lack of transparency, which is an essential feature of an autocratic regime, allowed corruption to flourish. It is a system that is based on patronage in which different groups compete with one another. Corruption exists in every level of society. Autocracy flourishes because those features that could be obstacles, such as an involved citizenry and a sense of public responsibility, have not yet come into existence. It is difficult to tell at this point what the chances are that in the near future institutions could develop which would limit the power of the autocrat.

Transparency International year after year places Russia among the most corrupt countries in the world. The petty and on occasion not so petty corruption is a major brake on the modernization of the economy of the nation. Even more important than the spectacular examples of corruption, such as contracts connected to the 2014 Winter Olympics in Sochi, when Putin's friends were able to pocket billions, are the examples of everyday corrupt acts that citizens have come to take for granted. To receive a license to open a small business requires bribes; to place a child in a prestigious university requires connections; to receive a fair hearing in a court case requires money and connections. It is these conditions that are the major drag on the development of the economy and that distinguish contemporary Russia from the successful modernizers of the East Asian variety.

Putin Returns

THE MEDVEDEV INTERLUDE

The 1993 constitution limited the president to two four-year terms. Putin's second term ended in 2008. How Putin dealt with this problem was characteristic of the political system that he had created: he observed the letter of the law without paying attention to its spirit. He needed to have a new president in order to demonstrate his observance of the constitution, but at the same time he was determined to be able to retain his power. He chose an old associate from his Leningrad days to run for the office while implicitly understanding that he himself would remain supreme master.

That associate was Dmitrii Anatolevich Medvedev. Medvedev was born in 1965, that is, he was considerably younger than Putin. He came from an intellectual family and was a much better-educated man than his sponsor. Like Putin, he attended Leningrad University Law School and had a genuine scholarly interest in the law. Unlike Putin, however, he had no Soviet career; he could not be regarded as a Soviet man. He had neither the opportunity to join the party nor the chance to acquire a reputation as a prominent dissident. He came to intellectual maturity at a time when liberalism and thoughts of political and economic freedoms were in the ascendant. After defending his dissertation, he became a docent at the university and taught Roman law there until 1999. Like Putin, he worked in the administration of Mayor Sobchak and in this capacity got to know the former. From the very beginning of his political career, Medvedev worked together with Putin, and they came to be personally close. Given their different backgrounds it is remarkable that they had managed to work well together through many decades. As Putin rose in the hierarchy in Moscow, he brought his younger colleague, his protégé, to the capital. In 2000 Medvedev managed Putin's campaign for the presidency. As a reward, Putin appointed him chairman of Gazprom's board of directors. Medvedev continued to serve in this most

important and profitable segment of the economy. In 2003 he became chief
of staff to the president and in 2005 became first deputy prime minister.

Putin became president because Yeltsin chose him. In the same way,
Medvedev became president because his mentor chose him. The constitution
allowed two consecutive terms for the president, and at the time of the
completion of Putin's second term there was considerable speculation about
changing the constitution. Putin's support in the Duma was strong enough to
allow him to make this change, but he decided to observe the letter of the
law. The governing party, United Russia, nominated Medvedev but what
really mattered was Putin's support. Since the former had such a different
past and demeanor than his mentor, there was reason to believe that the new
president would initiate a new era. That Putin chose him, a man of such
different background and ideological commitments, implied that the president valued loyalty above all. Putin was aware that both for domestic and
especially for international consideration it would be an advantage to choose
a person with softer edges than himself. When Medvedev spoke of freedom
and especially about the need to fight against corruption, the younger man
had greater credibility than his predecessor. During the election campaign,
the past and future presidents made it clear that they would be working
together. Putin represented continuity, which is what the majority of the
Russian people desired at the time. Some Russians may have been surprised
by Putin's choice given how different an image Medvedev projected; in
retrospect it was not a surprising choice at all. There was no other candidate
who had demonstrated his loyalty to Putin as thoroughly and for as long a
time as Medvedev. At the time of his nomination for president he announced
that he would choose Putin as his premier. Thus the two would govern
together.

The reaction of Western observers and Russian intelligentsia was enthusiastic. In March 2008 Medvedev was elected with more than 70 percent
of the vote. The opposing candidates were the Communist Party leader
Zyuganov, and Zhirinovskii, who was regarded by almost everyone as a
buffoon. These two men were representatives of a different era.

Would Medvedev's succession as president advance the cause of liberalism, as many expected? Would his often-announced willingness to struggle
against corruption make a major change in Russian life? Given his background, there was no reason to question his sincerity. However, ultimately
his achievements in liberalization and the eradication of corruption
remained limited. Medvedev immediately named Putin premier, and the
governing party had an overwhelming parliamentary majority in the Duma.
As a consequence, a new political order came into existence. Russia
remained a presidential republic but how much power remained with the
president was not self-evident because of the personality of Putin. The two
men seemingly worked well together, and the system was referred to as
tandem leadership. Remarkably, although Putin ceased to be president, the

system that he had gradually established remained in force. The status quo remained: there was a premier who had overwhelming parliamentary support in the Duma as well as in the Federal Council. There was a president whose constitutional powers had not been reduced, who, however, depended on the cooperation of the premier, whose power was based on popular support. Medvedev had formal authority and theoretically could have dismissed the premier, but that act was simply unthinkable given the relationship of the two men and Putin's genuine public support.

All through Putin's presidency, factions competed with one another for power and financial benefit. Putin's achievement was that he succeeded in maintaining equilibrium. Medvedev did not belong to any of these groups, and he acquired his post because of his loyalty to Putin. Putin chose him partially because this choice did not unbalance the system by giving one group added strength.

Medvedev came to power with a program of economic modernization, political liberalization, and struggle against corruption. He repeatedly spoke of the importance of observing laws and freeing the legal system from political influence. At the same time, during his tenure Khodorkovskii was resentenced, adding additional years to his imprisonment. Medvedev's analysis of the problems, economic and political, of the country that he headed was impressive and not very different from the analyses of Western observers. These tasks turned out to be more difficult than he himself envisaged, demonstrating that the problems Russia faced were more profound.

He did manage to present a somewhat different political persona than Putin. When he spoke of democratization and fighting against corruption, there was no reason to doubt his sincerity. But analysis was not enough. The reforms introduced as a result of his actions were either too small in scale or altogether unsuccessful. The Russian political system involves close cooperation between business and government. Ministers and high administration officials sat on boards that oversaw major corporations. Medvedev recognized that this was a source of corruption and an obstacle to the establishment of an open and modern economy. He explicitly rejected the state capitalist method of modernization and stressed the need for private investment and initiative, leaving to the state the task of protection of assets.[1] He also advocated decentralization and strengthening the independence of the judiciary.

As Medvedev's four-year term as president was drawing to a close, the question was whether he should or could run for a second term. However, the correlation of political forces had not changed: even after four years in office Putin still possessed the support of the government bureaucracy and Medvedev still had no independent constituency. If anything, Medvedev had succeeded in alienating a segment of the business elite who feared the potential results of his lectures concerning the struggle against corruption.

PUTIN RETURNS

During Medvedev's tenure the law was changed extending the president's term from four to six years, making the next election all the more important. Medvedev hoped to run for another term. However, the constitution did not bar Putin's return in 2012, and indeed in September 2011 Medvedev announced that Putin would be a candidate in the following year. When the decision was made to trade positions is uncertain but both Medvedev and Putin said that they had long ago agreed to take such a step, implying that Medvedev's presidency was only temporary.[2]

The transfer of power, Putin's return to the presidency, did not go as smoothly as the chief actors in the drama must have envisaged. In the winter of 2011–12 there were spontaneous demonstrations, larger than Russia had seen since the early 1990s. The protests of December 2011 started in response to the parliamentary elections in which the governing party, United Russia, did not perform as well as expected; even the official results showed that it had received somewhat less than 50 percent of the votes. Approximately 30,000 people demonstrated against electoral fraud. The demonstrators rightly believed that the figures were even lower and that there had been large-scale cheating in tabulating the votes. Those who demonstrated came onto the streets not only because of the parliamentary elections, but also because since September 2011 they had known that there would surely be presidential elections to bring Putin back to office. The demonstrations could be regarded as a small step toward the development of a civil society. People – at least implicitly – were not only protesting against electoral fraud, but were also expressing dissatisfaction with the political system that promised Putin's return to office.

In May 2012, when Putin was reelected, about 20,000 people demonstrated in Moscow, engaging in some scuffles with the police, who detained about 400 people. The authorities brought criminal charges against the organizers. Putin received fewer votes than he had in the previous two elections, the decline being most noticeable in the major cities. In Moscow, for example, he did not even receive 50 percent of the vote. In organizing the protests, modern methods of electronic popular communications played a major role.

Medvedev's reelection would have ended the Putin era and could possibly have transformed Russian political life. As it was, Putin's return to power cemented the system. Had Putin left politics willingly in 2012 and allowed Medvedev to have another term, there might have been a chance of a gradual transformation of the political system. During his second term, the reelected president might have had the political capital to introduce meaningful reforms. However, given Putin's character and convictions, such an outcome was highly unlikely.

The nature of the political system during Putin's third term was different from the first two. That was because now, more than before, opposing voices could be heard; public opinion came to be more polarized. More voices were directed against various aspects of Putin's illiberal regime. Some opposed the socially conservative, conformist, repressive nature of the regime. Among these the most notable were members of the group Pussy Riot. This was a feminist-rock protest group attacking Putin, the Orthodox Church for its support of the president, and Russian conservatism for not tolerating gay people. For their guerrilla performances, including in churches, some members of the group have been regularly arrested and kept in prison for short periods.

The most charismatic person to emerge on the political scene was Aleksei Navalnyi. He was a young man – born in 1976 – with a legal education, who communicated with his followers via an electronic blog. He started his political activities within the liberal Yabloko Party, but was excluded for his extreme nationalist, anti-immigrant beliefs. His ideology has been a mix of nationalism and liberalism. He came to prominence at the time of the 2011 Duma elections when he described the United Russia party as a party of crooks and thieves, which then became a catchphrase. In his blog, Navalnyi pointed out the illegalities of the Putin regime and called attention to examples of corruption by members of the president's circle. The authorities dealt with him as they usually did with troublesome opponents: they arrested him and charged him with embezzlement, a phony charge.

To make matters worse for the reestablishment of Putin's type of political order, important personages such as the finance minister, Aleksei Kudrin, who had served in the government since 2000, resigned and made common cause with those who opposed the existing political system. Kudrin's case was exceptional. He had known Putin from their days in St. Petersburg, and he had become minister of finance in 2000, retaining his position until 2011. He was credited with moving Russia to financial stability, which then enabled the country to weather the economic crisis of 2008–09 better than most other industrialized nations. Remarkably, in spite of his high-profile resignation and his criticisms of the Medvedev–Putin regime's policies, he was not jailed, but was allowed to continue to act as a legitimate critic, implying a degree of maturity in the political system.

The government did fight back. Undoubtedly the leaders of the regime were well aware of the example of the revolutions, most immediately in Ukraine and in Georgia, where in the name of liberalism, with Western support and encouragement, people came onto the streets and overthrew oppressive regimes. One strategy against what seemed to them to be foreign subversion was to take measures against social, nonprofit organizations that were receiving support from abroad. In 2012 the Duma passed a law that branded sixty organizations as foreign agents since they had received money from abroad and at the same time had carried out political activities in

Russia. The leaders of such organizations were harassed and on occasion arrested. The government was afraid of a Ukrainian-type revolution in Moscow. The move was aimed at the repression of dissent.

The most outrageous and high-profile political assassination was that of Boris Nemtsov in February 2015. Nemtsov had been deputy prime minister for a time in the Yeltsin era. He had been a liberal critic of Putin from Putin's assumption of office, accusing the president of turning Russia into an autocracy. He made several attempts to point out examples of corruption among people close to Putin. For his work he had been arrested several times. He had extensive contacts in Ukraine and at one point acted as an economic adviser to President Viktor Yushchenko. From the time of the collapse of the Soviet Union, Nemtsov had been one of the few liberal voices consistently advocating Western-style liberal economics and politics. He was by far the best-known organizer among the Russian liberal intelligentsia who opposed Russian involvement in the Ukrainian civil war. The circumstances of his assassination remained murky. As with other political assassinations and murders of politicians and journalists, it is impossible to establish that Putin actually ordered the killing. On the other hand, it is fair to call the government to account for creating and tolerating an atmosphere in which such a murder can take place, and it is unlikely that those actually guilty of the acts will be found and held responsible.

The regime defended itself not only through repression, but also through winning over or retaining the support of a large segment of the population by emphasizing Russian nationalism, conservative values, and the active support of the Orthodox Church. In his third term in office, Putin and his followers repudiated Western-type liberalism more explicitly than ever before. His call for the defense of conservative values obviously found an echo among Russians, but also beyond the borders of the country. Conservative, nationalist, antiglobal movements in Europe have found much to admire in Putin's Russia.

We will never know whether in the absence of Putin Russia would have taken steps toward the development of a liberal democratic polity. It is possible – indeed, likely – that it is not Putin who made contemporary Russia what it is, but that Putin represents a country that has a troubled past and must take many steps in developing those institutions that are needed in the modern world.

The Duma elections of December 2011 followed by the presidential elections in March 2012 constituted a turning point in Russia's political history. The return of Putin as president, an office that he can hold until 2018, when he once again can compete for another turn, demonstrated the personalization of Russian politics. On the other hand, his return created opposition, thereby also signifying the appearance of a public sphere, which was unlikely to vanish in the future. From this point on there would be critics of the president's policies. To a certain extent political life has opened up.

THE INTERNATIONAL CONTEXT

The era of Yeltsin saw a precipitous decline in Russia's influence around the world. An economically weakened Russia had no means to enforce its will beyond its borders. The United States and the European Union saw no reason to take into consideration Russia's national interests. Contrary to the promises of the Gorbachev era, NATO expanded to the east. Poland, Hungary, and the Czech Republic joined in 1999, and they was followed in the era of Putin in 2004 by the Baltic states, Bulgaria, Romania, Slovakia, and Slovenia. Five years later even Albania and Croatia were admitted. Not only had the Warsaw Pact, envisaged as a meager counterforce to NATO, ceased to exist, but also the states that had constituted it were now in an alliance system that, from the point of view of Moscow, could have no purpose other than to keep Russia in check. Policymakers in Moscow saw such policies as the violation of the explicit and implicit agreements that were constructed in the heady days of 1989–91. When the cold war ended, there were no attempts made to reintegrate Russia into the international scene and recognize its legitimate interests.

At the time of assumption of office of the president Putin could envisage nothing other than a Western orientation of Russian foreign policy, although in the new era he was determined to give fewer concession to his Western partners. How did the outside world look from Moscow's point of view? The policymakers must have had three major policy goals. The primary goal of the Putin administration, as that of any country, small or large, is to ensure security. Second, the policymakers wanted to see Russia's significance acknowledged on the international scene, and to regain the prestige that the country had lost during the Yeltsin era. Third, an important goal of foreign policy was to create an international atmosphere that was helpful for improving the economy. These goals inevitably pulled the country in different directions. Although the goals remained constant over time, methods of bringing about results varied.

How could Russia's security be improved? The country faced external and internal threats. The most significant external threat was the appearance of a hostile bloc at Russia's most sensitive western border. NATO came into existence in 1949 to resist Soviet encroachments in Europe. Now there was no more Soviet Union, what were the goals of NATO? No amount of assurance by spokespeople for Western governments could have alleviated Russian fears that the alliance was still aimed against them. Once the Baltic countries joined, policymakers in Moscow felt that the citizens of these countries as well as Poles, whether justified or not, had long-standing hostility to anything Russian. The Baltic countries demonstrated this attitude by how they were treating their Russian-speaking minorities. Although the majority of Russians had supported the independence of the countries where they lived at the time of the collapse of the Soviet Union, nevertheless they were transformed into second-class citizens. The Putin administration had legitimate fears that the Baltic countries, once they had the backing of a powerful NATO, would host Western armaments aimed at Russia.

NATO expansion created a paradox. The newly established independent states joined in search of security in opposition to a presumed Russian expansionism. But the very fact of their inclusion in a military alliance in reality reduced their security by creating an area of instability and conflict. The inability of Western leaders to appreciate how their actions would be perceived in Moscow was a major reason for the making of a new cold war. A united Europe – united not only economically but also explicitly militarily – from which Russia was consciously excluded was perceived as a major security threat. During the course of the second administration of Putin the pro-Western orientation of Russian foreign policy shifted. The Russian response was an improvement in the country's military capacity.

The West also represented a different kind of threat, the threat of subversion. Subtly and not so subtly the liberal West advocated and supported regime change in all or almost all authoritarian countries. It is another matter whether such change would have been beneficial for the inhabitants of those countries, yet it is understandable that such policies were perceived by the authoritarian leaders as dangerous to themselves. The possibility of Western-supported and -influenced plans for regime change in Russia itself was never far from the mind of policymakers. They took it for granted that encouraging these revolutions was not motivated by a desire to bring about genuine democracy in different parts of the world, but was aimed at furthering Western, above all, American, strategic interests.

The large and radicalized Muslim population represented another major security threat. No European country has been as endangered by Islamic terrorism as Russia. Russia has had the largest Muslim minority, and minorities in the Caucasus have been fighting Russians for centuries. The sympathy Putin expressed to President George W. Bush immediately after the terrorist attacks of September 11, 2001, was no doubt genuinely felt. Muslim terrorist threats acted as a bond with Western nations, in particular, the United States. Leaders in Moscow must have been glad to see the United States taking on the Taliban in Afghanistan. The necessity of fighting against terrorism on an international scale contributed to the formulation of a pro-Western foreign policy in the early years of the Putin administration. The Russians supported US intervention in Afghanistan but, much like other European governments, opposed intervention in Iraq. Even after the drastic deterioration of Russian–United States relations at the time of the Ukrainian crisis, American diplomats still found it possible to cooperate with the Russians around the danger of Muslim terrorism. American diplomacy on occasion received help from the Russians, for example, in the case of Syria and Iran.

As Putin brought stability in domestic affairs during his first and second terms in office, Russian policymakers attempted to refashion foreign policy to the extent that their country would once again appear as a strong power on the world scene. Such an attempt was bound to lead to conflict with Western powers, especially the United States. As Russia became stronger internally, it attempted to play a greater role in world affairs and at the same time the policymakers could not but be aware of Russia's vulnerability. They saw the creation of a unipolar world in which the United States could act anywhere without taking into consideration international organizations, most importantly, the United Nations. From the point of view of Moscow, the West – especially the United States, acting on its own as in the case of invading Iraq without the United Nations Security Council's agreement – came to be perceived as a potential threat. Policymakers came to see the West increasingly as a hostile force willing and able to intercede in sovereign foreign countries.

Russia is the biggest energy producer in the world. It produces as much oil as Saudi Arabia and one-fifth of the world output of natural gas. The great wealth of natural resources is both a boon and an obstacle for further modernization of the economy. It is an obstacle because Russia is affected disproportionally by changes in the demand for energy in world markets. It is also a problem because the great share of foreign currency income that comes from the export of raw materials, primarily gas and oil, frees the country from carrying out reforms that might be difficult in the short term but are necessary in the long run. The ability to supply or to withhold supplies of gas and oil from Europe came to be a major component in the formulation of foreign policy. As a major supplier of energy to European countries, Russia has used delivery or withholding of energy as a foreign-policy tool. It has been able to punish countries that took positions contrary to Russian interests. Ukraine, which used to receive Russian gas at subsidized prices, was particularly vulnerable to decisions made in Moscow concerning the delivery of gas and oil.

The third goal of foreign policy was to open up the economy to the rest of the world. It has been a relatively open economy with low taxes and tariffs. Because Russia has been able to export raw materials it has accumulated currency reserves that have enabled it so far to weather several economic downturns and political crises. After a long struggle, it succeeded in gaining admission to the World Trade Organization in 2012. (It had been member of the G8, which represented eight of the largest economic powers in the world, until 2014, when it was suspended as a result of the Ukrainian crisis.) In spite of corruption, and the lack of a reliable legal system at different times, the country managed to attract a not insignificant amount of foreign investment. Russia has been better integrated into the world economy than it has ever been before in its history.[3]

Ironically, the more Russia was on the losing end in foreign conflicts and as its influence in major international affairs diminished, such as its preferences in the conflicts over the former Yugoslavia, and much later over Iraq and Libya, the more Russia was perceived as a country determined to carry out aggression against its neighbors. Western, primarily US, encouragement for the "color" revolutions in ex-Soviet states, such as Ukraine, Georgia, and Kyrgyzstan, was seen in Moscow as a direct threat. Such policies both undermine Russian security by bringing anti-Russian regimes into power in the immediate neighborhood and jeopardize Putin's power by providing examples of countries overthrowing their autocratic rulers.

GEORGIA AND UKRAINE

In August 2008, under the presidency of Medvedev, Russia fought a war against Georgia. It was the first time since the collapse of the Soviet Union that Russia had sent soldiers abroad in defense of what it considered to be its vital interests. Of all the former Soviet countries, Moscow had the most strained relations with Georgia after the so-called Rose Revolution in November 2003, which brought Mikheil Saakashvili to power. The new president immediately assumed a pro-Western and anti-Russian stance. At the Bucharest summit in 2008 NATO promised eventual membership for Georgia and Ukraine. The war against Georgia was a direct consequence of this promise.

The Georgians overplayed their hand. Counting on Western support, they sent their army into South Ossetia, a rebel region that was de facto independent. The Russians now had a casus belli. The war lasted only five days. Russians did not mind that they gave the appearance to the outside world that they were willing to defend their interests even with weapons when necessary. The response to the criticism that Russia had circumvented international law by violating the territorial integrity of a sovereign country was that they were following the Western example when in 1998–99 NATO intervention freed Kosovo from Serbian rule. Serbia had been a Russian ally. Like Kosovo, South Ossetia and Abkhazia became nominally independent, but of course the tiny states – with populations of only approximately 50,000 in South Ossetia and a quarter of a million in Abkhazia – could exist only with Russian protection. The war had significant consequences. First, it encouraged the military to introduce reforms since, even though it had been victorious, it had betrayed weaknesses. Second, the short war against Georgia foreshadowed a far more serious conflict over Ukraine.[4]

Ukraine presented a special problem. First of all, the country was unstable, with a wide divergence between the Russian-speaking east and south and the Ukrainian-speaking west. Galicia, which had not been part of the Soviet Union until the end of the Second World War, was the birthplace of

Ukrainian nationalism. For understandable reasons, these nationalists considered Russia to be the greatest threat to the survival of a united Ukraine. In their conception a Ukrainian nationalist by definition was anti-Russian. If a nation is defined by having a shared history and set of experiences and myths, Ukraine was a state, but not a nation. Although the gap was largely cultural, it also constituted matters of economic interest. The eastern part of the country had been the economic heartland, although it was an area that badly needed modernization. There were two Ukraines. They came to be symbolized by two colors: yellow for the west, blue for the east. The flag brought the two colors together, but in reality bringing the two sides together was much more difficult. The two colors represented different conceptions of the state.

Ukrainians failed to create a viable modern state. Among the European successor states to the Soviet Union, Ukraine was the least successful economically. At the time of the beginning of the crisis of 2014 it still had not reached the per capita GNP of the last Soviet years. Not just the Baltic states and Poland, but even Belarus did better. For the economic problems political uncertainty could be at least partially blamed. The degree of corruption in Ukraine was similar to that in Russia itself. The economic and political failure of Ukraine was a threat to Russia. The western Ukrainians who regarded Russia as the main threat to their sovereignty sought help from primarily the United States and Western Europe. From their point of view, the worse the relations between the United States and Russia were, the greater the support they could expect from the West. Their Western orientation was not so much the consequence of attraction of Western liberalism, but as a counterweight against perceived dangers from the East.

The history of Ukraine between its establishment as an independent state and the political crisis of 2014 was a series of upheavals, quasirevolutions. These political upheavals and the high degree of corruption condemned the country to economic stagnation. Before the overthrow of Viktor Yanukovych's presidency, the governments alternated between two different conceptions of Ukraine. People in the east and south of the country were likely to vote for candidates who stood for a multinational, more or less pro-Russian government, as against people in the west, who stood for a more exclusivist, nationalist Ukraine and were likely to see Russia as the main enemy.

The Ukrainians fought a war of symbols. Should the memory of men who had fought on the side of the Nazis in the Second World War such as Stepan Bandera be venerated? Was the great famine of the 1930s, the *Holodomor*, a Stalinist attempt at genocide, or was it a tragedy that other people of the Soviet Union also suffered? Should statues of Lenin be removed? When a president came to office who had received most of his support from the western part of the country, the government introduced symbols that the other half of Ukrainians considered offensive. In 2010, President Viktor

Yushchenko rehabilitated Stepan Bandera and named him a hero of Ukraine. A year later, when Viktor Yanukovych came into office, he annulled the award. Bandera came to be one of the heroes of those who demonstrated against Yanukovych in 2014. Yushchenko attempted to make it a criminal offense to deny that the great hunger of the Stalinist 1930s was an act of genocide aimed against the Ukrainian people. Years before the events of 2014, it was clear that Ukraine consisted of two people with different histories and political beliefs.

While Yushchenko was in office as a result of the "orange revolution," relations with Moscow deteriorated. Putin's spokesmen repeatedly announced that Russia would not tolerate Ukraine joining NATO. Nevertheless, the two presidents met several times, and Russia continued to supply Ukraine with oil and natural gas at prices lower than those on the world market. Yushchenko, unlike Saakashvili in Georgia, understood that he had to balance a fundamentally Western orientation against Russian interests, and not to alienate Russia too much, because doing so would alienate a large part of his countrymen.

The revolution of 2014 ended the delicate balance that had kept the two parts of Ukraine together. What occasioned the upheaval was the fundamental issue that separated the nation. In May 2013, President Yanukovych signed an agreement with representatives of the European Union envisaging deeper cooperation. The agreement was incompatible with the interconnectedness of the Russian and Ukrainian economies. The EU also demanded harsh economic reforms, which in the long run no doubt would have been beneficial, but that were painful in the short run. The Russians, by contrast, promised a $15 billion loan package and drastically lowered gas prices. Yanukovych's decision in November not to sign the agreement with the European Union sparked the uprising. Crowds gathered in protest on Maidan square, and the size of the protests increased day by day. Although the immediate issue for the protesters was the signing of the agreement, people who joined did so in opposition to a corrupt regime in general. Indeed, the president, although he had been repeatedly elected by his eastern and southern Ukrainian constituency, was an uninspiring, corrupt leader with a murky past. The authorities mishandled the situation. They used too much force in dispersing the demonstrators, thereby intensifying the revolutionary atmosphere. Within a few weeks, the demonstrations were transformed into a civil war.

The antiregime activists were at first part of a coalition. As time went on, extreme right-wing groups, some avowedly fascist, played increasingly important roles, making compromise impossible. The paradoxical result was that right-wing, nationalist movements called for integration into Europe, not because they shared European values, but because of their hatred of Russians.

The attempt to find a compromise failed. The two sides in the conflict, with the involvement of Western diplomats, signed an agreement that called for an end to the fighting, a decrease in presidential powers, and, most importantly, early presidential elections. Yanukovych, by this time deeply unpopular, was likely to lose that election. The revolutionaries who gathered in the Maidan found any deal with Yanukovych's forces unacceptable. They took over governmental buildings, and the president, fearing for his life, escaped.

With Yanukovych's removal, a long civil war commenced. The delicate balance between the pro-Russian and anti-Russian Ukrainians was broken. The country that had served as an intermediary between the European Union and Russia was no more. With the establishment of a government in Kiev whose authority was based on support from nationalist forces, Russia's security came to be endangered more than at any time since the demise of the Soviet Union. Any desire for compromise evaporated from the government in Ukraine. Expecting support from the West, especially from the United States, they found it possible to provoke Putin's government.

In this new and volatile situation the Russian government, having a weak hand, reacted the best way it could. It started to supply the eastern Ukrainians who opposed the new regime in Kiev with arms and a quantity of fighting men. Most likely, such military support would have enabled the pro-Russian Ukrainians to hold out for a long time, thereby preventing NATO from having hostile forces on Russia's immediate borders. Putin's forces occupied Crimea, a peninsula that had been attached to Ukraine only in 1955 and had a relatively small Ukrainian minority. The main reason for this was that the new government had made it clear that it would not renew the lease to the only naval base Russia had on the Black Sea, Sevastopol, which was to expire in 2017. According to the last census less than a quarter of the population of the peninsula considered themselves Ukrainian.

The Maidan revolution of 2013–14 had far-reaching and mostly negative consequences. The greatest sufferer has been Ukraine itself. The large number of people killed will not easily be forgotten; the material devastation will not be easily remedied. Even in the unlikely case that the pro-Russian elements are defeated, such a defeat would not win people over to a concept of nationalism that denies their past and heritage. Being included in the European community will not in itself turn Ukraine into a Poland or a Czech Republic. Economic reforms have costs, and corruption is not easily overcome. The prerequisites of liberal politics and a modern free-market economy are not yet present.

The government of Petro Poroshenko, elected president in 2014, has done nothing to bring about reconciliation of the two parts of the Ukrainian nation. On the contrary, the government has further embittered the conflict: it failed to repudiate the assistance of an admittedly small group of neo-Nazis; it has been willing to use the help of Muslim Chechen fighters who are in Ukraine simply because of their hatred of Russians; Poroshenko named as governor of the Odessa province Mikheil Saakashvili, a man who had not even been a Ukrainian citizen and had no qualification for the job other than hatred of the Putin regime. Odessa is perhaps the most pro-Russian major city in the country.

West Europeans and the United States in particular have also been losers. The United States, by supporting the most narrowly nationalistic elements in Kiev, made compromise in a civil war more unlikely. The only desirable outcome of the conflict would be a compromise that would reestablish Ukraine as an intermediary between East and West. An impoverished, weakened, and humiliated Russia that has no choice but to look for allies in the East cannot be in the American national interest.

The establishment of a hostile state on Russia's western border, governed by people whose nationalism is based entirely on hatred of Russians, is a grave threat to Russia's security. Of course, the Ukrainian army by itself would not be a threat. But Western, primarily US weapons and military experts on Ukrainian soil do present a threat. The Russian people are impoverished by the necessity of further investment in the military. Western sanctions imposed on the economy also hurt. It is difficult to comprehend the purpose of those sanctions. Only the most naive would believe that they would make the Russian government change its position and behavior. So far the consequence of the sanctions has been to illustrate Putin's argument to his people that the West is irrationally anti-Russian, thereby improving his popularity rating to a remarkable high of 89 percent.

The Western orientation of Russian foreign policy during Putin's first two tenures as president did not exclude the revival of the old Eurasian ideology. In the minds of the makers of Russian foreign policy, there was no contradiction between pursuing a foreign policy in concert with Western powers and at the same time insisting that Russia was a separate civilization. In their understanding, Russia was both European and Asian. Russia, after all, is a major Asian power, and it has longstanding interests in Central Asia. Eurasianism had a tradition of Russian intellectual life, which meant that Russia was a separate civilization in contradistinction to Europe. This was a nationalist ideology stressing the uniqueness of Russian history and ideology. The reemergence of this ideology was a consequence of the growing recognition that Russia was excluded from a united Europe.

The consequence of the conflict over Ukraine is a sense among the majority of the Russian people that the West is hostile, disregards Russian concerns, and does not respect Russian interests. The United States has never been regarded with as much hostility as it is today. The Russian sense of exclusion from Europe increased the appeal of Eurasianism, which is an ideology that is not conducive to liberal values. For many citizens, the warlike atmosphere justifies the repressive measures the government has been implementing. Russian democracy has taken several steps back from a presumed road to European liberalism.

The foreign-policy consequence of the crisis has been that Russia has had to look for friends and allies outside Europe. In the modern world it is not difficult to find such friends. The Chinese, the Indians, the Brazilians, and others have common perceived interests in working against United States hegemony.

The chances for the development of a liberal, tolerant Russia, integrated into Europe, where it really belongs, now seem more remote than at the moment when Putin came to power in 2000. If he suddenly died, it would not make much difference. Whatever is unattractive in the current Russian regime cannot be associated with the peculiarities of the character and personality of the president. The country's problems are more profound.

Chronology

Dates until February 1918 are given according to the old calendar.

1917

February 23	International Women's Day; demonstrations in Petrograd begin.
February 27	The last tsarist government under Prince Golitsyn resigns.
February 28	Formation of the Petrograd Soviet.
March 2	Abdication of Nicholas II.
April 3	Lenin arrives in Petrograd.
June	Kerensky's unsuccessful offensive.
July 3–5	"July days": armed demonstrations of workers, soldiers, and sailors result in repression of Bolsheviks.
August 26	Kornilov's mutiny collapses.
September	Bolsheviks win majorities in the Petrograd and Moscow Soviets.
October 25–26	October Revolution: the Bolsheviks take power.
October 26	Lenin issues decree on land and peace; Soviet government is formed.
November	Elections to the Constituent Assembly.
December	Creation of Cheka (Extraordinary Commission to Combat Counterrevolution and Sabotage).

1918

January 5	The Bolsheviks disband the Constituent Assembly.
January	The anti-Bolshevik volunteer army is formed.
March 3	The Soviet government signs a peace treaty with the Central Powers at Brest-Litovsk.
March	Allied intervention begins.

May	Czechoslovak troops traveling on the Trans-Siberian Railroad rebel against the Soviet government, making it possible for the Whites to organize their movement in Siberia.
Summer	Introduction of policies of war communism.
July 6	The revolt of the left Socialist Revolutionaries.
August 30	Attempt on Lenin's life and beginning of Red terror.
November	Admiral Kolchak assumes leadership over anti-Bolshevik forces in Siberia; end of the war in Europe transforms Allied intervention.

1919

March 2–4	Founding of the Communist International.
Spring	Kolchak's armies threaten Moscow.
October	Denikin's armies occupy Orel, 200 miles from Moscow.
November	Iudenich's army threatens Petrograd.
Winter	Red Army victorious on all fronts.

1920

April–October	Soviet–Polish war.
September	Baku Congress of Working People of the East.
November	General Wrangel, leader of the last White Army, abandons Crimea for exile.
Winter	Soviet rule is established in the three Caucasus republics; Allied intervention ends.

1921

March	Rising of the Kronstadt sailors; Tenth Party Congress passes resolution against factions, inaugurates NEP; Treaty of Riga with Poland.
1921–22	Famine.

1922

February 6	Cheka renamed GPU.
April 2	Stalin becomes general secretary of the Central Committee of the Communist Party.
June	Trial of Socialist Revolutionaries.
December 30	Establishment of the USSR.

1923

Summer	"Scissors crisis."
October 23	Forty-six leaders criticize ruling group.

1924

January 21	Death of V. I. Lenin.

| January 31 | Constitution of the USSR is ratified. |
| March | Introduction of stable ruble. |

1925
| January | Trotsky loses his position as commissar of war. |

1926
| | Trotsky, Zinoviev, and Kamenev lose out in the political struggle and are expelled from the Politburo. |

1927
May	War scare.
Fall	Beginning of procurement crisis: the government fails to collect sufficient grain from peasants.
December	The Fifteenth Party Congress approves the first five-year plan and registers Stalin's complete victory over Trotsky, Zinoviev, and Kamenev.

1928
January–February	Stalin in Siberia reintroduces forcible grain collection: "Ural–Siberia method."
January 16	Trotsky exiled to Alma Ata.
May–July	"Shakhty trial" of innocent engineers.
1928–32	Stalin's "cultural revolution."

1929
	Defeat of Bukharin and his comrades as "right-wing deviation."
Fall	Beginning of mass collectivization and "elimination of the kulaks as a class."
December 21	Stalin's fiftieth birthday and the beginning of the Stalin cult.

1930
| March 2 | Stalin's article: "Dizzy with Success." |
| 1930–31 | A series of show trials aimed against "bourgeois specialists." |

1931
| June | In a speech Stalin explicitly abandons the egalitarian promise of the 1917 revolution. |

1932
| December | Reintroduction of an internal passport system. |

1932–33
| | Famine in Ukraine, north Caucasus, and Kazakhstan. |

1933–37

Second five-year plan.

1934

January–February   Seventeenth Party Congress: "Congress of Victors."

August   Congress of Writers adopts principles of "socialist realism."

December 1   Murder of Sergei Kirov.

1935

February   Model collective farm statute.

May   Soviet–French treaty of mutual assistance.

July–August   Seventh congress of Comintern adopts policy of popular front.

Fall   Stakhanovist movement begins.

1936

June 27   Anti-abortion law and new family code.

August   First great show trial: Zinoviev, Kamenev, and fourteen others sentenced to death.

September 25   Yezhov replaces Yagoda as head of NKVD.

December 5   Adoption of new "Stalin constitution."

1937

January   Second great show trial: thirteen sentenced to death.

May–June   Purge of the Red Army.

1938

March   Third great show trial: nineteen, including Bukharin and Rykov, sentenced to death.

July   Soviet–Japanese border clashes in Manchuria.

December   Beria replaces Yezhov as head of NKVD.

1939

May 3   Molotov replaces Litvinov as commissar for foreign affairs.

April–August   Fruitless negotiations with Western allies.

August 23   Molotov–Ribbentrop pact.

September 1   Germany invades Poland.

September 17   Red Army invades Poland.

November   Soviet Union annexes western Ukraine and western Belorussia.

November 30   Soviet–Finnish war begins.

1940

March 12   Soviet–Finnish war ends.

April   Murder of Polish officers at Katyn forest.

June 26	Draconic labor legislation introduced.
June 28	The Soviet Union annexes Bessarabia and northern Bukovina (from Romania).
August 3–6	The Soviet Union annexes Estonia, Latvia, and Lithuania.

1941

June 22	Germany invades the Soviet Union.
July 3	Stalin's radio broadcast: "Brothers and sisters ..."
September	Beginning of the siege of Leningrad; fall of Kiev.
December	First major Soviet victory on the outskirts of Moscow.

1942

June 11	Lend-lease agreement.
August	Germans reach Stalingrad.
November 19	Soviet counteroffensive at Stalingrad begins.
November 23	German Sixth Army encircled at Stalingrad.

1943

February 2	Paulus surrenders.
July–August	Battle of Kursk.
November 28–December 1	Tehran conference.
1943–44	Deportation of entire peoples to Central Asia.

1944

January 27	Siege of Leningrad lifted.
August–September	Warsaw uprising.

1945

February 4–11	Yalta conference.
May 9	End of the war in Europe.
July 17–August 2	Potsdam conference.
August 8	The Soviet Union declares war on Japan.
September 2	End of the war.

1946

	Tightening of discipline in collective farms and extending the collective farm system to the newly annexed territories.
August 14–15	Zhdanov's speeches in Leningrad attacking Zoshchenko and Akhmatova; call for reimposition of ideological discipline.

1947

	Famine.
December 14	Currency reform.

1948
February 20   Coup in Prague.
June 28   Yugoslavia is expelled from Cominform.
July 31 –August 7   Lysenko's theories imposed on genetics.
1948–49   Berlin blockade.

1949
                           Struggle against "rootless cosmopolitanism."
January 25   Formation of Comecon.
September 25   Announcement of the testing of the first Soviet
                           A-bomb.
October 1   Founding of the People's Republic of China.

1950
June 26   Korean War begins.

1952
October 5–14   Nineteenth Party Congress.

1953
January 13   Disclosure of arrest of nine Soviet doctors:
                           "doctors' plot."
March 5   Stalin dies; he is succeeded as general secretary and
                           premier by Malenkov.
March 14   Malenkov resigns as general secretary.
April 14   Exoneration of surviving doctors in "doctors' plot."
June   Riots in East Berlin.
June 26   Beria is arrested.
July 27   Korean armistice.
August 12   Soviet Union explodes an H-bomb.

1955
February 8   Malenkov resigns as premier and is replaced by
                           Bulganin.
May 14   Warsaw Pact is established.
July 18–23   Geneva conference.

1956
February 14–25   Twentieth Party Congress: Khrushchev's "secret
                           speech."
October   "Polish October."
October 23   Hungarian revolution begins.
November 4   Soviet troops suppress Hungarian revolution.

1957
June   "Antiparty group" attempts to unseat Khrushchev.
October 4   Sputnik is launched.

1958

| February 26 | Abolition of MTSs. |
| March 27 | Khrushchev assumes title "premier" (in addition to first secretary). |

1959

| September 15–27 | Khrushchev visits the United States. |

1960

| May 1 | Beginnings of Sino-Soviet polemics; Soviet Union shoots down U-2 spy plane. |

1961

April 12	Gagarin is first man in space.
August 13	Berlin Wall seals border.
October 17–31	Twenty-Second Party Congress: Stalin's body is removed from mausoleum.

1962

| October 22–November 2 | Cuban missile crisis. |
| November | Bifurcation of industrial and agricultural sectors of the party apparat. |

1963

| July 25 | Nuclear test ban treaty. |

1964

| October 14–15 | Khrushchev is removed and replaced by Brezhnev. |
| November 16 | Bifurcation reversed. |

1966

| February 10–14 | Siniavskii–Daniel trial. |
| March 29–April 8 | Twenty-Second Party Congress. |

1967

| June | Arab–Israeli war leads to diplomatic break with Israel. |

1968

| | "Prague spring." |
| August 20–21 | Warsaw Pact forces invade Czechoslovakia. |

1969

| March 2 | Fighting at Sino-Soviet border. |

1970
October 8   Solzhenitsyn wins Nobel Prize for Literature.

1972
May 22–28   Nixon visits Moscow.
June 3   Four-power agreement on the status of Berlin.

1973
October   War in Middle East leads to US–Soviet confrontation.

1974
February 13   After the publication of *The Gulag Archipelago*,
                              Solzhenitsyn is expelled from Soviet Union.

1975
August 1   Signing of Helsinki accords.
October 9   Sakharov wins Nobel Prize.

1977
June 4   New constitution is published.

1979
December 24–27   Soviet army invades Afghanistan.

1980
January 22   Sakharov is exiled to Gorky.
August 14   Strikes begin in Poland, leading to victory of
                              Solidarity.

1981
December 13   Martial law introduced in Poland.

1982
November 10   Brezhnev dies.
November 12   Andropov named general secretary.

1983
September 1   Korean airliner shot down.

1984
February 9   Andropov dies.
February 13   Chernenko chosen as new general secretary.
December 15–21   Gorbachev in Britain.

1985

March 10–11	Chernenko dies; Gorbachev is named general secretary.
May 16	Anti-alcohol program introduced; Gorbachev introduces arms control proposals and calls for economic reforms.
November 19–21	First meeting between Reagan and Gorbachev in Geneva.

1986

February 25–March 6	Twenty-Seventh Party Congress: Gorbachev criticizes Brezhnev era.
April 26	Chernobyl disaster.
October	Gorbachev and Reagan meet at Reykjavik in Iceland.
December	Sakharov is allowed to return to Moscow.

1988

January	Disturbances in Stepanakert, Nagornyi Karabakh.
March 13	Nina Andreevna's letter expresses frustration of hardline communists over changes introduced by Gorbachev.
June 28	Political changes introduced at Nineteenth Party Conference.

1989

March	Competitive elections for a national assembly.
April 9	Suppression of demonstrations in Tbilisi.
May 25	Congress of People's Deputies convenes.
August 24	Noncommunist government comes to power in Poland.
November 9	Berlin Wall is demolished.

1990

December 20	Shevardnadze resigns as foreign minister.

1991

January	Attempts at repression in Lithuania.
March 17	Referendum on national unity.
July 10	Yeltsin takes oath of office as president of the Russian Federation.
August 18–21	Attempted coup.
December 12	Russian parliament ratifies establishment of Commonwealth of Independent States.

1992
January 2   Freeing of prices.

1993
April 25   Referendum on Yeltsin.
September 21   Yeltsin dissolves congress.
October 4   Bombardment of the parliament.
December 12   Vote for a constitution and a new parliament.

1994
December 11   Beginning of First Chechen War.

1996
May 27   End of First Chechen War.
July 3   Yeltsin reelected.

1998
August   Devaluation of ruble.

1999
September   Bombings in Moscow and other Russian cities.
December 31   Yeltsin resigns.

2000
March 26   Putin elected president.

2003
October 25   Khodorkovskii arrested.

2004
March 14   Putin reelected.
September 25   Putin abolishes election of governors.

2006
October 7   Politkovskaia murdered.

2007
February 15   Ramzan Kadyrov appointed president of Chechnya.

2008
May 7   Medvedev assumes office as president of Russian Federation.
August   Russia–Georgia war.

2011
October   Thousands demostrate against electoral fraud.

2012
May 7   Putin assumes office as president of Russian
                             Federation.

2014
February   Beginning of Ukrainian revolution and civil war;
                             Crimea annexed by Russian Federation.

2015
February 27   Nemtsov assassinated.

Soviet History: A Bibliography

The best and most balanced one-volume history of Russia in English is Nicholas V. Riasanovsky, *A History of Russia*, 5th edn. (New York: Oxford University Press, 1993). Jerome Blum, *Lord and Peasant in Russia* (Princeton: Princeton University Press, 1961), is an economic history that complements Riasanovsky's book. James Billington's *The Icon and the Axe: Interpretive History of Russian Culture* (New York: Knopf, 1966) is an interesting though somewhat idiosyncratic interpretation of Russian intellectual history. Richard Pipes, *Russia Under the Old Regime*, 2nd edn. (New York: Collier, 1992), is an interesting essay showing the Russian roots of Soviet communism. The best and most detailed history of nineteenth-century Russia is Hugh Seton-Watson's *The Russian Empire, 1801–1917* (New York: Oxford University Press, 1967). For the last decades of the empire, see Hans Rogger, *Russia in the Age of Modernization and Revolution, 1881–1917* (London: Longman, 1983). For the history of the revolutionary movement, see the extremely detailed Franco Venturi, *Roots of Revolution: A History of Populist and Socialist Movements in Nineteenth-Century Russia* (New York: Knopf, 1960).

General

Among the numerous histories of the Soviet Union, the relatively brief volume by Geoffrey Hosking stands out: *First Socialist Society: A History of the Soviet Union from Within*, 2nd edn. (Cambridge, MA: Harvard University Press, 1993). John Thompson's *A Vision Fulfilled: Russia and the Soviet Union in the Twentieth Century* (Lexington, MA: Heath, 1996) is more detailed but has the flavor of a textbook. The same can be said about Martin McCauley, *The Soviet Union: 1917–1991*, 2nd edn. (London: Longman, 1993), and M. K. Dziewanowski, *A History of Soviet Russia and Its Aftermath*, 5th edn. (Upper Saddle River, NJ: Prentice Hall, 1997). Martin Malia's *The Soviet Tragedy: A History of Socialism in Russia, 1917–1991* (New York: Free Press, 1994) is a passionate and intelligent essay aiming to show that the utopian idea of socialism was the source of the "Soviet tragedy." Mikhail Heller and Aleksandr Nekrich's *Utopia in Power: The History of the Soviet Union from 1917 to the Present* (New York: Simon and Schuster, 1986) was written by two people who knew the Soviet system from the inside;

it is bitterly anti-Soviet, very detailed, and extremely useful. A new and readable work is by Orlando Figes, *Revolutionary Russia, 1891–1991* (London: Penguin, 2014). A very good and detailed study is Ronald Suny's *The Soviet Experiment: Russia, the USSR, and the Successor States* (New York: Oxford University Press, 1998). For the Soviet political system, see Merle Fainsod's *How Russia Is Ruled* (Cambridge, MA: Harvard University Press, 1965), in spite of its age still the best account. Leonard Schapiro, *The Communist Party of the Soviet Union* (London: Eyre and Spottiswoode, 1970), is in fact a history of the Soviet Union. T. H. Rigby's *Communist Party Membership in the USSR, 1917–1967* (Princeton: Princeton University Press, 1968) is an essential work for the understanding of the character of the Communist Party of the Soviet Union. The most insightful and by far the most readable study of Soviet foreign policy is Adam Ulam's *Expansion and Coexistence: Soviet Foreign Policy 1917–1973*, 2nd edn. (New York: Praeger, 1974). There is no first-rate history of the church under Soviet rule, but see J. S. Curtiss, *The Russian Church and the Soviet State, 1917–1950* (Boston: Little, Brown, 1953); W. C. Fletcher, *The Russian Orthodox Church Underground, 1917–1970* (Oxford: Oxford University Press, 1971); and T. Ware, *The Russian Orthodox Church* (Harmondsworth: Penguin Books, 1963). The best economic history by far is Alec Nove, *An Economic History of the USSR, 1917–1991*, 3rd edn. (New York: Penguin, 1992). See also L. Volin, *A Century of Russian Agriculture: From Alexander II to Khrushchev* (Cambridge, MA: Harvard University Press, 1970). For the position of women in Soviet society, see Dorothy Atkinson, Alexander Dallin, and Gail Warshofsky Lapidus (eds.), *Women in Russia* (Stanford: Stanford University Press, 1977), and Gail Lapidus, *Women in Soviet Society: Equality Development and Social Change* (Berkeley: University of California Press, 1978). For the nationality question, see R. Suny, *The Revenge of the Past: National Revolution and the Collapse of the Soviet Union* (Stanford: Stanford University Press, 1993), and Robert Kaiser, *The Geography of Nationalism in the USSR and Russia* (Princeton: Princeton University Press, 1994). An excellent introduction to Soviet history is through biographies. Outstanding ones include A. Ulam, *Lenin and the Bolsheviks* (New York: Macmillan, 1965); A. Ulam, *Stalin: The Man and His Era* (New York: Viking, 1973); S. F. Cohen, *Bukharin and the Bolshevik Revolution* (New York: Knopf, 1973); R. C. Tucker, *Stalin as Revolutionary, 1879–1929* (New York: Norton, 1973); R. C. Tucker, *Stalin in Power: The Revolution from Above, 1928–1941* (New York: Norton, 1990); Bertram Wolfe, *Three Who Made a Revolution* (New York: Dell, 1964); Isaac Deutscher, *The Prophet Armed: Trotsky, 1879–1921* (Oxford: Oxford University Press, 1954); Isaac Deutscher, *The Prophet Unarmed 1921–1929* (Oxford: Oxford University Press, 1959); and Isaac Deutscher, *The Prophet Outcast, 1919–1940* (Oxford: Oxford University Press, 1963). Yuri Slezkine's book on the role of Jews in Russia is the most thoughtful treatment of the issue: *The Jewish Century* (Princeton: Princeton University Press, 2004).

1917–1929

Abramowitch, R. R., *The Soviet Revolution, 1917–1939*, London: Allen and Unwin, 1962.

Anweiler, O., *The Soviets: Russian Workers', Peasants' and Soldiers' Councils, 1905–1921*, New York: Pantheon Books, 1974.

Ascher, A. (ed.), *The Mensheviks in the Russian Revolution*, Ithaca: Cornell University Press, 1976.

Atkinson, Dorothy, *The End of the Russian Land Commune, 1905–1930*, Stanford: Stanford University Press, 1983.

Avrich, P., *Kronstadt 1921*, Princeton: Princeton University Press, 1970.

Ball, Alan, *And Now My Soul Is Hardened: Abandoned Children in Soviet Russia, 1918–1930*, Berkeley: University of California Press, 1994.

Ball, Alan, *Russia's Last Capitalists: The Nepmen, 1917–1929*, Berkeley: University of California Press, 1987.

Benet, Sula (ed.), *The Village of Viriatino*, New York: Anchor, 1970.

Bennigsen, A., and C. Lemercier-Quelquejay, *Islam in the Soviet Union*, London: Pall Mall Press, 1967.

Bennigsen, A., and S. Wimbush, *Muslim National Communism in the Soviet Union*, Chicago: University of Chicago Press, 1979.

Brandenberger, David, *National Bolshevism: Stalinist Mass Culture and the Formation of Modern Russian National Identity, 1931–1956*, Cambridge, MA: Harvard University Press, 2002.

Brinkley, George, *The Volunteer Army and Allied Intervention in South Russia*, Notre Dame, IN: Notre Dame University Press 1966.

Brovkin, Vladimir, *Behind the Front Lines of the Civil War: Political Parties and Social Movements in Russia, 1918–1922*, Princeton: Princeton University Press, 1994.

Brovkin, V. N., *The Mensheviks After October: Socialist Opposition and the Rise of the Bolshevik Dictatorship*, Ithaca: Cornell University Press, 1987.

Bunyan, J. (ed.), *The Origin of Forced Labor in the Soviet State, 1917–1921*, Baltimore: Johns Hopkins University Press, 1967.

Bunyan, J., and H. H. Fisher (eds.), *The Bolshevik Revolution, 1917–1918: Documents and Materials*, Stanford: Stanford University Press, 1934.

Burbank, Jane, *Intelligentsia and Revolution*, New York: Oxford University Press, 1986.

Carr, E. H., *The Bolshevik Revolution, 1917–1923*, 3 vols., New York: Macmillan, 1951–53.

Carr, E. H., *Interregnum*, New York: Macmillan, 1954.

Carr, E. H., *Socialism in One Country, 1924–1926*, 2 vols., London: Macmillan, 1958–59.

Carr, E. H., and R. W. Davies, *Foundations of a Planned Economy, 1926–1929*, New York: Macmillan, 1969–78.

Chamberlin, W. H., *The Russian Revolution*, 2 vols., New York: Grosset and Dunlap, 1965.

Chernov, V., *The Great Russian Revolution*, New York: Russell and Russell, 1966.

Clements, Barbara, *Bolshevik Feminist: The Life of Alexandra Kollontai*, Bloomington: Indiana University Press, 1979.

Daniels, R., *The Conscience of the Revolution: Communist Opposition in Soviet Russia*, Cambridge, MA: Harvard University Press, 1960.

Daniels, R., *Red October: The Bolshevik Revolution of 1917*, New York: Scribner, 1967.

Danilov, V. P., *Rural Russia Under the New Regime*, London: Hutchinson, 1988.

Davies, Norman, *White Eagle, Red Star: The Polish–Soviet War, 1919–1920*, London: Macdonald, 1972.

Day, Richard, *Leon Trotsky and the Politics of Economic Isolation*, Cambridge: Cambridge University Press, 1973.

Denikin, General A., *The White Army*, Gulf Breeze, FL: Academic International Press, 1973.

Dodge, Norton T., *Women in the Soviet Economy*, Baltimore: Johns Hopkins University Press, 1966.

Erlich, A., *The Soviet Industrialisation Debate*, Cambridge, MA: Harvard University Press, 1960.

Farnsworth, Beatrice, *Aleksandra Kollontai: Socialism, Feminism and the Bolshevik Revolution*, Stanford: Stanford University Press, 1980.

Fedyukin, S., *The Great October Revolution and the Intelligentsia*, Moscow: Progress Publishers, 1975.

Figes, Orlando, *Peasant Russia, Civil War: The Volga Countryside in Revolution, 1917–1921*, Oxford: Oxford University Press, 1989.

Figes, Orlando, *A People's Tragedy: A History of the Russian Revolution*, New York: Viking, 1997.

Fitzpatrick, Sheila, *The Commissariat of Enlightenment*, Cambridge: Cambridge University Press, 1970.

Fitzpatrick, Sheila, *The Russian Revolution*, Oxford: Oxford University Press, 1982.

Fleming, Peter, *The Fate of Admiral Kolchak*, New York: Harcourt, 1963.

Florinsky, M., *The End of the Russian Empire*, New York: Collier Books, 1961.

Footman, D., *Civil War in Russia*, London: Faber and Faber, 1961.

Getzler, I., *Kronstadt 1917–1921: The Fate of a Soviet Democracy*, Cambridge: Cambridge University Press, 1983.

Gill, G., *Peasants and Government in the Russian Revolution*, New York: Barnes and Noble, 1979.

Gitelman, Zvi, *Jewish Nationality and Soviet Politics: The Jewish Sections of the CPSU, 1917–1930*, Princeton: Princeton University Press, 1972.

Gleason, Abbott, Peter Kenez, and Richard Stites (eds.), *Bolshevik Culture: Experimentation and Order in the Russian Revolution*, Bloomington: Indiana University Press, 1985.

Goldman, Wendy, *Women, the State and Revolution: Soviet Family Policy and Social Life, 1917–1936*, New York: Cambridge University Press, 1993.

Haimson, L. (ed.), *The Mensheviks*, Chicago: University of Chicago Press, 1974.

Hasegawa, T., *The February Revolution: Petrograd 1917*, Seattle: University of Washington Press, 1981.

Holmes, Larry, *The Kremlin and the Schoolhouse: Reforming Education in the Soviet Union, 1917–1931*, Bloomington: Indiana University Press, 1991.

Holquist, Peter, *Making War, Forging Revolution: Russia's Continuum of Crisis, 1914–1921*, Cambridge, MA: Harvard University Press, 2002.

Hunczak, T. (ed.), *The Ukraine, 1917–1921: A Study in Revolution*, Cambridge, MA: Harvard University Press, 1977.

Husband, William, *Godless Communists: Atheism and Society in Soviet Russia, 1917–1932*, DeKalb: Northern Illinois University Press, 2000.

Kaiser, D. H. (ed.), *The Workers' Revolution in Russia, 1917: The View from Below*, New York: Cambridge University Press, 1987.

Katkov, George, *Russia 1917: The February Revolution*, London: Longman, 1967.

Katkov, George, *Russia 1917: The Kornilov Affair*, London: Longman, 1980.

Kazemzadeh, F., *The Struggle for Transcaucasia*, Oxford: George Ronald, 1951.

Keep, J. L. H., *The Russian Revolution: A Study in Mass Mobilisation*, London: Weidenfeld and Nicolson, 1976.

Kenez, P., *The Birth of the Propaganda State: Soviet Methods of Mass Mobilization*, New York: Cambridge University Press, 1985.

Kenez, P., *Civil War in South Russia, 1918–1920*, 2 vols., Berkeley: University of California Press, 1971–77.

Knei-Paz, B., *The Social and Political Thought of Leon Trotsky*, Oxford: Oxford University Press, 1978.

Koenker, Diane, *Moscow Workers and the 1917 Revolution*, Princeton: Princeton University Press, 1981.

Koenker, Diane, and William G. Rosenberg, *Strikes and Revolution in Russia, 1917*, Princeton: Princeton University Press, 1989.

Koenker, Diane, William G. Rosenberg, and Ronald G. Suny (eds.), *Party, State, and Society in the Russian Civil War*, Bloomington: Indiana University Press, 1989.

Landis, Eric, *Bandits and Partisans: The Antonov Movement in the Russian Civil War*, Pittsburgh: University of Pittsburgh Press, 2008.

Leggett, George, *The Cheka: Lenin's Political Police*, Oxford: Oxford University Press, 1981.

Lewin, M., *Lenin's Last Struggle*, London: Faber and Faber, 1969.

Lewin, M., *Russian Peasants and Soviet Power*, London: Allen and Unwin, 1968.

Lih, Lars, *Bread and Authority in Russia, 1914–1921*, Berkeley: University of California Press, 1989.

Lodder, Christina, *Russian Constructivism*, New Haven: Yale University Press, 1983.

Malle, S., *The Economic Organisation of War Communism, 1918–1921*, Cambridge: Cambridge University Press, 1985.

Mawdsley, E., *The Russian Civil War*, London: Allen and Unwin, 1987.

McCauley, M. (ed.), *The Russian Revolution and the Soviet State, 1917–1921*, London: Macmillan, 1975.

Medvedev, R., *The October Revolution*, London: Constable, 1979.

Meijer, J. M. (ed.), *The Trotsky Papers, 1917–1922*, 2 vols., The Hague: Mouton, 1964–71.

Melgunov, S. P., *The Bolshevik Seizure of Power*, Santa Barbara, CA: ABC-Clio, 1972.

Pereira, Norman, *White Siberia*, Montreal: McGill University Press, 1996.

Pethybridge, R., *The Social Prelude to Stalinism*, London: Macmillan, 1974.

Pipes, R., *The Formation of the Soviet Union*, Cambridge, MA: Harvard University Press, 1964.

Pipes, Richard, *A History of the Russian Revolution*, New York: Knopf, 1990.

Pipes, Richard, *Russia Under the Bolshevik Regime*, New York: Knopf, 1993.

Pipes, Richard (ed.), *The Unknown Lenin: From the Secret Archives*, New Haven: Yale University Press, 1996.

Rabinowitch, A., *The Bolsheviks Come to Power*, New York: Norton, 1976.

Radkey, O., *The Agrarian Foes of Bolshevism: Promise and Default of the Russian Socialist Revolutionaries, February–October 1917*, New York: Columbia University Press, 1958.

Radkey, O., *The Election to the Constituent Assembly of 1917*, Cambridge, MA: Harvard University Press, 1950.

Radkey, O., *The Sickle Under the Hammer: The Russian Socialist Revolutionaries in the Early Months of Soviet Rule*, New York: Columbia University Press, 1963.

Radkey, O., *The Unknown Civil War in Soviet Russia: A Study of the Green Movement in the Tambov Region, 1920–1921*, Stanford: Hoover Institution Press, 1976.

Raleigh, Donald J., *Experiencing Russia's Civil War: Politics, Society, and Revolutionary Culture in Saratov, 1917–1922*, Princeton: Princeton University Press, 2002.

Reed, John, *Ten Days That Shook the World*, London: Lawrence and Wishart, 1961.

Reshetar, J., *The Ukrainian Revolution, 1917–1920*, Princeton: Princeton University Press, 1952.

Rigby, T. H., *Lenin's Government: Sovnarkom, 1917–1922*, Cambridge: Cambridge University Press, 1979.

Rosenberg, W. G., *Liberals in the Russian Revolution*, Princeton: Princeton University Press, 1974.

Schapiro, Leonard, *1917: The Russian Revolutions and the Origins of Present-Day Communism*, New York: Basic Books, 1984.

Schapiro, Leonard, *Origin of the Communist Autocracy: Political Opposition in the Soviet State*, 2nd edn., London: Macmillan, 1977.

Service, R., *The Bolshevik Party in Revolution: A Study in Organisational Change, 1917–1923*, London: Macmillan, 1979.

Service, R., *Lenin: A Biography*, Cambridge, MA: Harvard University Press, 2000.

Shanin, T., *The Awkward Class: Political Sociology of a Peasantry in a Developing Society, Russia 1910–1925*, Oxford: Oxford University Press, 1972.

Siegelbaum, Lewis, *Soviet State and Society Between Revolutions, 1918–1929*, Cambridge: Cambridge University Press, 1992.

Slezkine, Yuri, *The Jewish Century*, Princeton: Princeton University Press, 2004.

Smele, Jonathan, *Civil War in Siberia*, Cambridge: Cambridge University Press, 1996.

Smith, S. A., *Red Petrograd: Revolution in the Factories, 1917–1918*, Cambridge: Cambridge University Press, 1983.

Steinberg, Mark D., *Proletarian Imagination: Self, Modernity, and the Sacred in Russia, 1910–1925*, Ithaca: Cornell University Press, 2002.

Stites, Richard, *Revolutionary Dreams: Utopian Vision and Experimental Life in the Russian Revolution*, New York: Oxford University Press, 1989.

Stites, Richard, *The Women's Liberation Movement in Russia: Feminism, Nihilism, and Bolshevism, 1860–1930*, Princeton: Princeton University Press, 1978.

Subtelny, O., *Ukraine: A History*, Toronto: University of Toronto Press, 1988.

Suny, R., *The Baku Commune, 1917–1918: Class and Nationality in the Russian Revolution*, Princeton: Princeton University Press, 1972.

Suny, R., *Looking Toward Ararat: Armenia in Modern History*, Bloomington: Indiana University Press, 1993.

Suny, R., *The Making of the Georgian Nation*, Bloomington: Indiana University Press, 1988.

Suny, Ronald Grigor, and Terry Martin, *A State of Nations: Empire and Nation-Making in the Age of Lenin and Stalin*, Oxford: Oxford University Press, 2001.

Taylor, Richard, *The Politics of Soviet Cinema, 1917–1929*, Cambridge: Cambridge University Press, 1979.

Thompson, John A., *Russia, Bolshevism, and the Versailles Peace*, Princeton: Princeton University Press, 1966.

Trotsky, L., *History of the Russian Revolution*, London: Gollancz, 1932–33.

Tumarkin, Nina, *Lenin Lives! The Lenin Cult in Soviet Russia*, Cambridge, MA: Harvard University Press, 1983.

Unterberger, Betty, *America's Siberian Expedition, 1918–1920*, Durham, NC: Duke University Press, 1956.

Vakar, N. P., *Belorussia: The Making of a Nation*, Cambridge, MA: Harvard University Press, 1956.

Wade, Rex A., *The Russian Revolution, 1917*, Cambridge: Cambridge University Press, 2005.

White, John A., *The Siberian Intervention*, Princeton: Princeton University Press, 1950.

Wildman, A., *The End of the Russian Imperial Army*, 2 vols., Princeton: Princeton University Press, 1980–87.

Williams, Robert C., *Artists in Revolution*, Bloomington: Indiana University Press, 1977.

Wrangel, Peter, *The Memoirs of General Wrangel*, New York: Duffield, 1930.

Youngblood, Denise, *Soviet Cinema in the Silent Era, 1918–1935*, Ann Arbor: University of Michigan Press, 1985.

1929–1953

Allilueva, Svetlana, *Twenty Letters to a Friend*, New York: Harper, 1967.

Andreyev, Catherine, *Vlasov and the Russian Liberation Movement*, Cambridge: Cambridge University Press, 1987.

Andrle, V., *Workers in Stalin's Russia: Industrialisation and Social Change in a Planned Economy*, Brighton, UK: Harvester, 1988.

Antonov-Ovseenko, Anton, *The Time of Stalin: Portrait of a Tyranny* (trans. George Saunders), New York: Harper & Row, 1982.

Applebaum, Anne, *Gulag: A History*, New York: Anchor Books, 2004.

Armstrong, John, *Soviet Partisans in World War II*, Madison: University of Wisconsin Press, 1964.

Bailes, Kendall, *Technology and Society Under Lenin and Stalin*, Princeton: Princeton University Press, 1978.

Barber, John, and Mark Harrison, *The Soviet Home Front, 1941–1945*, London: Longman, 1991.

Bennigsen, Alexander, and Chantal Lemercier, *Islam in the Soviet Union*, New York: Praeger, 1967.

Bereday, George F., et al. (eds.), *The Changing Soviet School*, Boston: Houghton Mifflin, 1960.

Berkhoof, Karel, *Motherland in Danger: Soviet Propaganda During World War II*, Cambridge, MA: Harvard University Press, 2012.

Bialer, S. (ed.), *Stalin and His Generals*, New York: Pegasus, 1969.

Brooks, Jeffrey, *Thank You, Comrade Stalin! Soviet Public Culture from Revolution to Cold War*, Princeton: Princeton University Press, 2000.

Brown, Edward, *The Proletarian Chapter in Russian Literary History, 1928–1932*, New York: Columbia University Press, 1953.

Brzezinski, Z., *The Soviet Bloc: Unity and Conflict*, 2nd edn., Cambridge, MA: Harvard University Press, 1961.

Carrere d'Encausse, Helene, *The Great Challenge: Nationalities and the Bolshevik State, 1917–1930*, New York: Holmes Meier, 1992.

Clark, Katerina, *Moscow, the Fourth Rome: Stalinism, Cosmopolitanism, and the Evolution of Soviet Culture, 1931–1941*, Cambridge, MA: Harvard University Press, 2011.

Clark, Katerina, *The Soviet Novel: History as Ritual*, Chicago: University of Chicago Press, 1981.

Colton, T. J., *Commissars, Commanders and Civilian Authority: The Structure of Soviet Military Politics*, Cambridge, MA: Harvard University Press, 1979.

Conquest, Robert, *The Great Terror: Reassessment*, New York: Oxford University Press, 1990.

Conquest, Robert, *The Harvest of Sorrow: Soviet Collectivisation and the Terror-Famine*, New York: Oxford University Press, 1986.

Conquest, Robert, *Kolyma: The Arctic Death Camps*, London: Macmillan, 1978.

Conquest, Robert, *The Nation Killers*, London: Macmillan, 1970.

Dallin, A., *German Rule in Russia, 1941–1945*, 2nd edn., Boulder: Westview, 1981.

Dallin, D., and B. Nicolaevsky, *Forced Labour in the Soviet Union*, London: Hollis and Carter, 1948.

Davies, R. W., *The Industrialisation of Soviet Russia*, 2 vols., London: Macmillan, 1980.

Davies, R. W., *The Soviet Economy in Turmoil, 1929–1930*, London: Macmillan, 1988.

De Witt, Nicholas, *Education and Professional Employment in the USSR*, Washington, DC: National Science Foundation, 1961.

Djilas, M., *Conversations with Stalin*, New York: Harcourt and Brace, 1962.

Dmytryshyn, Basil, *Moscow and the Ukraine, 1918–1953*, New York: Bookman Associates, 1956.

Dunmore, T., *The Stalinist Command Economy: The Soviet State Apparatus and Economic Policy, 1945–1953*, London: Macmillan, 1980.

Erickson, John, *The Road to Berlin*, London: Weidenfeld and Nicolson, 1983.

Erickson, John, *The Road to Stalingrad*, London: Weidenfeld and Nicolson, 1975.

Fainsod, Merle, *Smolensk Under Soviet Rule*, Cambridge, MA: Harvard University Press, 1958.

Fejto, F., *A History of the People's Democracies: Eastern Europe Since Stalin*, 2nd edn., Harmondsworth: Penguin Books, 1974.

Filtzer, Donald, *Soviet Workers and Late Stalinism: Labour and the Restoration of the Stalinist System After World War II*, Cambridge: Cambridge University Press, 2002.

Filtzer, D., *Soviet Workers and Stalinist Industrialisation*, Armonk, NY: Sharpe, 1986.

Fischer, G., *Soviet Opposition to Stalin: A Case Study in World War II*, Cambridge, MA: Harvard University Press, 1952.

Fitzpatrick, Sheila, *The Cultural Front: Power and Culture in Revolutionary Russia*, Ithaca: Cornell University Press, 1992.

Fitzpatrick, Sheila (ed.), *Cultural Revolution in Russia, 1928–1931*, Bloomington: Indiana University Press, 1978.

Fitzpatrick, Sheila, *Education and Social Mobility in the Soviet Union, 1921–1934*, Cambridge: Cambridge University Press, 1979.

Fitzpatrick, Sheila. *Everyday Stalinism. Ordinary Life in Extraordinary Times: Soviet Russia in the 1930s*, New York: Oxford University Press, 1999.

Fitzpatrick, Sheila, *Stalin's Peasants*, New York: Oxford University Press, 1994.

Geiger, K., *The Family in Soviet Russia*, Cambridge, MA: Harvard University Press, 1968.

Getty, J. Arch, *Origins of the Great Purges: The Soviet Communist Party Reconsidered, 1933–1938*, Cambridge: Cambridge University Press, 1986.

Getty, J. Arch, and Oleg V. Naumov, *The Road to Terror: Stalin and the Self-Destruction of the Bolsheviks, 1932–1939*, New Haven: Yale University Press, 1999.

Goldman, Wendy Z., *Women at the Gates: Gender and Industry in Stalin's Russia*, Cambridge: Cambridge University Press, 2002.

Goure, Leon, *The Siege of Leningrad*, Stanford: Stanford University Press, 1962.

Graham, Loren R., *Science and Philosophy in the Soviet Union*, New York: Knopf, 1970.

Hagenloh, Paul, *Stalin's Police: Public Order and Mass Repression in the USSR, 1926–1941*, Baltimore: Johns Hopkins University Press, 2009.

Hahn, W., *Postwar Soviet Politics: The Fall of Zhdanov and the Defeat of Moderation*, Ithaca: Cornell University Press, 1982.

Halfin, Igal, *Terror in My Soul: Communist Autobiographies on Trial*, Cambridge, MA: Harvard University Press, 2003.

Harbutt, F. J., *Yalta 1945: Europe and America at the Crossroads*, Cambridge: Cambridge University Press, 2010.

Harrison, M., *Soviet Planning in Peace and War*, Cambridge: Cambridge University Press, 1985.

Hoffmann, David L., *Stalinist Values: The Cultural Norms of Soviet Modernity, 1917–1941*, Ithaca: Cornell University Press, 2003.

Holloway, David, *Stalin and the Bomb: The Soviet Union and Atomic Energy, 1939–1956*, New Haven: Yale University Press, 1994.

Joravsky, D., *The Lysenko Affair*, Cambridge, MA: Harvard University Press, 1970.

Kenez, Peter, *Cinema and Soviet Society, 1917–1953*, Cambridge: Cambridge University Press, 1992.

Khlevniuk, Oleg, *Master of the House: Stalin and His Inner Circle*, New Haven: Yale University Press, 2009.

Khlevliuk, Oleg *Stalin: New Biography of a Dictator*, New Haven: Yale University Press, 2015.

Khrushchev, N. S., *Khrushchev Remembers*, 2 vols., Harmondsworth: Penguin Books, 1977.

Kochan, L., *The Jews in the Soviet Union Since 1917*, 2nd edn., Oxford: Oxford University Press, 1972.

Kolarz, W., *Religion in the Soviet Union*, London: Macmillan, 1961.

Kotkin, Stephen, *Stalin*, vol. I, *Paradoxes of Power, 1878–1928*, New York: Penquin Press, 2014.

Kuromiya, H., *Stalin's Industrial Revolution: Politics and Workers, 1928–1932*, Cambridge: Cambridge University Press, 1988.

Levin, Nora, *The Jews in the Soviet Union*, New York: New York University Press, 1988.

Mastny, V., *Russia's Road to the Cold War*, New York: Columbia University Press, 1979.

McCagg, W. O., *Stalin Embattled, 1943–1948*, Detroit: Wayne State University Press, 1978.

Medvedev, Roy, *Let History Judge: The Origins and Consequences of Stalinism*, New York: Knopf, 1971.

Medvedev, Zh., *The Rise and Fall of T. D. Lysenko*, New York: Columbia University Press, 1969.

Merridale, Catherine, *Ivan's War: The Red Army, 1939–1945*, New York: Metroplitan Books, 2006.

Miller, Frank J., *Folklore for Stalin: Russian Folklore and Pseudofolklore in the Stalin Era*, New York: Sharpe, 1990.

Naimark, Norman, *The Russians in Germany: A History of the Soviet Zone of Occupation, 1945–1949*, Cambridge, MA: Harvard University Press, 1995.

Nekrich, A., *22 June 1941*, Columbia: University of South Carolina Press, 1968.

Nicolaevsky, Boris, *Power and the Soviet Elite*, London: Pall Mall Press, 1966.

Pavlov, Dmitri, *Leningrad 1941: The Blockade*, Chicago: University of Chicago Press, 1965.

Pinkus, Benjamin, *The Jews of the Soviet Union*, Cambridge: Cambridge University Press, 1988.

Plokhy, S. M., *Yalta 1945: The Price of Peace*, New York: Viking, 2010.

Pospielovsky, D., *The Russian Church Under the Soviet Regime, 1917–1982*, Crestwood, NY: St. Vladimir's Seminary Press, 1984.

Rywkin, M., *Moscow's Muslim Challenge: Soviet Central Asia*, rev. edn., Armonk, NY: Sharpe, 1990.

Salisbury, Harrison, *900 Days: The Siege of Leningrad*, New York: Harper and Row, 1969.

Scott, John, *Behind the Urals: An American Worker in Russia's City of Steel*, London: Secker and Warburg, 1943.

Seaton, Albert, *The Russo-German War, 1941–1945*, London: Barker, 1971.

Service, Robert, *Stalin: A Biography*, Cambridge, MA: Belknap Press, 2005.

Shearer, David, *Policing Stalin's Socialism; Repression and Social Order in the Soviet Union, 1924–1953*, New Haven: Yale University Press, 2009.

Siegelbaum, L., *Stakhanovism and the Politics of Productivity in the USSR, 1935–1941*, Cambridge: Cambridge University Press, 1988.

Simmons, Ernest J., *Russian Fiction and Soviet Ideology*, New York: Columbia University Press, 1958.

Snyder, Timothy, *Bloodlands: Europe Between Hitler and Stalin*, New York: Basis Books, 2010.

Solzhenitsyn, A., *The Gulag Archipelago*, 3 vols., New York: Harper and Row, 1974–77.

Struve, Gleb, *Russian Literature Under Lenin and Stalin, 1917–1953*, Norman: University of Oklahoma Press, 1971.

Sullivant, Robert S., *Soviet Politics and the Ukraine, 1917–1957*, New York: Columbia University Press, 1962.

Thurston, Robert, *Life and Terror in Stalin's Russia, 1934–1941*, New Haven: Yale University Press, 1996.

Timasheff, N.,*The Great Retreat: The Growth and Decline of Communism in Russia*, New York: Dutton, 1946.

Tolstoy, Nikolai, *Stalin's Secret War*, New York: Holt, Rinehart & Winston, 1983.

Trotsky, L., *The Revolution Betrayed*, London: Faber and Faber, 1937.

Tucker, R. C. (ed.), *Stalinism: Essays in Historical Interpretation*, New York: Norton, 1977.

Tucker, R. C., and S. F. Cohen (eds.), *The Great Purge Trial*, New York: Grosset and Dunlap, 1965.

Vaksberg, Arkadii, *Stalin Against the Jews*, New York: Vintage, 1995.

Viola, L., *The Best Sons of the Fatherland: Workers in the Vanguard of Soviet Collectivisation*, Oxford: Oxford University Press, 1987.

Viola, L., *The Unknown Gulag; The Lost World of Stalin's Special Settlements*, Oxford: Oxford University Press, 2009.

von Rauch, G., *The Baltic States: The Years of Independence, 1917–1940*, London: Hurst, 1974.

Weiner, Amir, *Making Sense of War: The Second World War and the Fate of the Bolshevik Revolution*, Oxford: Oxford University Press, 2001.

Weissberg, Alex, *The Accused*, New York: Simon and Schuster, 1951.

Werth, Alexander, *Russia at War, 1941–1945*, New York: Dutton, 1964.

Wheeler, Geoffrey, *The Modern History of Soviet Central Asia*, Princeton and New York: Praeger, 1964.

White, D. Fedotoff, *The Growth of the Red Army*, Princeton: Princeton University Press, 1944.

Zhukov, Georgi K., *The Memoirs of Marshal Zhukov*, New York: Delacorte, 1971.

1953–1991

Aganbegyan, A., *The Challenge: Economics of Perestroika*, London: Hutchinson, 1988.

Armstrong, John A., *Ethnic Minorities in the Soviet Union*, New York: Praeger, 1968.

Ash, T. Garton, *The Polish Revolution: Solidarity, 1980–1982*, London: Jonathan Cape, 1983.

Bennigsen, A., and M. Broxup, *The Islamic Threat to the Soviet State*, London: Croom Helm, 1983.

Bourdeaux, M., *Patriarch and Prophets: Persecution of the Russian Orthodox Church Today*, London: Macmillan, 1969.

Brown, A., and M. Kaser (eds.), *Soviet Policy in the 1980s*, London: Macmillan, 1982.

Brown, A., and M. Kaser (eds.), *The Soviet Union Since the Fall of Khrushchev*, 2nd edn., London: Macmillan, 1978.

Brumberg, A., *Chronicle of a Revolution*, New York: Pantheon, 1990.

Brumberg, A. (ed.), *In Quest of Justice: Protest and Dissent in the Soviet Union Today*, New York: Praeger, 1970.

Brumberg, A., *Russia Under Khrushchev*, New York: Praeger, 1962.

Carrere d'Encausse, Helene, *Decline of an Empire: The Soviet Socialist Republics in Revolt*, New York: Newsweek Books, 1979.

Churchward, L., *The Soviet Intelligentsia*, London: Routledge and Kegan Paul, 1973.

Cohen, Stephen F. (ed.), *An End to Silence: Uncensored Opinion in the Soviet Union: From Roy Medvedev's Underground Magazine, Political Diary* (trans. George Saunders), New York: Norton, 1982.

Cohen, S., R. Sharlet, and A. Rabinowitch (eds.), *The Soviet Union Since Stalin*, Bloomington: Indiana University Press, 1980.

Conquest, Robert (ed.), *The Last Empire: Nationality and the Soviet Future*, Stanford: Hoover Institution Press, 1986.

Crankshaw, Edward, *Khrushchev: A Career*, New York: Viking, 1966.

Dallin, Alexander, and Gail W. Lapidus (eds.), *The Soviet System in Crisis*, Boulder: Westview Press, 1991.

Djilas, Milovan, *The New Class: An Analysis of the Communist System*, New York: Praeger, 1957.

Dunlop, J., *The Faces of Contemporary Russian Nationalism*, Princeton: Princeton University Press, 1983.

Ellis, Jane, *The Russian Orthodox Church: A Contemporary History*, London: Croom Helm, 1986.

Feshbach, Murray, *The Soviet Union: Population Trends and Dilemmas*, Washington, DC: Population Reference Bureau, 1982.

Furst, Juliane, *Stalin's Last Generation; Soviet Post-War Youth and the Emergence of Mature Socialism*. Oxford: Oxford University Press, 2010.

Goldman, M., *USSR in Crisis: The Failure of an Economic System*, New York: Norton, 1983.

Gromyko, Andrei, *Memoirs*, New York: Doubleday, 1990.

Hajda, L., and M. Beissinger (eds.), *The Nationalities Factor in Soviet Politics and Society*, Boulder: Westview Press, 1990.

Hayward, Max (ed.), *On Trial: The Case of Sinyavsky and Daniel*, London: Collins/Harvill, 1967.

Hopkins, M., *Russia's Underground Press: The Chronicle of Current Events*, New York: Praeger, 1983.

Hosking, Geoffrey, *The Awakening of the Soviet Union*, Cambridge, MA: Harvard University Press, 1990.

Inkeles, A., and R. Bauer, *The Soviet Citizen: Daily Life in a Totalitarian Society*, New York: Athenaeum, 1968.

Johnson, Priscilla, *Khrushchev and the Arts: The Politics of Soviet Culture, 1962–1964*, Cambridge, MA: MIT Press, 1965.

Juviler, P. H., *Revolutionary Law and Order: Politics and Social Change in the USSR*, New York: Free Press, 1976.

Kagarlitsky, B., *The Thinking Reed: Intellectuals and the Soviet State, 1917 to the Present*, London: Verso, 1988.

Kanet, Roger K. (ed.), *The Soviet Union, Eastern Europe and the Third World*, Cambridge: Cambridge University Press, 1987.

Karklins, R., *Ethnic Relations in the USSR*, Boston: Allen and Unwin, 1986.

Kaser, Michael, *Comecon: Integration Problems of Planned Economies*, 2nd edn., New York: Oxford University Press, 1965.

Keep, John, *The Last of the Empires: A History of the Soviet Union, 1945–1991*, New York: Oxford University Press, 1995.

Kerblay, B., *Gorbachev's Russia*, New York: Pantheon, 1989.

Kerblay, B., *Modern Soviet Society*, New York: Pantheon, 1983.

Khrushchev, Nikita, *Khrushchev Remembers*, Boston: Little, Brown, 1971.

Khrushchev, Nikita, *Khrushchev Remembers: The Last Testament*, Boston: Little, Brown, 1974.

Khrushchev, Sergei, *Khrushchev on Khrushchev: An Inside Account of the Man and His Era*, Boston: Little, Brown, 1990.

Lane, Christel, *Christian Religion in the Soviet Union: A Sociological Study*, London: Allen and Unwin, 1978.

Lewin, M., *The Making of the Soviet System*, London: Methuen, 1985.

Lewin, M., *Political Undercurrents in Soviet Economic Debates*, Princeton: Princeton University Press, 1973.

Lewytsky, B., *The Uses of Terror: The Soviet Secret Service*, London: Sidgwick and Jackson, 1971.

Linden, C., *Khrushchev and the Soviet Leadership, 1957–1964*, Baltimore: Johns Hopkins University Press, 1966.

Macintosh, J. M., *Strategy and Tactics of Soviet Foreign Policy*, New York: Oxford University Press, 1963.

Madison, Bernice, *Social Welfare in the Soviet Union*, Stanford: Stanford University Press, 1968.

Matlock, Jack, *Autopsy on an Empire*, New York: Random House, 1995.

Matthews, Mervyn, *Education in the Soviet Union: Policies and Institutions Since Stalin*, London: Allen and Unwin, 1982.

Matthews, Mervyn, *Privilege in the Soviet Union*, London: Allen and Unwin, 1978.

McCauley, Martin (ed.), *Khrushchev and Khrushchevism*, London: Macmillan, 1987.

McCauley, M., *Khrushchev and the Development of Soviet Agriculture: The Virgin Lands Programme, 1953–1964*, London: Macmillan, 1976.

McCauley, Martin (ed.), *The Soviet Union After Brezhnev*, London: Heinemann, 1983.

McCauley, Martin (ed.), *The Soviet Union Under Gorbachev*, London: Macmillan, 1987.

Medvedev, R., and Zh. Medvedev, *Khrushchev: The Years in Power*, Oxford: Oxford University Press, 1977.

Medvedev, Zh., *Andropov*, Oxford: Blackwell, 1983.

Medvedev, Zh., *Soviet Science*, Oxford: Oxford University Press, 1979.

Morrison, John, *Boris Yeltsin: From Bolshevik to Democrat*, New York: Dutton, 1991.

Nove, A., *Stalinism and After*, London: Allen and Unwin, 1975.

Peris, Daniel, *Storming the Heavens: The Soviet League of the Militant Godless*, Ithaca: Cornell University Press, 1998.

Ploss, Sidney L., *Conflict and Decision-Making Process in Soviet Russia: A Case Study of Agricultural Policy, 1953–1963*, Princeton: Princeton University Press, 1965.

Popovsky, M., *Manipulated Science: The Crisis of Science and Scientists in the Soviet Union Today*, New York: Doubleday, 1979.

Ragsdale, Hugh, *The Russian Tragedy: The Burden of History*, New York: Sharpe, 1996.

Ragsdale, Hugh, *The Soviets, the Munich Crisis, and the Coming of World War II*, Cambridge: Cambridge University Press, 2004.

Reddaway, P., *Uncensored Russia*, London: Jonathan Cape, 1972.

Ruble, B., and A. Kahan, *Industrial Labor in the USSR*, New York: Pergamon, 1979.

Rush, Myron, *Political Succession in the USSR*, New York: Columbia University Press, 1965.

Sakharov, Andrei, *Memoirs*, New York: Knopf, 1990.

Schwartz, Harry, *The Soviet Economy Since Stalin*, Philadelphia: Lippincott, 1965.

Smith, Hedrick, *The Russians*, New York: New York Times Books, 1976.

Suny, Ronald Grigor (ed.), *Transcaucasia: Nationalism and Social Change: Essays in the History of Armenia, Azerbaijan, and Georgia*, Ann Arbor: Michigan Slavic Publications, 1983.

Tatu, Michael, *Power in the Kremlin from Khrushchev to Kosygin*, New York: Viking, 1969.

Taubman, William, *Khrushchev: The Man and His Era*, New York: Norton, 2003.

Tokes, R. L., *Dissent in the USSR: Politics, Ideology and People*, Baltimore: Johns Hopkins University Press, 1975.

Tucker, R. C., *Political Culture and Leadership in Soviet Russia from Lenin to Gorbachev*, Brighton: Wheatsheaf, 1987.

Ulam, Adam, *New Face of Soviet Totalitarianism*, New York: Praeger, 1965.

Urban, Michael, *The Algebra of Soviet Power: Elite Circulation in the Belorussian Republic*, Cambridge: Cambridge University Press, 1989.

Vali, Ference A., *Rift and Revolt in Hungary*, Cambridge, MA: Harvard University Press, 1961.

Vardys, V. S., *Lithuania Under the Soviets: Portrait of a Nation, 1940–1965*, New York: Praeger, 1965.

Voslensky, M. S., *Nomenklatura: Anatomy of the Soviet Ruling Class*, London: Bodley Head, 1984.

Walker, Martin, *The Waking Giant: The Soviet Union Under Gorbachev*, London: Michael Joseph, 1986.

White, Stephen, *Gorbachev and After*, Cambridge: Cambridge University Press, 1991.

Yanov, A., *The Russian New Right*, Berkeley: Institute of International Studies, 1978.

Yeltsin, Boris, *The Struggle for Russia*, New York: Random House, 1994.

Zubok, Vladislav, *Failed Empire; The Soviet Union in the Cold War from Stalin to Gorbachev*. Chapel Hill: University of North Carolina Press, 2007.

1991–2015

Aron, Leon Rabinovich, *Yeltsin: A Revolutionary Life*, New York: St. Martin's Press, 2000.

Åslund, Anders, and Sergei Guriev, *Russia After the Global Economic Crisis*, Washington, DC: Peterson Institute, 2010.

Åslund, Anders, and Michael McFaul (eds.), *Revolution in Orange: The Origins of Ukraine's Democratic Breakthrough*, Washington, DC: Carnegie Endowment for International Peace, 2006.

Åslund, Anders, and Martha Brill Olcott, *Russia After Communism*, Washington, DC: Carnegie Endowment for International Peace, 1999.

Breslauer, George W., *Gorbachev and Yeltsin as Leaders*, Cambridge: Cambridge University Press, 2002.

Brown, Archie, and Lilia Fedorovna Shevtsova, *Gorbachev, Yeltsin, and Putin: Political Leadership in Russia's Transition*, Washington, DC: Carnegie Endowment for International Peace, 2001.

Cohen, Stephen F., *Failed Crusade: America and the Tragedy of Post-Communist Russia*, New York: Norton, 2000.

Dawisha, Karen. *Putin's Kleptocracy: Who Owns Russia?* New York: Simon & Schuster, 2014.

Fel'shtinskiĭ, Iurii, *The Corporation: Russia and the KGB in the Age of President Putin*, New York: Encounter Books, 2008.

Gaidar, E. T., *State and Evolution: Russia's Search for a Free Market*, Seattle: University of Washington Press, 2003.

Gessen, Masha, *The Man Without a Face: The Unlikely Rise of Vladimir Putin*. New York: Riverhead Books, 2012.

Gill, Graeme J., and Roger D. Markwick, *Russia's Stillborn Democracy? From Gorbachev to Yeltsin*, Oxford: Oxford University Press, 2000.

Gitelman, Zvi Y., Musya Glants, and Marshall I. Goldman, *Jewish Life After the USSR*, Bloomington: Indiana University Press, 2003.

Goldman, Marshall I., *Petrostate: Putin, Power, and the New Russia*, Oxford: Oxford University Press, 2008.

Goldman, Marshall I., *The Piratization of Russia: Russian Reform Goes Awry*, London and New York: Routledge, 2003.

Herspring, Dale (ed.), *Putin's Russia: Past Imperfect, Future Uncertain*, 3rd edn., Lanham, MD: Rowman & Littlefield, 2007.

Hill, Fiona, Mr. Putin: Operative in the Kremlin, Washington, DC: Brookings Institution Press, 2015.

Ioffe, Gregory, Tatyana Nefedova, and Ilya Zaslavsky (eds.), *The End of Peasantry? The Disintegration of Rural Russia*, Pittsburgh: Univeristy of Pittsburgh Press, 2006.

Judah, Ben, *Fragile Empire: How Russia Fell in and out of Love with Vladimir Putin*, New Haven: Yale University Press, 2013.

Kagarlitsky, Boris, *Russia Under Yeltsin and Putin Neo-Liberal Autocracy*, London, and Sterling, VA: Pluto Press, 2002.

Kotkin, Stephen, *Armageddon Averted: The Soviet Collapse, 1970–2000*, Oxford: Oxford University Press, 2001.

McFaul, Michael, Nikolai Petrov, and Andrei Riabov, *Between Dictatorship and Democracy: Russian Post-Communist Political Reform*, Washington, DC: Carnegie Endowment for International Peace, 2004.

Mitchell, Lincoln, *The Color Revolutions*, Philadelphia: University of Pennsylvania Press, 2012.

Politkovskaia, Anna, *A Small Corner of Hell: Dispatches from Chechnya*, Chicago: University of Chicago Press, 2003.

Putin, Vladimir Vladimirovich, *First Person: An Astonishingly Frank Self-Portrait by Russia's President*, New York: PublicAffairs, 2000.

Reddaway, Peter, and Dmitri Glinski, *The Tragedy of Russia's Reforms: Market Bolshevism Against Democracy*, Washington, DC: United States Institute of Peace Press, 2001.

Sakwa, Richard (ed.). *Chechnya from Past to Future*, London: Anthem Press, 2005.

Sakwa, Richard, *The Crisis of Russian Democracy: The Dual State, Factionalism and the Medvedev Succession*, Cambridge: Cambridge University Press, 2011.

Sakwa, Richard, *Frontline Ukraine: Crisis in the Borderlands*, New York: I. B. Tauris, 2015.

Sakwa, Richard, *Putin and the Oligarchs: The Khodorkovsky–Yukos Affair*, New York: I. B. Tauris, 2014.

Sakwa, Richard, *Putin Redux: Power and Contradiction in Contemporary Russia*, Abingdon, UK, and Burlington, VT: Routledge, 2014.

Sakwa, Richard, *Russia's Choice*. New York: Routledge, 2004.

Shevtsova, Lilia Fedorovna, *Putin's Russia*, rev. and expanded edn., Washington, DC: Carnegie Endowment for International Peace, 2005.

Shevtsova, Lilia Fedorovna, *Yeltsin's Russia: Myths and Reality*, Washington, DC: Carnegie Endowment for International Peace and Brookings Institution Press, 1999, 2004.

Snetkov, Aglaya, *Russia's Security Policy Under Putin: A Critical Perspective*, New York: Routledge, 2014.

Urban, Michael, *Culture of Politics in Post-Communist Russia*, Cambridge: Cambridge University Press, 2010.

Wegren, Stephen (ed.). *Return to Putin's Russia: Past Imperfect, Future Uncertain*, 5th edn., Lanham, MD: Rowman & Littlefield, 2013.

White, Stephen, *Russia's New Politics: The Management of a Postcommunist Society*, Cambridge: Cambridge University Press, 2000.

Zimmerman, William, *Ruling Russia: Authoritarianism from the Revolution to Putin*, Princeton: Princeton University Press, 2014.

Notes

Chapter 1

1. Sir George Buchanan, *My Mission to Russia and Other Diplomatic Memories* (Boston, 1923), vol. II, p. 46.

Chapter 2

1. From 1703 to 1914 the city was called St. Petersburg; from 1914 to 1924, Petrograd; from 1924 to 1991, Leningrad; from 1991 to the present, again St. Petersburg.
2. For example, D. Volkogonov, *Lenin: A New Biography* (New York, 1994).
3. Among the first group of historians, the most prominent are George Katkov, *Russia, 1917: The Kornilov Affair* (London, 1980); Leonard Schapiro, *The Communist Party of the Soviet Union* (New York, 1960); and Richard Pipes, *A Concise History of the Russian Revolution* (New York, 1995). A typical representative of the second group is a study by Dianne Koenker and William G. Rosenberg, *Strikes and Revolutions in Russia, 1917* (Princeton, 1989).

Chapter 3

1. Compare, for example, the treatment in Stephen Cohen, *Bukharin and the Bolshevik Revolution* (New York, 1973), and Moshe Levin, *Lenin's Last Struggle* (London, 1969), on the one hand, and Martin Malia, *The Soviet Tragedy* (New York, 1994), and Richard Pipes, *Russia Under the Bolshevik Regime* (New York, 1993), on the other.
2. Alec Nove, *An Economic History of the USSR, 1917–1991*, 3rd edn. (New York, 1992). According to Nove the figure was 60 percent (p. 62). It should be noted that the territories were not strictly comparable.
3. In March 1919 the First Congress of the Third Communist International took place in Moscow. Lenin succeeded in separating the left wing of the international Marxist movement and organizing a Communist International. The aim of the Comintern was to spread proletarian revolution beyond the borders of Soviet

Russia. Soon after, the organization was reduced to no more than an instrument of Soviet foreign policy.

4. This section is largely based on chapters 4–6 of Nove, *An Economic History of the USSR, 1917–1991.*

5. *Ibid.*, p. 84.

6. This section is largely based on my chapter, "The Evolution of Bolshevik Cultural Policies," in Theodore Taranovski (ed.), *Reform in Modern Russian History* (Cambridge, 1995), pp. 247–64.

7. Loren R. Graham, *The Soviet Academy of Sciences and the Communist Party, 1927–1932* (New York, 1967).

Chapter 4

1. This section is based on R. W. Davies, *The Socialist Offensive: Collectivization of Soviet Agriculture, 1929–1930,* 2 vols. (Cambridge, MA, 1980); Moshe Lewin, *Russian Peasants and Soviet Power: A Study of Collectivization* (New York, 1975); and Nove, *An Economic History of the Soviet Union, 1917–1991.*

2. For literature on collectivization, see Davies, *The Socialist Offensive*; Davies, *The Soviet Collective Farm, 1929–1930* (Cambridge, MA, 1980); Lewin, *Russian Peasants and Soviet Power*; Sheila Fitzpatrick, *Stalin's Peasants* (New York, 1994); and Nove, *An Economic History of the USSR, 1917–1991,* ch. 7.

3. *Narodnoe khoziaistvo SSSR za 60 let* (Moscow, 1977), p. 269.

4. Lynne Viola, *Best Sons of the Fatherland: Workers in the Vanguard of Soviet Collectivization* (Oxford, 1987).

5. Figures from Roger E. Clarke (ed.), *Soviet Economic Facts, 1917–1970* (New York, 1972), pp. 3, 23.

6. The process of urbanization continued in the rest of the 1930s. While in 1926 18 percent of the population was described as urban, in 1939 it was 32 percent: Robert Kaiser, *The Geography of Nationalism in Russia and in the USSR* (Princeton, 1994), p. 122.

7. Robert Conquest, *The Harvest of Sorrow: Soviet Collectivization and the Terror-Famine* (Oxford, 1986).

8. Mikhail Heller and Aleksandr Nekrich, *Utopia in Power* (New York, 1986), p. 270; and Peter Kenez, *Cinema and Soviet Society* (Cambridge, 1992), p. 108.

Chapter 5

1. My view of Stalin is formed on the basis of reminiscences by people who knew him, including M. Djilas, Stalin's daughter Svetlana Alilueva, and a few others. The published letters of Stalin to Molotov, one of his closest collaborators, are striking in how little they reveal: Lars Lih et al. (eds.), *Stalin's Letters to Molotov, 1925–1936* (New Haven, 1995).

2. The extent of opposition to Stalin in the first half of the 1930s within the leadership is a debated issue. By and large those who opposed the "totalitarian" school, i.e., did not wish to use Stalin's character as an explanation for the terror, saw more serious opposition, and those who believed that Stalin was the moving

force behind the mass murder minimized the strength and determination of the opposition. I agree with the representatives of the second group.

3. The definitive text on the purges is Robert Conquest, *The Great Terror: A Reassessment* (New York, 1990).

4. Whether Soviet society could be described as totalitarian has been the most passionately and fruitlessly debated subject in Soviet history. Scholars who wrote about Soviet society after the Second World War, when the cold war was bitterest, described Soviet society as "totalitarian" and thereby stressed the similarities between the Stalinist Soviet Union and Nazi Germany, distancing both from the democratic and pluralist United States. Beginning in the 1960s, younger radical scholars found such self-congratulatory attitudes unacceptable. They attacked and destroyed the totalitarian model. This debate, however, is based on a misconception. Leftist scholars have repeatedly shown that the government was unable to control every aspect of life and that society was not altogether inert. But, of course, no sensible scholar ever maintained that Stalin or the party or the government was able to control everything. Totalitarianism simply means the ambition and the attempt to control every facet of life and the attempt to demolish the private sphere. According to this understanding, Soviet society between 1929 and 1953 can fairly be described as totalitarian.

5. In 1954 Barrington Moore, an American sociologist, published a book on the Soviet system entitled *Terror and Progress* (Cambridge, MA). Moore's phrase aptly describes the 1930s.

6. Some scholars, most explicitly Robert Thurston, argued that it was only the upper levels of society that felt the burden of terror and that the working classes remained largely unaffected. A glance at the labor code should disabuse one of such ideas. See Thurston, *Life and Terror in Stalin's Russia, 1934–1941* (New Haven, 1996).

7. Nicholas Timasheff, *The Great Retreat: The Growth and Decline of Communism in Russia* (New York, 1946).

8. Andrei Siniavskii (Abram Tertz), *On Socialist Realism* (New York, 1960); Vera Dunham, *In Stalin's Time: Middleclass Values in Soviet Fiction* (New York, 1976); and Katerina Clark, *The Soviet Novel* (Chicago, 1981).

Chapter 6

1. Protocols of the meeting in party archives, fond 77, opis 1, delo 919.
2. Alexander Weissberg, *The Accused* (New York, 1951).
3. Party archives, fond 17, opis 125, delo 124.

Chapter 7

1. Wolfgang Leonhard, *Child of the Revolution* (Chicago, 1958).
2. Later revelations show that Stalin was involved in the commencement of the Korean War to a greater extent than we hitherto realized. See Sergei Goncharov, John Lewis, and Xue Litai, *Uncertain Partners: Stalin, Mao and the Korean War* (Stanford, 1993).
3. Interfax, December 1992 (from the Voenizdat statistical study).

4. *Narodnoe khoziaistvo SSSR za 60 let*, p. 40.
5. Nove, *An Economic History of the Soviet Union, 1917–1991*, p. 268.
6. Clarke (ed.), *Soviet Economic Facts, 1917–1970*, pp. 112–13.
7. Ervin Sinko, *Egy regeny regenye: Moszkvai naplojegyzetek, 1935–1937* (Budapest, 1988), p. 540.
8. *Iskusstvo kino* 1947, no. 1, p. 8, "Vosploshchenie obraza velikogo vozhdia."
9. *Khrushchev Remembers* (Boston, 1970); Svetlana Aliluyeva, *Twenty Letters to a Friend* (New York, 1967); *Molotov Remembers. Inside Kremlin Politics: Conversations with Felix Chuev* (Chicago, 1993); Konstantin Simonov, *Glazami cheloveka moego pokoleniia. Razmyshleniia o I. V. Staline* (Moscow, 1990).

Chapter 8

1. Roy Medvedev and Zhores Medvedev, *Khrushchev: The Years in Power* (Oxford, 1977), pp. 96–100.
2. Adam Ulam, *Expansion and Coexistence: Soviet Foreign Policy, 1917–1973*, 2nd edn. (New York, 1974), p. 669.

Chapter 9

1. Anthony D'Agostino, *Soviet Succession Struggles* (London, 1988), p. 212.
2. This observation was the central argument of Seweryn Bialer in his book, *The Soviet Paradox: External Expansion, Internal Decline* (New York, 1986).

Chapter 10

1. Jack Matlock, *Autopsy on an Empire* (New York, 1995).

Chapter 11

1. Sergei Stepashin, "How Much Russia Is Worth?" *Rossiiskaia gazeta*, June 29, 2005.
2. Oligarch is now the accepted word for those who created enormous wealth for themselves by dishonest means at the time of privatization.
3. Stephen White, *Russia's New Politics: The Management of a Postcommunist Society* (Cambridge, 2000), p. 130.
4. Donald D. Barry, *Russian Politics: The Post-Soviet Phase* (New York, 2002), pp. 67–68.
5. See two entirely different descriptions of the events of September and October 1993: Leon Rabinovich Aron, *Yeltsin: A Revolutionary Life* (New York, 2000), pp. 494–554; and Peter Reddaway and Dmitri Glinski, *The Tragedy of Russia's Reforms: Market Bolshevism Against Democracy* (Washington, DC, 2001), pp. 369–435. Aron is favorable to Yeltsin, and Reddaway and Glinski bitterly hostile.
6. Zoltan Barany and Robert G. Moser (eds.), *Russian Politics: Challenges of Democratization* (Cambridge, 2001), p. 136.

7. The statistical data are taken from Allen C. Lynch, *How Russia Is Not Ruled: Reflections on Russian Political Development* (Cambridge, 2005), pp. 99–105.

8. These paragraphs are largely based on the work of Louise Shelley, "The Challenge of Crime and Corruption," in Stephen Wegren (ed.), *Russia's Policy Challenges: Security, Stability, and Development* (Armonk, NY, 2003), pp. 103–22.

9. White, *Russia's New Politics*, p. 145.

10. Anna Politkovskaia, *A Small Corner of Hell: Dispatches from Chechnya* (Chicago, 2003).

Chapter 12

1. Timothy J. Colton, *Yeltsin: A Life* (New York, 2008), also makes this point.

2. Vladimiar Putin, *First Person: An Astonishingly Frank Self-Portrait by Russia's President* (New York, 2002), pp. 22 and 40–44.

3. Stephen Kotkin, "How Vladimir Putin Rules," *Foreign Affairs*, March 2015.

4. Ben Judah, *Fragile Empire: How Russia Fell in and out of Love with Vladimir Putin* (New Haven, 2013), pp. 138–39.

5. The phrase "illiberal democracy" was introduced by Fareed Zakaria in an article in *Foreign Affairs* in 1997. Since then it has been widely used by several observers and even leaders, such as Viktor Orban of Hungary describing his own regime.

6. Richard Sakwa, *Putin Redux: Power and Contradiction in Contemporary Russia* (Abingdon, UK, and Burlington, VT, 2014), p. 28.

7. Alena Ledeneva, *Can Russia Modernize?* (Cambridge, 2013).

8. Richard Sakwa, *Putin: Russia's Choice* (London, 2004), p. 134.

9. *Ibid.*, pp. 45–46.

10. Elizabeth Piper, "Russian Middle Class Slowly Stirred to Action by Economic Crisis," Reuters, April 10, 2015.

11. Robert Coalson, "Some Who Left: A New Wave of Russian Emigration," RFL/RL, April 21, 2015.

12. I base myself on the arguments presented in Grigory Ioffe, Tatyana Nefedova, and Ilya Zaslavsky, *The End of the Peasantry? The Disintegration of Rural Russia* (Pittsburgh, 2006).

13. Richard Sakwa (ed.), *Chechnya: From Past to Future* (London, 2005), p. 19.

14. Dzhabrail Gakaev, "Chechnya in Russia and Russia in Chechnya," *ibid.*, pp. 36–37.

15. Musa Basnukaev, "Reconstruction in Chechnya: The Intersection Between Politics and the Economy," in Anne Le Huerou, et al. (eds.), *Chechnya in War and Beyond* (London, 2014), pp. 76–90.

16. *Ibid.*, p. 85.

17. The title of Karen Dawisha's important book is *Putin's Kleptocracy: Who Owns Russia?* (New York, 2014).

18. Richard Sakwa, *Putin and the Oligarchs: The Khodorkovsky–Yukos Affair* (London, 2014), p. 5. Khodorkovskii remained a party member until 1991.

19. *Ibid.*, p. 16.

20. *Ibid.*, pp. 5–51.

Chapter 13

1. Sakwa, *Putin Redux*, in particular ch. 3.
2. *Ibid.*, p. 113.
3. Anders Aslund and Andrew Kuchins, *The Russia Balance Sheet* (Washington, DC, 2009), p. 69.
4. Richard Sakwa, *Frontline Ukraine: Crisis in the Borderlands* (London, 2015), p. 4. This book is the best description of the Ukrainian crisis.

Index